ELECTIVE AFFINITIES
VISUAL & PERFORMING ARTS

Columbia Themes in Philosophy, Social Criticism, and the Arts

COLUMBIA THEMES IN PHILOSOPHY, SOCIAL CRITICISM, AND THE ARTS PRESENTS monographs, essay collections, and short books on philosophy and aesthetic theory. It aims to publish books that show the ability of the arts to stimulate critical reflection on modern and contemporary social, political, and cultural life. Art is not now, if it ever was, a realm of human activity independent of the complex realities of social organization and change, political authority and antagonism, cultural domination and resistance. The possibilities of critical thought embedded in the arts are most fruitfully expressed when addressed to readers across the various fields of social and humanistic inquiry. The idea of philosophy in the series' title ought to be understood, therefore, to embrace forms of discussion that begin where mere academic expertise exhausts itself, where the rules of social, political, and cultural practice are both affirmed and challenged, and where new thinking takes place. The series does not privilege any particular art, nor does it ask for the arts to be mutually isolated. The series encourages writing from the many fields of thoughtful and critical inquiry.

Lydia Goehr and Daniel Herwitz, eds., *The Don Giovanni Moment: Essays on the Legacy of an Opera*
Robert Hullot-Kentor, *Things Beyond Resemblance: Collected Essays on Theodor W. Adorno*
Gianni Vattimo, *Art's Claim to Truth*, edited by Santiago Zabala, translated by Luca D'Isanto
John T. Hamilton, *Music, Madness, and the Unworking of Language*
Stefan Jonsson, *A Brief History of the Masses: Three Revolutions*
Richard Eldridge, *Life, Literature, and Modernity*
Janet Wolff, *The Aesthetics of Uncertainty*

Elective Affinities

MUSICAL ESSAYS ON THE HISTORY OF AESTHETIC THEORY

LYDIA GOEHR

COLUMBIA UNIVERSITY PRESS   NEW YORK

COLUMBIA UNIVERSITY PRESS *Publishers Since 1893*
NEW YORK   CHICHESTER, WEST SUSSEX

Library of Congress Cataloging-in-Publication Data
Goehr, Lydia.
  Elective affinities : musical essays on the history of aesthetic theory / Lydia Goehr.
    p.   cm.—(Columbia themes in philosophy, social criticism, and the arts)
  Includes bibliographical references and index.
  ISBN 978-0-231-14480-3 (cloth : alk. paper)
    1. Music—Philosophy and aesthetics.   2. Music and philosophy.   I. Title.   II. Series.
ML3800.G5756 2008
781.1'7—dc22   2008020307

∞

Columbia University Press books are printed on permanent and durable acid-free paper.
Printed in the United States of America
c 10 9 8 7 6 5 4 3 2 1

Most of the essays in this book were printed elsewhere in earlier or much shorter versions. I am
grateful for permission to reprint the material and to the editors who oversaw the initial production.
"*Amerikamüde/Europamüde:* On the Very Idea of American Opera," *Opera Quarterly* (2007).
"*Doppelbewegung:* The Musical Movement of Philosophy and the Philosophical Movement of
  Music," in *Sound Figures of Modernity: German Music and Philosophy,* ed. Jost Hermand and
  Gerhard Richter (Madison: University of Wisconsin Press, 2006), 19–63.
"Explosive Experimente und die Fragilität des Experimentellen: Adorno, Bacon, und Cage," in
  Spektakuläre Experimente: Praktiken der Evidenzproduktion im 17. Jahrhundert, ed. Helmar
  Schramm, Ludger Schwarte, and Jan Lazardzig (Berlin: de Gruyter, 2006), 477–506.
"Film Music: Doubling, Dissonance, and Displacement," in *Das Double,* ed. Victor I. Stoichita
  (Wiesbaden: Harrassowitz Verlag, 2006), 319–44.
"For the Birds/Against the Birds: Modernist Narratives on the End of Art," in *Action, Art, History:
  Engagements with Arthur Danto,* ed. Daniel Herwitz and Michael Kelly (New York: Columbia
  University Press, 2007), 43–73.
"The Ode to Joy: Music and Musicality in Tragic Culture," in *International Yearbook of German
  Idealism,* Vol. 4: *Aesthetics and Philosophy of Art,* ed. Karl Ameriks and Jürgen Stolzenberg
  (Berlin: de Gruyter, 2006), 57–90.
"The Pastness of the Work: Albert Speer and the Monumentalism of Intentional Ruins," in *The
  Philosophy of Arthur C. Danto* (LaSalle, Ill.: Open Court, 2007).

In some tones the nightingale is still a bird; then it rises above its class and seems to want to show every other feathered creature what real singing would be.

— Goethe, Elective Affinities

Contents

Preface

For a long time I conceived of this book with the title *Notes to Adorno* to recall Adorno's musical essays on philosophy and literature collected in his own *Noten zur Literatur*. However, though focused on Adorno's work, my terrain is broader. I begin in an earlier period of German aesthetic theory, with, among others, Goethe, Schiller, and Hegel and end in America, with, among others, Arthur Danto and John Cage. The title after Goethe's novel *Elective Affinities* with the subtitle *Musical Essays on the History of Aesthetic Theory* far better suits the themes I treat along the way.

The essays trace a history of attraction and reaction (hence, the elective affinities) of music to philosophy, drama, birdsong, crime, film, and nation-hood. As philosophical histories of thought and idea, they explore concepts such as movement, affinity, musicality, naturalism, experimentalism, displacement, actuality, and possibility. Tying the conceptual histories together, I make explicit the deep reliance that German aesthetic and social theory has had on a philosophy of history based on tendencies, yearnings, needs, and potentialities. Although I treat philosophy, society, and the arts conceived under the romantic-modernist terms of catastrophe, ruin, and death, I track the reversal of these terms to present critical arguments for continuation, persistence, and survival.

More than offering exhaustive presentations of any given thinker's work, I use the work of others to produce my own patterns of conceptual thinking. These patterns depend more on reading primary texts than on pursuing issues dominant in the large body of secondary literature. Nevertheless, I want to acknowledge how much I have learned from the writings of many excellent scholars working on modernist aesthetic theory. For the most part, I do not engage in theory production, presenting theories with the purpose of pulling them apart, then to reconstruct them in better terms. Instead, I read histories of philosophical, aesthetic, and musical thought to show substantial gains and losses of meaning regarding our use of concepts. To say that this book offers a critical history of concepts is thus to say that it offers a history of their reception and thereby of the complex adaptations, appropriations, and retrievals of some of the most dominant philosophical and aesthetic theses of modern times.

In a previous project, *The Quest for Voice,* I studied the works and writings of Richard Wagner. I pursued what I conceived of as a tightrope argument, according to which concepts that promise so much good may, by subtle and not so subtle alterations in their use, end up abetting enormous harm. Similarly, in this book, no concept is uncritically accepted or dismissed outright; each is explored from the inside out to show how a concept can turn against its own better or worse uses in our different theories and practices. I take this to be the procedure of a historically informed, immanent critique. This book also returns to the first interest I ever had, namely, the concept of a musical work (*The Imaginary Museum of Musical Works*). Though I have spent much of my writing life trying to show all that has been involved in its use, I have never argued that the concept should be discarded, whatever that would mean. Here I pursue the terms for the work concept's continuation, albeit under critical or deflationary conditions, to labor philosophically against the excessive authority it has attained.

For a critical history of concepts to be effective, it must be neither too abstracted nor yet excessively steeped in detail. In 1768, the German poet Christoph Martin Wieland wrote "Musarion, or The Philosophy of the Graces," in part to warn overly schooled philosophers seeking beauty against looking with their eyes wide shut: "Too much light often blinds gentlemen of this sort," so that they do not see "the wood for the trees." I believe this famous expression originates with him. However, his warning is double-edged, telling philosophers to compromise neither the philosophical need to see the larger picture nor the material presence of the trees. Seeing too much detail, in the sense of knowing all, one might see everything but not the whole that matters. I heed the warning as best I can, though with the result that the essays are longer than I originally intended them to be.

Their length is not surprising: each essay is written across disciplines—philosophy, history, and musicology. Though I deeply respect the history of the different disciplines, I believe that each works best when its formal and historical limits are acknowledged. That no academic discipline works alone means that each should be subjected to as much critical reflection as any other socially sedimented domain. The concern with disciplinary limits shows itself in this book in relation to its several discussions of philosophy's lifelong battle with history and the arts.

Although an essay collection, this book was always intended to be a book. That each essay is written as such reflects not only the distinct occasion for which it was written but also Adorno's particular engagement with the essay form. Still, the more I reworked the essays into their final versions, the more they transformed into chapters. Increasingly, I made transparent the overarching developmental strands, though not so much as to break entirely the internal movement of each essay. If the book rests in an ambiguous space as a result, at least readers are left with the freedom to read the eight parts in two ways, separately and developmentally.

To make transparent the development, I ordered the chapters according to when the essays were written. From the writing of one, I usually discovered the theme or concept for the next. At the beginning, my philosophical need was straightforward: to understand Adorno as best I could. There are few thinkers as central as he in the history of the philosophy and sociology of music. Like others, I was conscious of all the accusations regarding the difficulty and obscurity of his writing and the elitism of his thought. Still, I found these accusations tempered by an admission that it is to Adorno to whom even those most irritated turn when in search of something new or interesting to say.

Several years later, I no longer feel my initial need so strongly, though this does not imply its full satisfaction. Nevertheless, I have begun to see how I shall distance myself from this figure insofar as he continues to dominate my thinking. In this respect, this book reflects the passage of my learning, what I have come so far to understand about his project to produce a critical, philosophical, aesthetic, and social theory. There are tensions in this passage: from the first chapter to the last I changed my mind. I rewrote to resolve certain tensions, but I did not resolve them all. The passage as such would have been destroyed had I succeeded too well. In the end, I found myself respecting Adorno's thought more even than I did at the beginning, in large measure because I acquired a greater understanding of where the real problems in his thinking lie.

Studying Adorno, I tried to comprehend an incomprehensible period in which I did not live. I have only lived in and with its aftermath. Adorno started to write in the 1920s, fully aware of though not fully comprehending (who could have been?) the rise of National Socialism. While in exile in the United States, he continued to explore the social, aesthetic, and philosophical tendencies of Nazism and fascism. After the war, into the late 1960s, the extreme and polarized terms of his thought remained unabated as he assessed the possibilities of democracy in a divided Germany in a divided Europe in a cold and polarized world. He died as a professor in Frankfurt in his mid-sixties, a striking thought for those who read him as a writer penning his thoughts with the fully developed wisdom of a sage. He was in his early thirties when he left Germany and in his forties when he returned, having already written *Philosophy of New Music, Minima Moralia,* and, in collaboration, *Dialectic of Enlightenment.*

Against this background, I reject the unsympathetic attitude I have sometimes heard of those who choose to mock his references to Auschwitz or to the catastrophe of the Second World War as dangerous rhetoric or as inappropriate to philosophical thought. That he took history, society, and his own particular times seriously as a philosopher makes his philosophy neither happy nor comfortable. Yet it does not follow that what he wrote about philosophy, society, and the arts is relevant only to the times of his life or best thrown onto the Old European pyre of the pessimistic, nihilistic, and obscure.

This said, while writing, I often feared that I was tending toward a dangerous act of identification, as though trying to appropriate another thinker's experience and thought. Accordingly, I endeavored to distance myself in thoughtful ways but without losing contact with the perspective of a particular historical past that has also significantly shaped some parts of my own life. Closeness and distance became themes of the chapters themselves, as they are persistent themes of any modernist philosophy concerned with identity and difference, empathy and critical judgment.

Like Adorno, I have lived for longer and shorter periods of my life in England, America, and Germany—though I with a far greater freedom of choice. Also like Adorno, I have found myself caught continuously between genuinely different humors or temperaments, between all the upbeats and downbeats of what remain to this day striking differences between English, American, and German optimisms and pessimisms. The play between optimism and pessimism is an explicit theme of this book. Finding no comfortable resting place between the different humors, I have left the tensions uneasily standing as they do as different sides of a complex coin.

In this book, I usually draw on recent translations of German texts. However, I also offer new or amended translations—not because I regard myself able in this subtle art, but because my readings depend on specific concepts whose significance has been lost. Sometimes the loss is due to reception and sometimes to translation. I provide my own translations wherever this makes transparent the use and centrality of the concepts of my specific concern.

Rather than endlessly quoting, I usually reconstruct the thought of others in my own sentences though still using many of their words. To reconstruct thoughts as lying midway between translation and rewriting runs the risk of blurring the line between where my thought begins and another's ends. However, this risk should be balanced against issues of style and readability and then against the truth of what is involved when one tries to think through the thought of another. "To think through" means both to work out a thought and to think via another person's thought—the double task implicit in the transmission of thought.

I rarely focus on the normal range of criticisms of Adorno's life work. There is already a large literature on "what's wrong with Adorno." I focus more on how the philosophy and history of Europe and America conditioned his thought, though without aiming to either apologize for it or normalize it. To show how his thought is in and out of sync with his times—and with our times—is to defamiliarize both the thought and the times. Accordingly, I situate Adorno's work historically against the background of philosophers and theorists to whom he was reacting. While this approach tends to render his thought sometimes neither as original nor as obscure as some think, it shows more precisely where and how it stands apart. Moreover, I read the theories I interpret against the grain of their usual reception and so I hope in a new light. This applies to my readings as much, say, of Hegel, Schopenhauer, and Hanslick as of Adorno, Danto, and Cage.

One obvious way to approach Adorno would be to compare him with other thinkers of his times, with his like-minded and unlike-minded contemporaries. This I do to some degree. Walter Benjamin makes several appearances, although Max Horkheimer, Ernst Bloch, Siegfried Kracauer, and Georg Lukács make relatively few. A far less usual approach—the one I choose—would be to juxtapose Adorno with a thinker who at first glance seems to be poles, times, or continents apart. Finally, my story turns to Arthur Danto, the American philosopher of history and art.

My initial motivation for juxtaposing Adorno and Danto was not purely intellectual but partly a consequence of my coming in 1994 to work at Columbia University. Danto was born in 1924, twenty-one years after Adorno. Danto lives and writes on Riverside Drive two blocks from where I now live and about twenty blocks above where Adorno lived briefly in 1938. Knowing at first Adorno's work better than I did Danto's, I found it increasingly illuminating to read Danto with an eye to seeing where he diverged from Adorno and then, of course, where they converged. The more I looked—and specifically at their responses to John Cage—the more I found a way, first, via Danto, to bring Adorno into debates that are still current in aesthetics today and, second, via Adorno, to place Danto's work in a moment in the 1960s when Adorno was still living and writing, although by then back in West Germany. Much of what inspired Adorno to write as he did inspired Danto, albeit that they disagreed about the extent to which the 1960s marked pseudorevolutionary changes as opposed to genuine liberations for society, philosophy, and the arts. Whereas Danto has pursued this matter ever since, Adorno's life was cut short in 1969. Nevertheless, they stand side by side as two of the most significant thinkers in aesthetic theory in the postwar period, over whose shadows few have been able to jump. One aim of this book is to juxtapose these two figures as they have not been juxtaposed before, to say more than each has said or shown himself about his place in the modern history of aesthetic theory.

Two relationships have increasingly come to dominate my thinking: first, between the philosophies of history and art and, second, between aesthetic and social theories. Even where the chapters are differently focused, these tense and dynamic relationships are always present.

Chapter 1 was first written for a conference in 2003, in Frankfurt, at the Johann Wolfgang Goethe University, to honor the centenary of Adorno's birth. I begin with the conceit of rewriting a decisive moment in Goethe's novel from which the title of my book is taken, the moment of Eduard's performance of reading aloud, in which the concept of elective affinity is unfolded. I end by retrieving the form of Adorno's negative dialectic via the concepts, respectively, of movement and affinity. On the way, I contrast Hegel's lesser-known model of the affinity between philosophy and music with better-known models, based on metaphor and analogy, represented by Hanslick and Schopenhauer. Central to Hegel's account is the dialectical play between *the concept of movement* and *the movement of the concept*. While presenting Adorno's reworking of Hegel's model, I introduce many of Adorno's most advanced claims, claims to which I then return in the following chapters. The aim of the first chapter is to begin to show, through its own internal momentum, what may be learned about thought and expression when philosophy and music are brought into a critical-formal relationship.

Chapter 2 is not about Adorno, although it offers further background to his work. It explores the concept of musicality and its place in the cultural critique of the early nineteenth century. It was written for a conference in 2005 honoring Schiller, on the two-hundredth anniversary of his death. It interprets the end of Beethoven's Ninth Symphony with the entrance of Schiller's "Ode to Joy." Presenting the views of Hanslick, Schiller, Schelling, Schopenhauer, and Hegel, I argue that the substantive concept of musicality (*das Musikalische*) entered the discourse of poetry, painting, and philosophy notably in Schiller's writings before it explicitly entered the domain of music. Overall, I explore the period before Wagnerian opera was born out of the musical spirit of the Beethoven symphony. In addition, I challenge traditional alliances that were claimed between Schopenhauer and Beethoven and between Hegel and Beethoven, most significantly because, for both philosophers, their recognition of music's meaning and philosophical significance did not translate into a preference for the symphony but derived, rather, from their preference for opera.

Chapter 3 is the first to juxtapose Adorno and Danto. Its subject is art's relationship to nature and the commonplace. It was written first for a conference on "conceptualisms" in Berlin but then reworked to honor Danto's contribution to the philosophies of history and art. Attending to proclamations about the ends of philosophy, society, history, music, or art, I show that the arguments in which these proclamations are made are in fact *for* continuation, liberation, and survival. To bring out their differences, I pit Adorno's extremely polarized thought about polarization against Danto's tempered recognition of pluralism. Their arguments originate in the work of Kant and Hegel but are situated here in the context of more or less pessimistic and optimistic postwar tensions in Europe and America, specifically regarding the naturalizing work of John Cage and his vision of the bird cage from which he sought to liberate the human bird. Hence, the picture I chose for the book's cover: a painting by Magritte demonstrating the advanced state of the dialectic of enlightenment in 1933: *Les Affinités Electives*.

Chapter 4 was written for a conference in Berlin on the subject of "spectacular experiments." I describe the different historical trajectories of the concepts of *experiment* and of *experimentalism* in terms influenced by, though surpassing, Horkheimer and Adorno's *Dialectic of Enlightenment*. The narrative begins with the father of experimental science, Francis Bacon, and ends with the resistant father of experimental music, John Cage. My interpretation of both these figures contrasts with received interpretations that take each more to have initiated than countered repressive passages in science, society, and the arts. Toward the chapter's end, I turn to Adorno's critique of these repressive passages, which, though extremely harsh, is nevertheless directed toward retrieving from the same history a genuinely fragile form of experimentalism appropriate to late modernist forms of musical composition, on the one hand, and of philosophical essay writing, on the other.

Chapter 5 presents a narrative to show certain deep connections I have increasingly come to notice between the philosophies of history and art. Focused on the work of Hegel, Adorno, and Danto, I explore the idea of an intentional ruin to reflect on the work concept, to articulate the concept's social and aesthetic tendency toward monumentalization. Beginning around 1800, with the (Hegelian) development of a museum culture in Berlin, my narrative ends in the period of the Second World War when Albert Speer developed the idea of an intentional ruin to perform the monumental and murderous work of the Third Reich. I write the narrative, as in chapter 3, with the aim to show what both Danto and Adorno were reacting to when they began to work out the terms for the continuing conduct of postwar philosophy, society, and the arts.

Chapter 6 introduces a new concept and technique of philosophical argument for this book, that of displacement. Its themes are music's relationship to violence and murder as a fine art. My thesis is that artworks that seek to commemorate the victims of acts of terrorism, violence, or calculated destruction often end up mirroring—via various sorts of displacement—the rationale or logic of the acts themselves. The outcome of the argument makes transparent the theological remains that persist in many of the secular and humanistic claims of modernism. Though I focus again on the Second World War and its aftermath, I take recent events such as 9/11 as a significant part of my motivation.

Whereas chapter 6 focuses on the dangers of displacement, chapter 7 focuses on its advantages as a technique of critique. I renew the exploration of the concepts of movement and musicality undertaken in chapters 1 and 2. I also pursue a theme I became interested in when working on Wagner, that of doubleness. Written first for a conference in Wolfenbüttel, Germany, on "The Double," but here in much expanded form, I explore the many different sorts of arguments—specifically of duplication, dissonance, and displacement—produced in the first half of the twentieth century for fully integrating music into film. I discuss two sorts of resistance filmmakers and critics expressed toward so integrating music. First, they argued that, given a commitment to cinematic *movement*, film was *already musical without music*. Second, they argued against music's integration, given an anti-Wagnerian anxiety regarding film's ability to maintain an appropriate distance from life. One aim of this chapter is to show how most of the early anxieties about the status of film as an *art*—and the place of music within film—were displaced anxieties about modern *life*. (I also offer a reading of Adorno and Eisler's *Komposition für den Film*.)

Chapter 8 renders explicit a theme present in many of the earlier chapters regarding the elective affinities between Europe (particularly Germany) and America. I ask what it means to speak specifically about American opera, following an invitation I received to lecture at a conference on this topic at the University of Michigan. My argument is set against the background of a weary history in which those tired of Europe (*europamüde*) pin their hopes on to the New World only then to become weary in the New World (*amerikamüde*) when they actually arrive on the shores of the United States. Against the background of a narrative of Old World–New World pessimisms and optimisms, I show that, from its very beginnings (more or less around 1800), American opera has been an imported concept dialectically out of sync with music's empirical history in the United States. Whether supported by democratic, polyglotic, purist, or posthistoricist arguments, the concept increasingly survived by assuming the burdens of what national operas (and significantly German opera) were meant to bring to their respective audiences in Europe. Much of this chapter is devoted to Adorno's use of the concepts of actuality and possibility, as well as to his own youthful American, antiopera project based on Mark Twain's *Adventures of Tom Sawyer*. Given this interest, I describe what happened to the 1920s *Amerikanismus* in Europe when it was transformed in the 1930s and after into an *Amerikanismus-in-exile* in the United States.

My afterword continues the terms of the last chapter while returning also to those of the first. What sort of ending for this book, I ask, will least contradict the internal content and movement of its thought? I end as I began, by assuming the conceit to rewrite a moment from a great story. I began with a moment about performance from Goethe's *Elective Affinities* and end with another moment about performance described with wondrous wit by that "tramp abroad," Mark Twain. Concerned, for the last time, with the troubled distinction between art and life, I seek the significance of the fact that audiences separated by the Atlantic Ocean respond differently to art and to thought by applauding either before or after the ending has actually been reached.

Acknowledgments

I wrote this book over several years during which I traveled a great deal and met many people who helped me with my work. I cannot name them all but I do sincerely thank them.

To some, however, I owe specific gratitude.

To Arthur Danto, for his friendship and profound encouragement—and because he once told me that my gaze was too directed toward Europe and challenged me to think about America. The more I read his work, the more I was led along new paths.

To Richard and Peggy Kuhns and to Victor and Jacqueline Gourevitch, for their friendship, kindness, and inexhaustible knowledge and experience.

To my doctoral students at Columbia University, most of all to Jonathan Neufeld and Brian Soucek, who scrutinized almost every thought in this book. To Michal Gal, Hanne Hahonen, Dehlia Hannah, Felix Koch, Tiger Roholt, Sirine Shebaya, Edgardo Salinas, Martin Scherzinger, and Mario Wenning because I learned something from each of them.

To Susan Gillespie, Robert Hullot-Kentor, Eberhard Ortland, and Hans Vaget, for their inspiring conversation and indispensable help with translation.

To Daniel Herwitz and Gregg Horowitz, for many marvelous telephone conversations that have turned into productive collaborations.

To Patrick Calleo, for his passion for opera and life.

To Walter Frisch, for glasses of wine whenever the bell tolled.

To Boris Gasparov, for intellectual journeys in Riverside Park.

To Amy Ayers, for her painstaking reference checking.

To Wendy Lochner of Columbia University Press, to my inspired copyeditor Cynthia Garver, and to the two readers who vetted my manuscript for the press and who chose not to remain anonymous—hence, to Willi Goetschel and Richard Leppert in friendship and with deep respect.

To several fellow travelers in music, philosophy, and aesthetic theory, from whose writings or conversation I have learned something important regarding the arguments of this book. On one side of the Atlantic, to Carolyn Abbate, David Albert, Stefan Andriopoulos, Joseph Auner, Karol Berger, Jay Bernstein, Mark Evan Bonds, Taylor Carman, David Carrier, Jonathan Gilmore, Tom Grey, Berthold Hoeckner, Tom Huhn, Andreas Huyssen, Michael Kelly, Philip Kitcher, David Levin, Tom Levin, Susan McClary, Anne Midgette, Dmitri Nikulin, Max Pensky, Thomas Pogge, Gerhard Richter, Alex Ross, Fred Rush, Michael Steinberg, Rose Rosengard Subotnik, Richard Taruskin, Leo Treitler, and Lambert Zuidervaart. And, on the other side, to Andrew Bowie, Hauke Brunkhorst, Hermann Danuser, Albrecht Dümling, Johannes Gall, Stefan Gosepath, Michael Hagner, Espen Hammer, Brigitte Hilmer, Gertrud Koch, Reinhard Kratz, Christoph Menke, Herbert Molderings, Max Paddison, Roger Parker, Ludger Schwarte, Dieter Thomä, Christian Thorau, Albrecht Wellmer, and Janet Wolff.

To the Getty Research Institute, Guggenheim Foundation, Aby Warburg Haus, Wissenschaftskolleg zu Berlin, Royal Holloway College, British Library, Music Department at Cambridge University, and all those who made possible my fellowships and most pleasurable times in these institutions.

To the University Seminars at Columbia University for their help in publication. Material in this work was presented to the University Seminar on Romanticism.

Finally, for an unfathomable friendship that has spanned the writing of this book—from Los Angeles to New York to Berlin—my thanks to Ernst Osterkamp, a reader of Goethe par excellence.

New York/Berlin

ELECTIVE AFFINITIES

1 Doppelbewegung

The Musical Movement of Philosophy and the Philosophical Movement of Music

Was bedeutet die Bewegung?
—Goethe/Marianne von Willemer, *Suleika*

When Charlotte asks Eduard on one of those evenings at home to explain to her what is meant by an elective affinity, she clearly irritates him by interrupting his performance. Eduard has long enjoyed reading aloud in company, even, as it has been of late, a more technical book of science. In his deep, melodious voice, he likes to unfold the thought in his own time, pausing and pacing, surprising and consoling, where he sees fit. He doesn't want his company to know what will happen next, and certainly not the ending before he's reached it. He most dislikes it, therefore, when someone looks over his shoulder, as Charlotte now does, to read alongside him. "If I read aloud to someone, isn't it just as if I were explaining something orally?" he rebukes his wife. "The written or printed word takes the place of my own feeling, my own heart; and do you think I'd bother to talk if a small window were placed on my forehead, or on my breast, so that the person to whom I wished to tell my thoughts or feelings one by one would already know in advance what I was aiming at? When someone reads over my shoulder, I always feel as if I were being torn in two parts."[1]

Eduard is willing to explain the metaphor as he calls it, which so confuses Charlotte. With the help of the Captain, he describes the natural affinity with which different elements adhere to but also repel one another, as if each were choosing its own particular arrangement: *Wahlverwandtschaft*. Eduard speaks of chemistry and physics; the Captain, too, of how cohesiveness can be seen in liquids with their tendency to form into round shapes—falling drops of water or little balls of quicksilver or molten lead. At the same time, they all hear a description of human relations. They know they are playing with analogies; they notice the double meaning of the term. Elements and persons: each compelled to spring into activity to form novel and unexpected constellations, a lively movement that disturbs each along the way and of which the ending can't be predicted in advance.

Charlotte wants to believe she knows how things will turn out: she doesn't always need to look over Eduard's shoulder. Were she merely an observer of the story, she might have some understanding of the events, though mere observation would never be enough. No real understanding is acquired independently of experience, the Captain explains; everyone participates and experience takes time to unfold. What unrest Charlotte then feels when she finds herself drawn, as she quickly is, to the Captain, or when she notices days later that Eduard has taken up reading love poems again and is allowing the beautiful Ottilie to read alongside him. He even pauses longer than needed to avoid having to turn the page before Ottilie is ready. Ottilie prefers to read herself rather than trust the word of another; yet, though this obviously interrupts Eduard's reading, he no longer objects. With Ottilie he doesn't feel torn; sometimes, after all, *Verwandtschaft* means a "meeting of minds." So, too, is this seen when Eduard and Ottilie play music together. When Charlotte plays with Eduard, she always has to adjust her tempi to keep up with him. With Ottilie, the situation is subtly different: she learns the piece in her own way but also somehow perfectly to mirror his mistakes. A stronger affinity perhaps, an exceedingly pleasant experience, yet out of their union materializes a new piece—played at the wrong tempo.

The Aim

Goethe's novel—from which I drew my own telling of the story—enfolds a somewhat ironic description of its central principle, *Wahlverwandtschaft*, into a performance of Eduard's reading aloud. It shows the movement inherent in the principle, as well as the movement of its coming to be understood.

This is not surprising: the novel, as it has often been remarked, has the style of a recitation and "unfolds inside the categories of the 'story-teller.'"[2] As in Goethe's novel, my first chapter is also about a *Doppelbewegung*, about two sorts of movement brought into special affinity. Inspired by Goethe but focusing on Adorno, it tracks the affinity between philosophy and music in the German tradition.

When writing about philosophy and music, Adorno uses the terms "affinity," "convergence," "mediation," and "unfolding." For "affinity," he uses two German terms: *Verwandtschaft* and *Affinität*. He prefers these terms to the more traditional terms "analogy" and "metaphor." He often refers to Goethe's novel and to other works by Goethe. Arguing for a dynamic language of *becoming* to replace the static language of *Being*, he speaks of philosophy and music as dynamic modes of conduct (*Verhaltensweisen*). He works out his preferred schema through the general notion of *movement—Bewegung*. (I often use the German term to show its prevalent use.) Adorno believes that this notion can do more important dialectical work than the more commonly used notions of time and temporality. When late in life, for example, he argues in Darmstadt with composers such as Stockhausen, Boulez, and Cage about the concept of time, he assumes the broader vantage point of *Bewegung*.

Adorno employs the notion of *Bewegung* throughout his musical and philosophical writings to show the difference between the earlier German idealist dialectic and his own preferred negative dialectic. He uses it to work out an affinity between Hegel and Beethoven and to develop themes of *lateness* and *aging*. He uses it to explain why dissonance is the truth about harmony; disorder the truth about order; fragmentation, unity; infidelity, fidelity; and under what terms, finally, movement is the truth about rest.[3] He further uses *Bewegung* to describe the dynamic form and expression of music and philosophy. He takes the idea of unfolding a philosophical thought as seriously as that of unfolding a musical theme. The idea that one should read dialectical philosophy as though written with expressive markings is no mere rhetoric; nor is it a way to either reduce or elevate philosophy to the musical art. On the contrary, Adorno uses *Bewegung* to keep philosophy and music in a mutually productive relation, hence, in anything but a static or reductive relation of identity.

Although I describe Adorno's use of *Bewegung*, my attention does not rest there. From the outset, I recount part of a more general history of musical aesthetics. By moving backward through the figures of Hanslick, Schopenhauer, and Hegel, this story situates Adorno's use of the concept in a broad historical set of debates.

The Term

The concept of *Bewegung* has an extensive application going back to the pre-Socratic philosophers. In music, it covers the motion and tempi of sounding events through time and space, along with the horizontal and vertical structures provided by rhythm and counterpoint. It is also connected to clocks and timing, pendulums and metronomes. "Pull, pull, lift! It is moving [*bewegt sich*], floating [*schwebt*]!" writes Schiller in 1797 in *The Song of the Bell*. Normally when we speak of *Bewegung*, we assume that something moves or that something is being moved. Yet we tend to speak of musical forms as being *in* movement or as being *of* pure temporal movement, denying to music its presence or objecthood in physical space.

Bewegung conveys the idea of music as embodied dance: movement as metakinetic. When once Adorno described a Beethoven symphony as embodied, he made it evident that he was thinking less about an artwork's ontological embodiment in a physical object than about the musical work as a living body in performance. Defining "the relationship of the symphony to dance," he wrote:

> If dance appeals to the bodily movement of human beings, then the symphony is the [kind of] music that itself becomes a body. . . . The symphony moves, stirs "itself"; stands still, moves on, and the totality of its gestures is the intentionless representation of the body. . . . This corporeal nature of the symphony is its social essence: it is the giant body, the collective body of society in the dialectic of its moments.[4]

What a moving body admits, as a symphony admits, is a broad commitment to development and change. In contemporary theory, *Bewegung* appears most often in relation to sport and dance. When used in music, it also underscores the ontological and social necessity for a work to be performed and heard: a work considered in the aesthetic process of its unfolding.

Adorno used the term "bewegt" at least twice to name movements of his own compositions.[5] The term is not redundant. (After all, all music moves; how can it not move?) The term conveys the particular sense of energy and speed with which the movements are to be played. However, whereas in English, French, and Italian the terms "movement," "mouvement," and "movimento" refer to the distinct parts of a musical work—a symphony in four movements— the German term for the same is "Satz." This term stems from

"Gesetz" (law, principle, rule) and even more from "setzen" (putting, setting: i.e., composing).[6] The division of a work into discrete *Sätze* follows a modern analogy between music and language according to which, following Koch's *Musikalisches Lexikon* of 1802, the term "designates each individual part of a musical work that has for and in itself a complete meaning." Yet what remains in German, as in other languages, is the use of (Italian) "movement" terms (also called tempi and character terms), such as "largo," "allegro," and "presto," to mark the different sorts of *Sätze*.

Bewegung is used to refer to the modification, following Rousseau, of our passions or emotions: our agitations, excitements, and stirrings.[7] In music, as in other arts, it shows particular ranges of human gestures and expressions. In addition to Lessing's pathbreaking discussion of expressive movement in his *Laoköon* (1766), a documented English use from the 1770s notes the "rise and fall, the advance and recess . . . in the different parts of a building, so as to add greatly to the picturesque of a composition."[8] In this use, as in Lessing's, movement occurs within particular instances of particular arts and between the arts as demonstrated through an extensive exchange of their respective terms.

Bewegung is employed to capture the movement of thought—of thinking in process (*Gedankenbewegung*). In ancient philosophical texts, one may follow the movement and mediation of thoughts or propositions through syllogistic logic and dialectical reasoning. This usage is not far removed from other ancient and then modern usages, where one reads of the linear or cyclical patterns or vibrations of the celestial and earthly bodies. Kant speaks of the Copernican Revolution in terms of the movement of the heavens (*Himmelsbewegung*) in the context of reconfiguring his metaphysics. Merleau-Ponty's phenomenological existentialism depends significantly on his view of intentionality explored through the terms of the *mouvement* of body and thought: intentionality as embodied thinking in movement.

Across the board, *Bewegung* captures the dynamics of history and the evolutionary passages of nature. We speak of moves in a chess game, of movement in the stock market, of moving staircases, moving pavements, and, of course, moving pictures—about which an insightful comment is made in Tennessee Williams's *The Glass Menagerie,* in a conversation between Jim and Tom:

Jim: What are you gassing about?
Tom: I'm tired of the movies. . . . Look at them—. . . All of those
   glamorous people—having adventures—hogging it all, gobbling the

whole thing up! You know what happens? People go to the *movies* instead of *moving*. . . . But I'm not patient. I don't want to wait till then. I'm tired of the *movies* and I am *about* to *move!*[9]

Finally, there is a political meaning, originating in the early 1800s, used to refer to the German movement, to the Catholic movement, and later, as recorded in 1885, to student movements, about which it was once claimed that whereas Oxford is the home of "movements," Cambridge is the home of "men."[10] Since then, there have been historical or authentic performance movements, phenomenological movements, fascist movements, underground, workers', feminist, and student movements. Of course, not everything that claims to move actually does move or moves in the right way. Hence, Adorno's urgency to point to the *tendency* in a movement—promoting a new style, new performance practice, or new politics—to fall or degenerate into ideological or collective stasis.

In philosophy, politics, and the arts, the concept of *Bewegung* makes little sense unless used in relation to positive and negative notions of resting, waiting, ending, suspending, pausing, and stopping. These notions are connected to others: establishing, congealing, sterilizing, stabilizing, and solidifying. Adorno employs the latter terms when describing what he takes to be the rigidifying and reifying tendencies of ontology or metaphysics (in his critique, say, of Heidegger and Heideggereanism), of music (in his critique, say, of serialism and New Objectivity [*Neue Sachlichkeit*]), and of politics (in his critique, say, of totalitarianism).

The Concept

"Up to now, in the investigations of music's essence and effect, the concept of *movement* [*der Begriff der Bewegung*] has been noticeably neglected; yet it seems to me that this concept is the most important and fruitful." So wrote the Viennese music critic and thinker Eduard Hanslick in 1854 in his canonic text *Vom musikalisch-Schönen* (*On the Musically Beautiful*).[11] However, though he could not have made the point more explicit, the concept has continued to be neglected. Hanslick is partially to blame: he embedded his favored concept in an account that obscured it.

In his recent *Aesthetics of Music*, Roger Scruton notices the neglect of the concept and partially blames Hanslick, too. This shared observation leads Scruton in a direction different from my own and from Adorno's. As Scruton correctly sees, and as discussed below, Hanslick unfolds his concept of *Bewegung* within an overly anxious account of metaphor. Scruton dispenses with that anxiety, writing in summary of his own account:

> In hearing sounds, we may attend to them in the way that we attend to pictures, on the look-out, or listen-out, for imaginative perceptions. There then arises the peculiar double intentionality that is exemplified in the experience of metaphor: one and the same experience takes sound as its object, and also something that is not and cannot be sound—the life and movement that is music. We hear this life and movement *in* the sound, and situate it in an imagined space, organized, as is the phenomenal space of our own experience, in terms of "up" and "down," "rising" and "falling," "high and low." . . . Music is the intentional object of an experience that only rational beings can have, and only through the exercise of imagination. To describe it we must have recourse to metaphor, not because music resides in an analogy with other things, but because the metaphor describes exactly *what* we hear, when we hear sounds as music.[12]

In the text omitted from the quoted passage (indicated by the ellipsis), Scruton suggests that it would not be wise to move too quickly toward phenomenological accounts, as suggested by Sartre and Merleau-Ponty, or into Schopenhauer's metaphysics to explain the movement in music, because the foundations of these theories are too dubious. Other contemporary philosophers of music have been similarly skeptical and have confined their accounts as best they can to accounts of metaphor.[13] Adorno, too, is skeptical of these metaphysical views but worries, first, that by retreating too far from them, we might lose something from the concept of *Bewegung* we actually need or should preserve, and, second, that by tying the concept too closely to an account of metaphor, we might obscure the concept's independent import.

From a broader perspective, Scruton employs the concept of movement to develop a firmly principled, securely grounded, and normatively significant metaphysics in support of the harmonious development of music and the human soul. Within this project, he attributes the interruptions to, and unrest in, this development to the ruin and relativizing of culture. Here, Scruton and Adorno find common ground. Adorno also sees culture's ruin (and ruins) in terms of the interruptions and unrest in the history of harmony. However, rather than using the concept of movement to place philosophy and music safely on the side of the harmonious soul, Adorno uses it to expose a history whose movement culminated in the catastrophic end that was Auschwitz. "Every self-righteous appeal to humanity in the midst of inhuman conditions," he writes with reference to Goethe, "should be viewed with the very greatest suspicion. There are no words for the noble, the good, the true, and the beautiful that have not been violated and turned into their opposite— just as the Nazis could enthuse about the house, its roof resting on pillars, while torture went on in the cellars."[14] Adorno finds no philosophical safety in appealing to harmony to sustain in the modern world what he takes to have become deeply false or deceptive political conceptions of the good. He uses the concept of *Bewegung* as a doubling concept put to the service of philosophical and political critique. Hence, also, the title of my chapter: *Doppelbewegung*.

Hanslick

Hanslick articulates the objective conditions for an aesthetics of music to meet the standards of natural science. He names chemistry, mathematics, and physiology in particular. His aim is more Goethean than positivistic: "Ariel moves the song / to heavenly pure sounds" (*Ariel bewegt den Sang / In himmlisch reinen Tönen*)[15]—which means that though Hanslick sees in music what he sees in chemistry—namely, "natural connections" and "elective affinities" between the elements—he notices that the affinities are "strange" and "mysterious": "All musical elements stand to one another, according to the laws of nature, in secret connections and elective affinities."[16]

According to Hanslick, music's mysterious affinities are to be understood in terms of the autonomous relations between musical elements. The relations follow artistic and aesthetic principles or laws appropriate to music as a fine or beautiful art—principles or laws that are irreducible to those of any other science or art. They are almost impossible to describe, however. Only in Ariel's song, or in the pure listening experience of music itself, are we given comprehensive and comprehending access to music's mysterious movement.

Hanslick separates his account of music's beauty from a traditional, subjectivist feeling theory. Feelings aroused in listeners by music neither constitute nor account for music's beauty nor stand in any essential relation to its meaning: "The beauty of a musical piece is specifically musical, that is, inherent in the tonal relationships without reference to a foreign, extramusical arena of ideas."[17] He turns his attention to "the music itself." More or less following Kant, he finds a musical object of purely aesthetic contemplation and imagination and, following Hegel, the unfolding of a specifically or purely musical idea (*Gedanke*). The musically beautiful lies in the notes in their compositional arrangement and in nothing else. Music's content—*Inhalt*—is just its "*tönend bewegte Formen*" (where Hanslick himself gives double emphasis to the middle term).[18]

What Hanslick writes before and after he enters this celebrated but also untranslatable phrase into his account should lead one to think that he is deeply concerned with its middle term, "bewegte," used to suggest forms in movement sounded out through the medium of tones.[19] In the subsequent reception of his theory, however, the middle term is increasingly suppressed by the terms that sandwich it. In the development of musical formalism, more attention is given to the structured arrangements of sounds—the tonal forms—than to the *Bewegung*. Of course, no formalist ever denies that tonal forms move, but they do restrict the scope of the movement. Compelled by Hanslick's separation of musical forms from the subjective arousal of feeling and emotion, they believe it correct to separate, within the concept of *Bewegung*, music's more intangible aesthetic potential from the objective fact that tonal forms move in time. The term "bewegt" is accordingly interpreted to capture only the *motion* generated by music's rhythm and temporal sequence. Formalist theories of motion, rhythm, and meter abound in the literature and they are productive. Still, the theories often testify to a loss regarding the concept of *Bewegung*.[20]

Hanslick inadvertently encourages this loss, inadvertently because he is far more reacting to traditional accounts of musical beauty than prescribing a strict formalism for the future. When he divorces musical forms from the subjective arousal and representation of emotions, be they emotions conceived in general or particular ("joy" or "this particular feeling of joy"), he does not mean to separate the forms from their expressive or aesthetic potential. He means only to assert a separation to counter the reductionist collapse of music's meaning to merely subjective feelings. Hanslick uses the term "Bewegung" partly because it was widely used in earlier, enlightenment theories of musical meaning, but more, for his own times, because it points to the double truth that music is a temporal art and an art par excellence of lived experience and expression. Music moves and it moves us. Still, he insists, it does not move us by arousing or representing everyday feelings.

Hanslick wants to account for music's ability to move us aesthetically *entirely* in terms of music's ability to move itself: to move fast and to move slowly, to rise and swell in a thousand shades. He speaks of music as an audible kaleidoscope full of tension, dynamics, and contrasts. *Bewegung*, the argument goes, is the element that music shares with our emotional states. Even so, this should not encourage us to seek in music a *portrayal* of those states. Following a thought Goethe developed in his color theory, Hanslick argues that tonalities, chords, and timbres each have their own moral or emotional characters (ecstasy at A-flat major, melancholia with the key of B minor). However, that such elements are associated with the movements in the works does not mean that the musical movements merely *represent* or *portray* these elements. On the contrary, the suggested or isolated correspondences or symbolisms must be suspended in favor of the law or movement of the works themselves. Works unfold according to a purely musical logic of specific form and arrangement that cannot be translated entirely into any either particularized or generalized language, be it of emotion, character, or concept.[21]

Hanslick thus argues that music's beauty and expression lie in music's movement *alone:* "For its alleged purpose, music has no other means other than through the analogy of movement and the symbolism of tones."[22] Any other sort of appeal lies outside music's proper domain. Yet a problem is lurking in the analogy of movement and the symbolism of tones, as Hanslick explains here, in this most decisive passage:

> It is extraordinarily difficult to describe this autonomous beauty of the art of tone—this specific musicality [*dies spezifisch Musikalische*]. That music has no prototype in nature and expresses no conceptual content means that it can be talked about only through dry technical determinations or in poetical fictions. Its realm is in fact "not of this world." All the fanciful descriptions, characterizations, or paraphrases of a musical work are either figurative or erroneous. What in every other art is still description is in music already metaphor. Music wants finally to be grasped as music and can only be understood from the perspective of itself and enjoyed in and for itself.[23]

Hanslick cannot and does not want to dispense with metaphor even in a philosophical treatise. However, he constantly worries that even a necessary use of metaphorical language, tethered to music's movement, will fall into poetical inexactness. Preventing this fall, as the history of musical aesthetics has shown, is the hardest philosophical task of all.

After Hanslick, it is the threat of *inexactness* that seems most to encourage later, scientifically inclined formalists to confine their attention to the "drier" movements of musical form. Yet, what this accomplishes, as previously noted, is a narrowing of the concept of *Bewegung* to its most technical and least aesthetic and social use. When other theorists then judge these formalists to have become too restrictive, they take the obvious course: to reintroduce some of the aesthetic and other dimensions of movement back into the account. In doing this, they tend to make the theory of metaphor more central. As in Scruton's work, the two tasks are combined, with the consequence, however, that the importance Hanslick assigned to the concept of *Bewegung* is overshadowed by the task of explaining how music moves through metaphor.

The First Transition

In this chapter, I isolate the concept of *Bewegung* from the account of metaphor to retrieve something of the concept's potential. To this end, I return to the philosophical uses of this notion prior to Hanslick's. If Hanslick was reacting to the feeling theories predominant in enlightenment aesthetics, he was so by drawing on the philosophers of romanticism and idealism who had already developed an aesthetic of absolute music. The terms of that development are well documented; less documented, however, is the role given to *Bewegung* to connect absolute music to a metaphysics of the Absolute. In this context, and this is the crucial transition in my own argument, the concept of *Bewegung* plays as significant a role in shaping philosophy's conception of itself as it does in shaping philosophy's conception of music—to which, nevertheless, music answers back by asserting the freedom of its own expressive movement from the subsumptive conceptual tendency of philosophy.

In the following sections, I summarize the views of two key but contrary figures: Schopenhauer and Hegel. In the matter of *Bewegung*, Schopenhauer gives pride of place to music, Hegel to philosophy. Schopenhauer, like Hanslick, relies on a commitment to analogy and metaphor; Hegel does not. Schopenhauer has long been known as the musician's philosopher; Hegel has never been renowned for his philosophical interest in music. Yet, with the focus on *Bewegung*, it is Hegel's dialectical model that offers Adorno a means by which to show the deep affinity between philosophy and music: their moving toward one another and their moving away.

Schopenhauer

In Schopenhauer's account, music is a temporal and expressive art, an art of pure unfolding, that though expressive expresses no definite emotion or concept. It is expressive but not expressive *of*: it is expressive in purely musical terms. Yet, contra Hanslick, what makes the expression purely musical depends for its explanation less on the *Bewegung* of the tonal forms per se than on the *Bewegung* of the world Will. Drawing on a Pythagorean and Platonic use (as well as on certain strains of Indian or Buddhist philosophy), Schopenhauer sees the world on its nonrepresentational side as a Will in movement: a blind, active, and pure drive, undifferentiated in itself, but which shapes the constant and individuated urgings and strivings of men. Schopenhauer argues that, on the pure side, the world is as much embodied music as embodied Will.[24] Music stands to the Will not as a copy or representation but as its unmediated expression. Bypassing the world of individuated emotions and any mediating Platonic Ideas, it is separated from the other impure or mediated, representational arts. If, Schopenhauer concludes, we are tempted to say that music expresses the emotions at all, we should say that it expresses them at best "in themselves"—abstractly, universally, or essentially—as pure form without matter. But if, more exactly, we speak less about expressing emotions and more about music's expressive movement (which would circumvent the threat also of the mediation of Ideas), then all we have to say is that, as pure temporal process, music tracks the expressive course of the world Will from its innermost and most complete and undifferentiated perspective.

That music is so immediately related to Will leads Schopenhauer to articulate the deep romantic paradox of describing music in a necessarily inadequate philosophical language. How can a language, like philosophy's, that is essentially conceptual, grasp music's inexpressible or nonconceptual movement? This question concerns less the difficulties of translating one language into another and more Schopenhauer's difficult idea that, with its inexpressible significance as the unmediated expression of Will, music has a purer metaphysical and human import than the concept-bound philosophy. Whereas Leibniz maintained that music is "an unconscious exercise in arithmetic in which the mind does not know it is counting," Schopenhauer claims that "music is an unconscious exercise in metaphysics in which the mind does not know it is philosophizing."[25] But what value does a metaphysics that proceeds unconsciously possibly have? Perhaps the same epistemological value that a pure aesthetic experience has, at just the moment when this experience makes us most aware of the Will's dynamic pull: when we are drawn into the Will's movement though distanced from its ordinary or everyday representational forms, or when we experience ourselves released from the Will's movement in a moment of aesthetic stillness.

If music is embodied Will, then, on this account, to provide a perfectly accurate and complete description of music is to provide a description of Will.
"Whoever has followed me thus far," Schopenhauer writes,

> will not find it so very paradoxical when I say that, supposing we suc-
> ceeded in giving a perfectly accurate and complete explanation of music
> which goes into detail, and thus a detailed repetition in concepts of
> what it expresses, this would also be at once a sufficient repetition and
> explanation of the world in concepts, or one wholly corresponding
> thereto, and hence the true philosophy.[26]

To the extent that Schopenhauer describes music in its concrete form, he does
so by assuming a relation of perfect repetition and parallelism, to demonstrate
how, in its full melodic, harmonic, and rhythmic complexity, music's movement matches every movement of the Will: "In the whole of the ripienos that
produce the harmony, between the bass and the leading voice singing the
melody, I see the whole gradation of the Ideas in which the Will objectifies
itself."[27] Nevertheless, as Schopenhauer just reminded us, when we describe
music from the concrete perspective of the world as Idea and representation
or in terms that would give us a philosophy of music, we necessarily use an
indirect language of *analogy*.[28] For music expresses not the represented phenomena, only the inner nature as such regarded from the undifferentiated
perspective of Will, and philosophy can only capture this indirectly by its in-
dividuating conceptual means. If music is to remain pure, as the unconscious
metaphysics, it must retain its independence, therefore, from its concept-
bound and conscious competitor in philosophy.

Whereas Schopenhauer moves into the essential, abstract, or formal inside
of music to find the tracking of the Will, Hanslick moves only as far as the
objective-sounding forms, though he, too, finds in those forms something
mysterious. Whereas Schopenhauer significantly uses the term "analogy,"
Hanslick stresses the term "metaphor," though each also uses the other term.
Hanslick worries about fantastical falls into inexactness and seeks philosophical precision by referring only to the musical forms themselves. With far less
anxiety, Schopenhauer is convinced that he can produce a perfect analogy or
parallelism between Will and representation, and thus, by extension, between
music and philosophy.

But does his own philosophy successfully repeat or parallel music's essential
Bewegung? Thomas Mann, for one, believes it does when he describes Scho-

penhauer's metaphysical work as reading like the symphonic movement of a musical work: "I have often called his great work a symphony in four movements."[29] I think that Mann's observation is too quick. To be sure, Schopenhauer uses the term *Bewegung* to highlight the dynamic tensions in all the arts, from architecture to music. So, too, does he write about human and animal bodies in their willed actions and physical movements, as well as about the moving constellations of heavenly and natural bodies. In other words, he draws on the long history of the concept's most common uses. Yet, for all his attention to *Bewegung* and despite the special status he awards music, he does not bring the musical movement of the Will into the epistemological or structural conduct of his own philosophy.

Hegel on Music

Whether one should read this as a failure in Schopenhauer's scheme or, better, as a deliberate decision on his part to maintain philosophy's difference from music, it is this matter that differentiates his approach from Hegel and from many of his idealist and romantic contemporaries. Hegel, for one, makes *Bewegung* a central concept in his philosophy *and* a self-conscious concept of philosophy's operation. Though Hegel does not use only music's movement as his model, he does take seriously the rhythm of his philosophy conceived in significant part in musical and temporal terms. Dialectical rhythm stands at the core of his work, from its beginning to its end. What he sees in philosophy's movement, he sees in music's movement. When he chooses to speak about music in his lectures on the fine arts, he seeks the type of *Bewegung* he has already identified for his dialectic as a whole. He has a systematic or philosophical reason for doing so.

Only once in his remarks on music (recorded and amplified by his student Hotho[30]) does Hegel mention an affinity to his work on logic, which means to the dialectical *Bewegung* of the concept (*Begriff*). He introduces into these remarks not only the concept of movement (*der Begriff der Bewegung*) but also the movement of the concept (*die Bewegung des Begriffs*). The doubling-up is important: if we do not notice it, we tend to think that Hegel is only inheriting, which largely he is, all the usual thoughts about the art of music as a pure language of subjectivity or human feeling. For Hegel, music is such a language, but its operation also follows a decidedly dialectical logic: the necessary movement of dissonance—contradiction, opposition, unrest—within an overall harmonic structure. Already "in my [Science of] Logic," it is re-called in his lectures on fine art,

> I developed the concept as subjectivity, but where this subjectivity, as an ideal transparent unity, is lifted into its opposite, that is, into objectivity; . . . but it is only genuine subjectivity if it enters this opposition and then overcomes and dissolves it. In the actual world, too, there are higher natures who are given power to endure the grief of inner opposition and conquer it. If now, as art, music is to express both the inner meaning and the subjective feeling of the deepest things, for example, of religion and in particular the Christian religion in which the abysses of grief form a principal part, it must possess in the sphere of its notes the means capable of representing the battle of opposites. These means it gains in the so-called dissonant chords of the seventh and ninth.[31]

In the *Science of Logic* itself, Hegel develops more than his idea of subjectivity; he also explains something of what he means by movement in music, when, in a passage on elective affinities, he notes the correlation between series or rows of music and chemical elements. This is a remarkable passage and not well known (for its later Hanslickean and Schoenbergian overtones), so I quote it at length:

> The expression *elective affinity* . . . refer[s] to the *chemical* relationship. For a chemical substance has its specific determinateness essentially in its relation to its other and exists only as this difference from it. Furthermore, this specific relation is bound up with quantity and is at the same time the relation, not only to a single other but to a series [*eine Reihe*] of specifically different others opposed to it. The combinations with this series are based on a so-called affinity with *every* member of the series. . . . It is, however, not only in the sphere of chemistry that the specific relation is represented . . . ; the individual note, too, only has meaning in relationship and combination with another note and with a series of others. The harmony or disharmony in such a circle of combinations constitutes its qualitative nature which is at the same time based on quantitative ratios. . . . The individual note is the key of a system, but again it is equally an individual member in the system of every other key. The harmonies are exclusive elective affinities whose characteristic quality is equally dissolved again in the externality of a merely quantitative

progression. What . . . constitutes the principle of a measure for those affinities which (whether chemical or musical . . .) are [therefore] elective affinities between and in opposition to the others.[32]

In Hegel's view, the purely instrumental stratum of music is a purely temporal language of subjective inwardness. It is also a language of double negation: first, it cancels out its spatial situation, its stability in persistent material; second, it cancels out its own sounding-out in time. The first negation allows this sounding stratum to exist as pure movement or as pure sensuous vibration. It moves through itself or its material in transitional patterns of tension, discord, resolution, and rest. The second negation cancels out its own assertion of becoming. The sound vanishes or annihilates its objective existence in the moment it asserts it: a tone is heard and then it is gone.[33]

With its double negation, music as a sounding art is the mode of expression most adequate to the inner life, the self, experienced *in* its own pure movement *as* pure movement. Music is pure self-expression, expressive of itself alone, but, via mediation, expressive also of the self's movement. Within his overall history of the arts, music has the status of a romantic art in second place behind poetry. (Between purely instrumental music and poetry lies an especially valued space for opera, a form of art I describe in chapter 2.) In its particular movement, music not only matches the dialectical movement of the conscious self through a "sympathetic harmony"; it does this also to make explicit to the self its own movement. Moving through feeling, music's sounding stratum negates its mediation of the objective world to allow the self to experience itself as pure negativity in "its own formal freedom." The sympathy between music and self is premised on a relation not of "analogy" or "repetition" but of *mediation. Music's patterns mediate the self's movement toward formal freedom.* The freedom or inner life of the self is made intelligible to the self through the unfolding of the musical patterns. Although participating in the unfolding of music's movement is only *one* way the self comes to know itself, it is *indispensable* to the self's coming to know itself in a purely subjective way. This is how music plays its essential part in the dramatic passage of humanity toward absolute knowledge.

For Hegel, music and the self both engage the flow of time. The self, first, moves to time's flow by constantly interrupting that flow. It constitutes itself in time yet becomes conscious of itself just at the moment of its reflective withdrawal from that flow. The self exists neither as "an indeterminate continuity" nor as "unpunctuated duration." Rather, it becomes conscious of itself by concentrating on momentary experiences from which it then withdraws back into itself. In the movement between its "self-cancellation"—when it "becomes an object to itself"—and the return to itself, the self achieves "self-awareness."[34] Likewise, music's movement is significantly more than sounds merely moving in time. Through a successive or temporal dispersal of its moments, music dialectically achieves its identity. In the passage, the moments mutually relate in backward- and forward-directed patterns, in flowing and interrupted melodic and contrapuntal movements, such that each pattern (or whole) surpasses the particularity of its individual moments.[35]

It is important to repeat: music and the self meet not in parallelism but in formal mediation. Music, Hegel argues, "takes" the sphere of inner sensibility or the abstract comprehension of the self "for its own." So taken, that comprehension is transfigured into purely musical form. However, the transfigured form does not leave behind what it transfigures: instead, it draws or carries the self along through its own pure movement. Hence, the movement of our inner life becomes known to us through the pure movement of music, in the act of our engaging with music as attentive listeners.

In this matter, neither Hanslick nor Schopenhauer disagrees. Schopenhauer claims almost the same thing; Hanslick absorbs many of Hegel's claims. What distinguishes Hegel's view, however, is his emphasis on the mediation and transfiguration made possible by the formal and dialectical performance of the concept of *Bewegung*. With this emphasis, Hegel needs to neither resort to what in the most anxious moments of a philosophy of music looks like a compensatory language of metaphor nor apologize that philosophical description or conceptual knowledge distances us from the music. This said, his commitment to a theory of dialectic and mediation is what Hanslick and Schopenhauer reject and why they seek alternative accounts.

For Hegel, it is via the dialectical mediation that music's musical movement and thought's conceptual movement establish formal contact with one another and without which the two would forever remain separated. Not able directly to offer conceptual knowledge, music nonetheless shows in what conceptual movement formally consists. This, for Hegel, is already quite a lot, even if it is not everything on the total path toward absolute knowledge. In the movement of concepts, he thus reminds us, not all that is given is given at once: the movement, the passage, is indispensable. Although, he writes, "the true concept is an inherent unity, it is not an immediate one. Split internally and falling apart into contradictions on the way, it eventually resolves itself." And so, too, with music's eventual moment of resolution when the harmony "goes beyond" the "dissonant" chords that present themselves to the ear along the way as "nothing but a contradiction." From which he concludes:

"Only this movement, as the return of the identity to itself, is what is most true."[36]

"The true is the whole"—*Das Wahre ist das Ganze*—Hegel famously declares elsewhere.[37] Yet because *ganz* connotes *vollständig* (complete) as well as *ungeteilt* (indivisible), when he says "the true is the whole," he means "the true is the complete." Truth is *the completion of a movement,* be it the movement of the self, the concept, or the song. In this way, the movement of *Geist* is the entire method of cognition.

Hegel on Philosophy

Hegel remarks that when a law or principle becomes too general, it runs the risk of losing its concrete or substantial significance. The same is true of *Bewegung,* especially if we employ the concept indiscriminately to capture the dialectical movement of everything. To avoid this danger, Hegel works out his system through the mediation of abstract principles and general laws by their specific, particular, and concrete determinations (and vice versa). The mediations are neither static nor fixed but track the historical unfolding of *Geist.* He employs the concept of *Bewegung* to capture the passage of Absolute *Geist* from its first to final stages of completion.

Recognizing that the concept of movement is both the explanatory concept for the system and a concept within the system, he does what some Greek philosophers did earlier: he conceives of the *Bewegung* of *Bewegung* as *Selbstbewegung.* Self-movement is the *formal character* of *Geist's* activity through all its manifestations. It cannot be treated, therefore, as a fixed or unalterable first principle. Following Aristotle, nature is purposive activity, where, according to Hegel:

> Purpose is what is immediate and *at rest,* the unmoved which is also *self-moving,* and as such is *Subject.* Its power to move, taken abstractly, is *being-for-itself* or pure negativity. . . . The realized purpose, or the existent actuality, is movement and unfolded becoming; but it is just this unrest that is the self.[38]

In the preface to his early *Phenomenology of Spirit,* in which the preceding words appear, Hegel describes philosophy's mode of unfolding truth or of how it brings things to light. He refers to progressive development, the time of birth and death, ceaseless activity, working things out, traveling one's path, temporal processes, and periods of transition. He writes of science as a morphogenetic process of cultural development and of transformation as part of the scientific enterprise.

Along this path, Hegel warns specifically against the formalist danger of *repetition,* where a concept assumes the appearance of movement but actually remains stuck in the same place. In preference to a cold or shapeless repetition or to a monochrome formalism, he recommends a constructive unfolding through which a concept moves and changes through assertions of sameness and difference. To this movement he connects another: that bearing on the necessary role the subject plays in establishing objective and then absolute truth. He rejects the idea of a static and fixed subject position from which fixed knowledge of a fixed world can be gained. The subject acquires knowledge only through dialectical movement. In its abstract form, the subject starts out, like music, from a place of pure and simple negativity, a nonplace from which it propels itself into action. It sets factors into opposition, breaks up and differentiates between things, in its process of becoming. It comes to know itself by becoming other to itself, eventually returning to itself in self-knowledge. The process is twofold: each assertion asserts a position that it then opposes or negates, and so on similarly until the contradictory passage is resolved.

Inherent in the Hegelian movement is the act of *defamiliarizing the familiar* (from the term *Entfremdung*), because what is familiar is never fully or properly known. (This thought, as the next, has an enormous influence on the future of aesthetic and social theory, connected as it becomes to the theory of alienation.) In a movement Hegel describes as cancellation, each thought or concept must be turned back on itself for its truth to be expressed. To turn a thought back on itself means to reveal its limits or its immanent contradiction with reference to what it excludes as other to itself, until at the end of the movement, the all-inclusive, surmounting, or absolute thought is reached. Hegel notes that when philosophy prematurely rests content with the familiar, with a premature assertion of a thought's self-evidence, it declines into a deadly dogmatism whereby philosophical truth is reduced to a fixed and final, but not properly known, set of propositions. Philosophers, he remarks, tend too quickly to believe that they have found certainty or safe resting places on the way.

Toward the end of his preface, Hegel describes the rhythm of the dialectic. One description, here the first, is more dialectical than the other:

Th[e] conflict between the overall [developing] form of a proposition and the unity of the concept [*Begriff*] that destroys [that development] is similar to the conflict that occurs in rhythm between meter and accent. Rhythm emerges suspended in the middle [*in der schwebenden Mitte*] when the two are brought together. So, too, in a philosophical proposition, because the identification of subject and predicate, which the proposition brings to expression, is not meant to destroy the difference between them; their unity, rather, is meant to emerge as a harmony.[39]

Second, Hegel insists that in the process of philosophical thinking we ought neither to wander off nor to interrupt the movement. One sure way to break philosophy's rhythm is to float off into figurative presentations, foreign ideas, or associations and reflections that have no bearing on the thought's internal logic.[40] Hanslick and Schopenhauer would agree with this instruction: After all, what could be better than concentrated philosophical reading brought into deep kinship with attentive musical listening?

The Second Transition

In the preceding sections, I have presented Hegel's view in two brief parts to highlight an affinity between his conceptions of music and philosophy based on the concept of *Bewegung*. I have done this to anticipate my reading of Adorno, who followed Hegel's path. Adorno was also influenced by Schopenhauer and Hanslick and was often very critical of Hegel. What he appreciates in Schopenhauer and Hanslick is the attention they paid to the movement of aesthetic expression and sounding form; what he likes in Hegel is the attention he paid to the movement of the concept. In the end, he adopts Hegel's dialectical model to show the deep and tense elective affinity between philosophy and music.

Yet, to establish the particular affinity between philosophy and music does not preclude his finding other affinities for philosophy. Hegel himself often drew from developmental conceptions of science and history, and his mention of rhythm is drawn as well, if not finally better, from poetry. Adorno recognizes all these other affinities, but he accords an extraordinary importance to the affinity between philosophy and music. In the tradition I have begun to describe, music (conceived as a language of pure expressive form and no concept) is increasingly taken to stand at the most extreme point of difference from philosophy (conceived as a language of all concept and no expressive form). Adorno explains the difference historically, by reference to a bourgeois or modernist condition in which music and philosophy, like persons, after 1800 became increasingly isolated or alienated from one another. He asks what music and philosophy, conceived deliberately at the extreme of their difference and loneliness, can now borrow or learn from the other in their complex relations of attraction and reaction. Where and how can these extremes of language meet in modern times if, indeed, they can meet at all? His answer lies with the concepts of *Verwandtschaft* and *Bewegung* (affinity and movement). He associates these concepts with late modernist theses of retrieval, survival, and hope. In sum, to understand why Adorno gives pride of place to music in his conception of philosophy and to philosophy in his conception of music, one must consider the persistent use and mention of these two concepts as they drive his negative dialectic and modernist critique.

In the rest of this chapter, I introduce many themes in Adorno's work, themes that reappear throughout this book. I present them more kaleidoscopically than systematically, as variations on the ideas specifically of movement and affinity. I adopt this approach to show something about the dynamic form that mediates the content, material, and substance of Adorno's writings. I also freely move back and forth between his thoughts about philosophy and music to show the dialectical convergence of the arguments he offers on each side.

No Exit

Adorno shares with Hegel the fear of stasis and cold repetition but refuses that which dictates Hegel's movement the most: the teleological drive of absolute *Geist*. Hegel brought the dialectic to an end yet to a false or authoritarian end in the Prussian state.[41] Though he speaks of ends as well—in music, art, philosophy, and politics—they are, for Adorno, negative ends brought about through catastrophic decay, degeneration, and defeat. Ends are not to be conceived as metaphysical triumphs over history but, rather, as historically warranted expressions of metaphysical loss.

A completed movement is not now the true (*das Wahre*) but the false (*das Unwahre*). To hold onto the whole as the true sustains in modernity a desperately dangerous illusion of freedom and happiness in what has become an *almost* gapless or fully administered society. (I explain the "almost" below.) Between Hegel and Adorno lies the *Bewegung* of history—the dark and displacing movement of enlightenment culminating in the extreme terror associated with the Second World War. The historical difference between Hegel and Adorno has consequences for what both philosophy and music now can be: consequences for their contemporary conduct and continuation.

Despite Hegel's extensive, mediated and materialist descriptions of the history of the arts, of society, and of history itself, Adorno criticizes him (as Hanslick does, too) for giving the nonconceptual, individual, and particular only negligible roles in his overall scheme.[42] Favoring the overall achievement of *Geist* expressed by the universal, the general, the shared, the necessary, and the beautiful, Hegel failed to recognize "the temporal core" of truth.[43] Intending to retrieve this temporal core within the dialectic, and thus in philosophy, society, and the arts, Adorno seeks significance where Hegel ultimately did not, in the "non-fixed" and the "non-posited," or, much under the influence of Benjamin, in the material traces, remainders, and remembrances of the historical present. "All music making is a *recherche du temps perdu*," Adorno writes. "This is the key to the dialectic of music up to its liquidation."[44] Or elsewhere: "One can no longer claim that the immutable [alone] is truth or that the mobile or transitory is [just] appearance, or [simply] that there is a mutual indifference between temporality and eternal ideas."[45] Certainly, there is a difference between appearance and idea, but it should not be translated into an indifference between, or mutual isolation of, the two sides.

Whereas Adorno believes that Hegel's thought passes "through and beyond" negation to achieve resolution in a final identity and harmony of spirit, he seeks for his own dialectic the *ongoing* movement of negation. This explains my own emphasis given above to the word "almost," for, if the world were really fully or finally administered, there would be no point going on with philosophy or thinking. Although Adorno writes as though making a final claim—as, say, "the whole is untrue"—he intends through the dialectical movement of his argument to produce a rupture in the claim. He must produce a rupture in the claim because, in a genuinely immanent critique, the ongoing movement of the argument is the only way left to break through the world's contemporary deceit. One deceit is to claim that the world accommodates all differences while in fact it reduces everything to the always and everywhere the same. Yet, to break *through* the deceit can never be fully to break *out* of it with too certain another claim, whether positively or negatively formulated, since that would be to affirm what the negative dialectic denies. In a negative or immanent dialectic, there is no absolute exit, although there must be gestures of escape and breakage made from within. (In this book, I often bring attention to such gestures by use of the word "almost.")

In his *Minima Moralia,* Adorno similarly writes with reference to the Hegelian term "auflösen" that a "negative philosophy, dissolving everything, dissolves even the dissolvent." To dissolve something is not to dismiss it but to hold it in suspension or to preserve it at a critical distance. To distance it is to defamiliarize its familiarity, to let its truth be seen. Still, the idea is not to write as if one were setting the good in place by discarding the bad; this is neither feasible nor possible. The anti-utopian (or negative-utopian) idea is to keep the movement moving, the negative thinking in the process of being thought. Thinking neither begins from a fixed starting point nor ends with a pure liberation from an antagonistic society, from which Adorno concludes: "As long as domination reproduces itself, as long as the impure element re-emerges even in the dissolving of the dissolvent, [then] in a radical sense no [final, transcendent, or absolute] leap is made at all."[46]

Still, it is often claimed that though Adorno denies the final leap, he absolutizes the negative within his system just as others absolutize the positive, and thus, like the theorists he criticizes, he brings the philosophical movement to a halt. Aware of the criticism and to avoid his negative dialectic terminating in hardened declarations of nihilism or nothingness, Adorno makes gestures toward possibility and hope most often in the last lines of his argument. He describes these gestures or ruptures as the necessary nondialectical moments of dialectical thought.[47] As gestures of hope, however, they are neither blind nor pure but carry with them all the feelings of loss and decay that moved the preceding arguments. Sometimes he writes of gestures of hope not fully hiding the despair, sometimes of the "grayness of despair" that cannot appear unless set against "scattered traces of color."[48] Either way, he is methodologically interested in the double character of a final thought. He writes: "How the negative dialectic breaks through its hardened objects is via possibility,"[49] where the aim is to think something that is genuinely other than what is or, more accurately, to think something other than what appears to be the case.

Drawing on a long tradition, Adorno often speaks of knots—of dramatic, structural, and Gordian knots. At least once, in a discussion of the universal's relation to the particular in the movement of concepts, he refers to the music of Anton Webern (though, here, he is no more specific about the reference).[50] For Adorno, it is just as significant how one brings a philosophical thought as a musical thought to an end. Knots help convey the double character of a final thought or a thought along the path: the sense of a thought's standing firm, of the argument's having hit on the right constellation, or of an ending having tied the movement up—yet also the sense of its being possible to untie the conclusion, to begin the thinking anew, of there being a moment of freedom or possibility contained even in an argument that seemed only to be leading to death. Social thinking might come to a halt, but what remains is the *need* to think and with this, thinking by individuals goes on.[51]

Late in his life, Adorno wrote that in a final move (*in einer letzten Bewegung*) the dialectic turns "even against itself."[52] Although, in this move, we are allowed to think the absolute, the absolute remains in bondage to the thought that cannot rid itself of its conditioning. There is no final stepping out of thought. As much as we want to take this step, a negation of a negation yields no unconditioned positive. Dialectical thinking coerces us into thinking it does, as modern society coerces us. We want our thought to rest comfortably or happily with the world. Nevertheless, if the world is untrue, our thinking should do everything to resist this want. In this resistance or in our not stopping the thought, are we given the only form—a negative form— for our hope.[53]

Adorno finds this hope expressed in the last moment of Goethe's *Die Wahlverwandtschaften,* in an interpretation he borrows from Benjamin. At the end, the lovers, Eduard and Ottilie, "rest side by side. Peace hovers above their resting place, serene angels of common likeness [*verwandte Engelsbilder*] look down at them from the vault, and what a charming moment it will be when in time to come the two awake together."[54] Benjamin writes: "The more deeply emotion understands itself, the more it is transition; for the true poet, it never signifies an end," from which he concludes both for his own interpretative essay and for Goethe's novel: "Only for the sake of the hopeless ones are we given hope."[55] Adorno reiterates Benjamin's gesture in a last line of his own, written in this case about the last scene of Goethe's *Faust:* "Hope is not a memory that is held onto, but the return of something that has been forgotten."[56]

For Benjamin, given the movement of the argument as a whole, this hope is inseparable from the fact of Ottilie's having starved or become mute, having retreated almost into nothingness. Adorno again repeats the gesture when he argues that his own negative dialectic contains "almost nothing" anymore of the traditional metaphysical content of truth: "presque rien," he adds to recall a "modernist musical motif." What comes to an end comes, as with Ottilie, to a *diminuendo.* The negative dialectic tends toward the smaller, quieter, and micrological or toward "the smallest transitions of thought."[57] Adorno is still thinking about Goethe, only this time, with Benjamin, also about the parable of the *New Melusine.* Benjamin makes the contrasting diminuendi in Goethe's works explicit:

Whereas the characters of [*Die Wahlverwandtschaften*] linger more weakly and more mutely, though fully life-sized in the gaze of the reader, the united couple of the novella [a text contained within the main text] disappears under the arch of a final rhetorical question, in the perspective . . . of infinite distance. In the readiness for withdrawal and disappearance, it is not [however] bliss that is hinted at, bliss in small things, which Goethe later made the sole motif of "The New Melusine."[58]

If knots bring Webern's music to Adorno's mind, the smallest things or cells remind him of the music of Alban Berg, at least when he writes that, even as "permanent becoming" the music finally dissolves to a minimum, "virtually in a single note."[59] As in Goethe's work, the significance of the final note depends on the entire movement preceding it. Adorno remarks that in Berg's music he hears in the smallest cells and transitions something quite new, because each revokes its own structure in the overall movement of becoming. The cells resist "solidifying." Like the dissolving of the dissolvent, the cells put themselves forward only to turn back on themselves. What is the point of this dialectical *Doppelbewegung* as he here describes it? To reject the final positing of a hardened musical something—*ein musikalisches Etwas*—that has falsely assumed the character of Being.[60]

Affinity

"Affinity," Adorno writes (with Freudian and Marxian overtones), "is the point [or peak; *die Spitze*] of a dialectic of enlightenment."[61] It has the double character of enlightenment's thinking, both of identity thinking and of dissonant or resistant thinking. To find affinity with something is to identify with it; it is to desire it, become it, perhaps to mirror it or just to tolerate it. The less we feel the affinity, the more ruthlessly we seek it: an affinity strongly *elected*. However, the spell is broken by the very fact of choice or election: when we realize it was our own hand (as subject) that tried to establish the identity with the other in the first place. With every yearning toward identity comes (at best) the recognition of our difference from that with which we want to identify. Affinity is as much about difference as about identity. A drop of water seen under a microscope shows as much commotion as stillness. Under a microscope, Adorno writes, the drop begins to teem with life, for even though our "stubborn, spellbinding gaze" tries to focus on a firmly delineated object, the object remains "frayed at the edges."[62] Elsewhere, he refers (as Hanslick did) to kaleidoscopes, not, however, to support the production of cold arrangements or empty variations, as kaleidoscopes can do, but as a way to express resistance to the compulsion to achieve the sort of identity that does away with difference.[63]

The concept of affinity is employed to explain the relationship between music and philosophy. Affinity is a lively and complex relation that keeps its relata in movement. To keep things moving through their immanent movement is the point of a negative dialectic. Philosophy and music share less their form or forming process than a particular mode of conduct (*Verhaltensweise*) that at best prevents a loss of movement on each side. This requires further elucidation.

Music's Need for Philosophy

What distinguishes music's form is its sensuous unfolding of tones through time; what distinguishes philosophy's form is its movement of thought or concept. Each nonetheless yearns for what the other has. Having submitted to a bourgeois condition of pure or unmediated autonomy, the more alienated they have become from each other, so the more they yearn. Their historical yearning is the modern expression of their metaphysical affinity: philosophy yearns for music's immediacy as music yearns for philosophy's articulated meaning, given what both have become. However, neither succeeds by becoming the other. In their mutual failure to become the other lies the point of their ongoing yearning. Otherwise put, they cannot give up the yearning even if it is unsatisfied, since not to seek what the other has would be to accept a much too narrow conception of their modern or present possibility. Following Hegel, to recognize the limit is to recognize what lies beyond it; it is to recognize "the more" (*das Mehr*) or "the difference" that prevents something from forming either a reconciled, premature, or self-satisfied conception of itself. Yearning for each other, music establishes contact with *conceptual meaning* and philosophy with *expression,* each therefore gaining or regaining something thereby.[64]

For one thing to *yearn* to be another thing, or to *want* what the other has, expresses the *need* that one thing has for another. In writing about musical works, Adorno stresses the fact that they are enigmatic. Their enigmatic or riddled meanings are grounded in their technical procedures and in the particular constellations of their materials. In this sense, works are their *tönend bewegte Formen*. Yet, because their meanings are enigmatic, they need their decipherment, interpretation—thus philosophy. However, though philosophical interpretations must articulate the works' meanings in concepts, the interpretations are meant to be neither reductive nor subsuming. Something more than the conceptual articulations must be acknowledged by absence in the interpretations in recognition precisely of a work's difference from its interpretation. Adorno variously refers to this something more as something aesthetic, silent, or mimetic in a work's comportment or posture (*Haltung*). As the principle of affinity demands, philosophical interpretation attempts something and must attempt something that succeeds by not completely succeeding—a *schwebende* (suspended or floating) condition of holding back from fully subsuming under its concepts the objects of its attention. How do interpreters hold back from conquering the objects of their attention? By treating works not as the reified or petrified objects they have become in the bourgeois age—where their enigmatic meanings have become almost entirely concealed—but as objective dynamic mediums (if this is still possible at all[65]) of mimetic or aesthetic experience.

Adorno is considering here the traditional problem of how we interpret a musical work in a language foreign to it. Unlike many of his predecessors, however, he argues with Benjamin—and with all the tension that comes from combining metaphysical and historical claims—that interpretation aims not to produce a perfect correspondence or translation but to reveal something in the work that the work itself cannot directly say: the work's social or historical truth content. The social truth content that is already mediated by the work's sensuous musical language—its aesthetic character—must be "mediated a second time" by philosophical reflection.[66] Philosophical reflection brings aspects of the work to articulation that the work as pure sensuous form can indirectly *show* but cannot directly *say*.

Whereas Schopenhauer conceives of music as an unconscious exercise in metaphysics, Adorno argues for music's writing of the world's history. About what does music write? *About* nothing: for Adorno, there is no *simple* or *direct aboutness*. Music does not offer an immediate picture of a social or historical situation, as suggested when we claim, say, that Beethoven's *Eroica* is *about* the Napoleonic Wars. What music writes or, better, offers up to critique is the social and philosophical knowledge drawn from the movement of our concepts. From the philosophical or critical interpretation of a musical work, to repeat, we learn something philosophical about the dialectical movement of our concepts. And because philosophy, like music, is mediated by a concrete history, we also learn something abstract or conceptual—hence, the second reflection—about the age (*Zeit* or *Zeitgeist*) of the Napoleonic Wars.

What is true of philosophical interpretation is true of other kinds of interpretation. Despite his allegiance to the *Werktreue* ideal, Adorno rejects (as does Hegel) a pedantic literal or word-perfect (*buchstäblich*) allegiance based on cold or unconstructive repetition. Reading a score or performing or listening to a work stands to the work as philosophical interpretation stands, as also bringing out something hitherto unseen or no longer seen. Certainly the work is tracked as the same work throughout all these activities, but these activities should also do *something more*. If a *buchstäblich* commitment remains, it does so only as a demand that an interpreter read the meaning *out* of the work. By letting the work speak for itself, a meaning might be revealed that would otherwise remain concealed. Or, a meaning might be retrieved that would otherwise remain set aside by a history of misreading or inadequate listening based on a misconception of what constitutes the authority of the text.

More than once Adorno criticizes the pianist Arthur Schnabel for playing Beethoven's music like a positivist, for failing to bring out the music's tensions, for overstressing the melody and understressing the harmony or counterpoint, and thus for failing to reveal anything of the work's dialectical potential. (The form of the criticism is compelling even if one thinks that in Schnabel's case it is misapplied.) What is the point of playing Beethoven not like a positivist? To challenge what the very concept of a musical work claims most—not actually to need its interpretation or performance. A perfectly correct or positivistic performance of a work is one that, by stressing the work's overall melody, falls too dangerously under the authoritative spell of the work concept. (In this argument, Adorno moves between musical and philosophical uses of the terms "melody" and "harmony," where melody is associated specifically with a compromise of the dialectical counterpoint within a work in favor of sustaining its false, overall harmonious appearance.[67])

Following its absolutist development around 1800, the work concept increasingly allowed its instances—the works themselves—to assume the self-confident and self-sufficient appearance of being fixed, final, and fully composed: the phantasmagoria of total harmoniousness. To bring out a work's tensions through performance or philosophical interpretation has been one way to challenge this absolutist claim. Activities of performing and listening should reveal aspects of the concept that the concept itself conceals behind its own false assertion of each work's autonomy. In these terms, reproductive activities must surpass their tendency merely or coldly to reproduce. This, for Adorno, is dialectical activity at its best: one achieves something musical and philosophical, or aesthetic and social, simultaneously from these dialectically mediating perspectives.

Reproductive activities are thus understood as turning musical and social practice against itself—as in the Hegelian movement of a concept—as a way to preserve the movement of the practice against the ever-threatening stasis of its governing concepts. To faithfully perform or interpret a work, in the best sense of fidelity, is to see the work as participating in the enlightenment dialectic of freedom's relation to authority. To see a *particular* work participating in a *particular* way in this dialectic is to read the enlightenment dialectic at a *particular* historical stage—hence, Adorno's many detailed descriptions of different works and types of music according to the *particular* constellations they produce with respect to the *general historical tendencies* of modern society and culture.

Adorno describes by reference to Goethe the ability of works to "point beyond" themselves: to point beyond their own limits, ability, uniqueness, and particularity. Works unfold according to their internal forms but participate also in unfolding the social-aesthetic concepts, respectively, of work, music, and art. To speak of overstepping their particularity is one way to capture the mediation of concepts: how works come to be read as *ciphers* of the social history of music and art. Alternatively, he writes of works as having a sedimented tradition and history of musical material working on and within them. Yet, though he offers descriptions like these, he always looks at the works *from the inside out,* to avoid overstepping their particularity. Like Hegel and Hanslick, he insists that to interpret a musical work requires that we follow *without distraction* its particular unfolding structure, though in a manner now consistent with the demands of immanent critique. To concentrate on the object suggests not a confinement or limitation of particularized experience but an expansion of one's experience and knowledge. However, the expansion to the more general philosophical and social terms depends on the difference being grasped from *within the experience itself*—between the subject who experiences the object and the object that is experienced by the subject. Following Goethe, the unfolding of experience is indispensable to the acquisition of knowledge.

Adorno rejects the idea that when we interpret a work we feel as if we thereby become distanced from it. He thinks we move closer, for interpretation (even social or philosophical interpretation) requires that we turn our gaze inward toward the work's details. Still, neither interpretation nor performance should be regarded as thus imposing a schema of ready-made concepts upon the work, for that would be to presuppose that an identity between the subject as performer and the object as work could be achieved. Although Adorno recognizes the *need* for interpreters to identify with the work, he insists on a negative identification that brings to expression and recognition something that has been concealed under false or authoritarian claims about identity. Accordingly, or dialectically, interpreters should identify with what in the work (if there is anything in the particular work under consideration) that resists identification.[68] To be true to what is true in a work is different from being true to what is untrue in a work. With the first, we come to know the difference between the subject and object or the work's immanent difference from how it has come to *appear* over time in an overly authoritarian practice.

On one occasion, Adorno turns his attention to a specific detail in a specific work to make a point that is both musical and philosophical. He writes in a sentence most difficult to translate of how, "shortly before the close of the first movement of Beethoven's sonata *Les Adieux*," we hear "in three measures an evanescently fleeting sound" with which we associate "the sound of trotting horses." And of how, then, in this short "swiftly vanishing passage" or in the "sound of disappearance," we are able to grasp much more about "the hope of return" than any general reflection on the same theme could (ever) possibly teach.[69] What is the combined point? That the gesture of hope is likely to show itself under present conditions in the smallest details and transitions or, in Benjamin's terms, in the moments that most tend to escape our notice the more our former ability to absorb ourselves in a work is given over to damaged forms of modern distraction. "The splinter in your eye," Adorno remarks in *Minima Moralia*, is "the best magnifying glass."[70]

Reading Hegel or Philosophy's Need for Music

"Canonic for Hegel is Goethe's statement that everything perfect points beyond its own kind."[71] Adorno offers these words to suggest that if a musical work can point beyond itself, so can a philosophical work or thought, since each has an "elective affinity" to the other. Stated otherwise: if music calls for philosophical decipherment, then philosophy at its most truthful calls for music's expression. Philosophy calls for music's expression to keep itself in movement to fight against its own tendency toward isolation and conceptual congealment.

Constellation must resist becoming a system, even in philosophy: "Everything does not get resolved," Adorno writes, "everything does not come out even." The dialectic is not a matter of wrapping things up neatly. Allegedly, Hegel tried to do just this. In the end, he made his dialectic too systematic by stripping mobility from its movement. Adorno attributes the error to Hegel's attitude toward language. His language became doctrinaire, "sovereignly indifferent" (*souverän-gleichgültig*).[72] Although, or precisely because, Hegel betrayed his own early commitment to keeping the dialectical or rhythmic movement of his texts in motion, his texts are better read now against their own authoritative grain or, as a musical text, as hermetic and thus in need of decipherment. Only then will the movement of the thought, as the movement in a musical work, be retrieved.

Continuing the point, Adorno notes first that, following contemporary custom, Hegel's texts were not fully written out but written to be "read aloud." (Recall Eduard's performance in Goethe's novel.) It was also customary for texts to be accompanied by keywords that functioned as expressive markings function in music. Why not then read Hegel's texts, Adorno suggests in recall of Hegel's own early advice, as though one were moving musically or describing "the curves" of the intellectual movement? Why not "play" along with the ideas with a "speculative ear" as though the ideas were "musical notes?" Why not "float along" or let oneself be borne by the current of Hegel's thoughts? Nevertheless, Adorno warns, be careful not to linger too long with "the momentary." Certainly, one may "develop an intellectual slow-motion procedure" or "slow down the tempo," when the thoughts become cloudy, but be careful not to slow down too much so that the sight or sound of the motion is lost altogether.[73]

Again in Benjamin's terms, Adorno criticizes Hegel more than once for underestimating the mimetic or nonconceptual character of a concept—the expressive, unarticulated aspect of a concept's meaning that allows a concept, like a name, almost to touch an object, as the fingertips almost touch in Michelangelo's image. If the mimetic or aesthetic character is underestimated in the concepts, it is also underestimated in the texts. Accordingly, Adorno demands that a philosophical text resist its own static impulse and release its dynamic side. Hegel's texts should "murmur and rustle" as great music murmurs and rustles, for philosophy "is allied with art in wanting to rescue, in the medium of the concept, the mimesis that the concept represses." Too often, Adorno complains, Hegel behaves like Alexander with his Gordian knot. Cutting rather than untying the knot, Hegel "disempowers the individual concepts, and uses them as though they were the imageless images [*die bilderlosen Bilder*] of what they mean." From which he concludes that we should hold onto the Goethean "residue of absurdity" (*Bodensatz des Absurden*) in

Hegel's philosophy of absolute spirit.[74] What might Adorno mean by drawing on Goethe's phrase? Perhaps something of the irony that I put into my description of Eduard and Ottilie performing the music of lovers: entirely united but in the wrong tempo.

It is tempting to criticize Adorno (as scholars have) for introducing into philosophy's passage of rational or conceptual thought an external, irrational, or aesthetic element, thus rendering rational philosophy immune to its own immanent critique. In my understanding, however, Adorno introduces an element borrowed from a domain or sphere external to philosophy (i.e., the musical or aesthetic domain) only to show what philosophy has lost the more reason has subjected itself to a dogmatic, positivist, or authoritarian method. The point is that the mimetic, musical, or aesthetic element would already belong to philosophy or to reason's passage were reason free from its rationalized state. This said, Adorno aims neither to reduce nor elevate philosophy or reason to an expressive or moving art, even if he does aim to show what philosophy would be like were it seriously to approximate an aesthetic theory that was truly reckoning with the modernist condition. Put otherwise, to broaden out the scope of aesthetic theory to meet philosophy is how Adorno shows what remains of philosophy and its canonical texts under modernity's late condition.

Hegel and Beethoven

Adorno finds a special affinity between Hegel's logic and Beethoven's composition. He appeals to certain elements in some of Beethoven's works to challenge the authoritarian tendency of some of Hegel's works. He explains his thinking in this crucial passage:

> The central categories of artistic construction are translatable into social ones. The affinity [*Verwandtschaft*] with the bourgeois freedom movement [*Freiheitsbewegung*] that floods [Beethoven's] music is that of a dynamically self-unfolding totality. As his movements come together according to their own law, becoming, negating, affirming themselves and the totality without an outward glance, they come to resemble the world whose forces move them [*sich bewegen*]; yet they do this not by imitating the world. To this extent, Beethoven's position regarding societal objectivity is more like philosophy's position . . . than any ominous mirroring posture.[75]

The point is that, unlike philosophy, Beethoven's music cognizes society "*without concepts* [*begriffslos*]," though it shares with philosophy the posture of not being "painted" (*abgepinselt*).[76]

In the specific use in Beethoven's music of a reprise, Adorno claims to find just the sort of return and reminiscence that reminds him of Hegel's logic. In Beethoven's "highly organized music," there is a "multidimensional" movement, he writes, moving "forward and backward at the same time." The principle of temporal organization apparently *requires* this, because dialectical time can be articulated only "through distinctions between what is familiar and what is not yet familiar, between what already exists and what is new." With Hegel, he insists, we must "know a whole movement [of a work] and be aware retrospectively at every moment of what has come before."[77] Yet, if Adorno sees in Hegel's philosophy a tendency toward absolutism and authority, does he recognize the same in Beethoven's music? He does, but in Beethoven's music he also hears the formal movement of absolutism's undoing, to match his own undoing of Hegel's texts when reading them against their authoritative grain. In this moment, he takes the side of the composer against the philosopher to claim that especially the later and more fractured of Beethoven's works carry more truth than is found in Hegel's later and more authoritarian-sounding philosophy.

Adorno further argues that Beethoven's works test Hegel's idea that "the true is the whole," because, as great works, they show what identity considered as a *completed whole* really is: namely, an artistic appearance that is also a product of construction.[78] Again, Adorno's alliance with Beethoven, or with his more fractured works, is used here dialectically to retrieve something lost or increasingly concealed in Hegel's philosophy and, by extension, in philosophy altogether. A work of art should be understood not only in Hegelian terms as the sensuous expression of an idea but also in terms that Marx later made most explicit as a product of labor and construction. The more totalizing the sensuous appearance, the more we tend to forget the labor.

In this argument, what happens to the musical work concept under the totalizing conditions of sensuous form indirectly shows what happens to the work or text in the sphere of philosophy. Both conceal their construction or the movement of their thought. The works become increasingly rigidified in meaning according to an authoritarian method, preventing genuine interpretation. Or, interpretation gradually turns cold the more it assumes an antiaesthetic aim merely to reproduce in an age of rationalized reading and reproduction. Adorno holds Hegel partially responsible for submitting the dialectical philosophy to an authoritarian method, but only *partially* responsible so that he can demonstrate the potential the *dialectic* still has to resist the *method*. Attributing partial as opposed to absolute responsibility is another way to keep the dialectical movement going in immanent critique.

To see philosophy and music standing in an elective affinity is to see each as mediating and being mediated by the other. For this reason, Adorno writes that they stand in a relation to each other that far surpasses "mere analogy." This is the explicitly anti-Schopenhauerean strike, a deliberate strike against an "ominous mirroring posture" or any other static sort of picturing relation. The history of music is not merely analogous to the history of philosophy, as Schopenhauer assumes, so Adorno maintains: *it is the very same history*— "What Hegel calls the unfolding of truth is the same in the movement of both."[79]

This is a central claim in Adorno's work showing that music, despite or just because of its claim to autonomy, is part of the very same development as modern bourgeois or absolutist philosophy. Nothing, not even the purest music, is excluded from the social movement. Attributing purity to music is what the excluding social or bourgeois movement encourages. Adorno accordingly describes philosophy and music as *coinciding*, which means that though they travel by qualitatively different means they converge in truth, and thus both show something about what the social conditioning comprises. The term "convergence" (*Konvergenz*) carries the connotation less of *converging on*, if what this suggests is that they have finally reached the truth and, more, that they *meet in truth*—in negative truth, in positive truth, and thus also in untruth—*along the way*. Once more, the idea is not to assert an identity between philosophy and music only to assert a tense and complex affinity based on their shared and particular, same and different, interacting movements within the enlightenment dialectic.

Adorno does not seek just any kind of movement or antagonism in his conception of critique, only the kind that performs the dialectical work he wants it to do, although how a work does this work is always also (following the terms of a materialist history) a particularized matter. Even if a work follows the musical development corresponding, say, to sonata form, it does not necessarily do the requisite dialectical work. This means that we should not simply *generalize* over all of Beethoven's music or over all of any other composer's music. Thus, for example, though Beethoven's early Violin Sonata in C minor, opus 30, no. 7, is a work regarded by Adorno as being of the highest genius, its "antagonism," he believes, is still "unmediated." Its arrangement is "set out only in splendid contrast, like armies or pieces on a chessboard, that at most collide (like atoms) in a dense developmental sequence." Contrarily, in the *Appassionata,* another work of genius, Adorno hears an affinity to Hegel's philosophy just where "the antithetical themes are at the same time identical in themselves."[80]

Should Adorno be criticized here for making music's movements too comfortably match philosophy's movements and then his own dialectical aims? The criticism would be legitimate were one to assume that his descriptions of movement were only literal, the sort of descriptions a positivist musicologist might produce when focused on musical form separated from any social description or philosophical interest. Within his negative dialectic, Adorno's interpretations are not offered for the sake of this sort of descriptive accuracy, though he was quite capable of producing it. They are offered, instead, in accordance with the contemporary social condition, hence, drastically at the extreme, to retrieve the meanings and possibilities that history has destroyed in both the works and the philosophical thinking about them. In psychoanalysis, so in negative critique, he writes on one occasion, "nothing is true" other than the "overstatements" (*Übertreibungen*), which is a wonderfully overstated assertion playing as perhaps it does on the human drive (*Trieb*) to exaggerate when narrating one's life story.[81] Who, in other terms, would ever believe that there is only or literally a Hegelian dialectical movement in Beethoven's music? This question obliges one to ask what exactly Adorno is unmasking by his descriptions. His own answer lies in the idea that the concept of *Bewegung* can and should be used dialectically to both expose and resist the tendency in all thought and music—even in his own—toward a deadly and disciplined stasis. Modern times make this project all the more urgent and his statements all the more extreme.

Pent-Up Time

That Adorno is constantly thinking against the grain of identity thinking does not lead him to underestimate the role of momentary stops and pauses: that is, moments of identity. He accordingly writes about stillness, suspension, and standstill, and of repose, equilibrium, and compression, in the movement of music and thought. There is nothing wrong in stopping on one's way, taking pause to consider, before one moves on. In the natural beauty of romanticism, he observes, the "natural and historical elements interact in a musical and kaleidoscopically changing fashion." Yet in this kaleidoscopic arrangement, the natural beauty shows its history of movement when *punctuated* by its pregnant moments of becoming (following Lessing) and of explosions (following

Goethe). Punctuation in thought, as in music, gives structure and meaning to the form of thought and expression. We cannot do without punctuation. Of the first movement of Beethoven's *Pastoral,* he thus notes that the repetition is not, as it *sometimes tends* to be (as allegedly in Stravinsky), "the outcome of a repetition compulsion" but "a relaxation" or "letting go." "The bliss of dawdling," he adds, to capture this marvelous sense of suddenly staying still: "Dillydallying as Utopia" (*Trottelei als Utopie*).[82]

The Greek musicologist Thrasyboulos Georgiades once noted something that Hegel and others noticed before him: though we say that a work's first note depends on its last, as the last on its first, the dependence is sustained by the movement of the work that occurs in between. This is a trivial claim if read purely logically. But what Georgiades phenomenologically describes is the special character that a musical work achieves as a medium of experience: when it is listened to as if the first note had met the last in an illusion of "pent-up time" or as if between the first note and the last no time has passed at all.[83]

Adorno refers to this argument specifically to explain the *double charac-ter* of a work's both aesthetic and empirical movement. To become absorbed by a work's aesthetic movement is to break out of empirical time, although one cannot break out of it altogether. Nor should one try: music cannot do without empirical time. Certainly, our aesthetic absorption might bring the musical movement to a standstill or make us feel as if the movement all happened in an instant, although implied by that instant is the work's entire empirical movement. To conclude, therefore, that the movement had entirely been captured in the aesthetic instant would be to surrender to the illusion of purely aesthetic time. Not to surrender, contrarily, would be to recognize the double character of the experience—that the pent-up or timeless character of the aesthetic experience of music cannot do without the empirical time in which the music unfolds.[84]

If a work as a whole can be experienced *as if* in a single moment, then, in reverse, a work's single moment begs for the entire work to be heard. Drawing again on Benjamin, Adorno takes from Goethe's *Die Wahlverwandtschaften* a piece of a single line that gains luminosity only by virtue of the whole: "Like a star, hope fell from the heavens." Benjamin says he is following Hölderlin in identifying this line with the caesura of the work, when the embracing lovers seal their fate.[85] Adorno adapts the thought to music. "Many measures in Beethoven sound like the sentence in *Elective Affinities*: 'Like a star, hope fell from the heavens." He asks us to listen to certain measures in the Adagio of Beethoven's Sonata in D minor, op. 31, no. 2, bars 27–38, first in context, then in isolation, to recognize "how much its incommensurability, radiating over the passage, owes to the work as a whole." Somehow, the passage "becomes extraordinary," given the "concentration" of its "lyrical and humanized melody." As suspended or raised, Adorno concludes with Hegel in mind, the moment is individuated "in relation to the totality," though it might also produce a rupture in that totality.[86]

Bewegung Versus Time

Adorno often writes about the history of music's movement to criticize the regressive tendencies of contemporary music, especially of the 1950s and 1960s. Influenced by Ernst Lewy's essay on lateness and aging in Goethe, he separates the potential of late style from the regressive aging of what he terms the New Music.[87] He finds a preferred late style in Beethoven and Mahler but aging in the music of Stockhausen, Boulez, and Cage, while yet maintaining that lateness and aging are two sides of the same dialectical coin. Accordingly, there is a tendency to age in some of Beethoven's music and toward lateness in some of Cage's music. Furthermore, in his critique of contemporary music, Adorno notes that he does not want to judge contemporary music according only to traditional categories but also on its own terms. On its own terms, however, he sees a loss of dialectical potential. He describes this loss by reading the composers' claims for their new music against their own grain. He then reads the loss as having always been possible in the tradition stemming back through Schoenberg, Wagner, and Schubert to that early Beethovean moment. This is how Adorno reads the past through the present and the present through the past, in terms provided by the formal dialectical *Bewegung* of enlightenment's history.

Adorno could have compared Beethoven's early or middle undialectical works with the undialectical works of contemporary music. For the purposes of critique, however, he chooses instead to use Beethoven's late and only most dialectical works against them. In Darmstadt, in 1961, he pits Beethoven's dialectical use of the reprise against the use he sees in the fully rationalized, serialist works being produced in his time. What the reprise showed in Beethoven was the possibility of genuine dialectical movement: "the feeling of something extraordinary having occurred earlier."[88] But this is not shown in, say, Boulez's serialist works. If there is error in the use of the reprise, this is because contemporary composers allegedly misapply the general concept of time. By reducing temporal interrelations to static repetitions, contemporary composers lose in their music the sort of transformational movements once heard in Beethoven. By suspending categories such as of coming before or coming after, they similarly lose all sense of an immanent dynamic. With the consequent loss of tension, New Music begins to show its age.

This notion of aging recalls Goethe's remark that aging is a gradual stepping back from appearance, where Goethe reflects on beauty and nature's laws: in a flower's full bloom or at the physical peak of human existence, beauty appears at its best.[89] Like Goethe, Adorno sees the gradual movement toward decay, disintegration, and dissociation. In Beethoven's late works, there is a paring or peeling away of sensuous appearance, a renunciation of material: "as if the whole sensuous appearance were reduced in advance to the appearance of something spiritual."[90] Nevertheless, for this was allegedly still possible in Beethoven's time, spirit somehow remains in these works. This is not, however, what occurs in contemporary music when sensuous appearance is suspended altogether, leaving no possibility of spiritual remainder. Adorno rejects as false or regressive the claims he hears regarding the new immediacy, spontaneity, and naturalness of contemporary sounds: the return to nature. In rejecting aesthetic appearance, contemporary composers do not step closer to nature or spirit; they step further away. A large part of the problem lies in their rejection of aesthetic time. To step back from aesthetic time is to step back from aesthetic appearance, and to step back from aesthetic appearance amounts to rejecting the very possibility of art. Art cannot do without its sensuous appearance if art is to continue, just as beauty cannot do without nature's laws. Adorno consequently preoccupies himself lifelong with the question of what contemporary form art and nature can appear in, given that the whole *now* is false.

Although Stockhausen as theorist acknowledges Bergson's distinction between *temps espace* and *temps durée,* a distinction that keeps aesthetic and empirical time separate, Stockhausen as composer collapses the distinction in the production of his totally organized works. Or so Adorno argues, to show that even if music's relationship to aesthetic time has been erased by contemporary works, the relationship is only broken and therefore can be mended. The relationship is thus only *almost* completely erased, more in this case by the works than by the theories supporting their production. Sometimes Adorno reverses the claim: the composers' theories are more regressive than their productions. That the regression can happen on both sides is not the present point. The point lies with the "almost": that there might be something left over, given the severely reduced relation between aesthetic and empirical time, to be retrieved.

Adorno credits Stockhausen for having offered in theory a most advanced articulation of "how time passes" (*wie die Zeit vergeht*) but then criticizes him for reducing his actually produced works to static entities. With their fully stipulated electronic scores or realizations, the works are reduced to singular or identically repeated events. The performances leave and show no remainder *in* the works and, therefore, *of* the works. From these works is thus removed the possibility via their performances of their dialectical undoing. Yet, rather than destroying the work concept, which is purportedly part of the contemporary project, the performances only meet the concept's regressive or authoritative demand by reconfirming the work's claim to be self-sufficient and complete. Seamless and gapless, these total works, even when they are proclaimed to be antiworks, submit to the totalitarian tendencies of identity thinking.

In all these sorts of argument, Adorno assesses contemporary music's employment of the concept of time by reference to the idea of movement.[91] He regards time as having become immobile and the musical score as having lost its fluidity or informality—to pick up on his own preference for what he describes, following his friend and colleague in Frankfurt, Heinz-Klaus Metzger, as *musique informelle*. He describes how contemporary music has become too formed at the cost of form's mobility: the "material and compositional principles" no longer mediate each other; they simply "remain alien." Reduced to mere kaleidoscopic arrangements of elementary particles, the elements of pitch and duration no longer move in aesthetic time. Instead, they simply merge under the general and undifferentiated heading of time (*Generalnenner der Zeit*).

Yet, Adorno reminds his readers, there has always been this tendency toward the unification or reduction of time in music's history, ever since Beethoven and the development of the work concept. Given the movement of enlightenment, there has long been the tendency to move toward the merely mechanical and the technological and hence toward reified rationality. Does it now follow that *all* or *everything* is heading in a singular and catastrophic direction? Not for Adorno, though we might read his statements this way the more they seem to become too hardened or knotted at their own elected extremes.

Is there, now, an example of music that still has dialectical potential even though it has advanced beyond the traditional logic of development? Adorno offers the works of Webern by way of answering this question in the positive, works that in their extreme brevity or absolute momentariness register a protest against the social totality comparable, say, with the scream in Edvard Munch's most famous painting.[92] This means that not all works must move along the path of development in order to have dialectical potential. But then again, not all works that unfold in an instant succeed in registering a protest against the social totality: some just conform.

Adorno connects tendencies toward conformism to what he describes as the weak ego development in reified collectivities or in some contemporary political movements. He reads Cage's proclamations on chance, articulated in accordance with the Zen Buddhist movement, as such compensatory and exemplary expressions. Weak egos may think they are claiming control of themselves, but they are really relinquishing control every time they submit their thinking to the regressive myth of spontaneity and nature. I return to this argument in chapters 3–5 but introduce it here only because it brings together Adorno's thinking about political, social, musical, and aesthetic movement. Hence, he argues, the more movements fall into stasis, the more they are controlled by weak men who seek compensation either in barbaric acts of strength or in misguided claims suggesting that they act no longer as individuals or persons at all. Such claims Adorno finds mirrored perfectly in the alleged pseudoidentifications of contemporary composers who compose as though they were nonintentional or free-flying birds of nature released from the social cage. Adorno allows that the promise of this freedom might be a warranted expression, but he takes serious issue with the *means* of the expression for fear of its fascistic tendencies.

The Last Move

Adorno draws on the concept of *Bewegung* whenever it serves to make explicit the regressive tendencies of contemporary society, philosophy, and music and on the concept of *affinity* whenever it shows what might be left over and thus retrievable in a badly damaged relationship. To be sure, Adorno's criticisms and judgments often seem backward looking, misguided, nostalgic, or conservative as if he wished to return to a Goethean or Beethovean moment. Sometimes they are as they seem, though usually what he intends by so articulating them is to *compel* readers to revise their own judgments on the *present*. The movement and form of his thought count just as much as its content.

Still, Adorno does not argue for a return to a golden age. There never was one: the past, in its glory or even because of its glory, is after all the past that lies behind the catastrophic condition of his present. His apparent conservatism is deliberately counteracted by dialectical critique every time he uses the present to show the tendencies of the past and the past to show the tendencies of the present. The dangers felt in the last note are already implicit in the first, even if we cannot predict from the first note what will follow. History is as much about contingency as about patterns. At the same time, Adorno takes perhaps the singularly, most extreme moment in history, the catastrophe of Auschwitz, from which to articulate the extreme terms of his negative dialectic. In philosophy and in music he looks for ways to destabilize their inherent tendencies toward social order, not because order is always bad, to put the point at its most banal, but because it can be very bad and he is not inclined to ignore this fact.

Adorno recognizes the sometimes genius of the composers he most strongly criticizes. His purpose in criticizing composers and their music—or anyone and anything else—is to unravel the false rationalizations he thinks he can identify in the present with the purpose then to retrieve what in the present has been forgotten or cast aside. His critique is aimed at recognizing the hidden and the shadowed, what history has made into ghosts. Still, he is aware that constantly exposing false rationalizations can itself become a petrified and monotonous activity.

In one philosophical move after another, Adorno stresses affinity, convergence, and mediation over analogy and metaphor to sustain within philosophy and music the shared possibility of both emotive and cognitive transformation. The dialectic demands not mere movement per se but the sort of transformational movement that winds through a labyrinth of particular and general phenomena and theses. Similarly, musical movement is not merely the movement of tones through time; music also moves, and at best moves, to bring about transformations in musical, social, and philosophical understanding. Philosophical argument likewise moves at its best when concepts confront themselves through the movement of the particular, expressive instances of thought.

By "critique," Adorno understands not the philosophical activity in which we merely describe or comment on what is in the music, as if all a work's aspects were to be treated neutrally or on a par. There is no such thing as the philosophy *of* music if by this we mean that philosophy is the clean and established method by which to capture the musical object. Philosophy and music stand instead in a mutually informing relationship. The activity of performing and interpreting "conceptless" musical works tells us something both about music and about the social and historical tensions implicit in our philosophical concepts. What music tells us is then made explicit by philosophical critique.

Critique makes explicit, in each one of its movements, the tense convergence between music and philosophy in their antagonistic kinship.

In other terms, Adorno begins his inquiry by assuming that music as a language, a form, and an expressive medium is a social carrier of its own concepts and therefore as much part of the social world as is everything else. Thus, even if purely musical descriptions of music's content are given, these descriptions presuppose concepts that are not solely musical in consequence or authority. If this is true of music, the same is true of philosophy. This is a fact that he believes will become all the more apparent to philosophers the more self-reflective they become about the terms and concepts of their own thinking in the very act of thinking in these terms and with these concepts. If philosophical writing becomes frustratingly self-referring or self-destructive as a result, this is the cost of its own truthfulness, the admission of its own limits with respect to what it can say and do with concepts.

Although Adorno was obviously neither the first nor the last to seek in philosophy and music a way to think about politics and history, he stands significantly apart from many other theorists in having brought philosophy and music into so close an affinity and in having used the Hegelian *Begriff der Bewegung* to sustain this troubled relationship. Taking this concept as seriously as he does, he begs the interpreters of a mostly German history of philosophy and music to read and keep rereading that history against its grain. In this chapter, I have contributed further to this rereading by refocusing the history of the philosophy of music specifically on the concept of *Bewegung*, separating the theory that put this concept at the center from theories of analogy and metaphor. I have not argued that the theory of movement is better than that of metaphor and analogy, though I do believe that, given its historical breadth, it offers much to those interested in showing how music and philosophy relate to society as to each other. Given how much attention Adorno pays to the concept, as Hegel before him, it remains surprising to me how much the concept of *Bewegung* has been ignored in philosophy and musicology, even by scholars who profess no immediate antipathy toward the dialectical method.

There are obviously many questions that remain. Although I answer them quickly here, I leave the answers open so that they may be treated more thoroughly in the chapters to follow. First, is music's movement more philosophically revealing than the movement of the other arts, of poetry or literature, or even of anything else? The answer is no, though music does offer an exemplary case. At its wordless extreme or in its purely instrumental form, it shows what is at stake for a philosophy that has lost its capacity for expression under the late condition of modernity, if we accept in the first place that it ever either had this capacity or lost it. Many philosophers, including Adorno, believe that the tension began in ancient Greece when philosophy pitted itself, in its first great Platonic or authoritative act of disenfranchisement, against music, art, history, and even persons, given their then-prevalent patterns of social conduct.

Second, to what does dialectical *Bewegung* amount when it enters the plastic or nonperformance arts? A full answer would require investigation of the theories of movement implicit in the modern movements, say, of symbolist or cubist painting, or of mobiles in modern sculpture. Rather than going in this direction, however, I turn in chapters 2 and 7 to the concept of movement insofar as it assumes a special relationship to the concept of musicality.

Third, why should we accept that different languages, and most of all philosophy and music, stand to each other in any relation of affinity, need, or yearning? To answer this question, we need again to reconsider the original Platonic warfare between reason and emotion, thought and expression, or, simply, philosophy and the arts. I turn to this theme in chapters 3 and 6.

Fourth, why should anyone expect to find convergent sorts of dialectical movement in different languages? To be sure, Adorno acknowledges the differences between languages, but, given his interest in social theory, he often pays attention to what they share because they participate in "the same history." In large measure, he is always reacting to a bourgeois separation of the spheres according to which the different languages and disciplines increasingly retreat into their own spaces, denying relations with each other. Nevertheless, Adorno emphasizes that Hegel's thought, for example, approaches sameness or totality whenever it sets the specificities of the different languages aside in favor of asserting similarities. He constantly repeats this criticism as if to acknowledge the threat to which his own thinking is subject. This is why he tries to write in a sufficiently indirect way—to avoid the equalized and authoritative appearance his own writing will assume the more he writes and the more it is consumed within an industry of academic theory production.

To resist what he knows he cannot prevent leads Adorno to extremes, overstatements, and even arrogances that many readers will not accept. In one respect, however, Goethe's Charlotte insists on taking Adorno's side. For, as she remarks, if "it is your conscience that leads you to make such remarks," then we need not worry as much as we might. Barring the threat of turning philosophy into a blatant, empty, and persistent form of moralizing, it cannot be bad "to take a look at ourselves and give due thought to the meaning of . . . words" such as "elective" and "affinity" in connection to matters that matter most.[93]

Charlotte knows of what she speaks.

Similarly, it is the looking at ourselves, whether by means of music or philosophy, that motivates Adorno most to think about matters in society, philosophy, and the arts in the highly chemically charged manner that he does.

2 The "Ode to Joy"

Music and Musicality in Tragic Culture

Stop, stop this raven-black music! Are we not surrounded by bright mid-morning? . . . Who will sing us a song, a morning song . . . ? No! Not these tones! Let us rather strike up more pleasant, more joyous tones!
—Nietzsche, *The Gay Science*

Beethoven's *Choral Symphony,* also called the Ninth, was first performed in Vienna in 1824. From the start, it was considered a most troubled masterpiece. Thirty years later, the Viennese critic Eduard Hanslick declared it a "spiritual watershed" interposing itself "between embattled currents of conviction."[1] Reflecting widespread opinion, Hanslick regarded this symphony, with its momentous choral finale, as having more fueled than calmed the acrimony between composers producing symphonies as opposed to operas, or absolute works in contrast to programmatic ones. After three purely instrumental movements, why didn't the work continue in this specifically musical way to the very last note? During its long compositional gestation, Beethoven even posed this question to himself, although for reasons probably different from the one Hanslick offered when, in desiring once and for all to clarify the musical genres, he argued that it is logically impossible for a truly musical work simultaneously to obey the laws of specifically musical beauty and to adapt itself to the demands of extramusical expression.

In 1854, Hanslick was arguing against the emerging supremacy of a Wagnerian aesthetic that was declaring opera or music drama (as Wagner sometimes called it) to be more advanced than the symphony. Further, he was resisting the dominant materialist-historicist argument that, with Beethoven's Ninth, the symphony had reached the limits of its purely musical possibility—what it could achieve by tones alone—thus proclaiming now its need for the word. As Wagner summarized the thought: "Where music can go no further, there enters the word."[2] Hanslick observed that though the critics of the Ninth might admire Beethoven's abstract intention, this did not mean that they had to like what they were hearing. Or even if they admired the message sung—Schiller's expression of how persons of lonely suffering are brought to joy through the collective of human brotherhood—they might still find the accompanying tonal forms "unschön."

With some amusement, Hanslick recalled a review of 1853 written by a self-proclaimed musical numbskull, but still one of the foremost German theological "enlighteners," David Friedrich Strauss. Strauss compared Beethoven's composition of the four movements to a sculptor who carves the legs, torso, and arms of a figure out of beautiful colorless marble yet chooses, in a final disconcerting gesture, to fashion a colored head. Hanslick then recorded the contrary opinion of one most estimable Dr. Julius Becher, who in 1843, before his political death (he was shot in 1848 for treason), declared the Ninth a masterpiece incomparable with any other musical work though on a par in matters of poetical power with Shakespeare's *King Lear* or with the Dhaulagiri peak of the Himalayas. Hanslick sided more with Strauss than with Becher but feared any comparison that, instead of focusing on the pure beauty of the musical forms, would take extramusical sidesteps into far too fantastical or solemn disquisitions about what grandeur in music was supposed to mean.

There was something residually classical about Hanslick's bid to determine the laws of specifically musical beauty in the purely symphonic genre, something antiromantic and anti-idealist, something that rubbed against Beethoven's modern liberation of the classical symphony. In Hanslick's view, by making the symphony grand and momentous, Beethoven dispensed with the quiet simplicity of the classical genre, bringing it to a loud and somehow formless conclusion. Joyful, even triumphant, the ending might be, but the joy was tinged with the feeling that, with his Ninth, Beethoven single-handedly brought the naive ideals of classical beauty to a reflective or sentimental end.

Indeed, more recent critics have suggested that Beethoven's introduction of Schiller's poem into the finale of his final symphony was ironic, a sign of lateness or aging or of the weary detachment that artists exhibit in relation to their works the more reflective they become.[3] What, for example, are we supposed to make of Beethoven's own, most conscious baritonal words,

"O friends, not these tones," by which he introduced his adaptation of Schiller's poem into his symphony? What or which tones: the sad or suffering tones of the preceding three movements or the sort of tones produced merely by instruments? Wasn't Beethoven's aim to end the symphony with the joyful song of the human voice? Whatever Beethoven actually meant, his declaration has been interpreted as suggesting something reflective, even metaphysical, over and above what Schiller's poem said itself. But what?

The Topic

This chapter is broadly about the role of music and musicality in what Nietzsche called tragic culture. It traverses the fine and unstable borders within both philosophy and music that delimit classicism and romanticism, realism and idealism, pessimism and optimism, suffering and joy. Although I devote my attention to the German aesthetic theory of the idealist age, I preserve Beethoven's Ninth as exemplar, and especially that delimiting moment of transition from symphony to song. Many interpreters have situated this transition within emerging debates over the musical genres: the symphony and the opera, music with and without words or extramusical reference. Many have taken the transition also to imply grander moves: from the aesthetic to the moral, the purely musical to the purely poetical, emotion to thought, feeling to idea, nature to humanity, and the secular to the divine. On this grander stage, interpreters have suggested that when Beethoven turned to Schiller's poem, the transition came to stand for nearly all the tensions emerging in his own philosophical, political, and poetic age. They have then gone on to show how it has been possible to the present day to put the work to use or misuse in all sorts of national, political, and religious occasions.[4]

However absorbing this theme, my own argument is not concerned directly with the reception of the symphony. Still, my argument is no less ambitious even if prima facie it is more plainly philological. It concerns a single interpretation of the transition that seeks to expand our understanding of the contemporary philosophical and aesthetic context in which the symphony was composed. It begins by taking seriously the work's title, not as it is usually known by the English as "the choral symphony" or by the Germans as the *Neunte* but, instead, as by the French (as by Berlioz) as *Symphonie avec choeurs*.[5] This title, or Beethoven's own *Symphonie Nr. 9 mit Schlusschor,* best captures the thought that to the symphony something is finally *added,* prompting us to ask for that addition's meaning. After all, the work only becomes a choral symphony at its end, though perhaps not even then if we acknowledge the subtle claim of some notable critics that, despite the entry of the chorus, the work remains purely symphonic throughout.[6]

My reason for stressing the title is to bring attention to the term "chorus" so that I can ask why *its* addition, in contrast to others who ask why the addition of the word, the voice, or the poem. Drawing on German aesthetic theory of the early nineteenth century, I show how Beethoven's work can be read, and, indeed, was later read, as calling up in appropriate modern form the authority the chorus traditionally had in ancient Greek tragedy. In modern form, the chorus sings of the suffering of modern isolated individuals and of the potential joy made possible by the aesthetic-political collective. With this song, suffering is transmuted into joy—*Freude durch Leiden,* after a phrase Beethoven used himself.[7] In these terms, Beethoven's symphony looked backward to the drama of antiquity but forward also to the music drama or total work of art that, *already in Beethoven's lifetime,* was being claimed to be the most appropriate modern form corresponding to ancient Greek tragedy— thus even before Wagner and Nietzsche argued for the same.

In this chapter, I draw on the work of Schiller, Schelling, Schopenhauer, and Hegel, but only in passing of Wagner and Nietzsche, since the claims of the latter are already well known. I do not discuss Adorno's work, though I continue to interpret the philosophical-musical views of early-nineteenth-century philosophers via concepts that later play a specific role in the social and aesthetic critique of modernity. As in chapter 1, I trace the early development of a concept whose application extends beyond the domain of music: musicality. It is used for description but even more for evaluation: to describe components of the arts but more significantly to make judgments on contemporary culture.

Overall, my account shows how the new symphonic orchestra assumed the task traditionally performed by the chorus in modern music drama: to give complete musicality to the work. With this change, however, the concern arose that the broader concept of musicality that formerly constituted the core of the ancient music drama became so narrow as to pertain only to the modern production of purely instrumental music. "The Beethovenean symphony" was blamed first for confining musicality *to* music but then for separating music *from* musicality and thus for moving modern German culture toward its decline. In place of the symphony, theorists looked backward and forward toward Italian and French opera for the cure. Wagner and Nietzsche later turned the criticism on its head to show how Beethoven's symphonies, moving toward the Ninth, were historically necessary for the rebirth of the total artwork of the future that would reunite lonely music with her sibling arts in the musical spirit of ancient tragic drama—hence, in 1872, Wagner's landmark decision to conduct a performance of the Ninth to celebrate the turning of the first stone of his Festspielhaus in Bayreuth.

Das Musikalische

My history begins by reading the transition in the Ninth, in light of the aesthetic theory of its time, as marking the entry of not only the word and voice but also, with deeper implication, the chorus. The use of the word "entry" is neutral between restoration and progress. The entry may be regarded as a reentry, a return to what music formerly was before its so-called emancipation into an independent art of tones. Or it may be regarded as a move forward toward the completion of the totalizing concept of art, according to which music as the art of pure subjectivity is given full exterior expression by being allied—*verschwistert*—with its sibling arts. As an art of pure subjectivity, music is taken to be the art of pure feeling. In being completed, feeling is joined to Idea and thereby raised to a higher and more conscious moral state. The "Ode to Joy" signifies this raising of consciousness from the work's initial incompleteness to its final rational and moral fulfillment. By being *verschwistert*, the purely musical becomes purely and fully human through the means of aesthetic transfiguration. The entire process is reminiscent of the Schillerian and idealized unification of sense and thought, the aesthetic achievement of beautiful personhood that enters literally via the chorus or metaphysically via the spirit of music into a moral and political collective.

To speak of the (re)entry of the drama in the Ninth is to point to instrumental music's alleged limitation. To so speak captures the sense of something's having been lost to music when, without any accident of language, music was claimed to have become instrumentalized. In these terms, the move from the symphony to the (choric) drama is a bid to restore to the independent and modern art of music its expression: its freedom to be musical. It is necessary to notice in this discourse the difference between two concepts, music and musicality (*die Musik* and *das Musikalische*), and to recognize in the latter a metaphorical or metaphysical scope arguably much broader than that, for example, suggested by Hanslick when he wrote of the internal and specific beauty of tonal forms as *das spezifisch Musikalisch-Schöne*.

The noun term "musicality" is of surprisingly modern origin, which is not to deny that its meaning recalls the originally Pythagorean and Muse-inspired significance attached most famously to the instruction Socrates was given, as philosopher, to practice *mousikê*. Still, it was only in the late eighteenth century that, in German, the noun "das Musikalische" was explicitly introduced to capture a jointly aesthetic and moral meaning or reference that extended far beyond the independent art of tones.

My research suggests that Schiller was the first *reflectively* to use the noun "das Musikalische" in German literature. (The noun does not appear in the major musical and philosophical dictionaries of the period.) He used the term primarily to speak about the character of the literary and painterly arts, and this use continues today. With the full breadth of its meaning, the noun assumed a critical role, according to which any work belonging to any and all of the arts may be judged as having (or as having been inspired by) sufficient or insufficient musicality. However, we ought to remember that if Schiller first reflected upon the term, Rousseau inspired the reflection. For, without exaggeration, Rousseau influenced nearly every theorist who later came to associate musicality with the movement of the human soul or with the inner expressiveness connected to feeling or emotion.

At its broadest, "musicality" connotes some sort of pure *Innerlichkeit,* or powerful preconceptual or predeterminate expressivity, an emotional or sensuous energy or drive of deep aesthetic, moral, cultural, religious, and social significance. It bears a close relation to other developing terms of the period: "the lyrical" (*das Lyrische*) and "the aesthetic" (*das Ästhetische*). It captures the yearning toward collectivity, unification, or expressive synthesis as it surpasses both in origin and effect the divisions brought about by reason, representation, and concept. Its application extends from a single artwork to a culture or society as a whole—hence Nietzsche's profoundly musical conception of tragic culture. As far as I can tell, Rousseau did not use the French "musicalité," although he often used "musical" as an adjective. Everyone does that and, I assume, in most if not all languages. "Musicalité" entered the French language in the 1830s and specifically, so it is maintained in several etymological dictionaries, in Berlioz's writings around 1835.[8]

Schiller

In his influential essay on the musicality of Matthisson's poetry, Schiller argues that emotions cannot, according to their nature, be represented directly but according only to their form, which is why music is paradigmatically the art of emotion. Yet insofar as poetry imitates human nature, and therefore expresses our emotions, poetry also affects us musically: "musikalisch wirkt."[9] In fact, Schiller concludes that we may regard any composition that expresses emotion, be it poetic or pictorial, as a kind of musical art. He shifts between different aspects of the concept of musicality: from demanding that a painter's colors exhibit tone and harmony or that a poem have a certain modulation to demanding that the musical mood (*Stimmung*) or emotional attitude of a poem unify itself with its cognitive construction or thought. For Schiller, the perfect harmony of the inner and the outer, or of the work's mood with its thought, is essential to any fine artwork insofar as it shows the artist to have reconciled freedom with necessity and humanity with nature. Given this reconciliation, both the artist and the artwork attain a high aesthetic and moral worth. With this claim, Schiller approaches the idea of a total artwork, where part of what the totality suggests is a profound identification of humanity with art or, as he puts it, of the artist and aspiring human being with the artwork.[10]

When Nietzsche later interprets the "Ode to Joy," he does so precisely in terms of the Schillerean power of musicality to overcome deep ruptures in a humanity divided from both itself and nature. However, as the opening section of the *Birth of Tragedy* shows, Nietzsche has translated the power of musicality into the Dionysian drive. Accordingly, he writes, it is not only "the bond between human beings" that has been "renewed" and is now being "celebrated" by "the magic of" Dionysus but also the bond between nature and "her lost son, humankind": "Freely the earth offers up her gifts, and the beasts of prey from mountain and desert approach in peace." On this basis, Nietzsche interprets the jubilant song—and just that moment when "the millions sink into the dust, shivering in awe"—as the sublime moment when the spirit of Dionysus is approached, when all constraints on the imagination are suspended and we move into a place of aesthetic freedom. In this place, slaves become free: all "the rigid, hostile barriers" that have arisen historically through "caprice"—or what Schiller calls "impudent fashion"—are broken down. Nietzsche concludes with further reference to Schiller:

> Man is no longer an artist, he has become a work of art: all nature's artistic power reveals itself . . . amidst shivers of intoxication, to the highest, most blissful satisfaction of the primordial unity. Here man, the noblest clay, the most precious marble, is kneaded and carved and, to the accompaniment of the chisel-blows of the Dionysiac world-artist, the call of the Eleusinian Mysteries rings out: "Fall ye to the ground, ye millions? Feelst thou thy Creator, world?"[11]

Nietzsche's reading has all the resonance of a philosophically brief and most conscious poem of 1800 that Schiller titles "Tonkunst." In this poem Schiller distinguishes the life breathed by the visual arts and the spirit given by the poet from the soul that is spoken out fully only by the muse of the hymns:

> Leben atme die bildende Kunst,
> Geist fodr' ich vom Dichter,
> Aber die Seele spricht nur Polyhymnia aus.

> (Let the visual arts breathe life,
> From the poet I demand spirit,
> But as for the soul—only polyphony expresses it.)[12]

For Schiller, as for Nietzsche, the soul's direct expression requires the suspension of epistemological constraints on the imagination. This is confirmed in a letter that Schiller wrote to his friend Christian Gottfried Körner on May 25, 1792, a letter that is one of the first to show the explicit substantive use of "das Musikalische." In this letter, Schiller points to the deep tension that arises in the creative process between needing and not needing to have a conscious idea of what one is going to write before one puts words to paper—anticipating what Nietzsche later describes as the artist's need for the free inspiration of Dionysus to guide the creation of the Apollonian image if the work's conscious thought is ultimately to achieve perfect union with its primordial emotion or mood. Schiller writes:

> It often happens to me that I am ashamed of how I originate my projects, even the most successful ones. One usually says that the poet must be full [voll] of his object if he is to write. Often only one, and not always an important, aspect of the object will invite me to work on a poem, so that one idea develops out of another. . . . How, now, is it possible that out of so unpoetic [or incomplete] a procedure something nevertheless excellent develops? I believe it's not always the vivid conception of the content of a work, but often simply the want [lack] of a content, an indefinite urge, feelings seeking an outlet, that produces inspired works. When I set out to write, *the musicality of a poem* hovers [*das Musikalische eines Gedichts schwebt mir*] before my soul far more often than a clear notion of the content about which I have rarely made up my mind.[13]

Another conscious use of the concept of musicality is found in Schiller's essay of 1795, "On Naive and Sentimental Poetry," because just when Schiller declares Klopstock to be a musical poet, he deems it necessary to provide a footnote to explain the term:

> I say "*musikalisch*" to recall here the dual affinity [*Verwandtschaft*] of poetry to music and plastic art. Accordingly, as poetry either imitates a given object as the plastic arts do, or whether, like music, simply produces a given state of mind, without requiring a given object for the purpose, it can be called plastic or musical. The latter expression, therefore, does not refer exclusively to whatever is music in poetry actually and in relation to its material, but rather in general to all those effects which it is able to produce without subordinating the imagination to a given object; and in this sense I call Klopstock a musical poet above all.[14]

The fact that "musikalisch" is employed with a significance extending beyond that applicable solely to the art of tones produces a marvelous tension in the relationship between the arts. On one occasion, the German composer Johann A. P. Schulz was asked to set a poem by Klopstock to music, to which Schulz responded: "Why should I compose that? It's already music!"[15] where the rhetorical point is that, by declaring the poem already music or, more precisely, already *musical,* renders redundant the addition of the tones. Perhaps Beethoven also had something of the broader concept of musicality in mind when he declared, or so his pupil Karl Czerny recalled, that Goethe's poems are easier to set to music than Schiller's, because it is not possible for him, as composer, to "lift himself" beyond what Schiller, as poet, has already achieved.[16]

This concept of musicality also alters the meaning we give to a claim found in many writings of the time: that operas will only succeed in becoming fine works of art if composers choose middling or mediocre (*mittelmässige*) texts. For here, the sensible idea is that composers do not seek mediocre texts as much as texts for which the musical setting is not superfluous. This might well lead one to wonder whether it was not on this account that Beethoven chose once more to set "An die Freude" to music (for it was not the first time that it had been set), long after Schiller rejected his original drinking song as flawed or unsuited to the taste of the times.[17] Whether or not Beethoven actually knew of Schiller's reservations, might it still not be that he believed he could give the poem a new meaning or musicality that by itself the poem did not or did not any longer have?

In 1797, Schiller wrote to the composer Carl Friedrich Zelter to seek his help in setting a given poem to music. Zelter responded several months later, commenting that he did not know why he'd found this poem so hard to set, which led him to wonder: "You can well ask me what I mean by *musikalisch*, and I will therefore tell you at once that I don't rightly know, but that I know from other musicians that they also don't know, and that most of them are so ignorant as not to know they don't know. . . . We musicians have no exact definition for what we call *musikalisch*."[18] It is surely significant that whereas musicians of the period seemed not to be conscious of a need to define or even to have this concept, the literary, visual, and aesthetic theorists were. I want to suggest that the difference likely speaks to how far the concept was being articulated in this period, in relation less to the actual art of music and more to a reflective metaphysics within which the idea of a unified world was being conceived in analogy to a unified work of art. For, whether given the world or the work, it was musicality that was being called on to energize the (re)unification.

Schelling

The next significant use of "das Musikalische" appears in Schelling's *Philosophie der Kunst,* a text comprising the lectures he gave between 1801 and 1805. Quite suddenly, the noun appears, does its single piece of work, and then disappears, yet its meaning pervades the entirety of the text. It appears when Schelling speaks of rhythm as "the music within music." In the first instance, this phrase is written as "der Rhythmus ist die Musik in der Musik," but in the second, it occurs as "der Rhythmus ist das Musikalische in der Musik."[19] What credibly motivates the change is that, the second time around, Schelling, as Schiller, was developing a specific interchange of characteristics between the different arts. However, whereas Schiller was describing the musicality in poetry and painting, at this moment Schelling was investigating the art of tone alone. Still, even for this single art, he drew on a broad metaphysical view and a general concept of art to determine its three basic aspects: the painterly (*das Malerische*), the plastic (*das Plastische*), and *das Musikalische*.

For Schelling, "rhythm" means more than the musical beat; it is that which constitutes the musicality or entire movement (*Bewegung*) of the art of tones. By contrast, "modulation" constitutes the painterly element and "melody" the plastic element. Musicality or rhythm sustains the most reflective, self-conscious aspect of music and is given the highest standing. Modulation "qualifies" music only "for feeling and judgment" and melody "for intuition and the power of imagination."[20] However, given his philosophical idealism, Schelling argues that music's overall unity comprises all the elements, so that, in absolute oneness, rhythm overcomes its difference from the other two and thereby achieves an identity with them: "Rhythm conceived in absoluteness, is the entirety of music, or . . . the entirety of music is rhythm in its absoluteness."[21] In this absoluteness, musicality as reflective power synthesizes with the intuitive power of imagination and with the power of judgment.

Schelling speaks of his favored kinds of music as having rhythmic melody. ("Rhythmically modulated melody" would have better accorded with his triple-aspect view.[22]) In the synthesis, musicality as a totalizing concept becomes the determining concept for all his subsequent musical judgments. Yet, Schelling hardly ever refers to actual works or composers, which distinguishes his treatment of music from that of the other arts. In the one and maybe only instance where he explicitly offers a composer's name, it serves just to differentiate the painterly element of music from "musical painting," the sort of low-level creation of "sunken taste," as he puts it, that consists in using music to imitate the sounds of nature. Schelling denies that music's function is to imitate and cannot resist slighting Haydn's *Creation*, which he thinks satisfies only "degenerates" who enjoy listening to imitations of bleating sheep. With remarkably similar tone, Schopenhauer also "entirely rejects" imitative music and adds Haydn's *Seasons* to the already impoverished list.[23] The judgment of both philosophers derives from a metaphysical claim and not, evidently, from any particularly sensitive listening.

To compensate for his lack of independent research into the art of tones, Schelling is content to rely on the much more expert Rousseau. Referring specifically to the *Dictionnaire de musique* as "still the most intelligent work on this art form," Schelling looks back with an idealizing eye to antiquity's exemplary production of the arts. And though he knows that no real idea of Greek musical production is to be gained, he remains confident that the "realistic, plastic, and heroic principle" must have predominated, because all elements were subordinated to that of rhythm—*das Musikalische in der Musik*. From this he concludes with Rousseau that the rhythmic melody that defined Greek music is quite different from that which defines contemporary music: namely, polyphony or harmony.[24]

Schelling adopts Rousseau's judgment that it is only in the Christian chorales (the hymns and psalms) that we have come to know something about what the music of antiquity meant. Yet, apparently, by the time these chorales were sung in the developed churches of high Christendom, most of the tempo and rhythm, the "powerful energy" of the original music, had been lost. Increasingly, Schelling argues, the Christians rendered music secondary when they began to set either the prose of the Scriptures or secular forms of "totally barbaric poesy" to music.[25] As the barbarism grew, the contemporary forms of harmonic music started to relate merely as allegory or caricature to what rhythmic melodic music once was. Schelling now shows in his own terms how, via the appeal to allegory, modern art seeks to fight against its own barbaric tendency. Hence, as allegory, modern music yearns, but it can only yearn, for the character ancient music once had. The yearning defines romantic art. Although harmonic music strives to unite the Finite, Different, and Multiple with the Infinite, Same, and One, it necessarily fails, as Greek music did not fail, to express heroic satisfaction and vigorous passion. Analogously, though harmonic music strives to reunite alienated individuals with the collective, it cannot bring about this final desired state. Schelling offers to his "more musically uneducated readers" a comparison with drama. He distinguishes the "harmonic" Shakespearean tragedy from the "rhythmic-melodic" Sophoclean tragedy. Whereas in *Oedipus* we experience without distraction the monody or pure melody of the event, in *Lear* we experience a harmony or polyphony in the deliberate counterpoint of parallel stories: Lear expelled by his daughters juxtaposed with the story of a son expelled by his father.[26]

Schelling acknowledges that there are as many critics who approve as who disapprove of harmony, so it's unlikely that the dispute will resolve itself simply, on the one side or the other. He suggests that we should rather appreciate the contribution every aspect of music makes to our understanding of both the reality and the ideality of the world. Recalling the Pythagorean view, he concludes that music or, more accurately, musicality must be "nothing other than" *both* "the perceived rhythm[ic melody] and the harmony of the visible universe itself."[27]

Schelling's idea of a three-in-one unity of the musical, painterly, and poetic finally enables him to describe the ideal form of a musical work to which even the alienated, harmonic works of contemporary times may aspire. Is there a contemporary work to which he might refer as an example? Could *we* not now read the transition to song in Beethoven's Ninth as a deep but necessarily failing romantic yearning for the purportedly achieved collective of the Greeks, a yearning to put back into the advanced, harmonic structure of instrumental music the power of melody and musicality? Perhaps, but in the very last paragraphs of his lectures, Schelling offers his own tentative and arguably even more prophetic answer. Given his ideal of unity, he recommends the formation of a total and living work of art: the sort of artwork extending far beyond the boundaries of the singular art of tones. Before the composition of Beethoven's Ninth and almost half a century before Wagner (though he is not actually the first), Schelling describes a modern work of total theater that will reunite poesy with music, painting with dance, and pantomime with the plastic arts. He refers to a perfect synthesis and to a most complex theater manifestation. When he then looks around him for an example, he looks to the world of opera, which is by no means an odd place to look. However, what he finds there is not yet a *real* but only an *ideal* satisfaction. In its present form, he maintains, opera only presents itself as a caricature of what ancient drama once was. To bring it closer to ancient drama or to produce a better example, we need an opera of "higher" and "nobler" form.[28]

Although Schelling's ideal of opera fits a romantic project of yearning, it recalls Schiller's more classical vision, as we see now in the final thought of Schelling's text:

Music, song, dance, as well as all . . . types of drama, live only in public life, and form an alliance in such life. Wherever public life disappears, instead of that real, external drama in which, in all its forms, an entire people participates as a political or moral totality, only an *inward*, ideal drama can unite the people.[29]

Schelling's argument is allied to Schiller's in just this point: that the external body of a work, be it a drama or opera, ought to be the embodiment of something inward or ideal, where what performs the work of inwardness, and thereby also of ennoblement, is musicality in its broadest sense. From this both conclude that any adequate account of the future of art and society must pay equal attention to the inner/ideal and outer/real faces of the artwork and then to the essential relation between the two. With this argument, they both turn their attention to the chorus.

Schiller and Schelling on the Chorus

For Schelling, first, the chorus represents the real face of the work of art and musicality is the inner ideal face. He describes the chorus as a "sublime invention," given its capacity not to flatter but to ennoble an audience, thus moving the audience away from everyday deception toward the work's "symbolic portrayal." The idea of symbolic portrayal resonates closely with a by-then standard theory of aesthetic distance in which the idea of appearance (*Schein*) is given a central position. Thus, he writes, the essential role of the chorus in ancient drama is to bring *outer* attention to what, in the total symbolic appearance, is *inner*. To show what is inner by outer means is to show what is essential as opposed to what is accidental or a mere embellishment of the entire action (*Handlung*). Schelling describes the action's essence as "pure rhythm"; it enables the outer face to achieve both its completion and its perfection. (Wagner later repeats the thought, without reference to Schelling, with his idea of "musical deeds made visible.")[30]

In the modern, harmonic tragedy, the essential and accidental dimensions fuse in polyphonic structure; in ancient tragedy, they are separated when the chorus separates itself from the action. With its own separate standing, the chorus redirects the audience's attention away from the action's accidental aspects and toward the "pure rhythm." It assumes the task of commentary or "objective reflection," either anticipating or explaining the action. It raises and frees the spectators' attention, placing them in a contemplative space, distanced from the immediacy of the suffering they are witnessing. In its aestheticizing role, the chorus calms the spectators, offering them relief and the opportunity for serenity, reflection, and compassion. Schelling praises the ancient chorus for its impartiality—for truth is impartial—and thus for its ability to take the side of right and of fairness. Standing for truth, the chorus counsels peace, laments injustice, and gives support to the oppressed. At an aesthetic distance, the chorus assumes its final moral character and ultimate political purpose to bring joy to and through the collective, but it never relinquishes its emotion-driven musicality or song. In this way, reason and emotion are synthesized.

At the end of his description of the chorus, Schelling refers to Schiller's modern tragic drama, *The Bride of Messina,* as trying to imitate the distance— the indifference or impartiality—of the ancient chorus but failing to do so. What accounts for the failure remains unclear. Certainly there is considerable tension surrounding Schiller's use of the chorus in this play, demonstrated in the author's own decision to write a lengthy explanatory prologue.[31] In his prologue, Schiller distinguishes his preferred form of chorus (modeled on the ancients') from forms more "opera-like"—*oper[n]haft*. Already, for many of his other dramas, he had thought at great length about how best to use music in the theater (as it was then common to do) and whether, given his knowledge of opera—and he particularly liked the operas of Mozart and Gluck—he ought to employ specifically operatic devices. In *The Bride,* he mostly rejects these devices and opts for more traditional forms of choric song and lyric verse.

One wonders even more now why Schelling objects, given how close Schiller's descriptions in the prologue are to his own. Schiller also writes of the need for the drama, and for the chorus in particular, to raise spectators to a higher, more "ennobled" plane and of the need, too, for the sensuous side of music and dance to bring "life" (back) to the tragic drama. He addresses the function of tragedy to bring happiness and joy to a people in the form of a freedom of mind: a freedom given when they are liberated through art from the burdens of the everyday, but where the point of this liberation is that the aesthetic freedom be reincorporated into their everyday lives. Schiller also speaks of the chorus's purpose to denaturalize contemporary theater, to create within the play an ideal space of poetic freedom for combined sensuous and reflective response. He is most concerned to promote the correct balance between the inner lyricism and the outer appearance of the drama, and between the ideal and the real. And he is just as aware as Schelling that, given the conditions of modern times, a mere copying of ancient drama will not bring about the desired end.

In fact, he has already argued elsewhere that one cannot presume in modern times the morality that was the basis of ancient art; it is something that must now emerge out of art as ideal expression.[32] In other words, the ideal and real, or the natural and artificial, are separated in modernity as they were not in antiquity. To find the right contemporary form for art, one must seek appropriately modern devices. Yet, with Schelling, what is appropriate in modern times might well aspire toward what ancient drama once was. It comes as no surprise, therefore, to read in Schiller's prologue of how the chorus in *The Bride* will best perform its symbolic work to unify "the divided many" into "the collective one" if it conveys the inner musicality of the drama, where the latter is expressed in the sound and movement of the chorus. The chorus should be accompanied, he writes, by "the whole sensuous power of the rhythm and of the music in sounds and movements [*Tönen und Bewegungen*]."[33] This all sounds very like the conception of the chorus in ancient times. Through the musicality, or what Schiller also calls the "poetic act," the chorus purifies the tragic work by distancing the reflection from the action. The purification becomes a dignified act almost of exaltation—an intensification of language through tonal or musically sounded-out speech to reach the drama's inner core. As for Schelling, so for Schiller, the purification of the chorus is an aestheticizing process, a way to maintain an aesthetic illusion in which suffering is transmuted into a joy associated with serene reflection (*Gemütsfreiheit*).

If not Schiller's description of serenity, then at least his description of intense exaltation fits perfectly the "Ode to Joy." Or so Wagner later maintains in the program note he wrote for his early 1846 performance in Dresden of Beethoven's Ninth.[34] Wagner describes the poem as an expression of the highest transport, in which universal brotherhood and universal love find their identity in the victory of heroic action. Later, in his own works, he subordinates heroic action to universal love, though he does not completely dismiss the former, as shown in the complex roles he gives to his both male and female protagonists. Here, the point is only that connections between Wagner and Schiller abound. Consider just one, from 1873: in writing a "Prologue to a Reading of *Götterdämmerung* before a Select Audience in Berlin," Wagner mirrored the central claims of Schiller's prologue to *The Bride*. In the mirror, one sees Brünnhilde (though one might also see Senta or Isolde) as Wagner's cherished bride, whose role it is to give birth to his drama out of her internal and essentially "musical womb."[35]

Schopenhauer

Schiller and Schelling set the stage for a future for art in which modern (music) drama is ennobled through the principle of musicality combined with the emotional and reflective work of the chorus. They precede Wagner and Nietzsche by arguing that the best of modern art will be born out of the musical spirit of the ancient Greek total work of art. Yet, Schiller and Schelling do not provide—because in 1800 they did not need to—an argument to overcome the dominance of the symphonic genre and specifically the Beethoven symphony. Wagner and Nietzsche do have to provide this argument and do so often by drawing explicitly on Schopenhauer's views. However, something paradoxical occurs, because to use Schopenhauer's views to explain the achievement of the Beethoven symphony, they have to disregard his own argument as to when and how it fails. Mostly they proceed by adopting some of his metaphysical claims and by ignoring his particular musical assessments. Without a doubt, it is more they than he who generate what later comes to be known as the Schopenhauer-Beethoven alliance.

By the 1850s, Beethoven had long been declared the savior of the symphony, if not of music altogether. The story began with the pioneering works of the early romantic literary critics, notably E. T. A. Hoffmann's classic essay of 1810 on Beethoven's Fifth. Nevertheless, just a decade later, in 1819, when Schopenhauer published the first version of his *Die Welt als Wille und Vorstellung,* he had Beethoven's symphonies neither paradigmatically nor completely positively in mind. (The Ninth was not yet composed.) Instead, he praised the operas of Rossini, which was not an idiosyncratic preference, given the prevalent opinion of the time that this was the age, and no less in Germany than anywhere else, of Italian opera.

Nevertheless, though he highly appreciates Rossini, Schopenhauer mentions him in his entire published oeuvre almost as rarely as he mentions Beethoven or, in fact, any other composer or work. Like Schelling, the sparse reference again contrasts with their rather better illustrated discussions of the other arts. However, whereas Schelling acknowledges his ignorance regarding the technical art of music, Schopenhauer makes evident his musical education. Having studied the flute, he mentions more than once his enjoyment of playing adaptations of Rossini's melodies.[36] Even so, in his major philosophical opus, his concrete references are few, and when he makes them, they derive less from his musical education and more from a Rousseauean-inspired metaphysics of musicality and melody. Overall, in his writing, apart from the few references to Rossini, there is a once-repeated dismissive reference to Haydn's programmatic music, no reference to Bach, and a few passing references to Mozart, all made in later life (when he produced in 1844 the second version of *Die Welt als Wille und Vorstellung*). There is also his oft-cited judgment from 1854 that Wagner was a better poet than composer, which shows little grace given that it was Wagner who, in this same year, began almost single-handedly to bring Schopenhauer's work, after a long quarter century of disregard, into the public eye.

There is, however, a noteworthy reference in *Die Welt als Wille und Vorstellung* to a work of Italian opera, Bellini's *Norma,* which Schopenhauer favorably compares with Schiller's *The Bride.* The comparison occurs within a discussion of the art of tragedy. Decades later, Arnold Schoenberg proclaimed the favor accorded to this work to be one of Schopenhauer's greatest errors.[37] However, given the present argument, the favor should be interpreted as no error at all. Schopenhauer finds in Bellini's opera a superior demonstration of the "genuinely tragic effect of the catastrophe," and in the duet "Qual cor tradisti" a "conversion of the will" conveyed by the sudden entry of quietness into the music. From this he concludes that "quite apart from its excellent music, and . . . [with] its interior economy, this piece is in general a tragedy of extreme perfection, a true model of the tragic disposition of the [heroic] motives, of the tragic progress of the action." To strengthen the point, he praises the work for affecting spectators "as it should," through "natural and simple" means and not, he quips, through the presence of "Christians or even Christian sentiments."[38] If, at this moment, Schopenhauer is assessing the drama "apart from its excellent music," this does not belie what seems to be his general thesis (and I return to this issue below) that without music the drama would have no inner core and therefore no essential movement to guide its tragic disposition.

It is necessary again to separate talk about music from Schopenhauer's implicit appeals to musicality, where the latter is a "profoundly serious" metaphysical principle. The distinction pushes the whole argument in a new direction. The principle of musicality, earlier described in relation to the chorus, is now not only separated from the chorus but also comes to replace it, and at just that moment when Schopenhauer implicitly aligns it to the pure art of tone. Schopenhauer writes (and this is a sentence both Wagner and Nietzsche quote):

> The internal relation that music has to the true nature of all things can also explain the fact that, when music suitable to any scene, action, event, or environment is played, it seems to disclose to us its utmost secret meaning and appears to be the most accurate and distinct commentary on it.[39]

By being aligned with the musical movement of the innermost nature or Will of the world, music alone (*allein*[40]) assumes the all-important ability to disclose something reflective to the listener, which, to recall, was the traditional role assigned to the chorus. However, the question to which this change gives rise is whether the idea of music alone automatically translates into an endorsement on Schopenhauer's part of the symphonic genre over and above the total art of opera.

I argue that it does not. This is the most difficult conceptual shift in the argument: whether, having implicitly praised the concept of musicality though having explicitly admired what music can do *on its own* as an independent art, Schopenhauer must conclude that the symphony is the best or only truly musical art. The modern symphony might do the work of musicality, but still it might not do it as well as opera or the religious mass (or even, though not for Schopenhauer, another art altogether). Ultimately, the matter is settled by reference to which *particular* works (tonal or otherwise) Schopenhauer judges as most musical—divorced, that is, from the consideration of genre.

Given both metaphysics and preference of taste, Schopenhauer sides with the melody sung by the fluty soprano; he regards this voice as representing the highest humanity. To sustain the claim, he establishes a link between the metaphysical (metaphorical) and the physical (literal) basis of music. To establish this link, he uses the noun "das Musikalische," though this is his only reference to the term in *Die Welt als Wille und Vorstellung*. In Pythagorean-Platonic spirit, he argues that the link is sustained by the fact that when vibrating strings are "stretched and plucked," the movements that the vibrations produce in the music—and the tensions between the consonant and dissonant passages—track the strivings and resistances of the Will and, hence also, the satisfactions and dissatisfactions of the human heart. Following this, he argues that music's musicality or what he calls the "real musicality of the tones" (*das eigentlich Musikalische der Töne*) is found more "in the proportion of the rapidity of their vibrations" than in their "relative strength." From this he concludes that the musical ear always prefers "to follow in harmony the highest note" rather than "the strongest." Even in the most powerful orchestral accompaniment, the soprano stands out and demonstrates her natural right to deliver the melody. By best conveying the musicality of the notes, the soprano voice achieves the highest or most enhanced sensibility, a sensibility that Schopenhauer associates with "the most highly developed consciousness that stands at the highest stage of the scale of beings."[41] In this argument, what is truly musical becomes by association the most purely human—a movement that reaches from the most physical considerations to the most metaphysical.

Schopenhauer pursues the analogy between music and Will (or, implicitly, between musicality and humanity) when he argues that just as individuals demand the existence of the entire world and thus the other grades of the world of representation to overcome their loneliness, so melody cannot survive without harmony. The soprano—whether produced by the voice or an instrument—requires the company of the alto, tenor, and bass. Schopenhauer's argument shows the essential unity, completeness, and collectivity that are brought to the world of representation when all of music's parts are performed together. However, the togetherness derives ultimately from the essential *Innerlichkeit* and lack of differentiation that the Will's (as opposed to representation's) perspective provides. Described as the Will's direct and unmediated expression, actual music acquires its significance only as it is identified with what I am describing as the inner drive of musicality or only as the inner drive overcomes, in Schopenhauer's terms, any imperfection, separation, or division that is imposed on music regarded from the perspective of representation. Even if real or actual music as outer or represented cannot *perfectly* mirror the inner drive of musicality, it must aim to do so. What Schopenhauer thinks about in terms of a perfect parallelism or analogy, as that idea was introduced in chapter 1, Schelling described as a yearning or affinity on the part of contemporary art for what art originally was.

Schopenhauer's argument could well now lead him to propose a full conception of a total artwork. But it does not—quite—given his apparent restriction of the work of the total art to the work of music alone. The union of the voices of the instruments suffices to exhibit musicality. Shouldn't one now use this argument to ground a generic preference for the symphony over the opera? Not necessarily. Schopenhauer's argument here takes its decisive turn, leaving us with the conclusion that it is not a matter of favoring one genre over another, only a matter of deciding between good and bad examples of works of any given genre. And, in his view, what Rossini was then doing for the opera was more musical than what Beethoven was doing for the symphony.

To be sure, Schopenhauer approved of the symphonic genre as he did of any other genre, but only if it sought no programmatic aid and remained "pure." Music does what it ought to do when, entirely from its own resources, it mirrors the world in its aspect of pure willing and, in this aspect, no generic or any other individuation comes into play. Schopenhauer thus argues that whereas Haydn (or Beethoven in his more misguided pastoral moments) compromised the purity of his music by seeking programmatic aids, Mozart and Rossini did not. Neither of the latter, he notes (contra Adorno's reading), ever attempted to paint nature's objects in tones in whatever sort of music each produced.

In principle, a Beethoven symphony is capable of being pure. But it is so only when it allows listeners to move their ears without distraction through its moving forms.[42] At this moment, Schopenhauer appreciates how such a symphony might lead a listener through the greatest aesthetic experience: through the confusion and conflict of the emotional life to a serene and calm end. However, though this appreciation suggests an awareness of the symphony's complex, harmonic structure, a strong commitment to the principle of simplicity soon overrides it. As symphonies move toward increased complexity (harmonic or otherwise), they purportedly lose their freedom and therewith their musicality. "Purely instrumental" they may be, but meaningless and shallow they sound to the musical ear. Sometimes Schopenhauer connects the rise of complexity to the domination of dialectical theory propounded, as he quips, by that famous trio of "charlatans"—Schelling, Hegel, and Fichte. Clearly, he does not want to acknowledge how close their musical assessments are to his own or how, in musical matters, they would concur with him that proper melody at best exhibits simplicity, where simplicity, as he writes, "usually attaches to truth." Indeed, simplicity "is a law" as essential "to all art" as to all that is beautiful or intellectual. Fearing he has stated the point too strongly, he turns it around: "at any rate," to depart from simplicity, or from melody, always poses a danger. In his view, but not only in his, Beethoven seems to represent the danger associated with this departure most of all.[43]

By endorsing the principle of simplicity, Schopenhauer takes sides with Rousseau, as well as with Rossini. Without hesitation, he correlates simplicity with the preference for melody over harmony and complexity with the reverse preference. To favor melody is partially how composers keep their music "pure." Thus, in praise of Rossini, he writes that even in opera the "music speaks its *own* language so clearly and purely that it requires no words at all, and therefore produces its full effect even when rendered by mere instruments [*blossen Instrumenten*]." In the 1850s, he cries out with even more vigor: "Give me Rossini's music that speaks without words!"—but continues more soberly: "In present-day compositions more account is taken of harmony than of melody. Yet I hold the opposite view and regard melody as the core of music to which harmony is related as the sauce to roast meat."[44] The claim is straightforward: what is asked of the symphony is asked of the opera: that both give preference to melodic music because melodic music stands for the highest and most human expression. Without melody, musicality cannot appear at its best in works in *whatever* kind of works they are: that is, as long as we do not listen to the works purely musically.

If the symphony is tending toward decline, in Schopenhauer's view, then the opera is, too—and now we know for the same reason. Rossini is held up as one of the very few exceptions to this decline. Moreover, it is significant that when Schopenhauer dismisses the operas of his day as exhibiting insufficient melody or simplicity, it is enough to describe them as "unmusical" or as fit only for "unmusical minds." To declare them unmusical is to regard them as incapable of bringing listeners in touch with the pure quintessence of the world Will. He describes unmusical operas, and usually they're the ones that are "too long," as those into which too many foreign elements are imported or in which too many accidental features distract us from what is essential. He lists among the most distracting elements "absurd and insipid" plots, the "childish and barbaric pomp of the scenery," and, finally, the "antics" and "short skirts" of the dancers.[45] If nothing else (and Wagner takes up this theme, too), one reason for keeping the melody always present in the listeners' ears is to keep them focused on what is essential. If the point isn't already obvious, it may be simply stated: Schopenhauer gives the role once fulfilled by the chorus in ancient drama to the singer of melody who, under the condition of simplicity and transparency, focuses the audience's attention on the work's, and, by extension, the world's, unmediated and pure movement.

Schopenhauer's commitment to melody matches the argument he develops against what we might call on his behalf "programmatic associationism." What he especially admires in music, and especially now in the symphony, is its capacity to lead us through feeling, but only from the abstract or pure perspective of form, which means that no contact is made or even attempted with real passions or actions in the world. At every moment, music should maintain its immediate relation to the world as Will and fall into none of the traps or temptations offered by the world of representation. If music moves us, it does so only in relation to the Will's "innermost being," which is to say, "remotely" or far removed from the particularity of our everyday emotions, thereby leaving us in an abstract and pure musical mood (*Stimmung*). Schopenhauer acknowledges the extraordinary effort it requires on the part of listeners to meet the demand that purely instrumental music makes on them, which is why listeners, like composers, tend to seek programmatic associations. However, in resorting to these aids, they quickly lose contact with what the music expresses in truth.[46]

In a judgment of later life, Schopenhauer turns to the sung mass as arguably surpassing both the symphony and the opera in matters of musicality. For here, as he writes once more, the music takes priority over the word such as to become unimpaired by the miseries about which the words sing. Rather than "grovel on the ground with the oppressive puritan or methodist character of Protestant church music," the music of the mass should soar like a seraph upward into higher realms, analogously to how one of his beloved paintings by Raphael soars (as far as painting can) beyond the world of representation. Ultimately it is the mass, stripped somehow of Christianity, yet thoroughly permeated by religious-aesthetic feeling, that best offers what he describes as "pure and unalloyed musical pleasure."[47]

In sum, Schopenhauer's commitment to musicality does not automatically translate into a commitment to solely instrumental music, even if it does translate into a commitment to pure music alone. If music alone tracks without mediation, disturbance, or interference the deep and serious significance of our existence, then it can do this even when accompanied by words or images. For what matters is the presence of musicality, where musicality only indirectly concerns the question of genre but directly the assessment of whether meaningful melody is present. So, even if words are present, as in the opera or in the mass, it is the sole purpose of the melody, first, and accompanying harmony, second, to demonstrate music's "power and superior capacity" to express what is most "profound" in the work. Whereas words can never move beyond the world as representation, melodic moving forms can reach into the "innermost soul" of any representation they accompany.

Schopenhauer reminds his readers that sometimes composers begin to compose a piece by selecting the text first. However, when they do this, they should be guided solely by whether that text gives them the compositional opportunity to enter into a sphere beyond representation: one of profound joy or pure feeling, separated from any individuated aspects of the world. He reiterates a point made above: namely, that composers should not be guided by whether or not a text is mediocre; they should only consider whether the text can be rendered sufficiently musical by the provision of tones. Nevertheless, whether a text might already be musical *before* being set to music, making the setting superfluous, is a question his account leaves interestingly unresolved.

It is not necessary to turn now to Schopenhauer's anyway quite brief remarks on tragic drama because his remarks on music have done all the work for the present argument. Over and above Schiller and Schelling, Schopenhauer makes explicit for us the claim that the musicality of the drama or the aesthetic work of humanity need no longer be embodied in or performed by the chorus if it is already present in the movement of the melody. Melodic movement is the bottom line, even if, for its completeness, it requires the presence of an entire harmonic structure that will finally transmute the dissonance into consonance and, by analogy, suffering into joy. What matters is that the musical mood is completed. The ramification of this argument is profound. The argument encourages both Wagner and Nietzsche to seek further within the modern music drama something that is as much symphonic as dramatic—something more musical or expressive than (merely) representational. It explains why *Tristan und Isolde* later proves more suited to the rebirth of music drama out of the spirit of music than any other of Wagner's works. To be sure, in Schopenhauerean terms though not necessarily in his judgment, *Parsifal* would fit the mass and *The Ring* the conception of the total work of art. But *Tristan* or, better, *Isolde* proves the argument that shifts attention away from the chorus of ancient drama and toward the inner and now symphonic drive of musicality, but only, now, if the term "symphonic" is not automatically identified with the literal production of a symphony.

The impact of Schopenhauer's argument could not have been stronger. Still, there are potentially severe limitations in the view. For example, by implicitly equating music and musicality, or by attaching the concept of musicality so closely to the purely tonal art, the argument leaves open the question of how much work the concept can now do in artworks in which music is not present. (And remember that the concept's application in arts other than music was significantly what motivated its introduction in the first place.) Even if Schopenhauer does not equate what is purely musical with the pure production of instrumental music, it is not clear how he accommodates its presence in arts where music is not present. Of course, one could say that musicality is always present in the background of all art, just as the blind striving of the Will is implicit in every representational activity of life, but to say this would only raise more questions as to how one explains its presence in arts, including music, that are then deemed "unmusical." Maybe one would have to say, with Schopenhauer, that no art is, strictly speaking, unmusical—only insufficiently musical, given its distance from the pure expression of Will.

This raises again the overall problem: To what exactly does "music" refer when he describes it as the pure expression of Will: to actual music or to what I am describing as inner or pure musicality? If it refers to both, then this could be interpreted either as excluding the access any other art (without music) has to musicality or as implying that of all the arts, music comes closest to reaching the pure condition of musicality. If one opts for the latter interpretation, however, one would have to rethink what Schopenhauer wants when he so strictly separates music from all the other arts.

Further, when Schopenhauer separates unmediated music from the remaining mediated arts, it looks as though he removes the pure art of tone or the power of musicality from the sphere of anything cognitive or moral. "Music" might be the "most profound" of all the arts, but it also runs the risk of being *too purely* aesthetic. When Schopenhauer describes music as an unconscious metaphysics, he simultaneously threatens to impose a limitation: that even if it can lead us all the way along the aesthetic path of liberation from the torments of Will, it cannot even begin to tread the moral path. On that path, something more conscious or representational must reenter the picture, something that returns at least part of our attention to the world of human action and, with that, to the other arts. One ought always to keep in mind the "and" in the title of his book: *The World as Will and Representation*.

Thus, at the end of his remarks on music, which is also the end of his treatise's third part, Schopenhauer suggests his concern that music's beauty, though utterly profound, might still somehow lack sufficient seriousness (*Ernst*). He speaks, recalling Schiller, of its lightness or cheerfulness (*Heiterkeit*) and of the consequent need to turn to the serious ethical considerations of the fourth part. In this matter, remember that when Schopenhauer separated music from all the other arts, he left tragedy occupying the highest position in the remaining hierarchy. Imagine, then, that having completed his remarks on music, he had returned to tragedy to reestablish a connection between the aesthetic and the moral or between the immediate and mediated arts. Returning to the tragic drama and to the opera as an example of such, he would have encouraged precisely the transition that both Schiller and Schelling encouraged—as Beethoven arguably encouraged when he made the aesthetic drive of his first three movements culminate in the moral statement of the fourth. Indeed, aware of the purely subjective or emotional character of instrumental music, all of these theorists sought a total work of art that would maintain via the Schillerian chorus an essential connection to the cognitive and ethical. Could Schopenhauer have followed suit? In a sense he already had in the remarks he offered prior to those he made about music. But had he returned to these remarks after completing those on music, would he have been so successful in bringing our attention to this single thought: that the future of art or music lies less with determining the superiority of one genre over another, or even of one art over another, and more with asking whether, in contemporary times, *any* sort of art or artwork *any longer* expresses the spirit of music?

From another perspective, of all the theories I am considering, it was Schopenhauer's that brought most attention to the challenge that the symphony, and the Beethoven symphony in particular, had made to the reign of opera. With this challenge, his work profoundly influenced the theorists of future generations. However, it left them asking whether, in seeming to limit the concept of musicality to music or even to melody alone, he showed them how to use the concept to perform the moral and political work earlier theorists had conceived it to do in works without music. The question thus arises whether Schopenhauer effectively removed from musicality its full dramatic potential by distinguishing the art of the Will from the arts of representation. Or was this fundamental separation made in order for the two sides then somehow to be reconnected in the completion, so to speak, of his fourth movement? The answer depends, though I pursue it no further, on how one interprets Schopenhauer's remarks on music in relation finally to his opus as a whole.

In sum, Schopenhauer potentially produced a rupture between an aesthetic of purely musical meaning and an ethics or politics of drama, which is precisely what Schiller tried to overcome when he developed his modern drama out of the ancient choric spirit of music or musicality. However, Schiller himself never satisfactorily convinced those around him (or, arguably, himself) that a work in which the chorus was present but music absent could ever be *sufficiently* or *completely* musical. Perhaps this is why so many theorists of his day and thereafter turned away from theater toward opera. Nevertheless, that musicality remained a concept deeply relevant to the other arts continued to absorb the attention of theorists and artists in decades to come, especially when the concepts of musicality and movement joined metaphysical hands. I resume this matter in chapter 7 when considering the early development of film, for in this development, the future of art under the condition of a total work of art came again into question.

For now, let me suggest that the very best work for the times I have been considering was Rossini's opera of 1829. This work set Schiller's drama *Wilhelm Tell* to music, and, with this, transformed Rossini from being a composer (so it was said) of light opera into a composer of the music drama. Wagner saw this transition in Rossini's work though believed it had been preempted, if not already by Gluck and Weber, then a year earlier by Auber's *La Muette di Portici*. Wagner selected the latter work before he read Schopenhauer, but after he read Schopenhauer, he considered with even more urgency what impact the Beethoven symphony had had on his compositional conception and judgment. With Nietzsche, he considered how best to transfer the power of musicality to pure music drama to render the chorus redundant.

The possibility of this transfer motivated Nietzsche's thought that ancient tragedy disappeared when it lost contact with the spirit of music but could be reborn in a new form were that contact to be reestablished. It also motivated Nietzsche to argue that it is part of the power of the symphony to find correlative expressions in visual and poetic form. What Beethoven showed better than anyone else, in Nietzsche's view, was the demand the symphony finally made to be completed through an extension of the receptive mind or the purely listening ear into the domain of metaphysical, metaphorical, and symbolic representation. Even if the chorus did not fully return, this was because in the modern work of total art, the word and image were deemed capable of doing the necessary *outer* work of the drama and the symphony the necessary *inner* work of musicality.[48]

Perhaps Wagner was more willing than Nietzsche to relinquish the presence of the chorus altogether. Even so, the presence or absence of such did not imply a preference for the symphony over the opera. On the contrary, it led to an argument in which the condition of symphonism, metaphysically understood, became the condition for transforming an unmusical *opera* into a properly musical *drama,* where the term "musical" signified the presence or absence of (sufficient) musicality. Wagner made the point, in fact, at a moment just preceding his discovery of Schopenhauer: "*The chorus of the Greek tragedy,*" he wrote, "has bequeathed its emotionally necessary significance in the drama to *the modern orchestra* alone [*allein*]."[49] However, if one is tempted now to think that it was Wagner alone who then turned "opera" into a dirty word to preserve for the term "music drama" alone the inexhaustible hopes of modern musicality, then one ought to remember that he never actually dismissed the pure melodic power he heard in Italian and French opera. To this thought I now turn: how music drama was finally reborn—dialectically—out of the antagonistic spirits of *both* Rossini and Beethoven.

Hegel

I turn for this argument not, however, to Wagner but to Hegel. This is not because Hegel's musical view advances much beyond what we already know and not because he takes into account the challenge of the symphony. Hegel is considered here only because he offers us an explicitly dialectical way to think about how the symphony gives way to the birth of opera out of the spirit of musicality, or the rebirth of music drama out of the spirit of ancient tragedy. And this, I want to show, has an interesting result regarding the concept of musicality.

Closer to Schelling than to Schopenhauer, Hegel argues that the history of romantic or Christian art proceeds from music to poetry, reaching its end in tragedy. As discussed in chapter 1, music for Hegel is the art of pure subjectivity, the abstract art of *Innerlichkeit,* or the formal art of feeling that tracks the formal movement of the self. While this sort of characterization of music leads Schopenhauer to regard music as transcending the world of representation (and obtaining its essential or pure expressive nature thereby), it points, for Hegel, more to an inadequacy, meaninglessness, or one-sidedness on music's part regarding the objective world. Instead of stressing the positive side of music's pure negative status, Hegel now stresses music's limitation in our attainment of absolute knowledge. As a purely temporal art, it has no staying power in the world of objects. From this, he begins to express skepticism toward solely instrumental music as failing, without the aid of word or action, to do the complete artistic work of *Geist.* Following Schelling (and with reference to him), he considers a more adequate form, one that will do more spiritual work rather than less. He thus considers a solution in the domain of opera before he turns to modern (tragic) theater most notably because of their common origin in antiquity.

In so describing Hegel's view, I am adding something new to the view described in chapter 1. There, I showed the deep affinity between music, thought, and the self via the passage of dialectical *Bewegung.* Here I emphasize

Hegel's suggestion (less often attended to in interpretations of his work) that because music as a purely instrumental art can only be a negative art, given its double negation, it elects an affinity with image and word, or seeks totality, whenever it wants to achieve a fullness or completeness of spiritual content.

Hegel develops his thoughts about opera in closer relation to tragedy and poetry than to the art of music per se. When thinking about the latter, however, he relies on Rousseau to generate descriptions of melody, harmony, rhythm, tone, tempo, and modulation. Like Schelling, he expresses ignorance about music and offers few examples: "Remember that [I] Hegel [am] not knowledgeable about music."[50] When offering examples, he usually bases them on comparisons with the other arts about which he knows considerably more. Further, like Schelling and Schopenhauer, he employs his examples primarily to illustrate his philosophical claims, even if, like them, he enjoys making his musical tastes known to the audiences of his lectures.

His recommendation that opera as modern music drama might serve as an exemplary form for the continuation of the tragic art appears several times in his writings. The following sentence from his lectures on aesthetics of 1826 summarizes the justification:

> If, however, the artwork is a wholly complete totality, then it has this perfection only in the opera. The ancient drama was already [at the same time] opera. . . . [It had] music, dance, song; [and] the choir sang and danced to the accompaniment of instruments.[51]

However, if opera is to do the work of modern drama, it will do this work in alliance with, and sometimes even as an improvement on, modern theater. Such theater is represented by Schiller's plays—for example, *The Bride of Messina,* where the chorus, Hegel points out, clearly still plays an essential role. Sometimes Hegel criticizes Schiller's works as overly reflective, and works of theater more generally, as overindulging in externals or as producing collisions between subjective and objective themes, but he continues to regard some of these works as worthy models against which to judge the contemporary production of art. Hegel also speaks of the necessity of setting mediocre (*mittelmässige*) texts to music and of the awkwardness in particular of setting Schiller's text to music.[52]

When asked once to give an example of an exemplary opera for his times, Hegel mentions Antonio Sacchini's *Oedipus auf Colonus* of 1786, then a most successful opera and with a clear origin in tragedy. But he could also have mentioned Rossini's operas (especially the later ones), which, like Schopenhauer, he much admires. Finally, when asked from a metaphysical point of view what he likes about opera, he points to the potential of its formal movement of melody to raise the work's content to a level beyond the concrete: "The melody," he reminds us, "is the soul of music."[53] Whenever he states a preference for melody, he states a preference also for song, and for the song, particularly, of Christ's redemptive suffering.

Hegel's suggestion that the future or continuation of tragic drama could lie (at least in part) with the development of the operatic art is not well known, mostly because it is left rather too implicit in the version of his lectures published after his death by his student Heinrich Gustav Hotho. The scholarship in Germany that has recently presented Hegel's lectures on aesthetics from 1818 to 1826, independently of Hotho's sometimes misleading revisions, persuades us to reconsider Hegel's views.[54] From this literature, we learn, for example, that Hegel's profound liking for Rossini went so far that in 1824—the year of the Ninth—, having traveled to Vienna to give himself the opportunity to listen to Italian opera, he wrote to a friend in Berlin that as long as the money held out, he'd rather stay in Vienna.[55] Apart from Rossini, he also demonstrates a liking for Gluck's operas, the majestic works of Händel and Palestrina, and the instrumental music of several eighteenth-century composers, notably Mozart. He does not mention Bach, though the name appears twice in Hotho's version, perhaps because of a new appreciation Hegel acquired (with significant coaching from musical friends), after hearing Mendelssohn's historic performance of the *Matthew-Passion* in 1829.[56]

In Berlin, Hegel had many opportunities to hear the music of Beethoven. Yet he doesn't mention Beethoven in his lectures and generally expresses disapproval of the new and complicated symphonies with which his day was being challenged.[57] Finding instrumental music difficult to listen to, he argues against the complexity of harmony in favor of the simplicity of melody, for the reason that true feeling comes with simple melody. However, he knows that the feeling cannot simply be light or cheerful but must also show a form or potential tragic enough to transmute suffering into the joy of Christian collective. Like Schelling and Schopenhauer, Hegel recognizes the necessity for a complex (dialectical) movement in the art of tones, but his recognition does not automatically translate into a taste for the art produced. Also like the others, he stresses the need for a melodic line to guide the harmonic or contrapuntal structure. As with Schopenhauer, whatever generic preference he expresses, his preference has less do with musical genre as such and more to do with where and what accounts for the presence of musicality in contemporary culture.

Hegel's editor and student, Hotho, underplays several of the theological aspects of Hegel's theory, both to secularize the argument and to give that argument a systematicity it does not originally have (so scholars have recently shown), thereby removing from the text Hegel's often more hesitant voice. (Recall Adorno's comment from chapter 1 on the live and unfinished character of Hegel's texts.) Recent research also suggests that Hotho took less seriously than Hegel the view that romantic art shows the full potential of Christian community in its ideality or essence, even if, for Hegel, not in its actuality or reality. If romantic art is failing in real or actual terms, it is significantly because of the increasing ironic condition of reflection that has come to characterize its production. Hegel connects this increase in irony to the general loss in culture of Christian morality and community (*Sittlichkeit*). In contrast, Hotho focuses more on the irony than on the claim about community to render more explicit Hegel's rational thesis that art reaches its end when it achieves its reflective self-understanding. (In Hegel's view, rational or philosophical reflection is one thing; ironic, artistic, or obsessive reflection another.) Apparently, Hegel is less certain of the thesis than Hotho's version suggests, a fact arguably evidenced in Hegel's bid to describe what can still count as meaningful art even at the moment that art becomes, as he puts it, a "thing of the past."[58] I resume this theme in chapter 5.

In his remarks, Hegel does not appreciate, as Schopenhauer does a little more, the ability of a virtuoso melody to float too freely over and above the word. For the sake of the moral aspect of art, he prefers that the melody remain tethered to the concept. However, that music is so tethered does not prevent it also from exhibiting to the highest degree a certain kind of freedom. In his lectures of 1820/21, he wrote: "The Italians are much freer, they allow the music to pour forth of its own accord." What Hegel encourages is less a freedom for music to be appreciated for its own sake than a freedom recognizing music's ability to raise the word to a higher level. For, in this raising, we experience the everyday being transfigured via the aesthetic into the moral: the suffering into the joy, hence, in this case, an aesthetic experience permeated by moral and religious content. Thinking also of Raphael, Hegel seeks a historical correlate in music, thus his praise of early Italian music for its freedom to float free though not completely free. In this floating-yet-tethered (*schwebende*) freedom, we experience a serenity and calm—even a Homeric "smiling through tears" or, with Beethoven, a "joy through suffering"—that raises us above the chaotic intensity below. When Hegel does not have Raphael's *Transfiguration* before his eyes, he seems to have in his ears the profound *Crucifixus* of Christ's suffering.[59]

When he writes of this suffering, he speaks of the *musikalische Seele*. This is something also apparently underplayed by Hotho, who prefers to find in the musical soul, and by extension in *die musikalische Stimme*, something more purely formal and abstract: namely, a purity of voice now separated from any thought of Christian embodiment. It is worth noting that one recent commentator, when describing Hegel's view of the voice, also writes about "die reine Musikalität der Stimmen," where presumably, for this critic, the newer term "Musikalität," probably derived from the French term, is meant to do the work of the older term "das Musikalische."[60] The question, however, is whether the newer term preserves the aesthetic, moral, or theological substance that the early-nineteenth-century theorists attached to the older term, or whether it more promotes the sort of formalism for the purely musical art that we later see defended by theorists after Hanslick. As far as I can tell, Hegel does not use the original term "das Musikalische," even if he does endorse its central association—namely, to capture the drive of *Innerlichkeit* that seeks its completion in the full external face of art. "In genuine opera," he writes, where opera is opposed to operetta, "an entire musical action (*eine ganze Handlung*) is performed musically throughout (*musikalisch ausgeführt*)." (To be sure, this sentence could belong to Hotho, or even to Schopenhauer, Hanslick, or Wagner, where everything depends on how much or how little is imported into the idea of performing the action of an opera musically.)[61]

Like Schopenhauer, Hegel is aware of the tendencies of modern opera qua operetta to turn into mere pomp or for an opera to stress the artificiality of the music over and above the work's drama. This is evident in his lectures of 1826. In this respect, it is not surprising to read of his turning toward the text (and thus eventually to tragedy) to guide and to constrain the spiritual development of the music, even if, in matters of taste, he sometimes sides with the sort of opera that others in his time dismissed as spiritually impoverished. However, the main point for the present argument is that, even if Hegel culminates his discussion of the ordering of the arts by reference to the spiritual perfection of tragedy, his immediately preceding discussion of opera plays a specific role and should not be underestimated. Good opera is the mediating and cultivating step between the second and first arts—between music and tragedy or poetry—and has its historical source and at least part of its justification as such in the once-existing total artwork of the ancients.[62]

So far, there is not much to distinguish Hegel's view from those of the other theorists. Still, the next and final point begins to give his view a distinctive character. Hegel enjoys comparing different kinds of music by explicit reference to their national origins. He writes of tastes and styles more suited to Germans than to Italians and of what the Italians are better at doing than the French: "In Italy, everyone has a voice"—and apparently the voice of a nightingale.[63] The other theorists write this way, too, but Hegel's comments encourage a new thought for his time and one that pervades aesthetic theory for at least a century to come. If there is to be a future for art, then this matter should be of most concern to the Germans because it is arguably only their art that is being threatened or promised (depending on how we read the thesis) with its end. "In Germany" (*bei uns*), Hegel writes, "anarchy reigns." [64] This thought quickly motivates another: though the Germans ought for the sake of art's future to look for models, say, in Italy or France, they need also, according to a dialectical logic, to identify the last and most reflective act of German art which the new art will then surpass. In looking across to foreign lands (even if they hear these works at home), composers and philosophers turn their attention to Rossini (and others). In looking inside the land for the last and most reflective act of German music, they turn their attention to Beethoven.

Cultural Loss

This double attention is the final step in the argument. It motivates the thought that the Beethoven symphony, as representative of the most modern German art, had to give way to the production of a different kind of art of either increased or even more advanced musicality. Why the lack of satisfaction with where German art presently stood? Because even if one thought that the Beethoven symphony showed the highest advance of musical form, it testified, and the Ninth paradigmatically, to a much broader cultural anxiety regarding the loss of musicality.

In the darkness of this alleged loss, theorists looked back to the distant past to understand what musicality once was to determine what German art ought (once more) to become. But they also turned their gaze outward or sideward toward contemporary forms abroad in which musicality still seemed to be present. Hence, Italian or French opera (or much later American opera) was offered as the model for the future of the German musical art, which, not incidentally, was a theme Wagner treated with the utmost fearfulness in the final scene of *Die Meistersinger*. Prima facie, the arguments of this period encouraged a turn (back) to opera, but this was less their purpose than to show dialectically how contemporary forms of German music must call forth what they no longer (allegedly) exhibited themselves: musicality. Given that musicality (and even being German) became both a metaphysical and a cultural principle, the argument technically committed itself to no future for a specific genre, despite the concrete and often conservative recommendations offered in favor of one sort of music over another.

Moreover, given the complex argument of restoration and progress in this period, it isn't surprising, however paradoxical this thought now seems, that, in the decades after the 1840s, Beethoven was allied as often with Hegel as with Schopenhauer. If anything, the present argument should persuade us to reassess the canonic alliances that have so dominated the discipline of musical aesthetics, even if, in a more subtle sense, the argument also gives strength to these alliances.

Thus, if we read Beethoven's Ninth as calling at its close for the instruments to *rejoin* their choric friends of serene and joyful voice, then, ultimately, it is this work that best exemplified the dominant aesthetic argument of the age more even than Rossini's late opera. This argument even fits Schopenhauer's account, as long as we accept two things: first, that Beethoven's Ninth remains purely musical or symphonic throughout, regardless of the addition of the chorus, but, second, that a symphony is not deemed musical in virtue of being performed by instruments alone. In this way, the Ninth does the philosophical work theorists wanted it do *either way:* as calling either for the continuation of the symphony or for the rebirth of opera as music drama. For its real concern was less with the question of genre (and this, even granting the enormous interest in genre in this period) and more with the question whether any kind of work of any kind of art was still capable of being musical.

When Schiller found musicality in poetry and painting, he did not intend to make all the arts approximate to the condition of music as an art. On the contrary, he tried to maintain for the concept of musicality its original connotation tied to the preconceptual inspiration of the muses. Wagner and Nietzsche also realigned the concept of musicality with what was once meant by *mousikê.* They did this in philosophical recognition that the concept of musicality had run the danger more or less since 1800 of having become overly identified with a concept of music connoting a far too independent art of tones.

In all the arguments presented, the terms "melody," "harmony," and "symphony," like that of "musicality," assumed meanings far more philosophical and cultural-political than either literally musical or purely aesthetic. This is evident especially in the argument regarding melody, which, by being allied with the concept of truthfulness and simplicity, persuaded theorists then to underestimate the merits, even if they saw the necessity, of harmony. Against this background, one might finally suggest that the Ninth could also have served as a *corrective* to judgments of taste had it drawn theorists away from their rather naive and conservative commitments to melody by showing the potential for social and aesthetic truthfulness also in contrapuntal harmony. This is the view that Adorno, though not he alone, later developed to the extreme by dialectically placing Hegel and Beethoven side by side. In this picture, however, Italian opera tended increasingly to be excluded or to be hidden behind the congealed dialectical paint, a paint that promising total color nonetheless ended up denying joy to those promised inclusion by the enlightened, symphonic song.

Hanslick feared the turn to metaphor or metaphysics in matters of musical meaning. Considering the Ninth brought home to him just how exemplary it was in raising metaphysical problems, the cultural and social significance of which far exceeded that which was grasped solely by the ear. Hanslick was right: the Ninth was a spiritual watershed interposing itself between embattled currents of conviction. Interestingly enough, it remains so even to this day.[65]

3 *For the Birds / Against the Birds*
Modernist Narratives on the End of Art

The First Deception

Thou wast not born for death, immortal Bird!
No hungry generations tread thee down;
The voice I hear this passing night was heard
In ancient days by emperor and clown.

These lines from John Keats's "Ode to a Nightingale" of 1819 sustain the rhetorical question Kant posed in 1790: "What is more highly extolled by poets than the bewitchingly beautiful song of the nightingale [sung] in a lonely stand of bushes on a still summer evening, under the gentle light of the moon?"[1] Kant spoke of the beauty of birdsong, as of nature more generally. He found beauty too in art. Yet the conditions of beauty were not, for either nature or art, what we would expect. For, from an aesthetic perspective, we find a natural object beautiful if we regard it as purposeful, as if its meaning were derived from something like human intention, but an artwork is beautiful if we regard it as purposeless, as though, through the creative act of genius, nature were its source. However, Kant continued, from a moral perspective and given the very same objects, we want to see them for what they really are and don't want to be deceived. So if someone tricks us into thinking we are hearing a song of nature when it is artificially produced, a basic condition of our appreciation is disturbed. Kant told of an innkeeper who determined to trick his guests into thinking they were listening to a bird when behind the bushes a young boy sang in imitation.

Kant is well known for having helped overturn a traditional demand on art that it should stand to a natural or to an ordinary everyday object in a relation of mere copying. Hegel extended the argument when he referred to the many examples of fully deceptive imitation in the history of art. He wrote of the grapes of Zeuxis that were long regarded as art's triumph: so like the real thing, the legend has it, living doves tried to peck at them. Like Kant, Hegel was unimpressed by these "tricks" of imitation: deception, at least of man, shouldn't be the aim of an art in service to absolute *Geist*.[2]

Keats further complicated the relation between art and nature, though now also between humanity and nature, because his ode in praise of the nightingale's natural song was sung under the condition of human suffering:

> My heart aches, and a drowsy numbness pains
> My sense, as though of hemlock I had drunk.

The last line offers no further clarity:

> Was it a vision, or a waking dream?
> Fled is that music:—do I wake or sleep?

Like Kant and Hegel, Keats drew on the possibility of deception to suggest that the nightingale's song is not always or purely a happy one, even when sung on a summer evening.

This was also Oscar Wilde's theme in his short story about a nightingale who tries in vain to help a young philosopher find a rose to please a girl. "What is the heart of a bird compared to the heart of a man?" asks the unhappy nightingale, and then immediately answers her own question: "Bitter, bitter was the pain, and wilder and wilder grew her song, for she sang of the Love that is perfected by Death, of the Love that dies not in the tomb." The young philosopher fails to get the point and instead of singing a *Liebestod* chooses to return to his books. What does logic give him that love does not? It gives him a guarantee against his ever being deceived again.[3]

The Second Deception

The interest that motivates this chapter originated in a piece I wrote for a conference in Berlin on "conceptualisms" in music and the other arts. I titled it "Against the Birds" ("Gegen die Vögel"). I read Adorno (as both philosopher and music-critic) as arguing against conceptualism in general, which is to say, against the regressive tendency of concepts entirely to subsume particulars such as works of art, as a totalitarian society subsumes its individuals, thereby denying to both the works and individuals their freedom of movement. I focused on Adorno's critique of the composers he met in Darmstadt, especially on John Cage. For just when Adorno argued against subsuming particulars fully under a concept, he argued against subsuming art entirely under the concept of nature and nature entirely under the concept of art. Adorno worried about the contradictions implicit to the naturalist claims about art he heard in Darmstadt. He thought it a misleading naturalism used to justify highly unnatural modes of production. Sometimes he objected more to the deceptive character threatened by the claims than to the actual music produced.[4] Darmstadt, he might have written, "as [*als*] mass deception."

My title "Against the Birds" played against a title John Cage once used for a book, *For the Birds*. Cage didn't do much with the title; nor at first did I. So I began to think further about Cage and then more broadly about the pervasive use of birds, birdsong, and bird cages in the history of music and opera, until I arrived at the thought that knowing this history might help further elucidate Adorno's critique. In this history, it was evident that birds had entered music's domain, first, by symbolizing all manner of freedom, escape, return, love, and knowledge, and, second, by demonstrating the many tense elective affinities between artistic making and nature's inspirations. From Mozart to Messiaen: this history corresponded to what Adorno, with Horkheimer, described as the dialectic of enlightenment.[5] They described a dialectic between nature and art, according to which nature came, in the civilized name of reason and art, to be dominated by humanity at the same time that it was reincorporated into an uncivilizing discourse of myth. Enlightenment, as they did write, "as [*als*] mass deception."

In their account, one end of the enlightenment dialectic occurred earlier than the 1960s with the catastrophic culmination of the fascist movement in Nazi Germany. Still, the tendencies they saw in Germany before the war they also saw afterward, in (West) Germany, as well as in postwar capitalist countries like the United States. Moving my attention from Europe to America (or from Darmstadt to New York), I noticed that the Manhattan philosopher and art critic Arthur Danto had also called on the dialectic between art and nature (nature now under the guise of the commonplace) to comment on the conceptualist and minimalist movements of the postwar years. At that moment, I realized that the two postwar accounts, European and American, might very well be illuminated by their comparison.

In general, Adorno wrote more about music; Danto has written more about the visual arts. Both have written about John Cage. Both, moreover, link thoughts about art's relationship to nature to those about art's relationship to the commonplace. Hegel originally provided the link when he spoke in the same sentence of "the hard rind of nature" and "the common world" as equally giving the mind more trouble than the products of art "in breaking through to the Idea."[6] However, the connection goes further: for the dialectic that starts out between art and nature becomes over time one between art and the commonplace, where the commonplace increasingly becomes a concept demonstrating the loss of what the concept of nature once implied: namely, beauty and freedom. If this is right, then it also plausibly follows that the artists of the 1960s (and after) who sought a meaning for art in the commonplace were too content to accept the loss of a certain sort of meaning in art. Or, those who still saw beauty in nature or art were too content not to find beauty in the commonplace. Whatever the attitude adopted toward art or nature, it has always been inseparable from an attitude adopted toward the common world.

Shared by Adorno and Danto is a deep philosophical commitment to preserving a *difference* between art and nature or between art and the commonplace simultaneously to reveal the deceptive character of what they both interpret to be contrary assertions of *identity*. In these assertions, both find the terms to articulate the idea that art has come to some sort of end. This is an end differently conceptualized: by Danto, as a triumph over deception or, better, as a triumph over the question of deception such that the question no longer obtains, and, by Adorno, as a calamitous triumph of social deception over us. In this chapter, I focus on how both philosophers assume theses about identity and difference to interpret the culmination of their particular historical narratives of modernist deception. I want to show that just as the arguments are about *identity* but for *nonidentity,* so similarly, however focused the arguments are on *ends,* they are, in fact, for *continuation.*

Cage's Parrot

In 1972, John Cage produced an event in downtown New York titled *Bird Cage.* It was named after a beer coaster from a working-class bar in Philadelphia. It took place over two evenings and consisted of twelve tapes of birdsong recorded in New York State, spliced by the voice of a speaking man, Cage himself. At a significant moment, Cage and his parrot engaged in a repetitive play of imitating voices. As the advertising declared, Cage wanted the tapes to be heard by people who were "free to move" and where birds were "free to fly"—and that, apparently, could still happen in the 1970s in downtown New York.[7]

Cage generally articulated the trajectory of music's bourgeois historical passage. He raised the question of music's relation to birdsong to render explicit what is involved in our concept of music. Less in reference to the works than to the proclamations he made on their behalf, his thought was that contra, say, the naturalist projects of Béla Bartók and Olivier Messiaen, birdsong need no longer be composed into musical form because it is already music or at least musical. We need not transfigure natural song or ordinary sound into music because it is already what the compositional act would show it to be. The traditional psychological, if not also ontological, gap that long maintained a difference between music and birdsong is closed. Music finds its origin by being returned to that from which it sought, under the condition of enlightenment, to separate itself: namely, from natural song. Through the reincorporation of natural song or everyday sound into the concept of music, the concept is brought to self-understanding by being shown no longer to need its artificial or deadening Western aesthetic history. In this passage, music meets its natural maker, finds its concept and identity, and, as paradoxical as it sounds, is liberated from its cage. "I make music," Cage insisted, "not cages."[8]

To present Cage's argument this way is to use it as we may use many of the proclamations of the Fluxus artists: to sustain an account of the end if not of music's *production* then of music's traditional enlightenment or bourgeois *conception.* To a significant extent, it is the tension between production and conception, or between product and concept, that motivates many of the modernist theses regarding the end of music and art.

Adorno and Danto

Both Adorno and Danto interpret the history of the arts in terms of the Kantian and Western dialectic between art and nature or in terms of the arts' bourgeois separation from the world of the everyday. Influenced also by Hegel and Nietzsche, they trace their accounts back to ancient Greece, to Plato's fear of the arts, generating what Danto in the early 1980s called the disenfranchisement thesis, of art by philosophy, and back to Greek myth, motivating Adorno's concentration with Horkheimer in the late 1940s on Odysseus and the Sirens.[9] Both read the movements such as of conceptualism and minimalism as challenging or at least polemicizing the basic distinction between art and life, to deny the difference in favor of proclaimed assertions of identity. "Art is Life, and Life is Art" proclaimed the Fluxus artists, or Cage, with much more of an edge: "Art has erased the dividing line between life and art. Now it is up to life to erase the dividing line between life and art."[10]

Both Adorno and Danto acknowledge that the identity claims are not straightforward, yet they read them at the extreme, as strong assertions of identity. Cage's birdsong doesn't really deceive the listener into thinking it is *the real thing*. Warhol's Brillo boxes (Danto's favorite example) don't look, as Danto's critics always remind us, *exactly* like their supermarket, storage counterparts. However, the strongest claim to identity or of perceptual deception—that we could mistake one for the other—is necessary for both their arguments to work.

Consider Cage's best-known work, *4' 33"*, of 1952. Even though there is nothing to hear except the real, ordinary, or natural thing, the noises that happen to be heard are still framed by institutional time and space and are deliberately so framed to bring attention to the traditional strictures of time and space in the concert hall. Contrast this work with Max Neuhaus's installation in Times Square called *Times Square* (1977–92). Unlike others who apparently encountered this work without anyone's help, when I visited the site, I heard nothing until I was told (in fact, by Danto) what to listen for. It was a monotone sound, a murmur or tremor, like the large chord of a cathedral organ, and hence a pillar of sound separated from the ordinary sounds of the square intended to be separated and experienced as separated, such that when one walked across the square, it would be like moving into a sound space and out again on the other side. Neuhaus's work was site- and sound-specific, a sound sculpture on which, Danto recently remarked in conversation, one could spray no graffiti.

Cage's work was more traditionally constrained than Neuhaus's by factors of time and space. Yet Neuhaus claimed his work to be a work, whereas Cage claimed with his work to challenge the very concept of a work. Cage used his work to make the constraints of the work concept explicit, though Neuhaus's work might still have been the more subversive. The question here is whether it is more effective to challenge the work concept from the outside or from the inside, by an external and explicit idea or by changing conditions that internally compel a change in our understanding. Adorno thinks the latter: a new aesthetics cannot be inferred from a philosophical idea or from empirical investigation; it can only be developed by reflecting historically from inside the musical experience itself.[11] I think Danto partially concurs. Neither he nor Adorno bases his account on works that proclaim themselves philosophical works, or, better, works of philosophy (if, indeed, any really do). Neither is so interested (despite sentences sometimes suggesting the contrary) in an account of an art *become* idea or philosophy. They are both more interested in a history of art production that compels at a particular historical juncture a philosophical interpretation and, with this, liberation from a certain sort of deception.[12]

Both more or less sidestep or criticize the actual, metaphysically styled statements made by artists themselves about their works. They do this to show, following Adorno first, that philosophical criticism articulates a significance for the works that the works cannot do themselves in the languages in which they are created and of which the artists are not necessarily aware.[13] Danto's point is different. For a long time, production of the arts fell under the same historicist master narrative as philosophical thinking about the arts. As philosophical critic, Danto aims to make explicit the terms of this master narrative, to release art from its authority, and thereby to bring the narrative to some sort of end. Danto describes how the concept of art was realized in or by the works themselves, though it was his own act of philosophical interpretation of the works that made the art act explicit.[14] Like Adorno's argument, Danto's depends on the relation he assumes between himself as philosophical critic and the works themselves. Although we speak as if the conceptual development occurred entirely in the works, it could not have done so (and the Hegelian or dialectical development could not have been completed) had there been no accompanying act of philosophical reflection and articulation.

For Danto, the concept of art is brought to its modernist fulfillment when art passes over via philosophical reflection into its posthistoricist condition.[15] Adorno also offers an account of such a moment, though his tone is different.

Rather than seeing the concept as realizing itself in any sort of positive gesture of self-knowing on the part of either artist or philosopher, he worries about an art production that has fully compromised itself to its concept. Art might meet its maker but the maker is now merely one of concepts. He thinks much about the contemporary impossibility of producing an uncompromised or literally nonconceptualized art. When he writes that there can be no poetry after Auschwitz (a statement he later modifies but to which he also often returns), one of the things he says he means is that society has so declined that there is almost no space left anymore for an uncompromised art to be produced. Almost all art has become conceptual in the very worst way. To have a gapless society is to have a society totally administered, where even the air is controlled, as in Walter Braunfels's opera *The Birds,* so that nothing slips out of the net.[16] Such a society prevents what at least great art was formerly able to achieve: namely, a refusal to conform to society's demand for a conceptually fitting art.

Danto reads art's history, with art's preoccupation with distinguishing itself from natural or ordinary objects, in terms of its ability to be the world's conscience: to take a stand at a distance or to interpret the world.[17] Adorno reads art's commitment to aesthetic appearance as a way to sustain its separation from a society that he regards as false. Through truthful forms of aesthetic appearance (whatever those forms might now be), art (which is to say, some art) destabilizes society's deceptive appearances. Adorno uses philosophical critique to expose the relation between aesthetic and social appearance. Danto pits art less against society or social appearance than against philosophy, given philosophy's positivist need to stabilize its concepts with definitions. Adorno does this, too, although he sees in this positivist philosophical need a corresponding and regressive social need. Danto isolates this philosophical need to show how it long dominated the practice of art, only ceasing when, in the 1960s, art went as far as it could in making the question "What is art?" explicit to the philosophical critic. Overall, Adorno makes the social theory embedded in his view explicit as Danto has generally been less tempted to do.

Danto

In a quite precise sense, Danto is a philosopher and critic of the 1960s.[18] He places the starting point of his philosophical work regarding art in Manhattan at a moment when he witnessed the production of art and music by artists such as Andy Warhol, Robert Rauschenberg, and Cage. In that moment, artists challenged the artworld to explain the difference between works of art and ordinary, commonplace, or real things (such as beds) from which the artworks were, most importantly, perceptually indiscernible. By erasing (intentionally or not) the perceptual difference between artworks and real things, the artists made transparent what the essential difference between them *is*. Danto describes the difference in terms of what he calls an "is of interpretation," as opposed to an "is of identity." He wants to explain how and why one may attribute all sorts of world-constructing (expressive, symbolic, and metaphorical) properties and all sorts of art-historical (expressionistic or representational) properties to artworks but not to their indiscernible counterparts. Artworks, contra everyday Brillo pads, as he has put it, show an interest in beautifying the world, not in cleaning it.

The interpretative context of the artworld, with its history of theories and styles, is what allows an object or image, considered ordinary when seen in the supermarket, to be transfigured into an extraordinary work of art when interpreted in the context of the artworld. The transfiguration marks not the act of making one thing into another thing or declaring one thing to be another thing as arguably in "found art." More, it recognizes with great consequence that how we encounter and interpret an artwork is categorically different from how we treat a perceptually indiscernible counterpart. Danto's use of the term "transfiguration," with its sacred history, plays perfectly into his modernist version of what was earlier called in Germany (by Hegel) *Kunstreligion*. By the 1960s, one might say, the religion of art was secularized once and for all—or desublimated to mark the loss of the sublime, as Danto has written—by a theory about the artworld that turned on just the moment when artists challenged that world to accept into its domain a work of art that looked no different from a supermarket commodity.

What in Danto's account marks the deep gesture of secularization on the part of contemporary art marks in Adorno's account also the calamitous triumph of commodification: art becomes commodity almost without remainder. For both Adorno and Danto, it is the theorizing of this remainder and hence the question of the continuation of art after its end that preoccupies them the most.

In his "Artworld" article of 1964, Danto describes the ontological victory won by modern artists (beginning with the Fauvists and the impressionists) when deception was no longer the issue for these artists in their art production. At this moment, something new became possible: namely, an artist could produce something that looked like the real thing without its being either a copy of the real thing or the real thing itself. "New entities" lying between traditional copies and real things were introduced into the artworld to explode the traditional two-sided mimetic ideology. Concerned with in-discernibles and not identicals (works that only *look like* but *are not* the real things), Danto shows why the question to sleep or not to sleep in this bed was the wrong question for anyone viewing a Rauschenberg bed. The ques-tion only seemed to be correct when the "is" was considered an "is" of iden-tity: when deception still seemed to be the issue or when it was mistakenly thought that artists were still trying to make viewers believe that imitations or copies were just the real things. When deception was no longer the issue and the "is" was transferred over to art-historical interpretation, the anxious question fell aside.

Danto argues that the attempt to erase the perceptual gap between art-works and ordinary objects only succeeded insofar as it made transparent to the perceiving philosopher what the correct philosophical task regarding art now was: to explain what the nonperceptual *gap or difference* amounts to. At that moment, the argument turned out to be thoroughly dialectical. To explain the essential difference to counter an incorrect identity being as-serted was not to render art philosophical but, rather, to grant art its libera-tion from a philosophy preoccupied with definition. In the attempt to effect what Danto calls a "logical symbiosis" between art and the ordinary, art was brought to some sort of end, although not to the end of its production. It was only released from a progressivist master narrative that was dominated by the thought that art should live up to philosophy's need for conceptual knowledge by coming to know art.

Burdened by this need, art was long disenfranchised from itself. This ended when art entered its posthistoricist stage, when, under much more demo-cratic conditions, it became no longer burdened by a developmental history of mimetic- and definitionally directed styles and materials. At this moment, art could be any style it wanted to be and could look anyway it wanted to look, no longer needing to look like the real world. Just when art *could* look like the real thing, it was freed from the philosophical stricture of *having* to look this way. Paradoxically, art only became *for its own sake* a century and a half after philosophy first declared art's freedom in these terms—a fact that proves that philosophy's declaration in 1800 suited philosophy far more than it ever suited art. Whatever the story in 1800, for Danto, it was only in the 1960s (and notably in America) that art was liberated from its history of pro-ductively repetitive art-historical attempts to say what art is and could now fly free as a bird, claiming its stylistic and material independence from philoso-phy's governance.

No problem it seems for art: art was liberated. But why not then speak less about art's end and more about its new and continued life in freedom? And why not now speak of philosophy's end or at least of the end of its domination of art? Is it not a consequence of Danto's view that by liberating art from its philosophical burden, a dominating philosophy of art was brought to an end, because, by so interpreting art's liberation, philosophy could finally ask and answer its own essential ontological question: What is art? Although, in Hegelian terms, philosophy had certainly achieved something by coming to *know* art, what now was there left for this old dominating philosophy to do?

Danto recognizes the possibility that the philosophy of art might have become gray, grown old, or left itself impotent with no more of a task than that of passive understanding. In freeing art from its dominion, philosophy seemed to lose not only its perpetual antagonist (they had always been at war) but also its own developmental form of ongoing thought. In a comparable gesture of release from the very idea of historical development, Philip Glass once declared that his music is best "experienced as one event, without start or end."[19] Without beginnings and endings, the music just happens. His posthistoricist demand was for spectators to lose their sense of time and perhaps even to release themselves from the burden of historical time altogether. For Danto also, this sort of release marked the moment of the so-called *happenings*. Is this, however, how we should now understand the philosophy of art as well, as having become the kind of activity that just happens?

In a certain sense, the answer is yes. In attempting to overcome its age, or, rather, to suit its own newfound maturity, the philosophy of art recognizes that art now just happens, though this does not mean that art releases itself from the need to be interpreted. Danto argues that the philosophical answer to the question "What is art?" is that a work of art has an *aboutness* and that it *embodies,* as it were, this *aboutness*. Philosophical criticism, as Danto now introduces this theme, amounts to showing how works embody and are about their meaning. That's it. While the traditional metaphysical philosopher must sit back, without either irony or cynicism, satisfied to let the criticism take place, he must nevertheless make sure that the new criticism does not assume a developmental direction of its own. Rather, the criticism must work with the fact of art's new pluralism, with the fact that art is no longer constrained by having to move according to a historicist philosophical development and may now be, as Danto likes to put it, anything it wants to be, as long as it retains its status as art.

The implication is not, however, that philosophy gives way to criticism altogether. To the extent that philosophy of art continues, it does so under the nondominating terms of what Danto calls "analytical philosophy," which assumes no historicist course. In this matter, Danto links the liberation of art and, with this, the philosophy of art to the sort of freedom felt or asserted by the early logical positivists who, in celebrating their access to the ordinary world through new forms of common sense and logic, claimed to sever all contact with the grandiose metaphysicians of historicism and idealism. The new positivists claimed, as artists also claimed, that access to the world was far less muddy than the metaphysicians had led us to believe. For them, the birds could now fly forward in a pure flight of scientific progress unobstructed by a historical gaze. Many have said in either celebration or despair that this move also marked an end of philosophy altogether, as its different branches, one after another, gave way to science. To be sure, Danto has not always been entirely convinced by the positivist flight, but he has not then retreated to the disenfranchising historicism of idealist metaphysics. He has always sought a place for his own analytical philosophy between the extremes. I return to this matter explicitly in chapter 5.

In a recent book *The Abuse of Beauty* (though he began to develop this example in 1964[20]) Danto employs for an epigraph a saying from his imagined character named Testadura, the hardheaded one: "Art is for aesthetics what the birds are for ornithology." In 1967, as Danto reminds us, Barnett Newman reversed the terms of the saying to turn it into a criticism of aesthetic theory: "Aesthetics is for art what ornithology is for the birds." Apparently, Newman had the philosopher (of music) Susanne Langer in mind when he said this. If, as in one of Puccini's operas, Pinkerton falsely promised Butterfly that he would return from America with the robin redbreasts, so aesthetics, Newman was telling Langer, is "for the birds": worthless, useless, impotent—and perhaps even "sharpless." My reference to *Butterfly* is quite relevant: when Pinkerton fails to return, Butterfly asks Sharpless whether the happy season comes less often in America. Sharpless holds the truth from her and declares himself "ignorant about . . . ornithology." "Orni?" she asks; "thology," he repeats.

The same verbal rupture is found in Hans Christian Andersen's tale "The Nightingale," a story motivated by his deep passion for the singer Jenny Lind, later turned into an opera by Stravinsky. In this tale, which plays on the difference between a real nightingale and an almost indiscernible mechanical copy, we hear that the "whole city talked about the remarkable (mechanical) bird" and that "whenever two people met, the first one needed only to say 'Night—!' before the other said 'Gale!'" The verbal rupture suggests a society fractured by heartless or mechanized design—a "tin ear" or a "tin heart"—which is also what one might well accuse Pinkerton of having, even given the modicum of regret he expresses having brought Butterfly to her death. Somehow, the heartlessness gives everyone a comfortable, even if false, sense of security. On hearing the mechanical nightingale's song, the towns-folk thus proclaim it the very best bird they can imagine, whereupon the narrator remarks that they made the bird sing again, although it was the thirty-fourth time. Unable to learn its tune, they declare that they prefer this bird to the real thing: "With the real nightingale you never know what's going to come next, but with the artificial bird it's all set. That's the way it is, and that's the way it's always going to be. You can explain it, you can open it up and see the human ingenuity—how the pieces are put together, how they work, and how one thing follows another."[21] Since, however, the mechanical bird cannot produce what the real nightingale produces—namely, a song of art—the tale is meant to persuade us that this difference should have proved more important to the townsfolk than the convenient substitution they evidently preferred to celebrate.

The phrase "for the birds" found its common currency during World War II, when enlisted men in the U.S. Army had to perform menial tasks regarded as no better than picking up the shit of the officers, an idea that mirrored the original meaning in which birds eat the droppings of horses and cattle. Recall, Cage used the phrase for a book title but did not do much with it; Danto suggests far more, asking whether aesthetic theory can tell us what it is for art to be art if ornithology can't tell us what it's like for a bird to be a bird—perhaps, as Butterfly, in love. His nicely dialectical answer is that, as soon as aesthetic theory tells us what art is, the bird that is art is set free from its traditional philosophical cage. Butterfly was not so fortunate.

The phrase "for the birds" reminds me of another of music's more historical associations with the shittier side of life. If Butterfly suffered from the false promise of Pinkerton, so the nightingale once suffered from the words of our Viennese music critic, Eduard Hanslick, who already in 1854 attempted (and later influenced Langer) to fix the terms, as described in chapter 1, for a philosophically respectable aesthetics of music. Hanslick denied in Kantian terms what Cage claimed: humanity doesn't learn from nature how to make music. Nature does not give us the artistic materials for a finished, pre-made tonal system but only the raw stuff that we make serviceable in producing music. So far, so good, but his derision came in his next remark. It is not even the voices of animals that matter, only their entrails, because with the latter we make the strings of our musical instruments. The promise of the nightingale's song is thus best left for the birds or, even better, for the sheep, since, so one may conclude, violins are better played by humanity with guts.[22] (That music is "for the intestines" was an idea later picked up and played with by Duchamp and the surrealists.)

In the 1950s, Danto attended the lessons on Buddhism by Dr. Suzuki at Columbia University. So did John Cage. To record his experience and his memories of Cage, Danto recently wrote an essay titled "Upper West Side Buddhism":

> [Cage's] *4' 33"* was inspired by Robert Rauschenberg's white paintings, done when he was at Black Mountain College in 1951. Cage said that he saw them as "airports for shadows and dust"—or as "mirrors for air." The deep point was that they were no more empty than his own 1952 composition was silent. The panels themselves collaborated . . . with the environment, so that the ambient lights and shadows became part of the art, instead of being aesthetically erased in order to allow a response to the pure, unsullied blank. If a wayward pigeon dropped shit on the white, that would be part of the work, at least in Cage's view. (Rauschenberg, on the other hand, stipulated that the panels be repainted, to keep them fresh.)
>
> Those who took Cage's course in experimental composition at the New School in the 1950's enlisted the surrounding world to create compositions. A case in point was Dick Higgins's 1959 *Winter Carol*. The carolers decide on the length of time within which they go out to listen to the sound of falling snow. Snow, of course, is naturally poetic, because of the hushed beauty it creates when it falls. But when Cage talked about the environment becoming art, he was not thinking about an agenda of beautification. It was, one might say, like applying phenomenology's "brackets" to experience, letting things be, just as they are, without imposing any interpretations.[23]

In focusing on how a natural environment becomes art, Danto highlights a crucial aspect of Cage's composition: namely, that naturalness resides less in the material per se than in the emergent experience of the work in the process of its performance. Cage's works are not static or fixed objects but open works—processes of becoming that show the natural world in its dynamic state. *Performance* art, which music can be as soon as it gives up its attempt to be an *object* art, stresses more the *becoming* of nature than it does any static notion of *Being*. Music is the paradigm (alongside dance) of the would-be objectless art. "You say: the real, the world as it is," Cage writes. "But it is not, it becomes! It moves, it changes! . . . You are getting closer to this reality when you say as it 'presents itself'; that means that it is not there, existing as an object."[24] The call here is for an art that imitates nature in its manner of operation, where it is the manner of operation not the demand for copying that governs the thought. The conclusion is profound. The point is not, after all, that musical sound should *sound* identical to natural sound but that art should reproduce the world by actualizing what is already going on in the world.

By stressing the manner of operation and not the copying, Cage claims to close the gap between art and nature by returning us to a world from which our human experience has been severed. His aim is to expand our experience and thereby also our understanding of what constitutes music. Here, he seems to approach one of Danto's most central points: that the ear, like the eye, has proved insufficient or, for Cage, inadequate to tell us whether what we see is art or what we hear is music. In Danto's view, we used to believe that the sensuous eye was sufficient and art production sustained this belief. Given recent art production, however, we have been shown that the eye is and was never enough. More is and has always been involved in one's experience than merely looking and listening when we wanted to know what made something art: namely, all the historically mediated knowledge provided *internally* by the artworld. For Cage, the point is a little different. Trusting the ear to tell us what is and isn't music is not possible as long as the overly restrictive parameters of the world of contemporary classical music remain in place. To expand our experience and to restore trust in the ear means moving no longer inside the traditional parameters of the music world but *outside.*

It is consistent with Danto's account to maintain that some of the greatest masterpieces of art were produced while the artworld was dominated by mimetic ideology. Nothing follows about the greatness of art from any theory according to which art is more or less produced. This means also that nothing directly or straightforwardly follows regarding art's evaluation as to whether the art is produced in freedom from or in bondage to philosophy. Put otherwise, and I pursue this matter again in chapter 5: in Danto's account, the entire tradition of Western art is kept in place both metaphysically and historically; nothing is diminished about art's history by its having reached its end. Nevertheless, he has always taken note of what external appeals to the East did by to help the Western artworld and its attendant philosophy come to its internally motivated knowing state. "Overcoming the gap between art and life," he writes, "became a kind of mantra for the avant-garde artists of the early sixties. It was certainly a point of principle with Fluxus artists, so many of whom came to art through music as conceived of by Cage. Yoko Ono, trained as a musician, had studied Zen before joining Fluxus." Although Danto recognizes that many of the significant steps were taken earlier by Duchamp in the permission he gave to "make art out of anything," he sees in "the combined force of Cage, Duchamp, and Zen . . . an artistic revolution of an unprecedented kind."[25] "Unprecedented," I want to say, the step *must* have been in Danto's view, if this was the first and only time Western art had realized its end in a philosophical self-knowing. But, then, given the obvious parallels with Hegel's view, maybe the unprecedented character was at least a partial repeat of something that happened once before, most interestingly, at the 1800 start of "the philosophy of art."

Overcoming the gap between art and life was central to Cage's project. Nonetheless, his project was governed by his attempt to get over the urge to identify a fixed object called a work with a static object from nature or the commonplace world. The idea was to allow the natural world to emerge within the making or performance of music. I call this view "emergent naturalism." Its fundamental question demands reformulation. The question no longer asks in an *ontological* vein what makes musical and natural sound different or the same; instead, it asks *psychologically* how we can come to experience the natural world through music in the right naturalistic way. Cage answers: we come to experience both nature and music if we open our ears—to another sort of thinking and listening—by putting our Western institutional mind to rest. Sound, like experience, must be freed from "all psychic intentionality." It must "be itself" and not be used merely as a vehicle of Western human theory and feeling. We are "part of nature" and must learn to exist like nature, simply existing without purpose.

As is well known, Cage was inspired by Eastern religious doctrines of chance and indeterminacy. Nevertheless, it should be emphasized, first, that Cage's implied *equation* between Eastern doctrines and claims of naturalism was only justified as a negation of what Western theory had done to separate man and music from nature. Which means, second, that Cage's instruction as to how one should listen was a Western instruction for those who listen with Western ears. His music, one might say, like Warhol's Brillo box installation, would not have been *needed* had Western mistakes of identity regarding music and its concept not been made in the first place.

As I said, although Danto has always been firmly committed to the internal claims and history of the artworld, he has never ignored the inspiration he experienced in Cage's relinquishing of intentionality, in how Cage "represented the world" without either "mind or hand." "Represents" is no longer quite the right word; it would be more accurate to now speak of how artists allowed the world, allegedly nonintentionally, to *emerge* in their art. Regardless, Danto writes of how the artists of the Suzuki class committed themselves to producing art without effort, intention, or design and of how in this commitment he found the "secret promise of politics, of art, of writing—a knowing effortlessness in which the object and the agent collaborate[d] to achieve a mutual fulfillment."[26]

I would like to believe that Danto less concurs with this view than simply finds in it the unprecedented revolutionary moment from which he drew his conclusion regarding art's end. Were Danto fully to concur, he would have to separate himself more radically than perhaps he wants to from the Kantian–Hegelian legacy regarding art's relation to nature. For, in this legacy, it was never the aim to deny to the artist or to the aesthetic contemplator of the arts the effort of human labor, discipline, and knowledge. On the contrary: the appearance of effortlessness in an artwork was always considered a hallmark of genius. That no effort is purportedly made or demanded at all—well, that's another thing and probably better left to the birds.

It helps here to recall Cage's book *For the Birds* and to suggest that we read it as dedicated to the birds but thereby also to those humans who try to listen as birds listen, as though they were already inside nature listening as natural beings. However, to listen *to* nature is one thing; to listen nonpurposively, as though *from* nature's perspective, is another. To describe birds as listening to sounds as music is already to attribute to them the character not merely of being human but of being *most* human, as though the very best humans are those who listen with a thoroughly naturalized intention. From this, the question arises whether Cage was demanding that the intentionality of our human listening be relinquished altogether or, more plausibly, only the downfall of a certain Western conception of intentionality or purposiveness—just, in fact, as Danto describes the downfall of an equally Western disenfranchising master: namely, the old philosophy.

Understood this way, it follows that the continuation of art making under the terms of effort and labor need not necessarily be aligned to a thesis regarding art's allegiance to a dominating philosophy or ideology. All Danto needs to say is that what sustained the paradigm change in the 1960s, or what artists historically had both to claim and to do in order for him as philosophical critic to do what he had to do, was different from what art is and what it continued to do after the philosophical claim was made. Accordingly, Danto writes in the last passages of *The Transfiguration of the Commonplace* of how the Warhol gesture with the Brillo box installation was meaningful only while it was not understood; when it was understood, the gesture was no longer necessary. In my understanding, it is the tension between what was said or gestured and what happened thereafter that allowed art to assume a new form more conscious of itself but freed from philosophy's demand for art's definition. Equally, for Cage, the relinquishing of Western intentionality or the freeing of music from the burden of a Western or European museum aesthetic did not mean that artists had to give up on discipline. It only asked that the discipline of a Zen artist be understood differently from how discipline had been understood in the West. For there, discipline had come to be associated with the alienating terms and restrictive conditions of industrialized labor, and it was these terms and conditions that Cage had found governing the routines of the concert hall.

For Danto, what counts for the "is of interpretation" is what artists and critics master in both their art and their eye by way of artistic theory and history. For Cage, what counts is also the history of craft, hence, what has been done by way of technique in the actual making of art. Danto argues in the case of Warhol that an artwork's being made "entirely . . . by hand" falls out of the vocabulary in an artworld devoted to producing copies that are also no longer copies as the objects of art. Yet Danto's point is to show that, ultimately, the making of art is retained. After all, Warhol made his Brillo boxes one by one (even if their design necessarily belonged to another). Nevertheless, from the perspective of his philosophy of art, Danto concluded that nothing would be an artwork "without the theories and histories of the artworld"—a conclusion that somehow led to his diminishing the attention he paid thereafter to craft.

Cage retained the element of art making despite his decision to turn much of the hands-on compositional activity over to increasingly less intentional performers: computers, telephones, and birds. As in Warhol's case, the appearance no longer fits the facts: the artists are everywhere and at all times present in the production of their art. Further, when Cage turned toward theory, it was only to sustain his productive turn toward an alternative or naturalized view of art discipline. In the end, Cage as composer performed what Danto brought to philosophical articulation: that despite all the theoretical moves that allegedly brought art to its end, art's consequent liberation would not have been possible had artists relinquished their art-making acts.

What more is at stake in separating claims about relinquishing a Western or philosophically dominated intentionality and relinquishing discipline or intentionality altogether? The answer takes us now to Adorno and to the matter once more of the conditions of continuation for both philosophy and art, given a thesis that an end has been reached. Not always fair to Cage, Adorno reads his claims at the extreme to expose in them, and in music, the potential for deception in the dialectic of enlightenment. Thus when Cage insisted that we put our minds to rest in the production of art, Adorno read the claim as advocating a future governed by a wholly mindless philosophy—and this he feared more perhaps than anything else.

Adorno

Adorno argues, with recourse to Kant, that to relinquish control or to deny labor is to give up too easily the tension that long governed the relation between art and nature. More or less around 1800, but increasingly thereafter, art and nature were made into stark opposites, assigned as each was to its own sphere, according to the dialectic of enlightenment. Having been overly separated from each other, each began to call on the other or to elect an affinity without seeking to become each other in a false claim of identification. Nature called on art for its construction and form, as art called on nature for its spontaneity and immediacy, though each still recognized its difference from the other. With this argument (which tracks the argument in chapter 1), Adorno refuses both the harsh separation of nature and art, as their identity, to encourage the preservation of a dynamic tension or play of differences between them. Yearning to have what the other has, without becoming the other, each gains something thereby. To assert an identity between art and nature or between art and life, or to maintain that an identity has finally been achieved as a matter of historical progress, is to break from an aesthetic past that formerly sustained itself as a dialectical movement between differences. To assert such an identity to overcome the feeling of separation has profound consequences for art and society, increasing their loss of freedom in a culture of compartmentalized constraint.[27]

One argument against a false naturalizing aesthetic (in which art is identified with nature) Adorno offers in amended Nietzschean and Freudian terms. It shows how, in the 1960s, artists like individuals came to feel socially emasculated (Nietzsche called it "chestlessness"; Freud, "alienation"). To compensate, artists felt compelled to produce the sort of art that was formerly produced in the heroic or revolutionary age of the early nineteenth century. Yet they could not actually produce heroic art. So, to compensate again, they declared their desire to renounce control of their art as though renouncing control of their weakened egos. Recognizing their impotence, they preferred "to drift and to refrain from intervening" or to stop speaking, so that, "as in Cage's *bon mot*," the music itself would speak in their place. Rather than trying to produce a heroic art for humanity as evidenced in the humanist development of bourgeois music around 1800, contemporary composers sought to produce an art for the birds, as if giving up on humanity altogether. But how exactly could an intentionless art contribute to the production of what, with their weak egos, they still claimed to desire: an aesthetic of heroic strength? Finding no convincing answer, Adorno proclaimed their products as impotent and as paradoxical as their aim.[28] We should at least ask whether this argument does not apply also to the pop artists of the 1960s, who so intrigued Danto. But if we ask this, then we also must ask whether these artists were, in fact, ever really feeling as emasculated as Adorno says they were, or so emasculated as to seek a compensatory aesthetic associated with heroic strength. The latter *sounds* or *seems* both un-Cagean and un-Warholian. So what was Adorno up to when offering such an unsympathetic argument?

To liberate art from intention is, for Adorno, to liberate art from effort, thought, and philosophy and thus from humanity's development overall. He describes the relinquishment of development (as an extension of his commitment to dialectical *Bewegung*) in terms of art's having fallen into a stasis or into a social or positivistic congealment. Art might now just happen, but it has nowhere to go, and if it does try to go somewhere, it tends not to go where we want it to go, and where we think it is going is where it cannot go: namely, back to nature. Adorno doesn't want philosophy to go the way of art if what this means is that philosophy will deceive itself into thinking self-reflectively that it has reached some sort of self-understanding. If philosophy reaches an end, it does so only when it genuinely puts on the table, as art also should put on the table, the question whether it can continue at all. The continuation of philosophy and art (and everything else) is possible in a negative dialectic only when its continuation is no longer positively assumed or positivistically construed.

Adorno argues that claims of immediacy end up at the same dangerous extreme as claims of total control, whether that control is one that masters the artwork or the society within which the work is produced. He writes repeatedly of how concepts and categories become naturalized, self-evident, or commonplace so that their historicity or social meaning and construction is sublimated in the name of Being, product, or essence. Adorno meets Danto with an argument against the totalitarian trajectory of German historicism. Adorno's *Aesthetic Theory* distinctively begins with a strike against everything in art, as in modernity more generally, that has come to assume the appearance of self-evidence, only to ask whether art and everything else has not thereby come to an end of its genuine possibility.[29] To assume a naturalized appearance is tantamount to following enlightenment's move into unfreedom. The naturalism is false insofar as it conceals the total control of labor and construction that is actually required for the naturalized appearance to sustain itself as such.[30]

Adorno differentiates this sort of false naturalism from the necessity or naturalness that attends a beautifully constructed work of art, when it strikes a viewer as if it could not have been created otherwise. From the moment of its creation, an artwork has "elements that appear natural and self-evident." However, these moments are natural only as a "second nature,"[31] and a second nature, being the product of art, is different from a first nature that's claimed to be the work's model, matter, or inspiration. Only with the idea of second nature is an artwork recognized to have its basis or mediation in human labor and effort and thus recognized to be both beautiful appearance and ordered construction. Adorno moves here between two meanings of "nature": between a work of art's appearing natural as if spontaneous and its being naturalized through the imposition of order. To confuse second with first nature or order with spontaneity is to establish an identity, reduction, or phantasmagoria, where the tension ought rather to be maintained. (This is the tension also made manifest in Wagner's *Die Meistersinger*). Adorno notes that Kant recognized the crucial difference when he described the work of art as a product of genius, *as if* no labor were involved in the production—the purposiveness without explicit purpose. But, after this, Kant forgot his own insight when he reduced his judgment of birdsong to a concern only with the little creatures that produce it.[32]

There is another double use to which Adorno puts the idea of second nature that will bring some clarity to the argument. First, there is the labor that goes into making the artwork even as it appears natural (this idea invokes Kant's "as if"). Second, something appears as second nature when its labor is concealed in such a way that we proclaim that the artwork is produced naturally or without force, as when we declare that some activity has become second nature to us or that we did something without thinking. When Adorno comments on Kant's failure to distinguish birdsong from the creatures that produce it, he shows how easy it is for the first idea of second nature to be confused with the second. For what birds do, they do without thinking at all, whereas what geniuses do, they do by transcending or, better perhaps, by transforming the enormous body of thinking and know-how that contributes to making them the first-class artists that they are.

Adorno reads much of the proclaimed radicalism of the postwar artists as regressive, as taking a further step toward social conformity. In the threatened collapse of the gap between art and nature, he sees a fall into a totalitarian pattern of identity thinking. Instead of maintaining their difference from nature, artworks now assert an identity (or the artists do on their behalf), because nature is now believed to stand for everything society is not. Artists would rather their works be like nature than like social products. However, because the nature in which artists now seek art's identity has been destroyed by the society, just as the art has been destroyed, the nature is not in fact alive or indeed anything like that to which artists now claim to have immediate access.

In a world given over to the praise of commodity, Adorno argues, natural beauty has been "transformed into a caricature of itself." It is, therefore, not the sort of nature that artists claim to reveal. To appeal (as Cage allegedly did) to an immediate nature to differentiate one's art from that which is produced in a world of artificial products is perversely to accept the social alienation one is trying to overcome. In other terms, Adorno argues that, given the total expansion of the exchange principle, nature is increasingly invoked to fulfill "a contrasting function": to mark the difference from that from which people want to distance themselves. Yet, by being so invoked, the idea of nature is reintegrated into the reified world to serve what the social world wants of it.[33] This is a typical argument in Adorno's philosophy (as it is in Schiller's and in Nietzsche's): certain kinds of appeals to nature, beauty, freedom, individuality, and truth are used to oppose the existing social order, yet, when reabsorbed through appropriation back into the social order, the order is kept in place and the appeal to something different is rendered futile.

Adorno sees little difference in his critique—regarding music, philosophy, or society—between a mystical union with immediate nature or, at the other end of the spectrum, with the pedantic following of rigid rules (as one sees criticized in *Die Meistersinger*). He regards both as symptomatic of the sort of totalitarian or positivistic thinking that demands certainty to overcome ambiguity, immediacy to overcome mediation; directness, indirection; sameness, difference; and order, chaos. With Cage in mind (but it could also have been Wagner), he describes the cruelty with which composers throw culture "into people's faces," even if, he adds with his own cruelty, this is a fate that both culture and people deserve. That it is deserved means that when composers act this way, they do so not out of a desire to be barbaric but because they want to show, reflectively, what people have done to culture and culture to people. Yet, their acts backfire when by appealing to an "exotic, arty-crafty metaphysics," they find themselves back in the same place from which they were trying to escape. Adorno sometimes remarks that what he most admires in Cage is his protest against "the dogmatic complicity of music with the domination of nature," as well as his refusal to yield to the terror of the technological age. However, what he cannot accept is Cage's rationalizing tendency to retreat into claims of phenomenological immediacy, which, linked to the "enclaves of sensitive souls," remind him of something fascistic, with which he also associates Rudolf Steiner's eurhythmic or "healthy-living" sect.[34]

A different way for us to think about the interaction between art and nature is to recall the pioneering work of Pierre Schaeffer and his *musique concrète,* out of which a principle emerged for contemporary music—that it should be heard as we hear it in urban and natural space, without attention paid to its mechanical source. Still, it is not so easy to distinguish the purportedly radical nature of this claim from Wagner's own rationale for concealing the orchestra at Bayreuth in the name of creating a pure space of sound and aesthetic illusion. By contrast, in David Tudor's *Rain Forest,* the principle seems to reverse itself, insofar as all we see in this work are the instruments of sound production, even if what we hear is something approximating a rain forest. The point of this work is that you have to *be there* visually to understand it, since it is *not* a work made for pure audition or recording, even if, on some level, it is all about the technology of sound production. Listeners have to see the mechanical sources and participate actively with the mechanical means while yet experiencing something that tells them about the audible world of natural or everyday sounds. The issue, here again, is whether a work that wears its artifice on its sleeve tells us more about the workings of nature than a work that hides behind the phantasmagoric veil of immediacy or naturalness.

Adorno always seeks a dynamic place between extremes—between, say, pure chance and total control, or, in Cage's case, between his works of chance and those of total preparation. He increasingly distinguishes the concept of *art* from that of a *work* of art to show how the former moves toward its demise the more it gives itself over to what the concept of a work wants most: to preserve as fixed the labor, preparation, and articulation that individuates it. The more fixed or articulated the *work,* the more *art* loses what it wants to preserve: namely, the resistant aesthetic dimension of what is not prepared or what Adorno variously calls (as discussed in chapter 1) the work's mimetic, spontaneous, silent, or speechless comportment.

Danto reads the challenge of the supermarket commodity or its indiscernible look-alike as helping to bring the concept of art to its self-knowing; he celebrates the Warholian excitement about the commodity look-alike for the philosophical knowledge it made possible. Adorno contrarily emphasizes the pyrrhic victory of an *art* that concedes to its commodification or to its being entirely a *work* or *product* of art. For, to reach the extreme of workhood or objecthood is to concede to what the culture industry has come to demand of the work: that it should *look* like but then also *be* no different from any other product of exchange.

Adorno is not convinced that artworks will continue to hold onto their expressive artness, or what Danto calls their "aboutness," given the social pressures of their objective, product-based commodification. Nor is he convinced that an artwork can survive by retreating into a pure condition of total speechlessness or nonintentional immediacy. Claiming that one's music or art is pure does nothing to diminish its status as a commodified work. In fact, with its claimed isolation from the social or Western production of art, art renders itself more impotent, not less, to do what it wants to do: namely, show the Western world that art production could be different from how it presently is. In this argument, total isolation or retreat assumes the same ideological character as total compliance—as two sides of the same historical coin. Only an artwork that remains true to itself will overcome the general impotence the artworld allegedly feels. Such a work is one that maintains in aesthetic form the materially mediated social tension between its inherent but contradictory impulses, thus appearing as both made and unmade, fixed and spontaneous, product and process. After that, however, the question arises: Under what conditions does the contemporary society allow such artworks to exist?

For Adorno, what survives at this moment of transition or triumphant commodification are *works* that in a deep sense have betrayed the aesthetic concept of *art*. However, that they have betrayed this concept does not mean that they have also betrayed history; on the contrary, history as society demands what art has become in the form of its works and deserves what it itself has brought about. Still, Adorno often remarks on the banality of the thought that allows one to rest too comfortably with the belief that because history has made the world ugly, art should now be ugly, too.[35] Recognizing the tension between social history and the ongoing need for aesthetic expression, the philosopher's critical task is now to differentiate among contemporary works those that too happily comply with the times from those that refuse to do this.

To comply with the times is to comply with the horror of the times but in denial of the horror, as Adorno sees the profound amnesia "after Auschwitz." Accordingly, he expresses utter skepticism when he hears this sort of claim made by Cage that his music does not "attempt to bring order out of chaos nor to suggest improvements in creation" but serves "simply" to wake us up "to the very life we're living, which is so excellent once one gets one's mind and one's desires out of its way and lets [the music] act of its own accord."[36] An excellent world? Maybe, though perhaps not so excellent a youth. Apparently Cage's emergent naturalism was motivated partly by the insult he felt in younger days when one of his works, *The Perilous Night* (1943–44), was dismissed for sounding like "a woodpecker in a church belfry." Erik Satie, who inspired Cage, had asked that one of his own works (humorously titled *Sonatine bureaucratique*) be played "like a nightingale with a toothache."[37] Cage worried that his work, like Satie's, would not be taken seriously; for Satie, at least, this was the point. But Cage wanted to be taken seriously and couldn't apparently set aside the memory of his mother telling him that his music was "for the birds!"

Recall Danto's remark that Cage was not "thinking about an agenda of beautification." Perhaps this is right, though certainly Cage was not seeking his naturalism in a world of horrid sounds. Adorno is also looking for beauty and shares with Cage the belief that this has nothing to do with an *agenda* of beautification. However, unlike Cage, Adorno finds that he cannot put his Western mind sufficiently to rest, no longer to see the horror of the world around him; indeed, he insists, there is something false in even so trying. "Excellence" is a term often used in reference to human labor. Cage spoke, instead, of the excellence of the world around him. Adorno contrarily argues that if excellence in human labor is still sought, it should be sought in the shadows and ruins of human labor—in what the world, in its arrogance and overconfidence, has discarded through other much more destructive acts of labor. "Consciousness," he writes, "does justice to the experience of nature only when, like impressionist art, it incorporates nature's wounds."[38] If nature is wounded, this is because of what humanity has done both to nature and to itself.

The composer Terry Riley once wrote that "music has to be the expression of spiritual categories like philosophy, knowledge and truth, the highest human qualities. To realize this, my music necessarily radiates balance and rest."[39] Why "balance and rest," Adorno asks again of his contemporaries, in a world that no longer admits of either in truthful form? If art is to mirror life, why think of the life or nature that appears under the spell of society's untruth? Why not focus on the concealed or lost life, on the life brought historically to death, on the life that no longer appears to the eye? Here, an interesting difference emerges. Danto is brought to distrust the eye for the perceptual illusion it may promote of a false identity between an artwork and an ordinary object by those who cannot see or properly recognize the difference. Through theoretical reflection, he surmounts the distrust. Adorno, contrarily, is brought to distrust the eye as an extension of a greater distrust of the illusions that modern society promotes in the name of the true, the good, and the beautiful—the forerunners of the more contemporary term "excellence." He never surpasses the distrust.

With Cage, Adorno argues against a static relation of art and nature in favor of a dynamic one. Yet he rejects the idea that nature shows its beauty directly. "Natural beauty," he writes, "is the trace of the nonidentical in things under the spell of universal identity. As long as this spell prevails, the nonidentical has no positive existence."[40] However, and this is the last dialectical move, even in administered society, there remains the possibility of beauty in both nature and art.

To explain the conditions of this contemporary possibility, Adorno appeals to indirection. If beauty shows itself again, it will be in the form of an intimation or splintered glance. Why this extreme (Keatsian) "negative capability"? Because, though beauty might come momentarily to be glimpsed, the glimpse will come in works whose forms are most likely dead, degraded, or liquidated, reflecting in their darkness what art and nature have become. If beauty appears, it will be in ruined or fragmented form: as both remainder and reminder of what art and nature once stood for. In this argument, Adorno appeals to an allegedly better past, not to overvalue the past but to bring strategic attention to the present through an acknowledgment of difference. Dialectically, artworks point to something lost or dead but also to something hopeful: this way, they genuinely pose the question whether they can survive as art in contemporary times. Genuinely to pose this question, however, they must resist regressing into either empty or happy forms of conformity.

"The song of birds," Adorno wrote at the end of his life, "is found beautiful by everyone; no feeling person in whom something of the European tradition survives fails to be moved by the sound of a robin after a rain shower." However, "something frightening lurks in the song," though not so much in the song itself as in the spell within which the song has historically become enmeshed.[41] With this remark, Adorno points to one outcome of enlightenment's passage—how nature fell into myth when it was subjected to the demands of fate or when the song of the bird assumed a false mythical status in an artificial world that forbade exactly the expression of this song. During the enlightenment, natural beauty was increasingly repressed, transfigured into an idea solely for art or into a myth for contemporary (in)humanity.

On this basis, Adorno draws his most optimistic conclusion: only an artwork that could free itself from the myth of nature would help nature or natural beauty recover. Such a work would be autonomous or true to itself—an
artwork that sought its justification *not in nature but in art*. This would mark
the determinate negation of art under the modern condition of autonomy—
the idea that art does not give itself up to a false heteronomous or unfree
claim of naturalism, by being true to what art *is* in its *difference* from nature.
An artwork committed to art, responding to art's internal material needs or
developmental logic, would have the potential to rescue both nature and art
from their mutual spells of mastery and thereby to show between them the
continuing possibility of a fragile interaction. This would be an artwork that
had not complied with the times and which, by not complying, would have
taken the side of destroyed nature—precisely by not trying to *be* nature.

The idea that we should not give up on either nature or art forms part of
an argument for preserving in the artworld a resistant stand against a society
that has almost submitted fully to an anything-goes principle, a principle that,
for many Europeans, connotes an unbridled power and optimism associated
with a totalitarian society in which leaders, biblically inspired, do anything
as an everyday banal commonplace, even the most evil things, just because
everything is now possible.[42] This sort of principle is different from Danto's
pluralist principle: when he speaks of art as being able now to be anything it
wants to be, this want only marks art's liberation from what the old philosophy wanted art if not to *be* then at least to *look like*. Danto's end-of-art pluralism does nothing to challenge his essentialism about what art *is* and hence has
always *been*.

Adorno concludes his argument appropriately with a negative utopian gesture. One such gesture comes from one of the most critical pieces he ever
wrote on Darmstadt. The gesture draws on Kant's promise of "perpetual
peace" to show that what was once possible as a positive dialectic is no longer
possible. Whereas Kant was able to see in and articulate for that promise a
genuine possibility, Adorno can offer only a negative expression historically
appropriate for modern times. Hence: "The form of every artistic utopia today is to make things of which we do not know what they are."[43] By "not
knowing," Adorno by no means advocates a mindless philosophy or art. He
only asks us to give up our trust in social domination (a trust he says we have
actually come to desire) to open up a space in which good thought and art
might be produced. He argues strongly for the continuation of unforced social labor and individual thought: art and philosophy in dialectical tension.

He argues this way to avoid the suggestion that to him alone the bird now sings, since he desires to be no Siegfried. Then he reminds us that the bird does not directly sing to anyone else, either. When all the metaphysical bird catchers leave town, the people left behind are given nothing by way of substitution or certainty to tell them whether the song they now hear from the birds is truthful. All they know is that they may no longer *blindly* place their trust in metaphysical claims regarding truth and nature. This loss is a desirable loss, leaving open the question whether art, society, and philosophy will continue at all. For Adorno, hope resides in the posing of this question.

The Song of the Pipes

Danto sees in "the end of art," in the 1960s, a positive moment of liberation, when art was released from the philosophical burden to come to know itself, because, at this moment, philosophy came to know art. Art production did not cease and the philosophy of art came to answer its essential definitional question. Dialectically, this was far less art's end than the end of a dominating philosophy. How art continued in its free state and what new conditions of art making pertained was where the excitement of the new art and its criticism resided, even if nothing followed directly about the value of the new art. In this free state, the philosopher was left sometimes celebrating art's liberation but sometimes bemoaning art's apparent loss of productive value. I return to this theme in chapter 5.

On Adorno's part, he sees an end of art when art's production compromised itself to identity thinking. He understands this end to have come to dominate both philosophy and society. He rejects the terms of any absolute or positive ending of an authoritarian, Hegelian-styled dialectic that precludes the real possibility of continuation, for to announce such a positive end is tantamount to agreeing to its terms. Unlike Danto, he does not stress the liberation or severing of art from philosophy and seeks more to distinguish autonomous from compromised art, and then autonomous from compliant philosophy. Not only does he stress the continuation of art and philosophy in their fragile and necessarily antagonistic relationship to each other; he also describes that continuation in terms of the specific challenge it potentially presents to an administered society under the extreme condition of modernity. Whereas Danto more or less celebrates the advent of *pluralism* for a philosophically liberated art, Adorno takes the side of an art and nature deeply wounded by society's extreme *polarization*.

In this chapter, I have begun to show how well the theories of Adorno and Danto are interpreted as offering for art and philosophy the terms for their *continuation* over and above their ends, and, between art and nature, their *difference* over and above their identity. Endings and identities are points reached on the way. They might be devastating or catastrophic, yet they are not thereby the last points in the discourse of either philosophy or art. The continuation of art, whether it reflects a positive liberation for Danto or a negative autonomy for Adorno, follows from specific acts of criticism performed in the shadow of philosophical critique. For the birds or against the birds—this is a false choice if, in assuming a critical position in relation to birdsong, Adorno and Danto seek not messages but, instead, a philosophical and social significance. A critical part of this significance consists for both in a continued search for beauty and, attendant on this, a truthful release from the various deceptions of eye, ear, and mind.

So I return to Keats, to join his song of the nightingale finally to his human song of the pipes. For if the argument has gone through, it is only when the two songs are brought together (as they were composed the same year) that beauty remains connected to truth, as truth to beauty. For, in the end, this "is all Ye know on earth, and all ye need to know."[44] Still, the urgent question remains: Under what conditions should truth and beauty now appear? This remains a central question in the chapters to follow.

4 Explosive Experiments and the Fragility of the Experimental

Distance is not a safety zone but a field of tension. It is manifested not in relaxing the claim of ideas to truth, but in delicacy and fragility of thinking.
—Adorno, *Minima Moralia*

The English "to explode" has at least one origin in the theater, in the term "to applaud"—*ex-plaudere*—where the idea is not necessarily to keep the actors on the stage but to drive them away by clapping, hissing, or booing, as though an audience were imitating the sound of a failed experiment or reacting to something that had just blown up in their face. When experiments succeed, they typically result not in explosions, unless they aim for such, but, instead, in the silent concord of the elements. From this, the thought arises that perhaps one should respond in the theaters of art and science with quiet murmurs of awe and not with the loud bravos and eurekas to which we have become accustomed.

Adorno writes about applause differently, beginning with the assumption that applause means praise, though what he thinks is being praised is not what we would expect. Writing about the "Natural History of the Theatre," he claims that applause "is the last vestige of objective communication between music and listener." When listening to music under advanced conditions of administered society, the now distracted listeners fail to listen even as the music goes on. When the music stops, they applaud anyway. Adorno sees in this behavior something approaching an ancient ritual sacrifice as when our ancestors applauded the slaughter of animals. Applause, he argues, was always ceremonial or ritualistic and remains so in our modern institutions. When we applaud at a concert, it is less a liking of the music that we express than our appreciation of the ritual. However, the pleasure we find in the ritual is false and displaced, emanating as it does only from a borrowed remembrance of something once done when humanity bore a nonalienated connection to the world.[1]

The Background

This chapter is not directly about applause but about the surrounding history of modernity in which both scientists and artists articulate the terms of meaning or experience by confronting the breach they take to have emerged between human beings and nature. It concerns those who, through experimental science or experimental art, claim that nature can still exist as a living presence within human experience. I focus on two distinct historical moments. Somewhat rhetorically put, the first moment marks a new beginning at the beginning of modern science, and the second, a new beginning at the end of modern art. Each moment is represented by a single figure: the first, by one of the fathers of experimental science, Francis Bacon, though being *the* father of experimental science is usually the definite description awarded to him; and the second, by one of the fathers of experimental music, John Cage, though to speak here of the father is to give authority to someone who lived his life in overt refusal of such.

Despite obvious differences, Bacon and Cage assume in their modes of experimentation a shared attitude toward nature, characterized more by nobility and respect than by violent intervention. Neither seeks to torture or manipulate nature through technological means. Both look for a way to let nature's mystery and secrets reveal themselves to the inquiring mind. For both, experimentalism has an emergent character; they want to know what can emerge out of nature to the observing eye or listening ear. Both of them argue for preserving an element of magic or chance in their languages of, respectively, science and art. Both, finally, ponder the nature of their inquiry. Bacon was an essayist who wrote in aphorisms to separate himself from traditional writers of method. Cage was a composer and writer who rejected anything approximating an authoritative grammar.

To bring the two figures together is not altogether original. Adorno did this before me, though in not so shared a philosophical breath. He brings them together in his overarching description of the dialectic of enlightenment and in far more devastating terms than mine. Despite their pleas for genuinely open inquiry, Adorno sees in both the tendency toward an absolute domination of nature. With Horkheimer, he regards Bacon's early "hounding" after absolute knowledge as having encouraged thinkers along a path that ended up in Cage-like attempts to restore life to a nature that humanity had already put to death. Horkheimer and Adorno write in their opening lines:

> Enlightenment, understood in the widest sense as the advance of thought, has always aimed at liberating human beings from fear and installing them as masters. Yet the wholly enlightened earth is radiant with triumphant calamity. Enlightenment's program was the disenchantment of the world. It wanted to dispel myths, to overthrow fantasy with knowledge. Bacon, "the father of experimental philosophy," brought these motifs together.[2]

Although Adorno describes enlightenment's path in the bleakest of terms, he hopes that the world might one day be different from how it currently appears. With Bacon and Cage, he seeks the aesthetic, scientific, and philosophical seeds of a free or nonadministered mode of experience (*Erfahrung*). Though he finds error in the path that leads from the scientific Bacon to the artistic Cage, he shares their aim to find in experience the dimension of the genuinely experimental. The connection or even (as in French) the identity drawn between the terms "experience" and "experimental" is anything but accidental. Adorno shows that though he takes Bacon to task as the father of experimental science, he is willing to continue Bacon's essayistic or aphoristic approach toward philosophy: "The English empiricists . . . called their philosophical writings essays, because the power of a freshly disclosed reality, upon which their thinking struck, continuously forced upon them the risk [or trial] of experimentation [*das Wagnis des Versuchs*]."[3] Or:

> Since Bacon—himself as essayist—empiricism has been as much a "method" as rationalism. In the realm of thought it is virtually the essay alone that has successfully raised doubts about the absolute privilege of method. The essay allows for the consciousness of nonidentity, without expressing it directly; it is radical in its non-radicalism, in refraining from

any reduction to a principle, in its accentuation of the partial against the total, in its fragmentary character.[4]

With these words, Adorno mirrors Bacon's own:

> Another diversity of Method, whereof the consequence is great, is the delivery of knowledge in Aphorisms, or in Methods; wherein we may observe that it hath been too much taken into custom, out of a few axioms or observations upon any subject, to make a solemn and formal art, filling it with some discourses, and illustrating it with examples, and digesting it into a sensible Method. But the writing in Aphorisms hath many excellent virtues, whereto the writing in Method doth not approach. . . . Aphorisms, representing a knowledge broken, . . . invite men to inquire further; whereas methods, carrying the show of a total, . . . secure men, as if they were at [their] furthest.[5]

The Topic

In this chapter, I make explicit the concept of the *experimental* by tracing its course in an enlightenment history that is well described as having become dominated by the contrary concept of the *experiment*. Though Bacon and Cage promote the experimental, they end up, Adorno maintains, walking the more dangerous path of the experiment. In dialectical terms, what the experimental shows about the experiment is the latter's tendency, despite itself, to control and thus eventually to kill nature through tortures performed in enlightenment laboratories of science and art.

Whether and with what deliberation Adorno misreads the work of Bacon or of Cage is only part of my concern. I am more interested in showing what is at stake in distinguishing the experimental from the experiment. However, given the first remark, one should remember that Adorno is by no means alone—and independently of his collaboration with Horkheimer—in interpreting Bacon as having started experimental science off on a route that led to humanity's most deadly experiment on nature. This was an experiment in which the experimentalists or philosophers sought in their rational pursuit of absolute knowledge to overcome the respectful distance that their predecessors kept from the objects of their inquiry. Goethe and Schiller also severely criticized the Baconian path, as later did Nietzsche, Heidegger, Popper,

Marcuse, and, finally, Cassirer, from whom, in fact, most contemporary critics have taken their cue.

Cassirer began his criticism by seeing in Bacon's rules of experimental operation a radical demarcation of "the modern from the medieval age." With these rules, Bacon renders knowledge indistinguishable from power. All this Bacon admitted himself. However, instead of regarding nature as a given, something to be speculated about at a distance or observed through sensory experience, Bacon, so Cassirer objected, brings nature into conformity with the man-made experiment. He introduces into scientific inquiry an essentially juridical, even inquisitorial, character, leading Cassirer finally to find in the father of experimental science also the first torturer of nature:

> Bacon sits as a judge over reality, questioning it as one examines the accused. Not infrequently he says that one must resort to force to obtain the answer desired, that nature must be "put to the rack." This procedure is not simply observational but strictly inquisitorial. The witnesses are . . . brought face to face; the negative instances confront the affirmative ones, just as the witnesses for the defence confront those for the prosecution. After all the available bits of evidence have been gathered together and evaluated, then it is a matter of obtaining the confession which finally decides the issue. But such a confession is not obtainable without resorting to coercive measures. "For like [and here Cassirer is quoting Bacon] as a man's disposition is never well known or proved till he be crossed . . . so nature exhibits herself more clearly under the trials and vexations of art than when left to herself." This is obviously not the language of the contemplative thinker who is confident of the harmony between the human mind and reality and entrusts himself lovingly to the pure revelations of nature.[6]

I return to this reading of Bacon below, but note immediately that it was not actually Bacon who wrote of "putting nature to the rack," as traditionally claimed, but Leibniz in 1696.[7] Still, Bacon's critics have always ranged from one extreme to the other: from those who regard him as the instigator of the most violent experiment to those who see in his work a profoundly aesthetic or experimental core, and the latter despite the inquisitorial nature of his language. It is my impression that the particular debate that has so shaped Bacon's reception has always been paradigmatic of the larger debate concerning the concepts of the experiment and experimental—so to this distinction I now turn.

The Distinction

Over the course of their undeniably overlapping histories, the two concepts have come to track increasingly opposed tendencies toward violence and non-violence, loud noises and quiet sounds. Nevertheless, it has not always been clear which concept has embodied which tendencies at which particular time. Not everything is bad about the experiment and not everything is good about the experimental, although the need to say this already suggests something about the different connotations of the terms. Over time, they have become competitor concepts. One sees this straightaway if we look at how the concepts have guided the development and procedures in science and art, as well as in society, religion, and politics.

It surprises me that in not one of these areas has the distinction been explicitly conceived, although it has broadly been assumed. One might claim that the distinction has always been so self-evident that it requires no explicit acknowledgment, but I do not think this is correct. Or one might claim that the movement between the two concepts over the entire range of their extensive use has been sufficiently smooth that it has not been necessary to draw a hard distinction between them. To be sure, one may speak of experiments in terms of the experimental techniques involved or the experimental data produced, just as one may speak about an experimental procedure as involving experiments with various kinds of materials, tools, or instruments. Hence, one may obviously move between the terms without semantic loss or gain. Still, it not only makes sense to say, but sometimes it is most revealing to claim, first, of a particular experiment, that it has nothing of the character of the experimental, and, second, of the experimental, that it has nothing of the character of the experiment. This secures my thought that between the two concepts there has emerged at least a strong difference of connotation.

To render the distinction explicit is to expose some of the most antagonistic tendencies of modernity. The difference has grown the more it has become implicated in occasions of critique, in cases where, as with Bacon, Adorno, and Cage, the purpose is to develop new ways of conceiving nature's relation to humanity or to art. In this content, the terms "nature" and "art" are used both to distinguish the sadly separated spheres and to separate thoughts about the natural, spontaneous, and free from thoughts about the artificial, intentional, and man-made. If the history of the experimental and the experiment is a story of modernity, it is because of what it contributes to our understanding of our relation to both nature and art. With this, the focus quickly turns to matters of life and death—equally of humanity, nature, and art—and with the focus so turned, the term "experiment" assumes the more negative connotation.

Consider the various domains in which the general concepts of the experiment and the experimental have acquired a particularly significant use without yet attending to their difference. There is obviously the history of experiments in the laboratories of experimental science stemming back to the seventeenth century. There is also the complex history of political and religious experiments, the oft-named "wonderful experiments" associated with the developments of socialism, communism, fascism, and democracy. To speak of political experiments was particularly common after 1900. However, as early as 1845, Marx (quoting Bruno Bauer) described the French Revolution as "an experiment," a bourgeois one that by belonging more to the eighteenth than to the nineteenth century was dialectically out of date. With political experiments came all the social experiments: Jeremy Bentham's so-described "humane experiments in penal reform," Friedrich Engels's industrial experiments, and John Dewey's later pragmatist experiments in education. Then there were the philosophers' thought experiments, with John Stuart Mill and Ernst Mach encouraging the exercise along an increasingly positivistic path. Then, finally, there is the history of modern art in which it has long been assumed that the more experimental the technique, technology, or artistic principle, the more avant-garde the art.

In none of these areas have the concepts of the experiment or the experimental been applied neutrally. From modernity's beginning, they have both been caught up, for better and worse, in value-laden theories of progress. Some theorists have claimed that all new art is necessarily experimental, where what "the new" and "the experimental" immediately suggest is the idea of trying things out that haven't been tried before. With this sense of trial has come the admission of the possibility of failure: to be experimental is to take a risk. And with this has come a recognition of the essential ambiguities or indeterminacies in our ways of knowing. Other theorists have contrarily stressed more the experiment than the experimental, seeing in the experiment a sober way to develop a risk-free or secure path to advance knowledge: to get things right or to reach certainty by incrementally differentiated means and finely controlled testing.

Recall a moment in a movement in art's history that will nevertheless quickly return us to science. The movement was Italian futurism. In part of their famed manifesto (written by Luigi Russolo in 1913), the futurists celebrated their noisy experiments by proclaiming with loudspeakers a new "art of noises" explicitly to oppose the purported silence of an "ancient life" and "nature" that purportedly once existed in happy accord. "If we over-look such exceptional movements as earthquakes, hurricanes, storms, and avalanches," they wrote, nature "is silent." Only now has noise been born to triumph over our once quiet sensibilities. For many centuries, life went by in the most muted and musical of tones; now, however, the modern world is all "Rumbles, Roars, and Explosions."[8]

For the futurists, though not only for them, the new noises were brought into the traditional arts of both ear and eye. Photography and film—the new forms of visual art—were forced to acknowledge or even to rejoice in their noise. Consider, at least in English since the 1890s, the prevalence of the violent language of "the shoot" or of "taking a shot" to describe how a camera captures its images. Maybe it was only the clicking mechanism and less any actual bang that generated the latter description—although perhaps not if one recalls the use of the camera-cum-gun in Kurt Weill's 1927 one-act opera, *Der Zar lässt sich photographieren*. Whatever the reason, noise was certainly the issue when early filmmakers realized that they did not know how to prevent the noise of the droning camera in the transmission of silent images and decided to introduce music as a mask, only then to discover that a droning phonograph, when such was used, worsened the situation.

Another motivation for introducing music into film regarded its potential to complete the new art. Henceforth, film, it was claimed, could accommodate all sensorial dimensions in a single construction and, with this, offer a total (synthesizing) and a totalizing (all-absorbing) experience. Moving beyond the grand Wagnerian synthesis, film could create the absolute illusion, indeed the perfect copy of modern life—although to use the word "copy" was no longer deemed suitable for a medium claiming to surpass all differences between the fictional and the real. Whereas, formerly, in the mimetically imperfect and divided arts, the illusion of the real was protected by a distancing disbelief that sustained the illusion as an illusion, film claimed to overcome the gap. Some theorists, as shown in chapter 7, celebrated what they took to be the new control and mastery of the real. Others did not and bemoaned the loss of an old, quiet, and noble realism as it was increasingly replaced by a new, noisy, and overtly authoritative idealism.

Much of what was written about the end of modernity was written also about its beginnings: the moment, for example, when experimenters in science began to see nature no longer as something standing at a safe distance from their observing eyes but as something into which they could pierce their experimental knives. Even in this period, so it was written at the time, the scientists separated themselves from the magicians. In the 1930s, Benjamin drew on just these terms to describe the emerging analogy between the film-maker and the scientist in the modern age of technological reproducibility. In the age of ritual or cultic art, he argued, artists acted like noble magicians, creating illusions of the natural world without cutting it up. However, by the end of Benjamin's age, artists had become fully what scientists already were—experimenters who sought not to leave nature as it is but to instrumentalize it in the name of progress. Most critics held Francis Bacon responsible for initiating the entire surgical movement.

A similar discourse on science and art was offered again in 1963 by Edgar Wind when he declared in his marvelous book on art and anarchy that art had become "experimental," to which he then added:

> It is significant that this word "experiment," which belongs to the labo-ratory of the scientist, has been transferred to the artist's studio. It is not a casual metaphor: for although artists today understand far less of science than they did in the sixteenth or seventeenth century, their imaginations seem haunted by a desire to mimic scientific procedures; often they seem to act in their studios as if they were in a laboratory, performing a series of controlled experiments in the hope of arriving at a valid scientific solution. And when these astringent exercises are exhibited, they reduce the spectator to an observer who watches the artist's latest excursion with interest, but without vital participation.[9]

In this passage, Wind moved automatically from using the term "experimen-tal" to using the term "experiment," with the result that he transformed what might have begun as a positive claim about art into a negative one. Here at least, he did not acknowledge the possibility that art might have become exper-imental without its having fallen into the controlling traps of the experiment.

Over time, the idea of the experiment (be it in science, politics, or art) has increasingly exuded the aura of complete control over what it seeks to investigate. This prompted a colleague of mine recently to ask whether when one speaks of political experiments one immediately associates the idea with tyranny. Indeed, the German noun *das Experiment* has assumed a connota-tion far more extreme than when one speaks of an experiment in politics or, even more, of the experimentation or experimentalism involved in this or that political system. To try things out in a democratic process sounds a lot better than imposing democracy as a prepackaged system on a country, as though the outcome were decided in advance. Analogously, when Goethe offered his theory of colors, he proposed an experimental method that was quite different from the analytical attitude of Newton's method, just because Newton as "Inquisitor" tortured nature to extract the confession of what he'd "already decided."[10] Goethe was drawing on two already-entrenched ideas: first, that of torturing nature to extract a confession; second, given the experimental methods of his time, that outcomes are decided in advance of testing.

Put at the extreme, reference to the experiment suggests a type of control whereby one attempts to subsume in advance that which one seeks to explain; whereby a method of testing is devised in which the outcome is predicted at the outset; whereby the testing is a matter merely of confirming or falsifying the hypothesis under strict conceptual conditions and optimal conditions of observation; whereby maximal control of material, sample groups, questions, and observation procedures is encouraged, given advanced statistical and measuring methods that control patterns of similarity, uniformity, and variation; and whereby, finally, the criteria of correctness or success are clarified but in such a way that what counts as a failure of the experiment is absorbed as part of its truth content. In short, in an experiment, the planning happens in advance, clear objectives are laid out, and optimal conditions are sought; where errors occur, they are conveniently theorized and controlled.

At this extreme, consider Peter Cohen's 1989 documentary *The Architect of Doom,* which traces the aestheticizing ideology of Nazi Germany. Just when Hitler knew his war was lost, we are told, he absorbed the defeat into a world-historical myth of repetition, according to which, regarding the Roman Empire first and Nazi Germany later, empires rise and fall several times before final victory is secured. The defeat of Nazi Germany was, therefore, just a stage along the way in "the great experiment." Hence, even when experiments go wrong, the failure is absorbed as already predicted. In the worst or most dishonest cases, the undesired explosion does not force a change of method or theory but only leads experimenters ever more dogmatically to assert the truth of their hypotheses. In chapter 5, I describe this dogmatism further, in terms of an overarching commitment to a most dangerous version of historicism.

At the other end of the spectrum, the concept of the *experimental* exudes the aura of open-endedness, revisability, and incompleteness—a "wait and see" attitude. It recalls Montaigne's term "essai," a term used also by Bacon and Leibniz and by German writers (including Adorno) who titled their texts with "Versuch zur" or "Entwurf zur," expressions that became prominent in the eighteenth century to convey the dynamic sense of an incomplete journey. (Hence, also, the associated preference for experience understood as *Erfahrung* [from *fahren*], in contrast to the more complete or self-contained idea of an *Erlebnis.*) Most experimentalists associated their trials made along the ongoing investigative path not with courts of torture run according to strict inquisitional law but with theaters in which evidence could be weighed on quieter and more balanced scales. When Goethe described his colors as arranged in a circle, he contrasted his image to Newton's "analytical" image. Instead of looking at colors diffracted or broken (*gebrochen*) through a prism, he preferred to view a spectrum for the organic harmony it revealed between nature and ourselves as knowing subjects.

Bacon also wrote about this sort of organic harmony, but apparently he did not convince. What he described as a harmonious relationship was seen by others as little better than a patriarchal marriage or, even more cynically, as a "happy match," in which, in Horkheimer and Adorno's words, "the mind, conquering superstition, [rules] . . . over disenchanted nature."[11] Goethe also saw in Bacon's experiments the suggestion if not of disenchantment then of sacrifice: the sacrifice of nature for the sake of human progress. Thinking about the experiments of Richard Hooke, Goethe referred to Bacon's "experimentum crucis," where the term "crucis" suggested to him not only a crossroad or crucial experiment but also a crucifix, as when a person's vessels in being nailed to a cross are, to use Bacon's own language, "fractured."[12]

In Goethe's age, the worry over the dangers of the analytical experimentalist became ever more severe. Stressed by the demands of scientific or philosophical writing in opposition to those of poetic writing, Schiller warned in his very first letter on the aesthetic education of humanity of the paradox into which so many writers of his day were being thrown. His terms are again reminiscent of that for which Baconian science had already come to stand:

> Like the analytical chemist [*der Scheidekünstler*], the philosopher can only discover how things are combined by analysing them, [and can] only lay bare the workings of spontaneous Nature by subjecting them to the torment [*Marter*] of his own techniques [*Kunst*]. In order to lay hold of the fleeting phenomenon, he must first bind it in the fetters of rule, tear its fair body to pieces by reducing it to concepts, and preserve its living spirit in a sorry skeleton of words. Is it any wonder that natural feeling cannot find itself again in such an image, or that in the account of the analytical thinker truth should appear as paradox?[13]

Schiller continued the thought, however, by noting the necessity for at least some kind of violence when it comes to the making of art, when, say, artists are obliged to break down the materials for the sake of producing new forms.

Schiller shared this attitude with both Bacon and Adorno, implying that not all sorts of violence are to be dismissed. Goethe recognized the point, too, though he was prone to criticize his friend for his tendency to use harsh language and for the sometimes aggressive expression of his thought.

Cage

If Bacon's work initiated a deep quarrel between opposing tendencies at the beginning of modern science, John Cage's work did the same at the end of modern art, though admittedly not to the same degree. Even so, in 1939 and after, it was the dogmatism of the experiment that Cage determined to relinquish when he described his preferred form of experimental music. In his book pertinently called *Silence,* he rejected much of the loudness of the modern Western world. At first he expressed doubts about using the term "experimental," thinking it might lead to a confusion of his project with other avant-garde projects around him, though later he said he found comfort in the term, especially when he realized how far (now in my terms) his experimental music would avoid assuming the controlling character of the experiment.[14]

Cage separated his idea of experimental music from the high modernist approaches to composition such as those developed by Milton Babbitt and Elliott Carter. This was an approach, Cage quipped, that by adding "a new wing" to the already established academy, opens "no doors to the world outside."[15] Then he separated himself from those composers who, in his judgment, merely introduce popular or jazz elements without effect into their ever more eclectic compositional forms. Finally, he distinguished himself from those engaging in pervasive experimentation on new materials and instruments, even if, evidently, he sometimes enjoyed doing the same.

What made Cage's preferred conception of experimental music distinctive was the purpose it expressed to break with the sort of authoritative works produced in concert halls, where works had allegedly closed down the experience of performers and listeners, given their tendency to function like experiments with predetermined outcomes. Like Adorno, Cage believed that we could not overestimate the deadening impact the traditional work concept had had on the listening experience. When we purchase a ticket for a work-based concert, we know in advance what we are going to hear. Live concerts have become increasingly like living-room listening, where recordings are approached with the expectation that the ever-the-same is heard each time, where the risk or experimentalism of the experience has been suppressed in favor of the already known. If the criticism of the live bourgeois concert was being exaggerated, it was so to call attention to how much authority the work concept had assumed in the performance practice of classical music. Music as a *performance* practice had given itself over to the highly controlled assembly production of *products.*

Cage determined to open the work concept up to the paradoxical degree that it would relinquish all control or, more carefully, all *traditional* control over a performance event that continued nevertheless to occur in the work's name. He described the change in terms of indeterminacy and openness: to free the work was to open one's mind, which significantly meant releasing the mind and musical production from inherited dogma (as this idea was introduced in chapter 3).[16] He wrote enthusiastically with new words and designs on his pages about the events, happenings, or occasions of experimental music in which the genuinely creative activity would be done by performers and listeners in a new theater of happy and open collaboration. Insofar as composers and conductors would continue to contribute to the event, they would do so in "contiguous" or participatory roles *also* as performers and listeners. "The conductor of an orchestra," Cage quipped, "is no longer a policeman."[17] Or one might say in Cagean spirit: his experimental works would be occasions *for* rather than *of* experience (*Erfahrungen* rather than *Erlebnisse*). In occasions *of* experience, one would always know what would happen in advance of the actual experiencing of the experience, rendering the actual experience unnecessary. In Cage's happenings, by contrast, one would genuinely not know, musically at least, for what one was buying a ticket and that surely was liberating, especially because it would make the actual having of the experience once again necessary.

The critical element of Cage's own experimentalism was directed against institution and method and redirected toward the revival of the emergent musical experience. He used the term "experimental" to capture "an act" of which "the outcome" could not be judged for its success or failure before its occurrence. "What is the nature of an experimental action?" he asked. "It is simply an action the outcome of which is not foreseen . . . for nothing one does gives rise to anything that is preconceived." But then, even after the occurrence, still nothing can be judged, insofar as the performance is no longer a repetition or an exemplification of an already existing thing. There is nothing, therefore, in a performance that definitively "proves" anything about the work as such. If "work" language remains at all, then it does under the condition that one performance "of a work" will preferably or even necessarily sound quite different from any other. "The word 'experimental' is apt," Cage explained, "providing it is understood not as descriptive of an act to be later judged in terms of success and failure." It isn't an act that "moves in terms of approximations and errors . . . for no mental images of what would happen were set up beforehand; it sees things directly as they are."[18]

To argue against the bourgeois work concept was for Cage to argue against the human, or at least the traditional, control of sound. Music had been overly constrained by a human grammar or by a particularly high Western or European set of conventions. Too much had been excluded from this musical domain, and what was admitted had been overly exploited. To liberate sound was thus to bring everything into this musical domain or, better, to take everything to the musical outside, to overcome the artificial chasm between art and life or between music and natural sound. To "give up" on traditional music is to turn *psychologically* to "the world of nature," he wrote, where, gradually or suddenly, one sees that "humanity and nature, not separate, are in this world together; that nothing [is] lost when everything [is] given away [of our determinations]. In fact, everything is gained. In musical terms, any sounds may occur in any combination and in any continuity." Cage accordingly described the need to let sounds be themselves, to allow something unknown—the element of chance and surprise—to occur in the listeners' experiences. This would happen, he insisted, only when "the measuring mind" stops believing that one day it will have succeeded in measuring nature.[19]

It is important that Cage was describing a psychological turn, suggesting a profound change of perceiving the world around us. When he made it look like an ontological turn, which he sometimes did, it assumed a more contradictory or deceptive character. For, in an ontological turn, all that remained of the distinction between music and sound was an *identity*. It was the ontological turn or reduction to which Adorno most objected and with which he ungenerously associated Cage's view. As shown in chapter 3, the ontological turn that sought a gapless identity between music and natural sound risked falsely dehumanizing by overidealizing both sides.

Cage focused on the re-creation of musical experience that would occur under his guidance in a control-free, nonintentional, and naturalized environment. He declared his music purposeless, all-inclusive, and open to creating a new awareness of the surrounding auditory world. We are technically equipped, he told us, to transform our contemporary awareness of nature's manner of operation into art. To where or what would this new sort of listening to nature's operation lead us? To the participation of our eyes and ears, he answered, in a theater of becoming based on the new idea of a naturalized or environmental theatricality.[20]

Having shed his vision of a worn-out European legacy, he adopted what he considered a truly American form of experimentalism, if only, he added, America would actually support it! "America has an intellectual climate suitable for radical experimentation. We are, as Gertrude Stein says, the oldest country of the twentieth century. And I like to add: in our way of knowing nowness." When once Cage heard someone tell him that "it must be very difficult for you in America to write music, for you are so far away from the centers of tradition," he responded to the contrary: "It must be very difficult for you in Europe to write music, for you are so close to the centers of tradition."[21] The contrast between America and Europe was more ideological than geographical. As shown in chapter 8, many Europeans were also contemporaneously trying to sever connections to a certain past.

Bacon

Cage went further than Bacon in his idea of experimentalism, and not just because his argument was offered several centuries later. Nevertheless, the question remains: How far did they track the same or different paths? To pursue this question, I go back to Bacon before going forward again to Cage. In an obvious way, it looks as though Bacon long ago denied explicitly what Cage promoted—that our experience ought to extend "beyond the actual experiment." Bacon insisted that one's wandering must never become "a blind or stupid straying"; the experiment must be controlled. Still, did it follow that a controlled experiment should then become all- or overcontrolling? Despite Cassirer's juridical reading of Bacon, Bacon seemed to think not. In his essay "De Sapientia Veterum," he confronted the situation. Here, the self-proclaimed servant to nature, having tried nevertheless to become its master by claiming God's omnipotent powers, was answered back by nature, the moment nature assumed a Protean, transformative, and restorative agency of its own:

> Nevertheless if any skilful Servant of Nature shall bring force to bear on matter, and shall vex and drive it [*vexet atque urgeat*] to extremities as if with the purpose of reducing it to nothing, then will matter (since annihilation or true destruction is not possible except by the omnipotence of God) finding itself in these straits, turn and transform itself into strange shapes, passing from one change to another till it has gone through the whole circle and . . . returns at last to itself.[22]

It is not completely clear how far Bacon wanted to go in thinking about the intervention of the scientific art into nature; hence the disagreement among his critics. Yet he did seem to argue that if nature could survive the intervention, both sides would get what they wanted: nature would have suffered no harm and experimenters would have gotten their knowledge. This reading is consistent with one of Bacon's best-known aphorisms from his *Novum Organon*, "Natura enim non nisi parendo vincitur," formerly rendered in English as "Nature to be commanded must be obeyed," though more recently as "Nature is conquered only by obedience," leaving it less clear in translation whether it is nature's or our obedience that is in question. Hence, perhaps, the continuing controversy. Perhaps, however, we should be guided by the aphorism that follows the more famous one. For, here, Bacon explicitly awarded nature an internal agency to do what it does *independently* of what scientists do when they either bring "natural bodies together" or take "them apart."[23]

To be sure, Bacon used a juridical language, as Cassirer says he does, but to what end? Taking Cassirer's lead, some recent critics have compared Bacon's proposed intervention into nature with the rape of a woman. Nature, feminized, is subjected to the experimenters' "shaking," "agitating," "disturbing," and even "hounding," to use Bacon's own words. I think the comparison goes too far. Bacon was plausibly seeking a more modest analogy, likely to the vexing or overstressing of the strings of a musical instrument, in recollection of Plato's description from book 7 of the *Republic* (531a). For, there, in a debate about the experiments of musical harmonies, the experimenters are heard quarreling over the measurement of the smallest tones while laying their ears to their instruments as if trying to listen through the wall to their neighbors. In coming so close to the object of their inquiry (though, for Plato, in coming *too* close), they were forced, so Plato noted, to rack, vex, and torture the strings on the pegs.[24]

Perhaps, however, Bacon was less disturbed than Plato by the proximity. Recall Bacon's description of Salomon's happy sound-house on Atlantis, in which under the kind rule of the king, the experimenters demonstrated "all sounds and their generation," investigated "harmonies of quarter-sounds and lesser slides of sounds," and transformed on "divers instruments" "small sounds" into ones "great and deep." They even reproduced the "tremblings and warblings" of the beasts and the birds.[25] In Bacon's description, it all sounds very good. In fact, I believe that Cage would have wanted to visit this house, too, to join in the happy experimentation, had it not by 1939 assumed a quite different task. For, having been purchased by the kaiser, it quickly became a place in which the experimentalists determined, through the loud-speaker, to exert control over all who lived there, ultimately taking the lives of those producing the sounds. In Viktor Ullmann's *Der Kaiser von Atlantis,* composed in Theresienstadt (and to which I return in chapter 6), the experiments produced as experiments in sound fast became experiments in death, just as experiments produced in the name of science fast became experiments in war. With this same trajectory in mind, Horkheimer and Adorno described the late catastrophic culmination of a tendency whose beginnings they also found in early modern science:

> The "many things" which, according to Bacon, knowledge still held in store are themselves mere instruments: the radio as a sublimated printing press, the dive bomber as a more effective form of artillery, remote control as a more reliable compass. What human beings seek to learn from nature is how to use nature wholly to dominate both nature and human beings. Nothing else counts. Ruthless toward itself, the Enlightenment has burnt [*ausgebrannt*] every last trace of its own self-consciousness.[26]

In recent work in the history of science, Peter Pesic (also a historian of music) has done much to explode the Baconian myth that Bacon was nature's first torturer. Following Pesic's reading, to speak of vexing nature is not automatically to speak of torturing it. Apparently, Bacon went to considerable lengths not to confuse the two types of language. He wrote of his own disapproval of torture, be it of nature, man, or animal, where torture was defined as physical abuse or as excessive and wrongful force, the kind, Bacon noted, one found in contemporary pursuits of justice. To the contrary term "vexation" Bacon attached only the straining and worrying of mental activity on the part of the experimenter who, in coming to know nature, took it to the extremes of transformational variation without yet attempting to insert the experimental knife. We vex our minds as we do the strings of our instruments—for the sake of hearing the secret harmonies of the world.

Bacon conceived of his experimental task, then, less to enter than to come as close as possible to nature, to discover its "genuine forms." Yet because these forms were "hidden in the depths and not easily discovered," experimenters, he realized, had to dig deep beneath the surface. One might say, the body of nature, as of an instrument, has to resonate if it is to sing. To reveal nature's depths was thus to reveal its mysteries or secrets. Given these thoughts, the Baconian experimentation approximated *disclosure,* where disclosing nature was far from torture and far more truthful. Whereas torture only produces false confessions, Bacon argued, nature's necessary vexation produces truth. Of this fallacy of false confession, he insisted, "it is one thing to put nature in a handcuff, another to fracture its vessels."[27] Many critics have not been able to see the difference, although others have, and when they have, they have seen respect more than rape to be the ideal of the legitimate experimenter. Even wanting to "handcuff" or "interrogate" nature, the act must not reach a tortured extreme. Perhaps the difference is too subtle; certainly, how one reads the difference—as making enough or not enough of a difference— makes all the difference to how one responds to the Baconian act.

When Bacon wrote of handcuffs as legitimate and torture as illegitimate, he urged that a little something be preserved in his method of the magician's art:

> Neither am I of opinion, in this history of marvels, that superstitious narrations of sorceries, witchcrafts, dreams, divinations, and the like, where there is an assurance and clear evidence of the fact, be altogether excluded. For it is not yet known in what cases and how far effects attributed to superstition do participate of natural causes: and therefore howsoever the practice of such things is to be condemned, yet from the speculation and consideration of them light may be taken, not only for the discerning of the offences, but for the further disclosing of nature.[28]

The potentially confusing phrase (in the English) is "light may be taken." If read as "throwing light on the matter," then the superstitious narrations will disclose something of nature, whereas if read as "lightly" in the sense of "not counting for much," then such narrations should be ignored. Bacon meant the former, given the logic of the preceding thought in which he distinguishes true from "impertinent" narrations based on superstition regarding "the prodigies and miracles of religions." Embracing something of "the history of marvels," the new science, he nevertheless insisted, should avoid the dogmatism inherent in too many narratives of natural religion produced in his time.

Pesic notes, following Cassirer, that Bacon was concerned to differentiate himself from his predecessors. In this context, Bacon rejected the sort of speculative or uncontrolled mode of inquiry that yielded more satisfaction of "the appetite of curious and vain wits" than knowledge proper. Nonetheless, to control the experiment was still not to overcontrol it. It had only to retain or establish criteria for the rigorous assessment of evidence. For Bacon, repeatability offered one such criterion and lay, as I would put it, at the experimental core of his experiment. To make the point, he used an undeniably aggressive, if not inquisitorial, language: to "hound nature in her wanderings is to be able to lead her afterwards to the same place again." Still, this sentence arguably captures two things: first, that the hounding of nature can be repeated; but second, that after the hounding, nature returns to where it began *as if* it had suffered no harm. (The question is whether it really had.) With this sentence, Bacon seemed only to differentiate himself from the sort of experimenter, who, arguably like Cage, preferred to go astray or to let what happens just happen. Bacon favored control, though for this he assumed full responsibility. When an experiment goes wrong, he argued, the experimenter, not nature, must be blamed. What errs in experimentation is usually *the prejudicial mind,* he reminded us, that constantly gets in the way of reliable observation.

Was Cage's attitude, I now want to ask, really so different from Bacon's? When Cage wrote of liberating music, he asked for a release of the mind from intention and attachment. Yet, arguably, all he wanted to release the mind from was an attachment to a Western or European tradition that had allowed composers to compose too determinately their works prior to the act of performance. To let what happens just happen might just have referred to what had thus far not been allowed to happen in the traditional concert hall. Read this way, his argument for the release from intention approaches Bacon's argument for cleansing the mind of its prejudices or "idols," as Bacon used the latter term, idols that subverted the truthful observation of nature. Whether nature was made the subject of Western science or of Western art, the sort of subjection wanted by Bacon and Cage seemingly suggested nothing harsher than a delicate balance between freedom and control.

This is all very well, but the questions are not all answered. For, one might still maintain that, given the distance of time, Cage went to an extreme of freedom in reaction precisely to the extreme of control for which the Baconian experiment was held responsible. And one may maintain this even if both theorists were really more reserved, neither relinquishing all control in their pursuit of knowledge nor yet intervening in nature at the extreme of torturous abuse. My purpose, now, is to distinguish between a harsher and a more charitable reading of their work in order to distinguish the sort of critique that focuses on historical tendencies from that which concerns itself with the specificities of particular views. I started with the former, moved to the latter, and now I return to and remain with the former for the remainder of this chapter. Henceforth, I show what is at stake in reading theorists against their own grain or in the light of their reception. For this, I turn to Adorno, not because he reads these theorists charitably but precisely because he does not.

Reading them at the extreme, he shows why it matters that we distinguish the history of the concept of the experiment from that of the experimental.

In presenting Adorno's arguments, I show how far modern science, society, philosophy, and art have come to share a set of concerns such that it would be mistaken to conclude that the experiment always takes the side of science and society and experimentalism always the side of art. However, though insisting on this, I present only those arguments of Adorno that are offered against artistic experimenters. For more in antithesis to these than to any others are we told something about his own version of experimentalism. Nevertheless, that I introduce this restriction does not mean (as it never means for Adorno) that his claims apply only to art.

Adorno

Adorno argues that at enlightenment's end, the Baconian extremes of the controlled experiment moved full circle to meet the Cagean extremes of experimental freedom, and when they met they did so in an authoritarian space. Why it was an authoritarian space is what his dialectical arguments of history are meant to show. Accordingly, he insists, when Cage called for relinquishing human control over nature to remove from the musical world its artificial or bourgeois constraints, he really reestablished complete control—and now comes the clout—much as the Nazis established control when they claimed an immediate relation to nature to justify the eradication from their society of all its unwanted and unnatural elements. Or, following the argument of chapter 3, when Cage claimed to reach nature, his liberated music sounded nothing like the song of the birds but resembled far more the music composed with and for the most advanced technologies of his day.

Adorno is not always critical of Cage, as he is not always critical of Bacon or, indeed, of the most advanced, serialist composers. Still, he is emphatic when it comes to exemplifying the regressive tendencies of enlightenment, which is almost always his chosen task. Consequently, he maintains, because what "appears not to be made is of course all the more made," those artists (from the most surrealist to the most aleatoric) who rely on "absolute involuntariness" end up converging with the artists they most oppose: namely, those who rely on totally integrated construction.[29] By dismantling claims of naturalness by showing the dependence of natural appearances on controlled human design, Adorno demonstrates not only his allegiance to Kant but also his own dialectic (most extremely worked out in *Philosophy of New Music*), between the *progressive* tendencies of serialism and the *regressive* tendencies of naturalism, each supporting a false side of a single, modern coin.

In another argument, Adorno claims that Cage went too far in his rejection of the work concept and thus failed to challenge successfully its authority. Rather than abandoning or even opening up the concept completely, one would achieve more, Adorno insists, were works performed *critically* to reveal the work concept's contradictions. To reveal these contradictions—say, the work's competing claims to authority and freedom—would be most productive because, as shown in chapter 1, it would help save the concept against its own worst authoritarian tendencies and redirect it toward a more truthful use.

Another option would be for composers to challenge the concept by producing what Adorno effectively describes as *antiwork works* of New Music: "Today, the only works that count are those that are no longer works."[30] Such "works," he believes, Schoenberg produced long before Cage consciously engaged in the attempt to produce something like (in my terms) *antiwork nonworks of anti-Western music*. For, what Schoenberg achieved with his works was the understanding that, even when composers exert control over the composition, no controlling assumption is (or ever was) made that anyone knows how works sound prior to their sounding-out in performance. In this way, Schoenberg's works, as all great works, work against the work's authoritative claim fully to determine the performances in advance:

> The idea that the composer is able to imagine every detail in advance is a legend that every composer finds refuted when he hears his own orchestrated sounds for the first time. . . . The tension between what is imagined and what cannot be foreseen is a vital element of the New Music. But in being a vital element, it cannot be turned into an equation that has resolved the tension in one direction or another.[31]

In his obituary essay on Schoenberg, Adorno remarks on how often his music was reproached for being "experimental." The idea was that Schoenberg broke so extremely with the musical tradition that he refused any continuity. That this might be a false view of both Schoenberg's music and his intention is obvious. Still, Adorno wants to show how the concept of the "experimental" came increasingly to be used maliciously against any modern composer who allegedly "sinned" against music or succumbed, to use the critics' words, to producing "vain" or "impotent" works that refused any organic relation to the tradition. However, rather than defending the attacked composer by showing that he *did* maintain an organic relation to the tradition, Adorno criticizes the very notion of an organic (harmonious) relation. Such a relation, he insists, has been belied by every great composer who has ever belonged to the tradition of Western music. Schoenberg belonged to a tradition in which what "went before" was overthrown by moving on according to a development of music's material and form. From this Adorno concludes with all the dissonance of his dialectic, that tradition is present "far more in works deplored as experimental" than in works either deliberately striving to be traditional or claiming to have nothing to do with tradition at all.[32]

If the experiment can go wrong at its extreme, the experimental can, too. This point is crucial. If music encourages too much immediacy, chance, or indeterminacy, to use Cage's own experimental language, it ends up floating, Adorno now argues, in a *random* and *purposeless* space of *becoming*. This might have been a very good thing for Cage but is very bad for Adorno, just because no criteria are any longer forthcoming to tell right from wrong or true from false. A space of *becoming* serves no one if it is guided by an "anything goes" principle. If a purposeless space is dangerous, then equally dangerous, in Adorno's view, is the consequence that seems to follow from Cage's purported total destruction of the imaginary walls of the musical domain—the destruction of not only the work concept but also the very concept of music. For what Cage allegedly achieved with this destruction was to get rid of one side of the relation between humanity and nature that his experimentalism was meant to preserve—the side of humanity. If nature or sound was left to itself because all intentionality had been laid aside, then what was betrayed was what was claimed most to be wanted—the retrieval of the relation.

Adorno does not read Cage as I do. I read Cage as wanting to relinquish one kind of human intentionality in favor of developing another, styled according to Eastern doctrines of chance and discipline (which may arguably be no better). Nevertheless, Adorno is completely justified in asking how artistic intention expresses itself through chance and whether Cage offered sufficient criteria for assessing his productions. However one reads Cage, in other words, Adorno's questions remain trenchant against a too-open positioning or, perhaps one should say, a too-open nonpositioning of art.

We know already from chapter 3 that it makes no sense in Adorno's view to ask artists to relinquish their intentional involvement with art. Since, when they do that, to reach nature in her immediacy, they usually end up with more human artifice—not less—and with just the sort of artifice forever severed from the nature they claim to want to touch. The longing to touch recalls the nostalgia with which this chapter began: that of alienated listeners who, longing to know what it feels like to be in real contact with music (whatever that means), displace their appreciation onto what, sometimes by their own admission, is a dead, empty, and outdated ritual.

With Cage, Adorno writes much about indeterminacy, spontaneity, and openness. However, he refuses to rationalize these elements of experience by purified appeals to nature. In a passage titled "Das Experiment," he argues for the necessary *mediation* of human consciousness in nature, which means for present purposes the mediation of art. If we come to know something about nature, it is not because nature directly reveals itself to us but because a certain form of experimental art does something to crack through the social fabric that holds nature apart from us in the first place. To come to see nature through art is to see nature as damaged as art: beautiful nature is not simply waiting in the background to be rediscovered. To see nature this way is falsely to assume that nature exists in an autonomous sphere separated from humanity, a violent assumption that lies at the root of the modernist problem. Once, in describing the passage of enlightenment to catastrophe, Adorno concluded with John Dewey that what we need is more or better enlightenment, not less. The conclusion in the present argument is similar: if we want to reestablish our relation to nature, what is needed is more art and more experimental antiwork works of art. Or, against the dominant experiments produced in contemporary laboratories, what is needed is more genuine experimentalism.[33]

What, now, does Adorno mean to capture by speaking positively of experimentalism? In his view, all genuinely New Art is experimental, which, to recall, is what Edgar Wind claimed, too. Whereas, however, Wind slid (at least in the passage I quoted) from the experimental to the experiment, Adorno more adamantly preserved the difference. One way he did this is by developing what in the 1950s Pierre Schaeffer pursued under the heading "vers une musique expérimentale." Following Heinz-Klaus Metzger, Adorno pursued instead "une musique informelle," where the idea of music's being or becoming *informelle* was meant to subvert the authoritarian production of music of their day. Only through experimentalism does art have any possibility of achieving a new comportment or posture that refuses to capitulate to the social or formal powers of administration. Only experimental works maintain their distance from the two deadening extremes—first, from a society that insists on constraint at the expense of freedom and, second, from an art that insists on complete freedom at the expense of constraint.

Experimentalism implies risk, failure and, in tandem, the recognition that a society that promises security usually gives its members anything but. Of the literary and musical experiments of the German artist Hans G Helms, he remarks that "the defamatory word 'experiment'" might be returned to its "positive sense" only if "experimental art" is allowed *not* to be "secure." Only those works prepared to "expose themselves to every risk" have a chance of "surviving" or of having an "afterlife." To produce a work that plays safe with the tradition is doomed from the outset to fall into oblivion, its failure being guaranteed by its own aim. The only chance a work has to survive is if, in not conforming, it shows that it is prepared to take a risk, to be unsure (*unsicher*). That it is prepared to take a risk, however, does not guarantee its success. It offers only the chance or possibility of survival: "The experimental [*Das Experimentelle*] is not automatically within the truth; it can equally well end in failure, otherwise the concept of the experiment [*der Begriff des Experiments*] has no reasonable meaning." Here, one should note the deliberate move from the term "experimental" to "the concept of the experiment," to see Adorno's attempt to return to the latter what the former still connotes.[34]

In Adorno's judgment, Cage did not take the risk. All he did was try to guarantee success by aligning his production with dubious philosophical claims about chance, but he took no risk within the production itself. This argument matches that offered in chapter 3, against conceptualism, according to which works, despite their success, do not survive when they willingly relinquish aesthetic appearance in favor of identification with, or subsumption by, a concept. Between the claim to be experimental and the production of experimental art clearly lies all the dialectical difference in the world, the difference between *art*'s genuine survival and a *work*'s either commercial or conceptual success.

Adorno's experimentalism is about trying out new possibilities within the arts. However, this idea is tempered by the recognition that, as an artist, one might well become more interested in experiments than in producing experimental art. When, as allegedly with Cage, the experimenters stressed the unforeseeable nature of the outcome, the works they produced ended up being of no surprise at all. How can a production genuinely surprise, Adorno asks, if there is nothing any longer at stake in what a composer decides to do or if no gap remains between what an experimentalist wants to prove and what is proved, because, in these cases, nothing counts as either a proof or a disproof of what the experimenter sets out to prove? In an argument similar to that of Karl Popper, Adorno describes the dangers of an experiment over which the experimenter exerts complete control so that nothing, according to design or decree, can go wrong. Only works that are not so controlled, and thus assume something like an agency of their own, are the ones that retain the real potential to surprise:

> The avant-garde . . . calls for a music which takes the composer by surprise, much as a chemist can be surprised by the new substance in his test-tube. In future, experimental music should not just confine itself to refusing to deal in the current coin; it should also be music whose end cannot be foreseen in the course of production. In genuine experiments there's always been something of a surplus of that objectivity over the production process.[35]

Adorno notes how often genuine experimentalists tend to prejudge their works failures because they are so aware of the risks they take. Yet, in so judging their works, they often end up conceding what the enemies of the New Music most like to tell them: that had they only played safe, they would have been assured of success. In Adorno's view, there is a tendency, even among the most committed of experimentalists, to conform to what society demands of its music and musicians. What threatens us today, he remarks, is not, unfortunately, experimental art but, rather, its *domestication* or *conformism*, which transforms the threat into no threat at all.[36]

This argument recalls another that Adorno often offered, regarding composers who declare their music difficult or incomprehensible even if in its construction it is entirely coherent and consistent. Why is it necessary to apologize for making thoughts, be they philosophical or musical, hard for readers and listeners? To declare one's work difficult is to give the audience the immediate opportunity to agree. From which it follows that one should know what one is saying when one apologizes. Or, as Stanley Cavell has made the point, one should understand what one *means* when one *says* what one says.[37] This is not merely a platitude. Nor is the point to encourage a philosophical form of moralizing over a society that apparently does not want to *think* or *mean* with its words. The point is intended to demonstrate the genuine difficulty either of writing philosophy or of composing music that does not immediately accommodate ears that tend to prefer to be accommodated. For Adorno, as for Cavell, to stress the genuine risk and fragility involved in the modernist project is one way to capture the sort of difficulty that really or philosophically matters.

Adorno's preferred experimentalism is distinct from what he takes to be Bacon's human hounding and Cage's human silence, even if, as I have shown, it actually absorbs many elements of both. Hence, he recognizes the necessary role that violence plays in what is for him, dialectically, a silent form of art. The violence of experimental art is the violence only of the inward refusal or withdrawal of art to conform to the more violent violence of a society in which the art necessarily exists and to which it therefore responds. Adorno differentiates his own encouragement of explosions, shocks, and fireworks from those of the futurists, surrealists, or aleatorists whom, he contends, tend to celebrate such things only "for their own sake." His encouragement is offered, contrarily, just to the extent that the explosions might help to shatter society's totalizing myths or *idola theatric,* as he writes clearly in reference to Bacon. To the violent world one shouldn't contribute more violence, even if one sort of violence (produced with extreme gestures and exaggerations, perhaps) is needed to dampen the power of another. This is an endorsement not of the "eye for an eye" principle, only of the idea that art must genuinely respond to a society from which it cannot separate itself.

Genuine shocks, in Adorno's view, are such as to explode the untruth of the increasingly authoritative works and the authoritarian society in which they are produced. Totalizing myths concerning art, nature, or personal happiness conceal their violence through aesthetic appearance in ways similar to how explanatory formulas tend to mask the very thing that needs explaining. The myths must be exploded by suitably explosive works, which, as he puts it, more truthfully show their own "scars of damage and disruption." To bear one's scars, as soldiers might bear their scars, is one way to shatter the myths of victory, to break out of "the closed confines" of what seemingly has come to be accepted as acceptable modes of conduct in society at large. To explode the myths is to implode the myths, to reveal the barbaric history hidden behind illusions of harmony. To make art explosive is to invest both the works and the myths with a "self-imploding" or "antitraditional energy":[38]

> Even tranquil works . . . discharge not so much the pent-up emotions of their makers as the works' own inwardly antagonistic forces. The result of these forces is bound up with the impossibility of bringing these forces to any equilibrium; their antinomies, like those of knowledge, are unsolvable in the unreconciled world. The instant these forces become image, the instant what is interior becomes exterior, the outer husk is exploded; their *apparition,* which makes them an image, always at the same time destroys them as image.[39]

Adorno looks to experimental art not to escape from "the crisis of experience" but to confront it. He asks repeatedly whether experience is possible in a world on which the most deadly experiment has been performed. He thinks it is, though only if it follows the terms of his negative dialectic. For such terms try to maintain as a live and constant question whether, in fact, any experimental art, science, or philosophy is, indeed, genuinely experimental. In experimentalism (and I pursue this theme in chapter 6), he finds a form of explosion that is sometimes loud and harsh in appearance but still metaphysically silent, given its withdrawal from contemporary conventions and structures of meaning. To withdraw is to refuse to communicate or to be complicit, while yet remaining answerable to questions regarding truth. All this suggests the sort of silence that is heard in self-imploding works. These are works that allegedly have a chance of doing genuine violence to the world of established social myths. Why is Adorno so convinced that Cage's most famous work of silence did not achieve even a little of this?

Adorno underscores how fragile the conditions are under which an artwork, a scientific theory, or his own experimental critique in philosophy is produced as experimental. Truth is fragile and has only the smallest chance of survival. An experimental act usually ends up as an experiment. The idea of fragility is crucial and returns us to the question with which I began: whether our appreciation of experimentalism should be quiet or loud. I think Adorno similarly wonders whether explosions have always to result in noise or whether, in preserving the character of the experimental, they have a chance of retrieving something of the fragility of thought characteristic of experience before the moment of, and during the long passage toward, its crisis. Fragility though violence as smiling through tears: Is this not what Adorno aims precisely to save in the original Baconian attitude?

Conclusion

In this chapter, I focused on the distinction between the experiment and the experimental. However, the point was not to come out in favor of one rather than the other. For that would be to assume that they are, in fact, different concepts rather than two sides of a single coin that has tended to flip on to one or other of its sides the more or less assertively it has spun in different domains. It would equally be in error to assume that the experiment belongs more to the discipline of science or politics and experimentalism more to art, even if it might seem that way given the form of my argument. With Adorno, my idea was to capture the sense of what is lost in experiments when they become too controlled and of what is lost in experimentalism when it travels too superficially under the naturalizing banner of freedom from human constraint. Still, I tempered and even complicated Adorno's interpretations of Bacon and Cage by presenting their views as they were offered and not only in light of their most extreme tendencies. Bacon was not completely a Baconian scientist as Cage never became entirely a Cagean in matters of art.

More than being concerned to judge these theorists, my overall aim was to describe their views as responses to a perceived crisis of experience that, in turn, gave rise to a long and complicated history of the concepts of the experiment and the experimental. Whether, in the end,w we have two concepts to deal with or one seen from two different sides matters less to me than my having shown what is at stake in the history in which experimentalism and the experiment have played—and continue to play—so central a role. In philosophy, society, science, and the arts, the antagonism that keeps the different impulses of the concept(s) alive—mostly in negative affinities—need no longer pass us by without account.

5 The Pastness of the Work
Albert Speer and the Monumentalism of Intentional Ruins

> Ah alas! in times of tumult . . . men [are] destined to come forth as the shaping spirit of Ruin, to destroy the wisdom of ages in order to substitute the fancies of a day, and to change kings and kingdoms, as the wind shifts and shapes the clouds.
> —Coleridge, *Biographia Literaria*

This chapter concerns the inseparability of philosophical attitudes toward history and art. Although I track particular narratives by Hegel, Danto, and Adorno, I take Albert Speer's monumentalist construction of intentional ruins as the primary example. Intentional ruins are those kinds of objects about which one could say that they were born to be old from the very first moment of their existence. Regarded this way, they are not nearly as atypical as we might wish them to be. Rather, they demonstrate a truth that holds all of the arts under the specific condition of *work* production: that, at a certain historical moment around 1800, the very idea of a work came to be constituted both as a social fact of production and as an aesthetic fact about experience as belonging to the past. It was an extraordinary development with far-reaching and potentially devastating consequences.

To think of the pastness of works is not first off to think about their form or content—about works of antiquated style or works with specific sorts of historical content.[1] It is to think more about the class of works in toto and thus more about the concept of a work than any work or kind of work in particular. Here, my interest comes close to what I once described as the historicity and historical emergence *of* the work concept.[2] In this new and more critical argument, I concentrate on the historicity *in* or implied *by* the work concept—that is, on the special form of pastness that attached itself to art objects when the work concept and the aesthetic and social theory on which it relied became inseparable from a specific development in the philosophy of history. Many philosophers of art have attended to art's history or to the concept of art's historicity, though few to the specific change the concept of history underwent itself when, hand in hand with art, it became the subject matter of a new form of systematic philosophy. That philosophy was named "the philosophy of."[3]

In 1800, philosophy transformed history's past into a *thing* of the past. Objectified, or turned into a repository for all that had happened and been produced, the past stopped being regarded primarily as a vital part of our extended historical present and began instead to be thought about, by analogy to an art museum of works, as existing in separation from us—as something complete, independent, unchangeable, and indestructible. Just as the historicizing of the arts underwrote the dominating role increasingly given to the work concept, so the almost aestheticization of history promoted a new conception of the past such that it was set apart from everyday life to be contemplated at a distance. In neither case did these historicizing developments suggest a relativism or subjectivism for their subject matters. They suggested, rather, both an objectivism and objectification, approximating, as Maurice Halbwachs once wrote, "a crowded cemetery" whose "constant" task it is to make room "for new tombstones."[4]

The reference to "a cemetery of tombstones" misleads, however, if it suggests that the past was now a site of mourning, even if for Halbwachs it somehow was. He was referring specifically to the tombs' inscriptions to emphasize the fragmentary, incomplete, and lost character of historical evidence. Contrarily, in the view I am considering at present, history entered not a cemetery of tombstones but only a museum of such, in which a disassociated reflective eye proved far more appropriate than a saddened one. "In recent times," Hegel wrote almost without exaggeration, "all . . . conditions have changed. Our culture [*Bildung*] is essentially intellectual and immediately converts all events into reports for intellectual representation."[5] By this proclamation, what was symbolic of loss was transformed into something symbolic of gain:

What traveler, amidst the ruins of Carthage, Palmyra, Persopolis, or Rome, has not been led to contemplate the transience of empires and of men, and to sorrow at a once vigorous and rich life that is now gone?

> This is not [however] the sorrow that dwells upon personal losses . . . [;]
> it is a disinterested sorrow [*uninteressierte Trauer*].[6]

This intellectualist view, as I call it for the moment, relied on two parallel changes. The first change was to the arts, when the *work concept* came to define a practice that was transforming itself from being a living, everyday practice into a public sphere, within which elite museums designed for the collection and preservation of objects were now given center place. The second change occurred to history, when the *past concept* assumed a dominating role in a society increasingly dedicated to creating public archives and historical associations for the collection and preservation of documentary evidence. Together, these changes supported the emergence of nationalist cults of posterity and preservation of which, much later, the Nazi cult of intentional ruins was an example.

In this view, if the past was turned into a thing of the past, so, by intellectual extension, were the present and the future: all history was placed in a closed domain and systematically controlled. Access to the domain was then given to those who had the right key, either to those with education and reason or to those with privilege and power. This key is well named the "key to the whole." It was forged predominantly within a German vision of *Weltgeschichte,* or what otherwise has variously been named a substantive, speculative, teleological, progressivist, or historicist philosophy of history. With the key turned, claims recognizing the temporal or tensed limitations of historical knowledge were transformed into grandiose claims about history as a whole. What from a historical perspective was once a claim about standing the test of time became a claim about the timelessly universal. To come to know history as a whole was to come to know it unhistorically, through a universalizing philosophy, theology, or politics.

If history could be so known, art could be, too, with the same universalizing principles. With the same key turned, the historical differences between artworks were overshadowed by claims of their shared timeless and canonic identity. Works of the past became works equally of the present and of the future—the moment, that is, that the works were de-tensed.

Hegel and the Key to the Whole

Hegel was the most important forger of the key to the whole. Interpreted as a thinker tending toward the authoritarian, he is often regarded as one of the first, if not the first, fully *systematic* philosophers of history and of art. Herder and Schelling were certainly predecessors. In this section, I read Hegel in this systematic way.[7] In what he called a "philosophy of world history," Hegel transformed both history and art by underwriting the relevant social changes in their respective practices with an extraordinarily influential conceptual narrative. According to its terms, he subjected history and art to a developmental dialectic of absolute spirit such that both came to their end at the right moments of their self-realization when reason or reflection effectively triumphed over them. Belonging to the real but lower world of contingency and appearance, they were absorbed into an ideal philosophy and politics revealing their "essential principles" and "higher goals." Speaking of the nation-states, he wrote: "The principles of the various National Spirits [*Volksgeister*], progressing in a necessary series of stages, are themselves only moments of the one Universal Spirit [which] through them . . . elevates and completes itself in history, [in] a self-comprehending *totality*."[8]

Two ideas dominated this narrative: first, history and art were given a still significant even if lesser role in a story in which philosophy triumphed. The control of their contingency and appearance and, with this, their proclaimed ends were seen to be all for the good. Second, art at least necessitated its turn to philosophical reflection when modern society and culture showed evidence of severe turmoil or spiritual decline. Hegel interpreted the revolutionary changes of his times as necessitating at least two different attitudes toward the end of art. The first demonstrated and celebrated the achievements of reason; the second more regretfully placed the art he admired the most into the museum of the past, to protect it from the fallen present, arguably to preserve it for a spiritual role it could or might play in a better or ideal future. From the second perspective, what he left in the present, to deal with the present, were the ironic artists for which he had little time. Since the time of Tieck and the Schlegel brothers, he wrote, "contempt for the public has become the fashion, especially in Germany. The German author insists on expressing himself according to his own private personality and on not making his works agreeable to hearers or spectators. . . . [He disclaims] against Schiller and maligns him for having found the right note for the German people. . . . The French act altogether differently. . . . In Germany [*bei uns*] anarchy reigns."[9]

Though regretful, Hegel did not settle with this observation but turned it to the philosopher's advantage. Art, he wrote, "considered in its highest vocation," has become "a thing of the past." The "genuine truth and life" it formerly had is now preserved in the form of an idea, which is to say, in a philosophy of art. The "*Wissenschaft* of art" that is needed today was not needed when art itself offered "full satisfaction," as in the Attic days of classical sculpture. Art, however, "invites us to intellectual consideration," no longer for the purpose of creating new art but "for *knowing* what art is."[10] Given the double perspective, these words, certainly some of Hegel's best known, show the new philosophy of art to be just as much a compensation for a loss in modern times as an achievement regarding what the philosopher has come to know.

In the new philosophy, whether of history or of art, Hegel increasingly subjected the particularities of both to the rule of the ideal, the essential, and, most important for the present argument, the timeless. Given the movement of spirit, the three modalities of time were absorbed into the greater movement of the whole: *das Ganze*. World history, he argued, regards everything as only a manifestation of spirit; it has finally only to do with the "essential now." From philosophy's perspective, there is no past, no temporary present, and no future. Far from being a loss, however, at least for philosophy, this is a gain.[11] Similarly, Hegel spoke about the sensuous appearances of art: what from the sadder perspective he put into the past for safekeeping and preservation, he placed from the overriding philosophical perspective into a repository of timeless ideals. If other theorists of the period were wondering how one could know either the past as it actually happened—"wie es eigentlich gewesen [ist]"[12]—or works of art as they are in themselves, Hegel offered them a productive solace and instruction: to assume the reflective gaze given to the philosophical mind in order to surpass the epistemological limitations of time or the aesthetic veil of appearance.

Hegel was largely motivated by claims that had long belonged to theology. He designed his philosophy either to substitute for these claims or to absorb them to render his own *speculative* claims theologically *substantive* under the guidance of reason. "Spirit knows all things," he remarked, following a saying from Corinthians II, "and penetrates even to the depths of the Deity."[13] Converting what the sciences of the time were developing as an art of lawlike prediction, he produced a rational art for comprehending the present and future (at least in principle) in the moment or even before the moment of occurrence. In the book of Genesis, the creator curbed control of the future by placing humans into sin but simultaneously into the space of moral possibility. In Hegelian terms, many of the freedoms associated with human action and art were made into "as ifs" belonging to the lesser world of contingency and appearance. What Hegel (and God) left standing on the world stage were the great artists and actors—die grossen Menschen in der Geschichte—who, defined by their passion and intuition, guided others toward the true, the good, and the beautiful.[14]

In great world acts of history or in great works of art, the particular determinate content was necessary only as the material or concrete means through which the acts or works were finally transfigured into embodiments of universal truths speaking to all persons for all time. Thus, Hegel wrote, David's Psalms still speak to us today "with their brilliant celebration of the Lord," as does "the deep grief of the Prophets." But so does a moral theme, such as Sarastro sings in *The Magic Flute,* "give pleasure to everyone, Egyptians included."[15] What was "merely shown" in art by way of its appearance or what "merely happened" by way of a person's actions was finally read by the philosopher from the perspective of what "eternally is" for the sake of the "substantial" development of "the National Spirit."[16] Thus, even if we were tempted to believe that to reach an artwork that was five hundred years old, we had to cross a historical gap that could not be crossed, for the substantive philosopher this was no longer a concern. The transfigurative potential of the work would make the leap, as it were, on our behalf—as long at least as we were content to gaze on it with an eye that had become rational, philosophical, or all-knowingly world historical.

In summary, there were two substantive turns made by Hegel's key to the whole. The first occurred with his declaration that art is a thing of the past. In this turn, the work of art was also turned into a thing of the past (*ein Vergangenes*) the moment it was placed into a museum that had also come to house the past itself (*die Vergangenheit*). The second turn occurred when the museum of the past was essentially de-tensed and transformed into a forever-lasting repository for history as a whole. With the turns combined, the outcome was momentous but potentially deadening. For the Hegelian thesis was increasingly interpreted as having turned both art and history into subjects only of reflection, as if both had always already completed the live passage of their becoming in the name of a rational Being that was always already known.

At this extreme, when art and history became things of the past, it was as though their entire outputs were made into complete collections, leaving the fact of *when* works were actually produced or *when* actions were actually performed somehow no longer essential to their meanings. This result motivates everything to follow. It suggests that, after the end of history and art—which is to say, after both gave way or submitted to their "philosophies of"—works entering museums or events entering the past were judged according not to what in them was new by way of what was genuinely unexpected but to what in them was new but already old by way of what was already or essentially known. Once more, it was as though works and events had to deprive themselves of the contingencies of life for the sake of assuming a timeless mode of existence appropriate to the rational law of spirit.

The Transition

Thus far, my reading of Hegel has been one-sided. By stressing the philosophical outcome of *Geist*'s passage, I have ignored the mediating role he gave to the sensuous, apparent, contingent, transitory, and material dimensions of the passage itself. I also stressed the authoritarian tendency of Hegel, the Hegel "of the right" in contradistinction to the more modernist Hegel "of the left." However, I presented his view as I did so that I could, first, paint the beginnings of a picture that was more or less appropriated by a later Nazi architectural ideologist and, second, explain why many philosophers, though deeply inspired by Hegel, argued against his view for its grandiose, authoritarian, or totalizing tendencies. (Unlike in chapter 2, I mostly ignore the differences between Hegel's view and Hotho's representation of it, differences that were unknown to the writers with whom I am here concerned.)

When I discuss the philosophers' arguments below, I again focus on Danto and Adorno. When they argued against Hegel, they did largely because of what happened to his view as it was transmitted through the nineteenth century into twentieth-century forms of totalitarianism. To a significant degree, they argued more against Hegelianism, or against what Hegel's philosophy had come to stand for, than more charitably against Hegel himself. But this approach left them with exactly what they wanted: a space to retrieve something from within the Hegelian philosophy, to be put to use in their own philosophical theories, that would work deliberately against the totalitarian tendency.

Whereas Hegel was increasingly interpreted as having seen in the ends of history and art only the achievements of reason, Danto, but even more Adorno, emphasized the condition of death, one brought about when reason was too comfortably attached to the spirit of political Will, to which they responded by articulating the philosophical terms of life. However, they were not the first to articulate such terms, nor did they completely approve of them. Nietzsche was their obvious predecessor. "Life," he once wrote, "is not an argument. The conditions of life might include error."[17] Nietzsche thought about the ends of history and art as a struggle between life and death, though with the natural order of things reversed. He looked for the conditions of life after death, where thinking about life after death, instead of death after life, was to think philosophically and culturally about rebirth after decline and emancipation after servitude. For Adorno, to think about life after death was to think about survival (*Überleben* and *Nachleben*) after the European catastrophe. For Danto, it was to think about a strikingly American liberation or move into democracy and pluralism after a long-standing European disenfranchisement.

In truth, Hegel, more charitably read, would not have disagreed with his critics nearly as much as they strategically thought he did. He, too, sought the "vitality" (*Lebendigkeit*) in history and art, just as he considered the terms of art's continued production after its end. In describing his view above, I emphasized the outcome of the philosophical pursuit far more than the lengthy duration or passage of the pursuit itself. But consider the last moments of his *Phenomenology*, when he described a "succession of Spirits" or "gallery of pictures" established to honor *Geist*'s passage. "Endowed with the complete riches of Spirit," the gallery persuades us to "move . . . slowly" past each picture with our eyes, at least if what we want is "to penetrate and absorb" the "entire wealth of its substance." To gain perfect knowledge, the eye like the self must withdraw from "outer existence" into what is "inner," so that the knowledge acquired may assume the "shape of recollection" (*Gestalt der Erinnerung*).[18] As emphasized in chapter 1, the passage of knowledge is coincident with the passage of lived experience. Without lived experience, knowledge cannot sustain itself as recollection. Without recollection, the achieved knowledge, even for Hegel, would be dead. Yet, to give our knowledge the character of recollection was, for Hegel, to give it the essential character of pastness, as though the philosopher were burying each piece of knowledge with full honors. Knowledge for the philosopher became reflective knowledge coming after the historical fact. Even so, until the final burial at the end of history or of art, the historical process was a "living spectacle."[19]

I made this brief excursus back to Hegel's thinking to show that however much he actually attended to the long passage of *Geist*, his view was interpreted strategically at the extreme, first by Nietzsche and later by Danto and Adorno, as having so systematized history and art that it effectively killed what it tried hardest to preserve. In fact, Hegel's philosophical method was increasingly believed to kill almost everything that crossed its path, including philosophy itself. Yet the response of the philosophical critics was not to give up on philosophy, or even necessarily on Hegel, but to argue for a development that might more successfully resist turning philosophy into a dominating or disenfranchising "philosophy of."

Before pursuing this matter further, I turn to a concrete, historical case—Albert Speer's monumentalist construction of intentional ruins. This case offers a material illustration of a conception of artworks where the matter of their historicity is paramount. It calls on an extreme historical moment that reveals as well as any could what is at stake when art and history are together absorbed into a totalizing philosophy that becomes a totalizing ideology. The moment shows what happens to both society and art when, in the name of everlasting life, life is what is eradicated. Though the discussion so far has focused on what happened around 1800, the Speer example addresses a moment when the sort of modernity those earlier revolutionary years instigated came to an extreme and catastrophic end. In considering Speer's view, I am tempted to retitle this chapter "The Ruin of the Work" or even "The Monumentalism of the Work," since both would capture the most grandiose conceit of historicism I intend now to expose.

Albert Speer

I was first inspired to think about Albert Speer's project on intentional ruins while reading Victor Burgin's *The Remembered Film*. This is a book about how films, despite their being experienced in collective acts of perception, remain with us as products of individual memory. Though a fascinating subject in its own right, it is not my subject here. I am concerned with only one passage and one comment in his book:

> In his proposals for the transformation of Berlin, Albert Speer recommended that buildings with an important symbolic function be built of materials that would superficially but rapidly deteriorate, clothing [the buildings] in the timeless authority of the ruin. A certain history was coming to an end in 1930, the year the German Pavilion was demolished. It began with the Enlightenment and passed through Goethe's Weimar and the Weimar Bauhaus. It [was] a history of political modernity, industrial modernization and aesthetic modernism: a history of "progress." In 1937, with the first aerial bombardment of a civilian population, the dream of progress was definitively shattered. . . . Whatever inhered in the original German Pavilion . . . could only ever be [re]built as a ruin, a memorial, a mausoleum.[20]

Let us start with some facts. First, there was one German Pavilion built in Barcelona for the World's Fair in 1929. Designed by Mies van der Rohe in "international style," it was dismantled the following year when, apparently, no one purchased it from the German government. In 1986, it was rebuilt on the same site in Barcelona in its original form, though not literally as a ruin, memorial, or mausoleum. Then there was the German Pavilion designed by Speer in 1937 for the World's Fair in Paris, also dismantled soon after, as constructions at these fairs usually are. That year, 1937, was also when Guernica suffered an aerial bombardment by the Franco-supporting German Luftwaffe, though this was not the first aerial bombardment of a civilian population. That occurred during World War I, in Antwerp, Coventry, and elsewhere—in fact, to many civilian populations in Europe.[21]

The part of Burgin's passage that requires most attention is that regarding Speer's recommendation that significant buildings be built using nonenduring materials, all the more quickly to assume the timeless authority of a ruin. The idea seems to be that the buildings are meant both to surpass their historical moment of creation to achieve their timelessness and to survive their inevitable material degeneration by being ruined, as it were, in the first place. That this recommendation asks for either the impossible or the paradoxical does little to lessen its ideological impact, which is surely one of Burgin's points. Yet, by describing Speer's recommendation as he does, Burgin potentially misleads.

His description does not exactly correspond with the text he cites. That text comprises an interview with Speer by Francesco Dal Co and Sergio Polano published in 1977–78. In this interview, as well as in Speer's own monumental recollections, titled *Erinnerungen* in German but translated in 1969 as *Inside the Third Reich*, there is no explicit reference to Speer's having recommended the use of superficially or rapidly degenerating materials.[22] On the contrary, Speer recommended using good, or at least the best available, materials to construct his buildings, since only then would persons of the future see what was created in a former, superior period of power.[23] "Periods of weakness are bound to occur in the history of nations," Speer reported Hitler as having said, "but at their lowest ebb, their architecture will speak to them of former power" and, by implication, of a power that will one day reemerge. Yet, if Burgin misleads, Speer did, too, though differently and with greater consequence. Speer articulated his architectural visions for Berlin and elsewhere under the rubric of a "theory of ruin value" (*Ruinenwerttheorie*). According to recent research, however, Speer only retroactively imposed these specific terms, since nothing suggesting them has "so far" been found in the surviving records.[24]

Maybe one could circumvent much of the present discussion were one to ignore Speer's retroactive reference to ruins. But this will not do. Partly why Speer looked back on his vision in these specific terms was to invest it with an additional authority deriving from earlier monumentalizing and classicizing theories of ruins. Consider the intentional or so-called false ruins of the late eighteenth century constructed in the aristocratic and public gardens, and then the rationale sustaining their construction, which was to establish an authoritative lineage back to great ages of the past. Set this beside John Ruskin's famed instruction to architects of 1849 that they build with the intent to build "for ever":

> Every human action gains in . . . true magnificence, by its regard to things that are to come. . . . Therefore . . . let it not be for present delight, nor for present use alone [that we build]. Let it be such work as our descendants will thank us for, and let us think, as we lay stone on stone, that a time is to come when those stones will be held sacred because our hands have touched them, and that men will say as they look upon the labor and wrought substance of them, "See! this our fathers did for us."[25]

Consider also Karl Friedrich Schinkel's neoclassical writings that idealized the construction of the ancient cities of Greece. Or Hubert Robert's late-eighteenth-century double paintings of buildings in present and ruined form—of the Louvre especially. Or Beethoven's not so successful "The Ruins of Athens," later recomposed, also not so successfully, as a longer and antiquated "entertainment" by Richard Strauss and Hugo von Hofmannsthal. Or remember Wagner's monumentalizing *Meistersinger* or even just the last line of Pfitzner's *Palestrina,* where we hear the aged protagonist casting the last stone for the sake of a future peace. Or, finally, Martin Heidegger's famous passage on the Greek Temple at Paestum as a model of what a future artwork might be, given an argument of modernist loss. All these examples illustrate—differently—what is at stake when a substantive philosophy of history imports itself into a philosophy of art that then has works produced in its image.

My point is straightforward: Speer's retrospective language, retroactively imposed, was neither arbitrary nor unique. Surely, still, one will object that there was a great difference between producing ruins in gardens and producing timeless cities such as the Third Reich intended to produce. Whereas the first idea was inspired by feelings, say, of sublime melancholy, the second was guided by increasingly misguided aspirations toward the progress and perfectibility of humanity and its state. This objection is well founded. However, the more romantic rationale of the one idea was certainly implicated in the idealist rationale of the latter, though this by no means suggests that all intentional ruins end up housing tyrants. In my view, it is necessary to recognize the nonuniqueness of Speer's vision for what it reveals about many of our more mainstream attitudes toward both history and art.[26]

Speer was instructed to design buildings as if they were already objects of the past to guarantee that they would last "for ever." Speer recalls that he was always thinking about "a permanent type of construction," where the point of the permanence was to overcome any decay that would inevitably occur to the buildings. What was wrong with decay? In general, it was something Hitler apparently disliked to see in any form, unless, of course, it was already aged, as were the ruins of Rome.[27]

In a Nazi propaganda film on architecture of 1938, directed by Speer, one of the first warning words to appear on the screen is *VERFALL*, which usually means decay or ruin but here marks only the sort of decay associated with the degenerate, dusty, and dreary. Images are shown of ruinous "Jewish" or "Bolshevik" buildings, of which the Nazis disapproved but which are not literally decayed. The images were produced solely to suggest the buildings' *inevitable* demise.[28] That is ideologically obvious enough, especially given the very first caption shown on the screen: "Die Kulturgeschichte ist der Spiegel der Weltgeschichte." But then Speer complicates the entire issue—both for the present argument and for Nazi ideology—by speaking of his own preferred ruins (*Ruinen*), some of which are shown in the film, as displaying a decayed state (*Verfallszustand*). All he means to capture by his reference to ruins is the idea that his buildings will show at the moment of their just having been built what ancient ruins already show—the fact of their everlasting survival. "Survival" overrides any normal meaning of "decay": one seeks a decayed state or a state of survival without any living sense of the thing's decaying. Speer knew, however, that he could not simply copy or imitate the ruins of old but had to construct them futuristically *as if* already old. This is the thought that shapes the claim regarding the pastness of works: that in being created as if already old, the works nonetheless have to strike their spectators as new. "It *looks* so old and is yet so new," one might have heard Hans Sachs singing had he been instructing a Wagnerian student of architecture instead of a student of music.

Speer's vision matched the monumental and mythic aspirations Hitler had for his country as a whole, according to which all ideas of construction and destruction were absorbed into an absolutist logic. Total architecture or total war: in both cases, the totality demands that an artwork or political state, given over to the past in recognition of its inevitable fall, be preserved in an idealized state of ruin for the sake of its future memory and revival. The idea of a monumental ruin thus suited a developmental conception of world history with the rise and fall of its great civilizations. To associate the term "ruin" with that of material decay was therefore to miss the point, as most of Speer's associates apparently missed it, or so Speer recalled when he remarked that only Hitler understood his idea as "logical and illuminating," in contrast to all the others who found it "blasphemous" and "outrageous." How, they asked, had Speer dared to associate the Reich with any thought of decay? Speer responded (long after the fact) by stressing that his reference to ruins was meant only monumentally or mythically, which is what Hitler apparently meant, too, when demanding that his overall Word, Work, and Will be built "out of stone."[29]

Still, how does one build a metaphorical ruin as if already aged that shows no signs of living or degenerate decay? This, Speer remarked, was the dilemma that he, as Hitler's architect, had to solve:

> The idea was that buildings of modern construction were poorly suited to form that "bridge of tradition" to future generations. . . . It was hard to imagine that rusting heaps of rubble could communicate these heroic inspirations which Hitler admired in the monuments of the past. My "theory" [of ruin value] was intended to deal with this dilemma.[30]

Speer found dealing with the dilemma difficult. His first problem was the contradiction implicit in the required act of production. Time's test, which usually requires time to pass, now allowed an object to pass without any time passing at all. One might think that no one saw this contradiction better than Speer's resistant contemporary Walter Benjamin, but this is not so. When Benjamin argued that objects produced for the sole and immediate sake of having historical spirit were typically those most lacking it, the propaganda minister, Joseph Goebbels, agreed. It was just that, for the sake of total war, Goebbels was willing, as Benjamin was not, to seek expedient solutions to all such kinds of contradiction.[31] And so was Speer.

One learns from Speer's description that Hitler was much inspired by Paris's Champs Elysée, Vienna's Ringstrasse, and Mussolini's Rome and that he conveyed his vision to Speer during the 1930s in a plan to rebuild Berlin. What Hitler most admired in Vienna were the independent but interrelated buildings, "freely visible from all sides." Hearing Speer's description of Hitler's vision, Speer's Italian interviewers asked him whether he wasn't trying to give them a vision of Berlin as "an empty capital, a city emptied to make room for the monuments." This, they remarked almost caustically, would have been a "really radical form of zoning." To which Speer responded that, indeed, he worried with Hitler that the streets would be emptied of life, so that in addition to erecting monumental buildings they decided to build streets for the sole purpose of producing the bustle of city life. Avowedly influenced by Russian and Spanish city designers, Speer noted that he was never interested in producing a city merely for exhibition, just as Hitler rejected "artificially constructed" cities of "nothingness," where "nothingness" connoted the absence of history and life evident in "dull" and "bureaucratic," modern capitals. Hitler offered Washington, D.C., and Canberra as examples of what he didn't like (sight unseen) and Vienna as their genuine and his preferred contrast.[32]

Consider Benjamin's thesis that an art (such as film) produced for exhibition is one that must fail if it tries to match the monumental aspiration of an outdated aesthetic, but will succeed if it gives itself over to what modern conditions of reproduction demand of it—that it openly be an art *without aura*. If art is to occupy a true rather than a false place in modern society, artists must acknowledge the technological conditions with which they are faced, which is nothing to bemoan if a suitable modern form of art is produced to take the place of traditional art. Put simply, for Benjamin, the Nazi aspiration to erect auratic buildings instead of works for exhibition was regressive and out of date.[33]

When Burgin misled us with his reference to rapidly decaying materials, maybe all he had in mind was Speer's construction for the Nuremberg Nazi Party rally, where the pattern of flags and night-lights was described by Speer as forming a "cathedral of light" and by British Ambassador Sir Neville Henderson as a "cathedral of ice." Describing the scene as a "solemn and beautiful" occasion, Henderson recalled that "the blue-tinged light from [the searchlights] met thousands of feet up in the air . . . to make a kind of square roof, to which a chance cloud gave added realism." However, that he offered his praise in a book titled *Failure of a Mission* shortly after his visit to Nazi Germany might suggest that his reference to a cathedral of ice was meant also to express his hope for its speedy melt.[34] There was no doubt in the case of Speer. When he referred to his "cathedral of light," he remarked that he was thinking only about what would survive the disappearance of the spectacle. For even if the spectacle couldn't survive, the idea of it could—and would. Indeed, his architectural concept of "luminescent architecture" was the only one of his ideas, he recalled with satisfaction, that survived the passage of time.[35]

Partly why his idea survived is because of the sort of permanence Leni Riefenstahl gave it in her most famous film. Speer recognized that even if live spectacles don't last, allegedly documentary reproductions of them do, given new forms of reproduction, although in recognizing this, Speer was reluctant to identify the documentary reproduction with the real event. Interestingly, he recalls how worried he became when he realized that the aura of the spectacle and, more specifically, the conviction of the political speeches delivered therein could equally well, if not better, be produced (as in fact they were) in a film studio as on the real podium, even when no responding audience is present.

On the other hand, that there might be no discernible difference between a genuine (documentary) and artificial (staged) production of aura was exactly the spurious identity on which the Nazi leadership relied in developing their ministry of propaganda. Speer was put in charge of reconstructing the ministry of propaganda in Berlin. Was he really so worried about what the ministry would produce inside its walls? Not really, as he almost admitted in describing his own contribution to producing "the demagogic element" of the Nazi spectacle. Worries put aside, what Speer ultimately appreciated in Riefenstahl's film was how far it achieved with a moving camera what he aspired to achieve with his stony design—an auratic site in which the Will triumphs the more the temporal spectacle gives way to something monumental and permanent.[36]

When Speer articulated his theory of ruin value he recalled looking for precedents among the original classical ruins of Greece and Rome, the romantic-classical ruins of the eighteenth century, and, finally, the neoclassical works associated with the movement known as New Objectivity. He described how he designed the party building at Nuremberg to assume an almost romantic Gothic beauty, which, "after generations of neglect" would be seen "overgrown with ivy, its columns fallen, the walls crumbling here and there, but the outlines still clearly recognizable." Perhaps, in the end, this is all that Burgin meant to capture with his reference to rapidly decaying materials. What decays is only the external "clothing" (Burgin's term) or the ornament that leaves the form intact. As long as the form remains visible to future generations, there may be ornamental crumbling here or there.[37]

In Speer's vision, therefore, there were three things that potentially lasted: the reproduction of a spectacle, the form of an actual building, and the idea or principle of the form. The third counted for the most. In his remarks, he focused on inner form to show the monumental transformation of one of the

most enduring principles of form—the Dorian principle of statics—a principle of simplicity and purity, he noted, still evident in Paris's Champs de Mars.
Again, he wanted to show a lineage to a tradition that would give his own
buildings authority. This is the key claim that turns the entire argument. In
whatever clothing the building appeared, and in whatever form it existed, it
was the endurance of the principle that finally secured the posterity of the vision. For the principle to endure was for an internal connection to have been
established between Speer's envisaged buildings and those of former great
civilizations, most especially the Roman, the rise and fall of which had served
as a model for Germany's own. Given Speer's vision of posterity, the past, the
present, and the future were all subsumed into an eternally present architectural space whose principle alone centralized and embodied the power and
authority of a great civilization.

So consider, finally, the description that Speer offered of Hitler's project to
build a *Grosse Halle* to stand at the center of the "civilized axis," visible from
all sides but spatially extending its authority over all of Berlin and thereby
over the whole of an ever-expanding Germany. The spatial extension was designed to coexist with a never-ending Autobahn. Speer then turned to explain
why the vision had not been realized. First, he noted that though Hitler took
great interest in the total control of space and time, he showed little pragmatic concern for where traffic lights would be placed or how traffic would
flow. Second, he wrote with far more clout that, whereas the "Romans built
arches of triumph or huge buildings to celebrate the big victories won by
the Roman empire . . . [,] Hitler built them to celebrate victories he had not
yet won." Most critics have read this sentence as evidence of Speer's postwar
betrayal, when he tried to distance himself from what he retrospectively described as Hitler's megalomania.[38] However, putting his remark together with
that noting Hitler's alleged disregard for practical details, a more stimulating
interpretation suggests itself. If what finally counts is the survival of the idea,
even more than the vision's embodiment in stone, then a city built to be a
monumental ruin might at best be a city never built. What others considered
a failure was implicitly turned by Speer, in a final step of recollection, into an
everlasting success.

The Waiting Game

To pursue this thought, there is no need to take sides with the Romans or to
comment on what we learn from arches of triumph about our celebration of

victories of war. Nor need one indulge in the irony (if that could ever be the right term) that Nazi Germany ended up with exactly the sort of ruin it didn't want. Instead, it is necessary only to pursue the difference that Speer identified between celebrating victories before and after they are won, because this reveals a crucial difference of attitude that one may assume toward history. Leaders who wait to celebrate the victory of war until the war is won are different from those who believe that winning is a foregone conclusion or that whether one wins or loses a local war makes no essential difference in an absolute plan in which final victory is assured.

This point is not altogether banal (or even, unfortunately, out of date). It is the difference between waiting and not waiting for the actual future to occur that has most often been appealed to by philosophers criticizing the worst conceits of a substantive philosophy of history. One of the first critics was Nietzsche's influential contemporary Jacob Burckhardt, who declared outright in his *Reflections on History* that to claim to know the future in advance is an arrogant absurdity. A later critic, Karl Löwith, exposed in his *Meaning in History* of 1949 the deep theological assumptions behind the arrogance of this substantive claim, and yet another was Danto, whose *Analytical Philosophy of History* of 1965 was designed specifically to favor waiting over the impatience of a substantive philosophy of history. There are other critics, too, among whom one must include Benjamin and Adorno, even if they more explicitly criticized the conceits of such a philosophy via concepts of progress and totality.

Henceforth, I focus on the work of Danto and Adorno, though I make a brief digression at the end. For both, as I wrote earlier, Nietzsche was their most significant predecessor.[39] What Nietzsche saw was that philosophy and not only ideology were responsible for shaping grandiose attitudes toward history and art. When Nietzsche looked back on what were for him still recent developments in the philosophy of history, he already feared an almost complete loss of historical life. History abused was a history tending toward the antiquated, monumental, and grandiose, written by historians born aged. History abused was comparable to art abused: in both, death killed life. Academic *Geschichte* had replaced a living *Historie,* just as bad modern art had replaced an art of truthful or tragic character. Tragic culture had become a ruins culture or a German culture, as Nietzsche described it, in which, because there is no genuine passion left, one finds only cults or conventions of passion in passion's place.[40] Yet, in the death and coldness of the culture that Nietzsche claimed to experience, he sought the seeds of a rebirth in an aesthetic philosophy and art designed, expressed, and acted out to subvert the murderous tendencies of a "philosophy of." In this matter, Danto and Adorno followed suit, though their proposals for an antisubstantive philosophy were as different from each other's as from Nietzsche's. Danto argued for a turn to "analytical philosophy"; Adorno, for a turn to "negative dialectic."

When describing Hegel's view above, I was already drawing on arguments that Danto produced when in the 1960s he articulated the terms for his own philosophy of history and in the 1980s the terms of his philosophy of art. In the first, he described the increasing errors of a philosophy of history, the more substantive or speculative it became; in the second, he described philosophy's historical disenfranchisement of art. Danto argued for a new analytical method for the philosophies of both history and art derived from positivistic philosophies of science and logic, with the belief that this would circumvent traditional substantive or disenfranchising conceits. Yet he always feared moving too far toward the opposite extreme. Accordingly, he rejected what in positivism he took to be the sort of eliminativism that explains away the artistic aboutness or historical meaning existing over and above basic or everyday properties of objects and events. Danto designed his analytical method to lie between the substantive and reductionist extremes to avoid committing the error of each.

However, to interpret Danto's design this way assumes a connection between his philosophies of history and art that he does not explicitly make himself. Whereas he does argue that the end of art is an outcome and overcoming of a disenfranchising philosophy, he does not explicitly say that this disenfranchising philosophy is itself an outcome of what he independently describes as a substantive philosophy of history. Mostly he keeps his philosophies of history and art apart, despite their tracking similar paths. Consequently, whereas he sees art as reaching a certain sort of end in philosophical self-knowing, he does not see the same sort of end reached by history. I think, contrarily, that he could have seen a shared end as having being reached by history and art when both were liberated from a disenfranchising philosophical method.[41]

Like Danto, Adorno articulated a thesis (or many theses) on art's end in terms inspired by Hegel while also criticizing Hegel's philosophy and Hegelianism for their totalizing tendency. More explicitly than Danto, he described how this tendency arrived at its most extreme expression in the ideology of the Third Reich. Yet he did not equate Hegel's view with this ideology but traced the dialectical passage of enlightenment that had led from one to the other. Against the European background, as well as his experience of the 1950s and 1960s in postwar America and West Germany, he argued against substantive metaphysical speculation and positivistic or scientistic reductionism as two different sides of the coin he called "identity thinking." Like Danto, he argued for differences and nonreductionisms to counter overwhelming claims of sameness. That was the topic of chapter 3.

Here, I read their arguments for difference as arguments for the continuation of life against the deathblow that identity thinking purportedly brought to philosophy, history, art, and society. Even if life continues as a life of bare or mere survival, or as a life of critical or persistent reflection, as Adorno seems pessimistically to describe it, it is still life. And even if life continues nondevelopmentally under a sometimes celebratory condition of radical pluralism— pacé the more optimistic-sounding Danto—it is still a life sometimes to be bemoaned precisely for its immediacy or presentness.

Further, though both Danto and Adorno recognize, with Hegel, that under the condition of modernity the academic disciplines have ceased to be naive, they equally see in the modern condition of reflection the need for ongoing modes of interpretation and redescription that are distinct from and preferable to the conceits of a pure, systematic philosophy. Neither seeks or finds a final resting place in a world that goes on, even if both sometimes offer claims of self-realized knowledge. And though both remain committed to the pursuit of reason to avoid their merely falling into the sentimentality, cynicism, or irony associated with the reflective age, they do all they can to protect the concrete temporality intrinsic to history and the material appearance and embodiment intrinsic to art.

Still they differ from each other: whereas Danto argues for the continuation or life of history and art in a democratic society of openness and pluralism, Adorno urges an ongoing negative dialectic to safeguard the *possibility* of history and art in a continuing condition of social polarization. If history and art have a life after death, they do so under social conditions that for Adorno are not yet met. Though Danto describes his philosophy of history as a waiting game that must allow the future to happen before the historian can say anything about it, this does not prevent him from placing quite a lot of faith (as I read him) in the present state of democracy. Adorno more adamantly sees the waiting game to be necessary in the disciplines of philosophy, history, and art and in social theory and practice for fear that any announcement of political achievement might encourage the same totalizing error to which comparable announcements led before.

Danto

Recall Speer's theory and how it finally encouraged surpassing the materiality of art for the sake of the lasting idea. With this claim, we immediately reach the middle of Danto's theory, because, in his view, to deny materiality for such a sake is to make a substantively false claim about "the transfiguration of the commonplace." Whereas the "substantive" ascent underplays material embodiment in favor of the Idea, Danto's ascent moves the philosopher toward the Idea without moving art toward its disembodiment.

The act of an artist who produces an artwork visually indiscernible from a commonplace object advances the philosopher's knowledge to the extent that the latter now understands what art (and an artwork) is—namely, that though it is more than what meets the eye (where the eye is regarded as an organ of pure sensory transmission), art cannot do without the eye altogether. Being an object both *of* and *for* art-historical interpretation, an artwork carries all the dimensions of art-historical meaning within itself. It is thus different from any ordinary object with which it might be perceptually and materially indiscernible. That the artwork is materially embodied (and is experienced as such) is not to be denied. The essential artness of art might give way to the idea of art when its end is recognized by the philosopher, but after this end, as shown in chapter 3, art carries on in production as art.

For Danto, to recognize the sameness and the difference between artworks and ordinary objects is to recognize the right connection in which artworks stand to the world. That connection is made up of a one-step removed, representational gap. An artwork should represent the world of ordinary objects but not be "at one" with this world. Set apart, the work is rightly conceived as materially embodied yet still as being essentially representational. Embodiment does not reduce the work to being *in* the world alongside real objects: the work remains *about* the world. For any given work, its art-historical meaning or its particular form of embodiment demonstrates the particular though also essential way it represents the world. The meaning becomes essential, given the definitive creative or intentional act that brings it into being, though this does not preclude more things coming to be said about the work as it starts to be interpreted and experienced in an ongoing world of style, influence, and comparative judgment. Following Danto's philosophy of history, what comes to be said about an artwork at later points in time about its style or influence, or the contribution it makes to the artworld, could not have been said or known at the moment of its creation. The question remains open, however, whether the more meaning an artwork assumes counts also as part of its essential meaning. After all, essential meaning, too, even if made in the creative moment, might need time fully to unfold or be known.

When Danto, in his philosophy of history, writes about what he calls narrative or historical sentences, he shifts the focus from the essential meaning of works to the realism of events. On the one hand, historical sentences are tethered to the ordinary or basic events to which they refer; on the other, they represent or interpret those events according to what is known about the events at a given point in time. By situating historical sentences or entire narratives between the realism of reference and temporally dependent description, Danto avoids two errors. The first is to reduce history to the writing of mere chronicle; the second is to transform historical claims about what can be said about past events up to now into ahistorical claims that now all about the events is known. The latter is the substantive conceit. Similarly, to speak of artworks as having essential and embodied meaning is Danto's way to solve what I earlier referred to as Speer's dilemma: to find a space between spirit and matter, or between absolute transcendence and material reductionism. By taking representation beyond mere copying toward expression, embodiment prevents the work becoming, in a total act of identification, either an idea that it might embody or an ordinary object with which it might be indiscernible.

For both history and art, then, the right connection to the world is maintained if no large step is made in the direction of absolute knowledge and no contrary assumption is made that either physicality or materiality exhausts their nature or truth. The gap that allows us to describe and keep describing events and works is sustained by the representational status of history and art. If art could perfectly replicate the world as the world is in itself, art's interpretational or even embodying functions would be largely redundant. The same failure that we cannot perfectly know the past, present, or future is what makes historical description, representation, and narration possible, necessary—and desirable. The failure is therefore no failure at all, only a limitation that becomes an antitotalitarian advantage. Art does not find perfect identity with the world and history does not find perfect identity with the past, let alone the present or the future, and because they do not, artistic and historical representations, with all their inexhaustible potential for saying or showing remarkable things, celebrate their ontological difference and distinction.

To recognize the representational limits of art and history has a further positive outcome if it persuades philosophers of art and history to be modest. Philosophers must no longer demand that history and art transgress their essential limits of representation through either philosophically substantive or philosophically reduced conceptions of themselves. Proper philosophies of history and art are those that recognize that history and art are forms of representing the world and that philosophy is such a form, too. Though Danto adapts many Hegelian themes, he also adapts themes from Wittgenstein and Dewey, the more he acknowledges limits and uncertainty or expresses antipathy toward any sort of all-knowing philosophy.

In Danto's view, by acquiring a piece of knowledge *about* the world, the philosopher does not, strictly speaking, change anything *in* the world. What changes is one's attitude toward the world or how the world, be it of artworks or of human events, is represented. Yet to change one's philosophical attitude might make all the difference in the world if what ceases as a result are the disenfranchising moves of philosophy that have tended to be too interventionist. One way to keep philosophers in their place is constantly to remind them that what they say about history or art they always say reflectively after the fact—after the event has occurred or after the work has been produced. Only what philosophers say about philosophy itself (as in claims of pure logic) may be articulated tenselessly. Even a claim about an artwork's essential meaning cannot be articulated tenselessly if one understands art to be mediated according to a history of development, unless, now in modified Heideggerian terms, the original authorial intention is taken to surpass this development the moment it is tied somehow to the metaphysical origin or essence of the artwork. (As far as I can tell, the historicity or ahistoricity of intention is not a matter Danto pursues in great detail; arguably, he leaves intention too comfortably in place.[42])

For Danto, as shown in chapter 3, when a philosophical understanding of art is reached, it marks less an end than a new beginning. Art is liberated from the long-term attempted *Anschluss* by philosophy to make it fit its own progressive desire to reach reason's end.[43] Danto never explicitly argues for such an end to history, although he could have. Once liberated from a substantive philosophy, he could have said, history, like art, may now do what it does according to its own nature, which is what analytical philosophers of history and art come to recognize when they more modestly remain on the representational border of the world of facts without further trying to intervene. Under the right philosophical account, history is given back its contingency, narrativity, and historicity, and art its essential aboutness and embodiment.

To see philosophy, history, and art all restored to their different representational ways of connecting to the world, they enter a postsubstantive and democratic age of analyticity, openness, and pluralism. Art can now be any style it wants to be. Perhaps this means that artworks conform to no strong concept of historical style at all but are more immediately responsive to their times, arguably as historical sentences respond to new events occurring in commonplace time, without assuming that the meanings will stay in place or remain relevant forever. As suggested above, even if the essential meaning of an artwork is determined at the moment of its creation, not all about that meaning is immediately thereby known. For the work's meaning might start to unfold, be altered, or even added to the moment the work begins to play its role either, before the end of art, in the grand, diachronic historical process (*Geschichte*) of style change or, after the end, in the synchronic or postmodernist, historical milieu (*Historie*) of style pluralism. To write this way, however, is to import more of Danto's philosophy of history into his philosophy of art than perhaps Danto would want to do himself.

However far the analogies reach, his analytical philosophies of history and art share at least the recognition that both history and art are representations of the world and only as such do they have active *lives*. Thus to adapt, finally, one of Danto's best-known examples from his philosophy of history: if one says today that a war has begun and after four weeks declares it won, one might later, in light of what happens in the world, have to redescribe it. The possibility of redescription keeps the past alive, given what happens in the ever-changing present. Comparably, a living art is one that does not enter the museum of the past already necessarily known or fully understood even if it does have (in Danto's view) an essential meaning. By extension, Danto's life as an art critic has long tempered the philosophical knowledge about art he acquired that day in 1964 in the Stable Gallery in New York and even if, as befits his philosophy of history, he was only later able to make that knowledge explicit. For, with his philosophical knowledge, he came to understand that he knew nothing more than what he had known before about how the uniqueness of embodied meaning shows itself as essential meaning in any particular work of art. In the end, it seems, a life in criticism is what is most needed to keep the philosopher modest.

At the end of this chapter, I discuss how Danto's view connects to a theory of ruins. Thus far, I have shown only how his design of analytical philosophy deliberately countered monumentalist or totalitarian attitudes toward philosophy, history, and art. Given this concern, it is reasonable to ask whether there has not always been something more at stake in Danto's maintaining the openness of history in contrast to the pluralism of art. Whereas so much went wrong in the world when history was substantively closed, far less went wrong in art under its disenfranchisement. As noted in chapter 3, the historicist artworld produced masterpieces one after another, and nothing in Danto's philosophy is designed to undermine this fact. Still, whether masterpieces were produced *because* of substantive attitudes is as complicated a question as that which asks whether history's worst events were a direct result of substantive intentions. In turn, both questions prompt another, equally complicated: whether postsubstantive conditions of democracy really suit the continued production of philosophy, history, or art, where, so the end of art thesis dictates, nothing substantial—or philosophically essential—is any longer at stake.

Of course, not every philosophy of art necessarily aims to make politics and art converge. Indeed, for much of his life, following his pronouncement of art's end, Danto has grappled with the contemporary state of art, which, though pluralist and liberated, has increasingly shown, so he says, since the celebratory atmosphere of the 1960s, a certain or even deliberate pointlessness. But, by this, he surely can only mean according to the terms of his theory, a philosophical pointlessness. As he has argued, nothing after the end of art is or can any longer be *new*, yet this is only because newness is gauged by the philosophical master narrative and that came to its end. Nevertheless, one cannot help but think, partly because he suggests this himself, that not enough has happened for Danto after the end of art to compensate for the necessary absence of the new.

Adorno

The question of compensation also preoccupies Adorno. As discussed in previous chapters, he is unwilling to leave philosophy, history, and art in a representational space unaffected by or removed from the complex dynamics of social theory and practice. Whatever the internal dynamics of Danto's artworld, for Adorno, it must always be assessed from a dialectically combined aesthetic and social perspective.[44]

Accordingly, Adorno insists that the concept of *art* be pulled away from that of a *work* to show, first, how much the social production of works has been caught up in the totalizing tendencies of modernity and, second, how art has then been called on to resist those tendencies. What he aims to capture with this distinction is the residue of aesthetic character and appearance in a practice of art that has given itself almost entirely over to the production of commodities. In this context, Adorno stresses the correlations he sees between substantive claims about history and postwar capitalist developments in European and American society.

In this chapter, I have not introduced Marx, but I could have—and often. Indeed, the argument could have focused on Soviet visions of totalitarian architecture to expose the substantive tendencies of a Marxist philosophy of history. Danto describes the Marxist errors, as he sees them, in his work on the philosophy of history, as Adorno does, too. But Adorno connects these errors also to the bourgeois and capitalist tendencies of Western democracies. Dialectically, he then turns to the early work of Marx, as to Hegel's early work, to retrieve possibilities that have been repressed, the more substantive and authoritarian the interpretation or practical realization of their views have become.

Like Danto, Adorno argues that artworks have a double character, but, unlike Danto, he writes about meaning and embodiment in terms of the expressive character of aesthetic appearance and the social character of the commodity. If Danto sees the tension between meaning and embodiment as occurring within the artwork, Adorno sees the tension as first existing in society's base conditions of production and reception. Whereas the *work* of art exhibits a drive toward order, harmony, internal coherence, and objectivation, the *art* or *aesthetic character* in a work exhibits a drive toward sensuousness, expressiveness, disorder, and appearance. The two drives antagonistically track enlightenment's course. The authoritative drive of the work tries to suppress and increasingly succeeds in suppressing the drive of art by subsuming art's appearance and ephemerality into the authoritarian or capitalist objecthood and permanence of the work. The drive of the aesthetic is consequently forced into a withdrawn position of resistance. So forced, the second drive becomes a negative drive dedicated to disrupting the authoritarian order that work production has sustained.

To be true to a work of art has unabashedly come to imply that one should be true more to the *work* than to *art*. Adorno argues for the relation to be revised, or for the terms to be turned back on themselves, yet thinks this will happen only if there is a social space in which it can happen. Accordingly, he enters into an almost Pygmalion struggle to find life in something that is paradoxically produced as if immediately (under the conditions of authority and commodification) to be voided of such. What brings art to its death is a social development in which works increasingly lose their ability to convey the expressiveness of art as their production and reception are identified with the production and reception of any other sort of commodity. Even if some artists try to maintain the dialectical relation between aesthetic appearance and social commodity, others willingly capitulate to the demands only of the latter.

Willingly to reduce one's art to commodified form is to accept what Adorno describes, following Goethe but now also Nietzsche, as art's aging. Like Danto, Adorno could have used the Brillo boxes as an example: Brillo pads might suggest sparkling cleanliness, but what they clean away is aesthetic appearance. What once was an artistic medium of *sensation* becomes a *sensationalist* commodity.[45] Speer's intentional ruins cleaned away appearance by denying the process of aging, a denial that matched far too well the most devastating expression of Nazi ideology with its program of clean, disinfected, and instant death.

Despite Benjamin's own changes of view regarding both history and art, Adorno maintains that he is repeating an argument Benjamin once, early on, believed about art and, later on, about history. This is the argument that, given present circumstances, an art that denies itself aura may show the residue of what is falsely claimed to be captured by (a false) auratic art: namely, sacred or cultic meaning. By being a negative, resistant, or withdrawn art, or by being an art that refuses in some sense to be a *work,* the art demonstrates its refusal to have aura in a commodified world and thereby negatively expresses what aura in art once was. Given this argument, Adorno opts neither for popular art nor for elite art as such, but only for particular exemplifications of any art that show—by refusing (á la Beckett) falsely to *show*—what the world has lost.

Adorno writes extensively about the ruin of art and the artwork as a ruin. Over time, the melancholy ruin of romanticism became the authoritarian monumentalizing of a city. Adorno wants to return the idea of ruin to the art that lies in the rubble of fallen cities, or to the art that was barbarically displaced by the monumental museums that failed, in the compromised name of pure or autonomous culture, to protect it. The more autonomy and purity the museums and culture claimed, or the more they retreated into a glorified past, the more they played into the monumental hands that contributed to throwing modern art onto the fire. When Adorno writes about art's future or retrieval by thinking about ruins that can hardly be viewed, he does so neither to divorce the mind from the eye nor to deny art's appearance, but only to reveal what was waylaid by the false ruins and monuments erected by the Nazis to a most certain future. Even in recollection, Speer did not find it difficult to look back, but Adorno does. With Benjamin and Nietzsche, he notes how false the comforts and recollections are of any history written on the basis only of alleged triumphs:

If Benjamin said that history had hitherto been written from the standpoint of the victor, and needed to be written from that of the vanquished, we might add that knowledge must indeed present the fatally rectilinear succession of victory and defeat, but should also address itself to those things not embraced by this dynamic and which fell by the wayside—so to speak, the waste products and blind spots that have escaped the dialectic.[46]

A resistant art is an art that refuses what society now demands of it. Yet, in that refusal, Adorno insists, the art must avoid regressively turning back to outdated forms (as the Nazis did) or progressively celebrating the reduction of the artwork to its material base (as pop or minimalist artists allegedly did later on). New Art is the art of the withdrawn in which beauty appears as trace or as a refusal to appear, and where the illusion the work promotes is an illusion that refuses to be one for the sake of an as-yet-unknown possibility. In my terms, resistant works are antiwork works of the new that refuse to have any positive "aboutness." It is as though they refuse their embodiment of meaning while yet refusing also to become concept or idea.

If art has been killed, history and philosophy have been, too, because (as I repeat throughout this book) they are all part of "the same history." This is not all; persons die when society gives itself up to total war with its murderous ideology of clean waste. For Adorno, there is no strict separation when it comes to matters of evaluation between what happens in the world of representation and in the world of facts. Even if he recognizes differences between theory and practice and recognizes, as he writes himself, that art produces no victims (see chapter 6), he still believes that no domain of thinking or production is free of responsibility or conditionality. He sees the truth of this statement to have been brought home to him by the Third Reich, when society itself was shaped overtly by Speer's and Goebbels's ministry of propaganda in the stony images of art and idea. Reason can no longer (if it ever could) protect us from the deceptions of our senses than common sense can protect us from the falsifications of reason. The outcome of the enlightenment is to have almost fully saturated all: reason, commonsense, and our senses.

However, though Adorno reads art's death as a catastrophic condition, he does not read this death as signifying an absolute state. A persisting dialectical movement of conflicting artistic and social drives shows that no final (re)solution has or ever could be achieved. Historical death is not an absolute. If Danto argues that the continuation of representation in art and history is only possible given the recognition of their limits (their being representations of the world), Adorno argues that the promise of the retrieval of life after death depends (as it depended throughout the bourgeois era) on that promise not being falsely fulfilled.

With Danto, Adorno maintains that an artwork, as aesthetic appearance, stands at one remove from the world. Nevertheless, what appears or what the artwork promises can only ever be that—a promise given in appearance, a truth forgotten as the work of art approaches either the totally synthesized artwork at one extreme or the totally reduced commodity at the other. At either extreme, appearance is made to coincide with a reality that is untrue and, with this, art dies. After its death, rather than going back to what it was before, art gestures toward what it once was to suggest what it might be again, if, indeed, it is to have a future. From this Adorno concludes that only by not being fulfilled does the promise of life remain in the form of art as future possibility. A commitment to residual possibility follows from his reference to the "almost." Or, according to the logic of the negative dialectic, only in an art that now refuses to *be* a work, or only in a historical narrative that refuses to *be* a total account, does the promise in the form of future possibility survive. Thus, rather than art and history giving way to a positive philosophy, they make way for a negative or critical philosophy of refusal that lives on, in philosophy, history, and art, in the shadow of death.

Coming Later and Coming After

Another way to articulate the difference between the views of Adorno and Danto is via a distinction I want to draw between something's coming *later* and something's coming *after*. What "comes later" presupposes a discrete separation between historical moments. For Danto, representation in history assumes a discrete difference between events, whereas representation in art assumes a discrete difference between ontological levels. Neither, however, automatically invokes the sense of loss captured by Adorno's idea of something's "coming after." Where there is loss, there is a longing to retrieve what is lost. Adorno rarely asks what something is but where something might go and from where something has come, though he is also conscious of things coming to a standstill. He stresses loss rather than gain. For Danto, contrarily, there is still overall more gain than loss, at least given the increase or expansion in what philosophers come to know over time about artworks and events.

One might say that Danto is concerned with what changes; Adorno more with what happens. Partly this difference is motivated by the types of art on which each focuses. Danto's focus on representation fits his focus on visual art; Adorno's focus on retrieval fits his focus on music. Representation better fits a world of permanently existing objects; retrieval better fits a world of ephemerality. Given this difference, each kind of art wants or needs what the other has—elective affinities. Representation (painting) wants to be aesthetic appearance existing in an object world of artworks; retrieval (music) wishes for something permanent or objectlike to counter the inevitable disappearance of its appearance. The point is not to choose between the drives, only to recognize that their struggle has been a constant in both the history of history and the history of art.

Danto is guided by the idea of representing the truth about the world; Adorno wants to retrieve that which a false society has destroyed. Danto rejects the substantive key to the whole yet still believes that the world somehow shows itself truthfully in our representations of it. He is willing still to turn the key, even if he denies that the turns reach an absolute or final end. Adorno more extremely declares the whole false and the world as it appears false; for him, retrieval and representation are turned into traumatic concepts the more he tries (while yet knowing he must fail) to tug the key completely out of the lock. To succeed would bring philosophy to its end.

Adorno often describes artworks as *Nachbilder* or afterimages, where the association of the term "image" is not detachable from an anxious history of prohibition and where the association of the term "after" is saturated with the trauma of producing images "after" (*nach*) Auschwitz. He argues for the almost impossibility of something coming *later* in a period *after* the sort of catastrophe that brought so much to its end. What coming after means is that it is almost too late (*zu spät*), to recall Nietzsche, for something to come later or for society now to save itself from itself. I stress the "almost" again, to prevent Adorno's making a final substantive leap. Rather than saying the whole is false, it is more accurate to declare it *almost false,* though to do so would undermine Adorno's conviction that in modern times dialectical argument only works if one extreme claim is turned over by another, equally extreme. Accurate description, he remarks, runs the danger of supporting a positivist myth, a myth that conceals that on which the establishment of facts depends. Why, he asks, when a thought diverges from the facts do critics automatically declare the thought rather than the facts false, which is also a subtle way of asking why one sort of fact is so often concealed by another more comfortable one? (Here, Adorno follows Lukács's analysis of *Tatsachenfetischismus*: fact fetishism).[47]

When Adorno returned to Germany from America in 1949, he was confronted with the fact of having survived (*überlebt*) the catastrophe. He asked what it meant for West Germany to become a democracy, given the continuation of social injustice and prejudice. He used his experiences in America to rethink democracy and the role art might play in a society showing still too many of its former barbaric tendencies. To continue to produce art or philosophical thought was one way to avoid indulging in either the irony or the despair of the present. Like Danto, Adorno became an active critic of contemporary art, though his criticism was always aimed, so he wrote, at doing justice to lost life. He connected the verb "to survive" (*überleben*) and the term for the production of afterimages (*Nachbilder*) with the noun *Nachleben* and the verb *nachleben* to suggest that for art to have an afterlife was for art to live up to the promise that life and art still have.

In a memorial piece he wrote for musician and writer Hermann von Grab, Adorno compared the attitudes of Valéry and Proust regarding the status of artworks now lying in museums as if buried. He described how the German term "museal" came to assume an unpleasant "color" (or, in English, "odor"), connoting the loss of a living (*lebendig*) relationship that spectators felt toward objects. The artworks became imbued with a sense of their own unreachable pastness just because the spectators' relationship to them had changed. (As Hegel claimed, so Adorno claimed, "all has changed" because nothing or not enough had really changed at all.) In a culture standardized by its own industry of production and reception, spectators began to appeal to the past tradition of art and for the need for art to be preserved and collected in museums, because they no longer experienced any connection to art or tradition at home. Adorno argued (recalling Nietzsche) that just as persons speak of happiness, aura, and authenticity when cut off entirely from the experience of these things, so the most urgent appeals for objective and public cultural tradition testify to the loss of anything that once substantively went by tradition's name. Against this background emerged what he referred to as a "cult of ruins."

Adorno accordingly distinguished the attention Valéry devoted to describing the mortified character of art *objects* from that Proust devoted to the remembrance of past *experience*. Whereas the former attention suggests an increasing fetishism of mortified objects, the latter suggests an infatuation with the survival of purely subjective experience. Adorno took the side of neither the pure object nor the pure experience; nor did he seek reconciliation between the two. He asked only after the critical potential for the one side to serve as the corrective of the other in a world that had become overall a world of the past. "What emaciates the life of the art work," he wrote, "is also [*zugleich*] its own life." What does the "zugleich" in this statement connote? It is a reference to how any form of life lives or should live on as the shadow of its own emaciated life.[48]

"The Past Is Not Dead; In Fact, It's Not Even Past"

To say more about lost life is to say more about remembered life, though to say more about this will do little to bring my argument to its close. Rather, it begs for the argument to move toward a new project, to show the role that philosophy, history, and art have all played in shaping forms of life in which a profound sort of meaning has been thought to be lost to the individuals who participate in them. This was the theme of Burgin's book, *The Remembered Film,* as indeed the theme of numerous others writers who have articulated ideas of life, lived experience, and individual memory as antidotes to a modernity they see to have totally objectified the world by absolutizing experience.

In brief, in this argument, the objectification of experience is inseparable from emerging dominant cults of posterity and cultures of preservation, which, in turn, are inseparable from attempts to shape the sort of public taste and opinion that seeks everyman modes of experience belonging to no one in particular. In this petrification and publicization of taste and opinion, the past is set apart as dead or as lost and becomes increasingly disembodied the more it is separated from any active, live, or personal commitment. Pierre Nora's famed sentence (mirroring Nietzsche's and Adorno's above) that "we speak so much of memory because there is so little of it left"[49] is directed at the substantive move around 1800, when, under the condition of reflection, living culture was unseated by *Kultur* and history by an academic *Geschichte.*

In this argument, the act of killing the past finds its analogue in the death not only of art but also of the writer, as Sartre argued about writers subsisting as cemetery watchmen, guarding over dead things. Contra Halbwachs, Sartre described not the fragmentary character of buried evidence but only the cold comfort writers experience the more they retreat (because they feel they *must* retreat) from the world of the living into the past, but where the past is only really the antidote to their dead or declined present lives.[50]

Thomas Mann also pursued this theme between the two world wars in his story about the historian Doctor Cornelius, who, instead of living in and with present life, leaped back into the past because there he believed he would find an order he no longer found in the present. In this story, the past was made into something certain as an antidote to present uncertainties and was even assigned by Mann the character of Being, connoting a place of "all Godliness."[51]

To retreat into the past in search of certainty also reflects the sort of modernist alienation described shortly after 1800 by Goethe in his story "The Man of Fifty" and by Sir Walter Scott in *The Antiquary*. Scott described the gap between present viewers and past artworks—or historians and the past—as comparable to the present selves of persons looking back at their past selves to which they feel, either because of age or because of some sort of rupturing experience, no longer any connection or commitment.[52]

A different tack was taken later by Yosef Yerushalmi, who described how reflective history as a totalizing and collective form of disembodied representation had destroyed the (Proustian) space for individual dreaming. Reading Jorge Luis Borges's story of 1944, "Funes the Memorious," Yerushalmi argued that collective representation had left everyone sleepless or with too much memory, the sort of memory that by being objectified and preserved was cursed just because nothing could now be forgotten.[53] So much for knowing *all* about *everything!* To warn against the collectivization of memory and representation, Yerushalmi wrote that no symphony could ever successfully be written collectively. I doubt that this is correct, but the desire for this to be true stems from what antisubstantive theorists of history most want to show: that art, like persons, should resist obedience to what collectivization demands of them, to demonstrate that something approximating the independent or free activity of individuals is still possible.

Comparably, Hayden White restored the contingent and ironic literariness of narrative strategies to counter the domination of a frigid or petrified world history. He sought better terms for writing history against a tradition that, as Hobsbawm in his *Invention of Tradition* and Habermas in his *Logic of the Social Sciences* also argued, had tied collective representation to dominating forms of political power. What had happened in this consolidation of power was that living history was brought to a standstill under dangerous conditions of naturalization and normalization. Power was most present but most petrified when rationalized by substantive assumptions about a would-be timeless present, for through this rationalization, the argument for change became a conformist argument effectively preserving the status quo.[54]

Iconoclasm

Obviously, in this chapter, I chose not to write in detail about these particular arguments, even though I knew how much they inflected the arguments to which I did attend. My aim was to describe certain connections between modern philosophies of history and art emanating from the Hegelian tradition. For a long time, I have been concerned with the concept of a work. Only recently, however, did I come to see how much the work concept is bound up with what I have been calling the past concept, given a specific conception of what philosophy is and what it takes to be its task.

Although I focused here on the pastness of history and art, I am aware that our modern anxiety to come to know an artwork or a past event is deeply connected to our anxiety to know our past selves. Much contemporary writing on history, art, and autobiography is about bringing something lost or gone back to life. Performances or readings bring works back to life as interpretation or analysis brings the past back into our present. But this very construction—nostalgic or productive—is only so pervasive because we construct something as lost to us in the first place. In itself, this is not a new point, though showing the extent to which it dominates and even motivates our modern philosophies of history and art I think is new, at least for those who have attended to either the philosophy of art or the philosophy of history but not to both together as deeply intertwined subjects.

In philosophy, much but not enough is made of the examples it uses to make its points. I discussed here an extreme moment in modern history when Speer planned to rebuild Berlin as a monumental ruin. I chose this story because of the ideological key it turned to the substantive terms of a world history that later philosophers took so profoundly to task. However, when these philosophers took these terms to task, they did not simply reject the ideological picture to which the substantive philosophy had become attached but rethought the very terms of the philosophy that had inspired the substantive conceit in the first place.

Many modern commentators criticize philosophy for its iconoclasm, for its perpetual displacement if not outright murder of history and art, given its censorious or disenfranchising tendencies.[55] However, it is less often acknowledged that it is these tendencies read as metaphysical *needs* which philosophy must retain to prevent its own reduction to that which it is not: namely, history or art. Danto and Adorno both show the need for philosophy to respect history and art by coming to respect its own limits. To disenfranchise history and art is for philosophy to disenfranchise itself. But for neither Danto nor Adorno is the answer to give up philosophy. That their philosophies are iconoclastic is the price they pay for pursuing the sort of thought that cannot help but try to subsume its subject matter. What matters after this price has been paid is whether Danto's continued pursuit of analytical philosophy or Adorno's pursuit of the negative dialectic grants a space for history or art then genuinely to answer back to philosophy. There is one iconoclasm that silences the opposition altogether but another, more complex one, that allows what it silences to speak back, paradoxically, in its own more liberated and liberating terms.

A Last Example

This chapter ends with an example Danto recently used in a piece for *The Nation*. It concerns the artist Robert Smithson and his 1960s theory of world entropy.[56] Given the theory of the inevitable fall of the world into disorder, Smithson argued that one ought to build monuments in the present to help us forget what the future will bring. Instead of causing us to remember the past as old monuments do, the new monuments make us forget the future. Materials, he added, must be chosen for this forgetfulness, materials that don't last, like electric light. The monuments must not be built *for* the ages but *against* the ages. Accordingly, Smithson constructed several monuments, one for the state of New Jersey about which he wrote: "Th[e] zero panorama seems to contain *ruins in reverse,* that is—all the new construction that would eventually be built. This is the opposite of the 'romantic ruin,' because the buildings don't *fall* into ruin *after* they are built but rather *rise* into ruin *before* they are built. . . . Has Passaic [New Jersey] replaced Rome as the Eternal City?"[57]

Danto interprets Smithson's project in terms with which we ought now to be familiar—from our reading of Speer: "The works . . . exhibit what Smithson calls 'a new kind of monumentality' [that brings] to mind the Ice Age rather than the Golden Age." This is "an allusion that suddenly vests his abstract ice-crystals with a certain prophetic meaning." What is this prophetic meaning? Danto answers: In "the ultimate future the whole universe will burn out and be transformed into an all encompassing sameness."[58] But what sort of sameness? Just the sort that one apparently sees in the aesthetic of boredom demonstrated by Andy Warhol. Boredom becomes another way for Danto to describe art's end, freed as art now is from the dogmas of a substantive philosophy of history that was always prepared to show why art should be interested in where it was going. Describing it so, Danto leaves us with the dilemma introduced above—that in a society we want, art seems to be associated with nothing mattering (perhaps only to the philosopher), but in a society we don't want, art seems to retain its purpose by being associated (though the question is how) with potentially dangerous substantive goals.

Had Adorno also commented on Smithson's work he would probably have concluded that to produce a monument or ruin for a future of absolute gain is no different from producing one for a future of absolute loss. To celebrate the gain, as Speer's ruins celebrated the gain, is no different from concealing the loss, as Smithson's ruins-in-reverse conceal the loss, in forgetfulness. From this one might conclude that neither work, constructed as a ruin, does justice to the historicity of either history or art or, more important, to a world that has never actually risen or fallen according to an absolutist logic. Whether one speaks of the pastness of the work or of its futurity, historical tense only becomes an interesting tension when one stops believing that one can simply glide across time with universalizing skates oblivious to the grooves one carves or finds already carved in the ice. If Danto leaves us with an interesting dilemma, Adorno does, too: that given a theory of intentional ruins, where the intention is to dispense or conceal the historicity of the work, the work cannot help but belie the intention by remaining historical through and through. What an artwork is and what is claimed on its behalf is one of the most basic tensions that keeps the necessary argument between philosophy and the arts alive.

6 The Musicality of Violence

On the Art and Politics of Displacement

The troops marched past the dead bodies. The music played.
—Maurice Merleau-Ponty, *Humanism and Terror*

This chapter develops specific arguments of modernism to reflect on twentieth-century musical works—operas, cantatas, requiems, and oratorios—that in different ways are connected to violence. I consider works less of domestic than of social or political violence (though one also has a strong domestic setting) and works combining sound with texts and images. The works treat ideals of justice, freedom, and hope as much as specific events and enduring situations. Sometimes they are composed *after* and sometimes *during* an event of extreme violence. As works of commemoration, mourning, or resistance, which these works tend to be, they inevitably adopt a stance toward the victims of the violent acts. I am most interested in the stance adopted.

As the argument develops, an analogy begins to emerge between the terrorist act and the artwork that memorializes the victims of that act. The terrorist act and the artwork share certain structural or internal logical features because they draw on a common history of aesthetic, political, and religious assumption. The analogy shows that works that aim to commemorate the victims of specific acts of violence sometimes come unwittingly to mirror the violent acts themselves—even though the act and the work have deliberately opposed aims. The unwitting mirroring occurs most strikingly when artworks so universalize their messages that they displace the object they seek to com-memorate—the specific victims—because an analogous displacement forms part of the rationale of the terrorist act itself. The analogy is not sustained by all works of commemoration. My argument does not dismiss the seriousness or pain with and against which such works are composed. I do not exclude recognition of the beneficial effects that a music of mourning may have; nor, finally, am I opposed to all forms of universalization. But I do make explicit a deep problem inherent in the very idea of using art to mourn humanity's crimes.[1]

First, I outline a broad modernist background focused on related themes: murder as fine art, the violence of music, and the attempted murder of art by philosophy. After that, I focus on arguments about the relationship between music, art, and violence that together fall under the umbrella term "displace-ment." Displacement means substituting, swapping, or even transforming one thing for or into another thing: it assumes various forms of mediation and indirection. It evokes all sorts of strategies for detaching, distracting, dis-tancing, despecifying, derealizing, discarding, and disadvantaging. Following Victor Klemperer's exposure of the tendency for ideologues to coin *de*-words, or *ent*-words in German, displacement is certainly not always a good thing, even if it is the formal principle and technique I am proposing for critique.[2] That is the point: in immanent critique, terms and techniques are not judged by foreign terms from above but are moved in internal ways for and against themselves to expose their own histories of use.

The Examples

I treat several works in more or less detail: Michael Tippett's oratorio *A Child of Our Time*—conceived in 1939 but delayed in its performance until 1944 partially because it was thought inappropriate to perform a pacifist work given the specific events of the Second World War—and John Adams's 1991 oratorio-opera *The Death of Klinghoffer*—later to become a film, thus helping to secure the survival of a work that was not well received. These works are contrasted with two of Schoenberg's late works: *Moses und Aron,* begun in the 1930s but never completed, and *A Survivor from Warsaw* of 1947. There are four more works I consider, divided into two pairs.

The first pair comprises not musical works but films about music. Both address the relation between aesthetics and politics. Both were screened in 2002 at a Lincoln Center film festival focused on the painfully glorious or gloriously painful history of the Berlin Philharmonic Orchestra. The first, Hermann Stöss's *Botschafter der Musik* (Ambassador[s] of Music) was made in 1951 in Berlin. It is a troubling documentary film about the postwar rise of the orchestra literally out of the ruins of its bombed-out hall. It praises the defeat of the Nazi dictatorship yet the survival of German music, symbolized by the return to public life of the "conductor-dictator" Wilhelm Furtwängler. Berliners, the narrator says, were never really taken in by the political dictator, only by the musical one. With Beethoven in the background, and *Die Meistersinger* in the foreground, the orchestra spreads its aesthetic across Europe with an iconography formerly reserved for the swastika. A map is displayed with the German symbol—now the orchestra—proudly broadcasting its arrows across Europe. The rhetoric proves disproportionate to the simpler truth that, for the first time since the war, the orchestra was allowed to perform abroad.[3]

Something of the same rhetoric is found in the second film, *Taking Sides*, made in 2001 by Istvan Szabo, after the 1995 play by Ronald Harwood. One of the orchestra players remarks in the play: "A conductor is also a dictator, . . . he is also a terrifying power who gives hope and certainty, and guarantees order. I wanted to be in the Maestro's power, too. The orchestra is a symbol, you see—."[4] This film also assumes a stance on the relationship between German wartime politics and aesthetics. It is about how, in having refused to take political sides by taking the "pure" side of art, Furtwängler took the wrong side and, arguably, even played one political side against the other. Szabo's film has been praised (when it has been praised) for *taking no side* itself. One would think that, given the film's title, this praise has been ironically intended; sadly this isn't so. Many works, similarly devoted to presenting difficult conflicts, have also been praised for taking no sides, but they shouldn't be if and when the fact of achieving such evenhandedness ends up feeling far less like fairness and far more like concession, apologetics, or compromise.

Compare one critic's remark regarding "the world premiere of John Adams's *The Death of Klinghoffer*," which "took place in Brussels in 1991, during the First Gulf War." The subject was

the hijacking of the Italian cruise liner *Achilla Lauro* by Palestinian terrorists in 1985. Peter Sellars's original stage production went to Lyons and Vienna, and thence to Brooklyn and San Francisco. Pickets from the Jewish Information League staged demonstrations outside the theatre in San Francisco. The problem was that Adams had dared to give an equal voice to both sides, making no judgement as to who is right and who is wrong. (Oh that politicians would do the same.)[5]

Regardless of what politicians do or ought to do, the question is whether, in making no judgment, Adams's work doesn't still fall into an ideological trap.

The second pair of works comprises two operas connected to recent acts of terrorism. The connection has an accidental motivation, stemming from two invitations I received in 2004 to speak, first, at a conference in Madrid on art and violence just months after the terrorist attack there, which made me think again of 9/11 in New York, and then to speak weeks later at the Hebrew Union College in Cincinnati about a strange and evidently most controversial double bill in the spring season program of the Cincinnati Opera.

The first work of this double bill was a contemporary opera by the Swedish composer Peter Bengtson based on Jean Genet's play of 1947, *Les Bonnes* (*The Maids*), and the second, Viktor Ullmann's 1943–44 oratorio-opera-singspiel *Der Kaiser von Atlantis, oder Der Tod dankt ab* (*The Kaiser of Atlantis, or Death Abdicates*). Genet's work is about a domestic murder based on an event that occurred in France in the 1930s: the murder by two sibling maids of their mistress. The story is about class and social oppression, but under Genet's hands, it becomes a work about crime transmuted into art. Ullmann's work, composed for performance in the camp at Theresienstadt, is about politics, technology, and death. In the contemporary production, this work was "updated" to render it unclear who exactly the perpetuators of terror are in our contemporary, so-called war on terror. (Whereas a "war on terror" rings biblical, a "war on terrorism" rings more suitably political, a difference that later proves relevant to my argument.) This updating apparently offended many members of the audience, less, they said, because it compared two arguably very different situations of terror and more because it relativized the absolute or radical evil of the systematic murder in the concentration camps by the very act of comparison.

In my own thinking about these productions, I attended to a comparison not at first between past and present situations but between the two original works, Genet's and Ullmann's. I wanted to know what more, if anything, they shared, other than their being approximate historical contemporaries. I decided eventually that they shared a de Quincean theme Sartre once applied to Genet's play whereby murder and fine art are brought into intricate relation. With this theme, all my examples started to connect.

Murder as Fine Art

According to Sartre, Genet's play is about the extreme derealizing or faking of reality to a point of pure artifice, whereby the murderous maids become other to themselves. In the loss of self or relinquishment of subjectivity, they become negative embodiments of pure evil. In their desire to surpass their subjugation as maids, they become their own oppressors. Sartre looks at the intense theatricality that allows the sisters to cross gender and identity into the dominating position of Madame and the Man. In this play of derealization, the real murder becomes an apparent murder and the crime merely the appearance of crime. Their crime is transmuted into art and finally even into an act of innocence associated with the purely sensuous appearance of angelic beauty: the *ange* in one of the maid's name, Solange. It is the sort of purity that leaves a perfume wafting over the blood or dirt that remains on the ground: the *sol* in Solange. The play accordingly ends with "the orchestra playing brilliantly" and the maids wafting in the delicate perfume of Madame's airy corpse, declaring themselves—in their beauty, their drunken joy, and their freedom—now holy.[6]

The theme of murder as fine art is also about the highly calculated and even cultivated character of murder performed for the sake of politics. Thus Ullmann's work, with its libretto by Peter Kien and subtitled *Death's Refusal*, is not about the resistance of prisoners who refuse to die. It is about death itself, about its metaphysical figure, an ancient warrior, who becomes so disgusted by the dictatorial and calculated terms of the killing around him that he goes on strike. War, he complains, or dying has none of the honor it used to have. He determines no longer to allow individuals to die on the terms set out by a kaiser significantly named Überall in reference, the music tells us, to Germany's national anthem. The kaiser hides behind the screen of modern technology, displacing the voice of a little aggressive man by that of the apparent All-Mighty:

Attention! Attention! In the name of His Majesty, of Kaiser Überall! We, by the grace of God, the one and only Überall, pride of the Fatherland, the blessing of humanity, Kaiser of both the Indies, Kaiser of Atlantis, . . .

> King of Jerusalem . . . have we with unerring instinct decided to declare
> over all our domain a great and blessed war of all against all.[7]

The loudspeaker is the source of Überall's power: the loud voice, the artificial voice, ruptures every scene, symbolizing the destruction of what is human in humanity. The technology gives to all who appear in this work a ghostly status hovering between life and death—"a life that no longer laughs and a death that no longer cries." In this work, it is technology not theatricality that derealizes life. If death is mistreated, this is because life is, too, as Überall finally comes to understand. In determining who shall live and who shall die, he realizes he has become no more than an adding machine (*Rechenmaschine*): murder as a perfectly calculated and calculating art. "Am I still a man," he asks, "or the calculating machine of God?" God is not disparaged in this question, only the thought that a person can assume God's role under the wrong instrumentalizing condition: God become human machine. As Death finally admits Überall to his realm, as the sole condition for ending the strike, the remaining characters sing the Lutheran hymn *Ein' feste Burg*.

One of Schlegel's final Athenäum fragments, number 447, states: "False [or inauthentic] universality is either theoretical or practical. The theoretical type is the universality of a bad lexicon, of a record office. The practical type originates in the totality of the interference."[8] Ullmann's work shows at least the theoretical type, the bad lexicon of Überall's record office, but perhaps, given the interference, the practical type as well.

Murder as fine art is about the transformation of crime into art, or, with Genet, the transformation of blood into aesthetic transcendence. It is also about calculation and planning, as in the fine art of murder. These two themes were combined in the 1930s by Benjamin, at the end of his essay on technological reproducibility, when he wrote about the aestheticization of the political. Describing the futurist and then fascist moves toward militarization in advanced capitalist society, he showed how war games approximate the condition of works of art. In the same period, Genet remarked that an artwork has the capacity to so exalt pain that it can expel that pain until nothing left remains—except the odd combination of beauty and blood: Solange. The pain is brought to nothingness, noted Genet, like a firework that ceases to exist after its explosion.[9]

As is well known, the composer Karlheinz Stockhausen commented on the terrorist attack of September 11, 2001, with approximately these translated words: "The terrorists brought about in one act what composers can only dream of—to practice madly for ten years, completely, fanatically, for a concert and then die. That would be the greatest work of art for the whole cosmos. Against this, composers are nothing." Had these been his exact words, they would have reflected the vainglorious envy of an artist who thought he was watching terrorists achieving in a singular fateful day what he had wanted his entire life to achieve—the creation of the greatest work of art.[10] But the words might also have referred to the aesthetic quality of the spectacle, captured by the camera, and then made, as if this had been one of the points, into an artwork for repeated technological reproducibility by those it had offended most. The firework ceased to exist, the blood lay on the ground, but, in reproducibility, the crime became art—again, again, and again.[11]

The Violence of Music

The idea of a spectacle that beautifies terror motivates my title: "The Musicality of Violence." This title has a deliberately distasteful tone. It suggests that violence may be so harmonized or aestheticized that it ends up satisfying a desire for beauty and pleasure more than revealing humanity's darker side. Writing about music in concentration camps, Tzvetan Todorov has suggested that music has always named the failure of humanity to be wholly inhuman.[12] Yet music has also named the success. To speak of the musicality of violence is to recognize music's sometimes inhumanity. We like to think that music is always put to good ends, that it consoles and reminds us of our humanity, or, as Lenin said (according to Gorky), that it leads us to say nice things even when we don't want to be nice. However, music no more guarantees humanity's positive side than does anything else. If music can be used well, it can be used badly. There is nothing in music's form or use that *guarantees* those who play or listen a safe haven from the world.

Plato argued this first with his recognition of music's power to move us but to move us sometimes in dangerous ways—hence his plea for music's censorship. Nietzsche followed later with his description of music's power to unleash the uncivilized impulses of humanity, thereby requiring mechanisms of civilized control. To render violence beautiful is to erect the Apollonian veil to protect humanity from direct confrontation with Dionysian power. Yet, he added, even if Apollonian art temporarily protects us from this power, the Dionysian instincts it represses rise again in another form of art or human conduct. The Apollonian illusion is after all illusion. Adorno later repeated this argument when he suggested that uncivilized impulses are not simply tamed by civilizing forces. For just when we most believe the impulses have been tamed, they reappear even more violently, indirectly to demonstrate the violence of the civilizing forces themselves. The violence plays itself out on both sides: the censorship introduced to tame music's resistant or uncontrolled violence is itself a form of controlled violence.

Adorno focused as much on music's capacity itself to terrorize as its ability to show the violence of civilizing or censorious society. Nowhere better did he express music's double function than when describing how the music that "stirs up the dance of the Maenads and sounds from Pan's bewitching flute . . ., rings out from the Orphic lyre, around which the figures of inner drives range themselves, pacified." The pacification, he explained, is sustained in its fragile state both by claims of contemporary taste and by the discipline "handed down" from Greek philosophy (Plato) "as a highest good." Yet, whenever there is this pressure to obey, a bacchanalian agitation emerges (as in Wagner's *Meistersinger*) to disturb the peace.[13] In extending his thought back to the Greeks, Adorno argued that neither the musicality of violence nor the violence of music is separable from the disciplining impulses of a philosophy that attempts, in the name of enlightened and civilized society, to control both the happiness and suffering of individuals—their pleasures and their pains.

The Attempted Murder of Art by Philosophy

Danto has also described the disciplining tendencies of philosophy in relation to art. His essay "The Philosophical Disenfranchisement of Art" reflects all the violence of its theme: philosophy's endless "warlike" attempt to render art "impotent," "futile," "neutered," "passive," and "useless." In rendering art impotent, however, philosophy brings itself to the same condition, leaving both attacker and victim incapable of making "anything happen in the world." Danto finds in this endless war a strain of inevitability, even necessity. The only way philosophy has been able to deal with art's undeniable power has been to treat that power as a danger and to make of it an enemy in need of domination and defeat. However, art has never entirely been defeated. Despite its disempowerment, art, at its end, finally releases itself from philosophy's dominion. Why the *need* for art's liberation? In part, Danto argues, to prevent works "of terrorism and torture" from simply being "rendered harmless and distant" from the very forms of life they are "meant to explode."[14] The language Danto employs himself is unremittingly warlike; the liberation of art is meant to bring the war to its end.

As critic, Danto seeks the philosophical significance in contemporary acts of art production. Finding in Stockhausen's words on 9/11 further evidence of his end of art thesis, he describes the history of art has having reached so pluralist a condition that not only is anything possible but also there are simply no constraints anymore on what can count as art. Danto acknowledges that there might still be moral constraints and constraints motivated by suffering, but such constraints are external to the absolute pluralism that now belongs to art's production. The very idea, he argues, that Stockhausen could have uttered these words at this moment underscores the total openness of art production, however monstrous the making of this art[15]—assuming, of course, that art was really being made on that day. Given his disenfranchisement thesis, Danto might also have shown how philosophy, despite art's liberation, was implicated in the monstrous act. At dusk, philosophy limps too late to the scene of the smoldering remains.

Sartre also attributed art's impotence to its overwillingness to believe the philosophical story told about it. When philosophy proclaimed art to be "for its own sake," art took that proclamation as its own but insufficiently investigated the terms. With Jean Paulhan, Sartre described the outcome as a form of "terrorism": literature's "lofty isolation" and its "scornful rejection of all efficacy" led to "the destruction of literature by itself." Dissatisfied with the celebration of literature's impotence, Sartre sought new terms for literature in a "literature engagée." We have the chance, he proclaimed, to overcome the historical "tangle of vipers": "Today we are beyond terrorism and . . . can make use of its experience . . . to set down the essential traits of a concrete and liberated literature."[16]

Adorno assumed a position different from both Sartre and Danto. He sought in art's proclaimed impotence traces of art's survival. Survival lies neither with art's liberating itself from philosophy nor with art's overcoming its own purported uselessness. Rather, in its refusal to proclaim either liberation or potency, art shows its negative potential to survive, while showing a society so terrorized that art has no choice anymore but to withdraw into a silent and shadowy form. "Authentic [*eigentlichen*] expression," he surmised, "probably only exists as the expression of negativity, of suffering."[17] I return to Adorno's position below.

Given this background, I turn now to specific arguments of displacement in which a new tension emerges, a theological tension between Christian and Jewish attitudes toward commemorative art. So far, I have written in this book about philosophy, society, history, ideology, and art, but theology has made only a rare appearance. Here, however, it appears as the stone guest to question the success of any attempt by modern aesthetic theory to humanize or secularize its principles too thoroughly.

Displacement of Politics by Aesthetics

One kind of displacement occurs when artworks are created or interpreted under an umbrella of aesthetic or artistic purity that somehow shields them from politics, society, and crime. Consider the oft-quoted response Picasso gave to the German soldier who asked him of his painting *Guernica,* "Did you do that?" to which Picasso replied, "No, you did." The soldier desired that the political issue be displaced by the aesthetic one so that his question would be turned into a question of art, whereas, in refusing the displacement, Picasso turned the issue back to politics.

The desire for this sort of displacement is also evident in the 1951 documentary about the Berlin Philharmonic where the failure of Nazi politics is displaced by the claimed victory of the musical aesthetic. Here the desire is to displace not merely our attention from politics to art but our responsibility, too (Did you do that?) to conceal the reality of the crime. In this displacement, following Genet, the crime is derealized into art as it assumes the aura of beautiful appearance: the music displaces the ruins of the concert hall. This displacement has extended roots in an aesthetic ideology that conceals grievous forms of social injustice behind the appearance of totality and harmony— the great symphony that desires to be the *Gesamtkunstwerk*. The defensive Furtwängler made the point succinctly (from the play version of *Taking Sides*): "I let musical beauty cancel out the political pain."

In the film version of Adams's *Klinghoffer,* there is a scene in which a dance is choreographed between a Palestinian kidnapper who glides over the deck of the "terror ship" with Klinghoffer in his wheelchair. The fact that this dance cannot help but conjure up those perfect routines danced under Hollywood skies forces us to pay attention to the extreme violence of the scene, while also inclining us to cancel out the pain for the sake of the song. Why portray the heated quarrel between the two men in this choreographed way—for the dance is certainly Klinghoffer's dance of death? It is an ugly death, Edward Said rightly notes; also, he adds, "gratuitous."[18] That an artwork can transmute violence into eloquence is one motivation behind Benjamin's claim, adapted from his philosophy of history to his philosophy of art, that an artwork is also a document of barbarism, whereby, in late modernity, the more beautiful the artwork, the more concealed the barbarism.[19]

Temporal Displacement

Another argument of displacement turns on historical time, on the allegorical use of the past to decipher the present or of the present to decipher the past. The philosopher Richard Kuhns insightfully remarked to me in quite some irritation with Adams's work, that it is one thing to watch Tosca jump off the scaffolding, another to watch Klinghoffer thrown off the boat. What is the difference, I asked: Is it a matter of taste, of tact, of what audiences are able to take in the form of art when the artworks confront contemporary events? Apparently, the work offended the family. It was thought to be composed too soon after the event, to transform pain into commercial profit, to take not enough of a side, to be too evenhanded. However, it was also thought to play into a commercial tradition of American anti-Semitic stereotypes: so much for being evenhanded! Overall, the work was not well received in the United States.[20]

If one of the thoughts is that an audience sometimes needs protection from the artwork that strikes their emotions with too much immediacy, conversely, the artwork sometimes needs protection from the audience. There is an old Aristotelian fear that audiences will interrupt performances if they are not made sufficiently aware of the distinction between fiction and reality. Clear separation of performances from audiences protects the former by not letting the audience members acquire false beliefs about the actions they are witnessing. It allows them to gain some distance from their own ordinary emotional reactions. Distance is required if we are to treat something as art.

In "going to the movies," Cavell makes the point, too, noting that some of our experiences are simply so overwhelming that we can't respond to them as art: "They hit you . . . like a circus does, or like an overwhelming sports event, or an automobile accident." And "that's not a response that you could really attribute to something that's artful. Or is it? Can you make of that something that's ponderable, something that has a sublimation into intelligible, sharable, responses?" Cavell argues that thoughtful and intersubjective communication of the kind we associate with art *requires* an act of sublimation that distances us from the immediate impact of the event.

Both Benjamin and Adorno acknowledge this distance but then argue for a different, historical distance, when they note in relation to Goethe's *Elective Affinities* that it took more than a century to see the inherent tendencies of enlightenment come to term. Artworks produced later sometimes say more about the past than those produced contemporaneously, and those so produced often need the passing of time before they are understood. Hence, past works might come to tell us more about the present than present works do.

Their argument is more complex than the familiar argument regarding the widespread use of allegory and other such displacing techniques to present the historical present under the often safer and more concealing guise of the past. Many present works set their stories in the distant past or future to protect both work and author from the censorious constraints of the present.

So far, these claims only indirectly broach the issue of how art might suitably commemorate contemporary events that still hurt. The feeling sometimes is that *now* is just not the right time and *here* not the right place to substitute real emotions with art's unreal, fictional, and distanced emotions. It is the real emotions that are needed. Does this imply that an artwork should strive to overcome its distance and confront the event head on? Were it to do that, by claiming that it could somehow replicate the real emotions, this would likely be met with a negative reaction, too. The audience might find the conceit of such a work redundant. A work that tried somehow to substitute for the event it wanted to commemorate in the act of perfect replication might well get the response that the real event was already quite enough, thank you very much. One might read this argument as an extension to the domain of emotions of Danto's argument regarding the preservation of difference given the challenge of indiscernibility. Hence, too distant, too close: there is something inherently problematic in what commemorative art is both able and wants to do. Like Greek tragedies, commemorative works face a grave difficulty. To generate an adequate response, they must promote the illusion of reality, for without the feeling of reality we wouldn't be moved. Yet, given the painfulness of the reality implied by commemorative works, the works must maintain an appropriate distance.

Consider works or constructions that try to commemorate past events that still carry pain—for example, the recently built Jewish Museum in Berlin. When the museum was still empty, and exhibited itself only through its architectural form, visitors were informed by the guide (or at least I was) that the aim of the visitor's passage through the building was to encourage a game of make-believe. One was meant to imagine what it was really like to be transported on a train to a concentration camp and finally to be locked alone in an empty space. In a game of make-believe, something different is at stake and occupies our attention, however. In having our attention displaced, we become interested more in how close we can get to the experience than in the experience itself. To assess how close we can get is to show our interest in the techniques of art.

Yet, suppose the building or artwork could replicate the experience. Would we want this? We say not, but surely our moral stance is not always so robust to protect us from our violent fantasies and pleasures. Think of the recent production of "terror" or "horror" films, from *Schindler's List* to the recent German-American film *Rosenstrasse,* films that are not sold as such but are marketed, rather, as films of commemoration and survival that attempt to portray a real situation of terror. Too often, for the sake of art—if not also commercial success—the works end up rendering the situation so gripping that somehow, rather than feel disgusted, we actually find ourselves envious that we were not there. True love, true heroism: we only come to know our deepest selves in such difficult times. Human aspirations are intermingled with shock. This intermingling is fraught with danger, however, especially when our fascination, desire, and longing become inseparable from a condition of life we claim most to abhor. Still, the point is less the obvious one that we sometimes enjoy deeply—with sublimity—our own feelings of disgust (the displacing of pain by pleasure). It is not even that watching situations of extreme terror tests our humanity or moral well-being at a distance. The point is more that in situations of disgust we look hard inside them for their redemptory potential. The more the disgust, the harder we look—add then music, and we find what we are looking for all the more quickly!

The issue of distance and closeness is just as pertinent in cases where art is either metaphorically or literally taken out of the museum and put on the streets, into rallying spaces perhaps like that of Nuremberg. Given advances of technology, even an unexpected event may be recorded at the moment of its happening, so that there seems to be no discernible difference between the real event that occurs and the artwork that the event becomes as record.[21] It might be that artists no longer need to employ strategies of replication or copying to get close because they can simply proclaim the recording of the real event to be the artwork. That this is possible, however, does not render questions of displacement redundant. Commemorative artists still have to consider how their works will relate to the event or situation, where and when they will be seen, and what aesthetic and political significance they might have. The confusion generated by the reality of the situation and the new virtual reality of art, as we might describe it, renders questions of distance and closeness more pertinent, not less.

False Consolation

Still another argument of displacement combines elements of the previous two: in some works, pain is displaced by consolation and hope, though sometimes the consolation is false. Consider music in the concentration camps. Often we read of how music was used to remind the prisoners of their and even their guards' humanity. In his carefully titled book *Music of Another World*, Szymon Laks, a prisoner in Auschwitz who survived as the "Kapell-meister," recalled:

> When [a guard] listened to music, . . . he somehow became strangely similar to a human being. His voice lost its typical harshness, . . . and one could talk with him almost as one equal to another. . . . At such moments the hope stirred in us that maybe everything was not lost after all. Could people who love music to this extent . . . be at the same time capable of committing so many atrocities?[22]

For his defense, Furtwängler (in the play) expresses a similar thought: "Human beings are free wherever Wagner and Beethoven are played. Music transported them to regions where the torturers and murderers could do them no harm." However, to temper Laks's memory and Furtwängler's dramatic defense, one should remember that the transporting music of another world was in truth the transporting music of their world—the world that was a camp in which prisoner-musicians were ordered to transport others (even if only indirectly) to the ovens.[23] Maybe some in the camp really did believe that music would somehow console those stripped of their humanity now walking to their deaths. But was the music not also used to pacify the prisoners, to strip them of any impulse to revolt? These thoughts constitute the dynamic of a consolation that is offered yet proves most false when it depends on individuals being reminded of their humanity in situations where they're actually being treated, as in Ullmann's Atlantis, as the living dead, or where, to recall the fictional Furtwängler's words, it's too late for harm to count as harm. "The orchestra played brilliantly," wrote Genet. Still, it played regardless of who lived or died.

Perhaps the last idea misleads. For Laks, as also for Primo Levi, the fact that the orchestra played "brilliantly" was anything but the point. Apparently, the orchestra (or, better, the "camp band") did not play "brilliantly" and what it played hardly even deserved the name "music," as long as "music," like "orchestra," was serving as an honorific or humanizing term. Laks describes how rarely great music was actually played and how often sentimental arrangements of sentimental tunes were offered from all countries and of all styles. Levi's description conveys the brutality even more:

The tunes are few, a dozen, the same ones every day, morning and evening: marches and popular songs dear to every German. They lie engraved on our minds and will be the last thing in [the] Lager that we shall forget: they are the voice of the Lager, the perceptible expression of its geometrical madness, of the resolution of others to annihilate us first as men in order to kill us more slowly afterwards.[24]

The tunes—the music—the last thing that will be forgotten: this is an extraordinary statement.

Displacement of Guilt

Those who have thought about radical evil ask whether it is appropriate to seek the humane in extreme, inhumane situations; whether it is right to ask prisoners in a camp that they come through music to recognize something like the Christian spirit of universal suffering and thereby the humanity of all: "Love thy neighbor as thyself." The thought is unwieldy. In an early writing, "The Spirit of Christianity and Its Fate," Hegel argued that reconciliation is achieved through reunification, especially when facilitated by the recognition of yourself in the other, by the trespasser in the victim. In this recognition, "the pricks of conscience . . . become blunt, since the deed's evil spirit . . . [is] chased away; there is no longer anything hostile in the man, and the deed remains at most as a soulless carcass lying in the charnel-house of actualities, in memories."[25]

In a contrary argument, not resolved by reconciliation, Adorno remained focused on the crime committed and not on any rationalization that would clean the blood from the floor. He was deeply skeptical of what he called "the utopia of a beneficent generality."[26] He bleakly described how victims were made under these spiritualized rationalizations of universal identification to assume the guilt of the trespasser. Rather than the trespasser identifying with the victim, the victim was made to identify with the trespasser (like Genet's maids). He then described how, with extreme displacement, music's beautiful melody was used to distract people from its use as a terrorizing weapon to rid them of their humanity in the name of humanity's higher calling. The paradox was that even when these people were stripped of their humanity by others, they were expected to recognize the humanity in their persecutors and to come to recognize it through the purportedly shared experience of the universal and great beauty of German music. The pity was that people on both sides showed a willingness to accept the argument: victims and persecutors alike. Laks admonished those who remembered music in camps this way as "bombastic claptrap."[27]

Todorov considers whether sensitivity to music increases sensitivity to moral values: whether in the camps, music helped produce connections between harrowed human beings—"'I' am communicating with 'you,'"—thus perpetuating moral life. He asks (in Kantian terms) whether, if music did play such a role, it followed that one could justifiably instrumentalize prisoners for the sake of a moral-aesthetic end, to counter their totalitarian instrumentalization. Could a human life ever be judged dispensable for the sake of art? No, he answers, especially if the view that music sustained hope and dignity, or that it was a way of expressing one's humanity in the most extreme of circumstances, was made to imply that dying was less important than performing music to the best of one's ability. Even, he concluded, if we think that "the life of the mind is admirable," it does not justify "the creative individual's making instruments of those around him."[28]

Displacement of Aggression

Consider what is nowadays sometimes called "sonic terrorism," where extremely loud music, usually rock, is blared out from speakers to torture a group of people by depriving them of sleep. This was used by U.S. forces in Waco, Texas, and in Panama. I suspect the response usually is that if the violent treatment is justified, it should be called neither sonic torture nor terrorism, but if unjustified, then the terms apply. The use of these terms and means cannot escape moral or political assessment. Consider, next, a contrary case of censorship as antisonic terrorism, when the Taliban deprived their people of listening to music altogether. Now compare both these examples with the situation where music might offer an "hour of respite" (a phrase I return to momentarily) to separate people from the political violence that unremittingly surrounds them. In this case, music offers not a useless escape but a constructive opportunity for displacement where people, and especially young people, channel their aggressions and frustrations into the mediums of music and art. Many living on violent streets say that they would rather produce culture than war—which is exactly the sentiment encouraged by Daniel Barenboim and Edward Said in their project to bring young Israeli and Palestinian musicians together in Goethe's Weimar, and in the shadow of Buchenwald. Collabora-

tive music making, they hope against hope, will help lead to a greater toler-
ance of political and religious differences.[29]

Displacement of Individuals

In a play written in response to 9/11, New York author Ann Nelson tells of
how a dance one night provided an "hour of respite"—a "dream intermission
in the middle of . . . all this."[30] Her play *The Guys*, later made into a film, is
concerned less with the type of displacement that is about channeling human
aggression into art with the aim to transform the aggression and more with
how artists treat victims of terrorist action in the aesthetic context of commemoration. In mentioning Hegel's view of Christian reconciliation above,
I began to describe a tendency to use music to move away from the specificity of horror toward the theme of universal suffering. In my understanding, it is Nelson's purpose to expose the dangers of this universalizing gesture
and thereby to reverse the displacement by moving back from universality to
specificity, from group to individual. Her play insists that those who died as
a group must be remembered as individuals. When this reversal back from
group to individual is not effected, the artwork begins unwittingly to mirror
the terrorist act.

Adorno uses the term "Vergleichung" when difference and individuation
are displaced for the sake of universal sameness: the making of everything
and everyone the same. He writes of how violence, in false and reactionary
modes, can befall an individual the moment it appears as "the surmounting of
individualism," when atomization (the alienation of individuals) and leveling
(the loss of individuality) come jointly to characterize a society.[31] His point is
not about defending individualism per se but about retrieving the sense of an
individual's concrete experience through critique of the many dimensions of
its destruction under the violent conditions of modernity.

Consider Adams's *Klinghoffer*, which tends dangerously to universalize
by neutralizing differences and does this, paradoxically, by trying to be evenhanded, by not taking sides. Taking both the music and Alice Goodman's
libretto into account, the work confronts the conflict between different victimized groups. Likely modeled on Meyerbeer's *Les Hugenots*, in which the
opposing sides duel it out in competing choruses, *Klinghoffer* awards the same
amount of time, first, to the Palestinian people to tell their story of exile and
displacement, then, to the Jewish people to tell theirs. This equal award is un-
doubtedly meant to make us think that each side has its story and justification.

Fine, but does this mean that the particular killing on the *Achilla Lauro* is then justified by being weighed on the larger historical scale? Edward Said congratulates the work for at least having taken, in the sphere of art, the Palestinian's cause seriously.[32] Certainly, the violence of the "terrorists" is portrayed less as felt than as duty. We're not really criminals, they sing; we have to do what we're doing. In an interview accompanying the DVD recording, the work's creators do not tell us what or how we are meant to think about these issues. (Said remarks that he is sure that Adams is not trying to justify the violence of the act.) Adams reports that he is little concerned with solving local questions because his work is meant to move from the specific event to what he describes as the spiritual content of the situation: its universal or poetic message. But all he tells us about that message is that it touches on the deepest human experience. His statement arguably leaves the work in a state of bad ambiguity.

Perhaps this is unfair. Maybe Adams and Goodman try, as other artists try, to counter the threat of bad or inauthentic universalization by giving the work's title the character of singularity. Maybe, in other words, the work tells us more than its creators tell us. The title points us to the singular individual who was killed on the boat. Yet, though Klinghoffer's singularity stands out, Klinghoffer's wife sings at the work's end that it counted for nothing: only if one hundred people had been killed would the world listen. To what, however, was the world meant to listen: to the kidnappers or to the captives? Presumably the latter since she despises those who killed her husband: she spits (in the opening scene) in one of their faces. Is her thought that somehow her husband's death would have been prevented had more or others been killed? That's a complex thought. More likely, she is saying that a singular death of an ordinary individual carries insufficient weight in times of political negotiation. With these questions, the work displaces attention onto Klinghoffer's wife. Certainly, it ends up being more about her torment than about his: she must survive the horror of the act. But does this mean that the work also takes her side?

It is not clear and becomes even less clear when we are shown her fury with the Italian captain who recognizes the doubt and therefore also the humanity of one of the kidnappers, shaking his hand as he is led away by the police. What should we make of this apparent gesture of sympathy? Are we meant to side now equally with the kidnappers and the kidnapped under the description of Palestinians and Israelis or Arabs and Jews? Or just with the captain from whose diaries the libretto was written? After all, he is the only person in the film who looks straight into the camera's eye. Maybe this is the work's point—to make us catch his gaze alone, insofar as he is the neutral outsider caught up in a great historical conflict that is not his own.

But why catch his gaze? Not, I assume, so that we will take sides with any particular individual, but only so that we will recognize the plight of any individual who becomes involved in a historical conflict that belongs to no one in particular. Is this the universal message to which Adams referred: that we should move beyond the individual suffering toward a recognition of what all humans share? I think so: in an early scene in the work, the captors and captives alike watch a television documentary presumably to remind them (and us) that in some original condition before exile, perhaps before history, the Jews and Arabs were cousins. The conflict, I think we are being told, belongs only to the historical world of fallen humanity. Paradise or the original condition promises something different, a world in which we are all "one," or where at least there are no undesirable differences that divide us.

Compare Tippett's oratorio, whose title also points to a singular individual, this time to "A Child of Our Time," after Ödön von Horváth's novel of 1938. One source for this title is Berlioz's *L'Enfance du Christ;* another is found in Hegel's preface to his *Philosophy of Right*. In Tippett's work, the particular child of his time is a young Jewish boy, Herschel Grynspan, who assassinated an official at the German embassy in Paris, one Ernst von Rath, for which the Nazi's "terrible vengeance" was what they called *Kristallnacht*. Apparently the boy was angered—because his family was affected—by the Nazi command to repatriate all Jews with Polish passports back to Poland. When he shot the German official, he did not try to escape and was arrested and killed. Tippett's work does not remain with the child, however, but moves (as *Klinghoffer*) through historical generalization to spiritual universality, to neutralize differences or to find commonalities between several different kinds of victims. Musical and literary references were thus produced not only to the victims of Nazism but also to the Irish prisoners who died in the Easter Rebellion in 1916 (after Yeats's "A Terrible Beauty Is Born"), to the African Americans who long suffered slavery, and even possibly to the plight of homosexuals, given the rumor—though it was only a rumor at the time—that the young boy had been the German official's lover. In this way, the plight of the singular individual is transformed into that of any victimized individual: the victim-everyman, the "nameless hero." Written against bigotry, scapegoating, and the violent destruction of human life, Tippett said that he knew from "the first day that the work . . . had to be anonymous and general, . . . to reach down to the deeper levels of our common humanity."[33]

Tippett's work differs from Adams's work: whereas *Klinghoffer* treats the different sides of the conflict evenhandedly because the conflict is between different groups of "victims," Tippett's work puts the "victims" on the same side. Maybe Tippett's task is easier: he does not have to articulate the terms of forgiveness or understanding for the violent acts of one oppressed group against another. However, no less than Adams, and perhaps even more, Tippett moves to deeper levels of our common humanity by engaging in a remarkable act of aesthetic and musical blending. (Perhaps the German "Verblendung" is the better term, suggesting as it does synthesis and concealment, blindness, delusion, and even façade produced though reconciliation—a smiling through tears.) To surpass the specificity of the act or excuse that motivated "Kristallnacht," Tippett chooses spirituals, taken from the south of the United States, as Bach drew in his Passions on Lutheran chorales, to express the universal suffering of humanity. (Adams's music recalls the Passions, too.)

In Tippett's work, the chorus of the oppressed is made to sing a hymn to Jesus, which is problematic because at another level the chorus of humanity is also the chorus of Jews, for whom, according to Hebrew law, there is a ban on singing in praise of a God that is not their own. Tippett does not disguise the theological (Christian) terms with the more neutral-sounding terms of his own enlightened humanism, a humanism that led him to conscientious objection and imprisonment, as well as to universal brotherhood. Tippett said he wanted to capture something common among all folk and that he used a sort of "folk music" to convey this commonality, "our total humanity." Under these conditions, he said he moved the work dialectically through generality to particularity to universality: from the general state of oppression of our time, to the terrible consequences brought about by the act of a singular boy who sought justice through violence, to the universal expression of hope. Notwithstanding, at the end of the third part, in the final moment of reconciliation and synthesis, the chorus of Jews is made to sing a Negro-Christian spiritual called "Deep River" about a promised land—on behalf of all.

Killing Versus Destruction

To make explicit the emerging analogy between the artwork and violent act, another argument of displacement—the Great Cause argument—addresses the suffering and justification of exemplary individuals who commit crimes— perhaps terrorist crimes—in the name of universal justice.

In Camus's 1947 play *Les Justes* (*The Just Assassins*), Kaliayev, the poet revolutionary, declares that he kills not a person but despotism itself. In Dostoevsky's *Crime and Punishment,* Raskalnikov claims he murders not a woman, only a principle. Dostoevsky links the claim to the Great Man argument, according to which a great individual is justified, like the genius in art, in transgressing the law for the sake of a new Word, Idea, or Ideal. This argument has roots in Schiller and Hegel, specifically in Hegel's philosophy of history, where he writes that different states with large ambitions inevitably conflict. These ambitions are acted out by specific individuals who assume heroic stances. Taken to represent the necessary movement of history, they often act in ways lesser persons can neither understand nor endorse. This argument fits Hegel's earlier one, according to which individuals who break the law set up for themselves an alien power or standard (under Christian law) to elevate "into an absolute what is only a fragment of the whole of the human heart."[34]

Dostoevsky believes that the argument that one is justified in killing for the sake of a great or alien principle rests on some measure of self-deception. This is perhaps why his murderous action is attended at first by a sickness associated with reason more than with Christian guilt. This sickness associated with reason is then overcome when the "murderer" finds reconciliation and redemption in Christian love embodied in the figure of a woman. In the general argument, however, there is more than self-deception at work; there is also self-denial. Individual egoism is displaced by a literal self-aggrandizement such that the individual or lesser self relinquishes itself to a greater self that represents the state as a whole. This self-denial is different from what Hegel describes in his *Philosophy of Right* in terms of externalization or alienation (*Entäusserung*), according to which a self moves through stages of self-withdrawal in the face of external subjects and objects, to develop itself as an authentic and reflective subject. The self-denial of concern here is used, rather, in the rationalizations for great or heroic projects, where what these might well necessitate is destroying external objects or taking away another's life.

Nowadays at least (because there is a complicated history here, too), terrorism seems to be aimed less at the killing of individuals than at the destruction of groups or world orders. Stated this way, the point is to reveal the double character of the act. Although individuals (or groups thereof) are killed as innocent individuals to provoke the necessary feeling of horror so as to achieve the desired political reaction—hence, the more innocent the better—they are nonetheless deindividualized in the name of a great cause or principle. Many said (perhaps wrongly) about 9/11 that the action was symbolically intended to destroy the most powerful capitalist center of the Western world, the locus of concentrated capitalist labor, just as the bombing in Madrid was allegedly focused on the central railway station when most people were going to work. Given this sentiment, individuals were killed only to have their individual deaths then rationalized away in the name of symbolic destruction. The question is how different the destruction of urban spaces is, where people are used as symbolic capital, from the systematic destruction of entire races or political groups, say, in Nazi Germany, to the extent that both are premised on deindividualizing individuals to render them token representatives of their groups. The argument usually also implies that killing innocent people is more effective than killing soldiers because the latter willingly suspend their individual identities to fight for their country. When they return home, they do so as body bags and number tags.

Andreas Huyssen has recently argued for a difference between the bureaucratic terrorism of Nazism and our contemporary situation on the grounds that what we are now experiencing is a condition within late modernity of an appropriation of state power by religious fundamentalists:

> This is not the banality of evil Hannah Arendt once analyzed as key to the bureaucratic mindset of Adolf Eichmann. It is rather the banality of a religious zealotry, which has caused so much suffering and destruction over the centuries whenever it has allied itself successfully with state power. . . . Politicized religious zealotry, . . . [of any] religion, is not the other of modernity, but its very product.[35]

If Huyssen is right, then the description of the symbolic capital of the recent terrorist attacks is couched less well in terms of capitalism or bureaucratic administration and better in terms of what one might call the terroristic condition of modernity, where what we witness at the core of contemporary experience is the willing relinquishment or metaphysical death of the individual subject to serve the state-supported enterprise of religion and apocalypse. Here, my own argument aims neither to explain contemporary terrorism nor to equate terrorism with state power, although it recognizes, with Huyssen, that deep alliances have been made. Nor do I claim that all political acts of violence are unjustified. I aim only to demonstrate the emerging analogy between the terrorist act and the artwork, where both displace individuals (intentionally or not) in the name of great causes, zealous aims, or universal messages. And as such, the important difference to which Huyssen points is subordinated to a similarity that still pertains.

Hence, consider three very different cases of deindividualization, where, however, though we speak about how victims of terrorist acts are treated, we run the danger of producing an analogous facelessness by generalizing over "the terrorists" to assume that they, like "the victims," are all alike. In the documentary film made about the filming of *Klinghoffer*, we are told that suicide bombers relinquish their lives in a proxy funeral (when a white shawl is placed on their shoulders), so that they are already effectively dead before they take the lives of others. Their proxy death, rationalized by a "great cause" argument, makes it possible for them to take, without permission, the lives of others.

The second case regards the notorious training of SS guards that concentrated on teaching them how to strip their prisoners of their individuality, names, and humanity to make their killing psychologically possible and bureaucratically desirable. Under the condition of false universality, they destroyed numbers, types, or groups but not individuals—a calculated coldness of fact recorded but then transmuted into the deepest sorrow at the Berlin memorial at Grunewald train station, formerly a station for deportation.

The third case regards the allied bombing of cities such as Dresden where the deliberate punishing or arguably gratuitous destruction of a city of such cultural pride—but without, some maintain, real military or political significance—displaced the responsibility for killing the citizens who lived there. Yet perhaps (albeit inadvertently) it was the cultural pride that was meant to be destroyed, given the crucial role it had played in Nazi ideology. Or, perhaps, the killing of citizens as a displaced way of destroying the leadership was meant precisely to bring home to those who survived the bombing the difference between citizens and leaders in an absolutist state that had thrived on their identification.

In these three cases, the contrast between *destruction* and *killing* is paramount, where killing individuals is subordinated to the greater logic of destruction. Before his premature death, W. G. Sebald wrote in his *Natural History of Destruction* about this pattern: of how the terms of killing became naturalized and congealed by the greater logic of destruction. He sought to denaturalize the terms. Implicit in these cases is also the thought that it is not bad but good people who kill—people with conscience—who convince themselves that killing others is possible under the disinterested and unprejudiced conditions of a cause.

Approaching a similar conclusion by different means, Borges, in an extraordinary short story titled "Deutsches Requiem," describes the reflections of a camp guard, regarding the torture he inflicted on a Jewish poet. The torture consisted in dehumanizing the man by using the poet's own humanist and culture ideals against him. Stealing the poet's ideals to make them serve the guard's own cause, the guard deprived the poet of all he had left, leaving him no choice (which really was no choice) other than to take his own life. As the war ends, the guard awaits his punishment. Continuing to identify the ideals of Goethe and Schopenhauer so neatly with those of Nazism, he goes willingly to his death, in full self-regard. If he goes to hell, it will be only as flesh: "I look at my face in the mirror in order to know who I am, in order to know how I shall comport myself within a few hours, when I face the end. My flesh may feel fear; I *myself* do not."[36]

What the guard says, Genet's Solange could almost have said, though she is less secure in both reason and feeling. As she approaches her end, she says she recognizes herself to be a criminal and to feel the pull of the hangman. But then she identifies herself with the other side, the police, as "the only ones who understand" her, because "they too belong to the world of outcasts." Having displaced herself, she declares herself not to be a maid at all because she has "a noble soul," though she simultaneously demands recognition for the work she did for Madame: "No, no she must not forget my devotion." Ultimately, her justification for murder lies in bringing her nobility as an outsider and her devotion as a maid into a relation approximating the master-slave dialectic. I described above how Genet, in Sartre's reading, derealized life through the means of artifice and theatricality and how life was differently derealized in Atlantis through the means of technology. To this, I add now another and perhaps the most harrowing form of derealization—that established by internal conviction, when the subject transforms without remainder what is subjective into something entirely objective. Whereas the guard succeeded in this act, Solange did not.

Belittlement

It is no historical or ideological accident that the Great Man or Great Cause argument is tied by its enlightenment or humanist motivation to the Genius or Great Artist argument. Here the artist is linked to the criminal, though more via sadistic or de Sadean transgression than via Kantian disinterest. One of the basic ideas in this argument of displacement is that if a society is sick, an individual may break its laws. However, whereas we tend to approve transgression in art as partly defining what makes art great, we are less comfortable when the transgression passes over to "great men of action." Not that we disapprove of heroism or great acts per se, only when a certain rationale is used to justify a real and consequent crime of which we as lesser or ordinary people disapprove.

Bertolt Brecht cracked the Great Man argument when in *The Resistable Rise of Arturo Ui* he reduced the great men of fascism and capitalism to the low life, petty bourgeois criminals of a sick, cabbage-covered society. He aimed to show that the gangster mentality of modern times belonged more to society than to its individuals, to its insiders more than to its outsiders, to its regular and not to its self-proclaimed extraordinary actors. How could this be a critique of the Great Man argument if it focused on society's most base and banal criminality? Exactly by refusing to displace the responsibility for the crime onto the individuals themselves and therewith removing the pride with which the worst great men act in the name of all. In this play, through artistic techniques of distance and displacement, Brecht displayed the untruth of the social displacement with the hope of effecting a reversal of its historical dynamic.

In Istvan Szabo's *Taking Sides,* a primary theme is the reduction by an ordinary American military officer of the extraordinary Furtwängler. "Let's just say I am a democrat. With a small 'd'," proclaims the officer; "I have more sympathy with the little people." The conductor tells the officer that he acted for the ideals of art alone, to preserve the "genius of great music." The officer responds that he acted more from "ordinary, everyday" reasons—in fact, from a petty jealousy of the younger conductor (Karajan), whose name he couldn't even utter. Furtwängler called that conductor "little K," where his own act of "belittling" was meant to confirm his own status as "the great-est conductor in the world." "As a musician," Furtwängler explains, "I was more than a citizen." The American officer has already decided that no one has special privileges: musicians, morticians—"they're all the same." He tells Furtwängler, with all the belittling terms he can muster, that he was used as "a pawn" by the Nazis: "When the devil died" they wanted their "band leader" (with all the militaristic connotations implied) to conduct his funeral march. (In my view, the grandiose reference to "the devil" ought also to have been belittled.)

At the end of the play that inspired the film, the officer is asked how he would have acted in such a situation, raising the issue of identification and empathy. The film leaves this ending out, to leave us asking whether the Great Man argument still holds, despite this conductor's "political" failure to live up to his own artistic greatness, or whether it collapses the moment it is confronted by images of corpses. "Have you ever smelt burning flesh?," the

American officer screams at the conductor, with almost the same volume that we are made to listen to Furtwängler's Beethoven and Bruckner. If the killing of individuals is the bottom line in moral assessment, it is used in this film to judge not only the political dictator but also the musical one. The officer asks: Wasn't your ability to fix the gaze of your orchestra players the same as Hitler's ability to fix the gaze of the German people? Is this really what you're putting onto the scales, your music against burning flesh?

The same gaze perhaps, yet different consequences follow. It is sometimes said that, even if art comes to look like politics, only the acts of the latter are consequential, because acts of art, like Furtwängler's gaze, have no victims. Still, it does not follow from this that music or art thereby contains no violence.

Sublimation

Consider an Adornian argument developed by Tom Huhn regarding an artwork's construction.[37] Traditionally, it is maintained that form liberates material by releasing its potential. In the Adornian argument, however, the form is seen to dominate material in a way that "rehearses" social domination. Yet precisely because we are dealing with an aesthetic "rehearsal," we tend to think that nothing is at stake and so ignore the analogy to the social. Calling on Kant's remarks on the dynamically sublime, Huhn shows (in terms that also recall my chapter 3) that through art we sublimate, pacify, or discipline what we experience as foreign and fearful into something tamed and familiar—and nature most of all. What causes us fear we turn into a positive pleasure by making it fit the comfort zones of a domesticated society. The more the pleasure, the more nostalgic our attitude becomes toward nature's violence. What sublimity in experience once was is itself forcefully sublimated.

To ask whether there is anything really at stake in art's sublimation of its violence might be just to accept the thesis of art's impotence, which is what we most want to accept when we most fear its power. In philosophy and politics, as in ordinary acts of human life, we render beautiful or impotent what we fear most. Art's impotent beauty, however, cannot be blamed on philosophy or politics alone. Art, too, must be held to account. For, all by itself, it shows both the form and the fact of the matter: hence, *how*, by artistic means, we disenfranchise what we fear and that we *actually do* disenfranchise what we fear, typically in the name of higher, enlightenment ideals.

Not to accept the violence of art is, accordingly, one disenfranchising strategy we adopt to remain oblivious to the violence of the domination performed in the world. Artworks stage the real violence of the world through their own internal formal structures of domination. Combining this argument with that about displacing individuals in the name of universality, this conclusion now seems right: that false universality is a central form of the enlightenment dialectic of domination and administration sometimes rehearsed—second time around in commemorative contexts—as heroic farce.

Art and Its Acts

The final argument of displacement asks what kind of art is most appropriate to mourn or memorialize those who have suffered by violent acts. It is offered by Adorno and commits itself to the Jewish law of the *Bilderverbot* for the sake of developing the negative dialectic. To avoid endorsing any sort of displacement that might erase the difference between work and act, Adorno recommends an art of silence. By withdrawing from speech, communication, and the completeness associated with the work concept, the residual art of the fragment takes the side of those who suffer. Adorno seeks an art that resists rather than repeats the acts of a society that displaces its guilt for the sake of its survival onto the shoulders of those it destroys. But what does an artwork that takes the side of suffering look like? One answer is that it does not look like anything—because it refuses to look.

Adorno notes that when artists confront horrifying events as the subject matter of their art, they usually expect to make afterimages (*Nachbilder*) of those events.[38] This is not an easy task, however. Often the afterimages feel too distant from the original event and may even promote some sort of perverse pleasure. Distance and pleasure are the dangerous consequences of images that are experienced more as ends than as means. Part of the power of images is and has always been to make us forget that images are just that: namely, images.

Adorno is most attentive to this argument when thinking about Schoenberg's *Moses und Aron*. This is no surprise. After all, this opera (or antiopera) has as its subject matter the craving for false comforts provided by Aron's easy images and fast, sophistic words. Adorno does not deal with the biblical theme directly. He asks, instead, whether in an age profaned by Auschwitz, one should even try to present a sacred work such as the offerings and passions of Bach. He provides a negative answer, not to dismiss the sacred promise of these earlier offerings but to suggest that contemporary works would be more truthful were they to show how at odds a sacred oratorio or even a biblical opera is with the secular acts of our times. He does not consider whether Bach's works were suitable for Bach's own times, but he is convinced they are not for his own time. An art that does not try to be a sacred work is more truthful under present conditions than a commemorative art that produces sacred afterimages as if to suggest that all is right with the world. When Schoenberg's Moses cries, "O word, O word that I lack," Adorno hears an admission of the failure for this work to achieve what might have been possible under different conditions. This means that this work takes most seriously the social or historical conditions in which it is produced—by not taking the sacred in vain.

In an article pertinently titled "'Not These Sounds,'" James Schmidt considers the use in 2000 of Beethoven's Ninth to commemorate the victims of the Mauthausen camp. He surveys the many arguments for and against using this work as a work of commemoration. Some argued that this was just the way to "take back" this work, restoring it to its "original" meaning, cleansing it thereby of any Nazi association. Others worried about the restoration because they thought either that the history could not and should not be erased or that the humanist ideal of universal brotherhood for which the work once stood had been established from the very start through exclusion. Others more simply worried about singing an ode to joy in so somber a commemorative occasion, whereas others saw no harm in expressing hope for a better future.

Schmidt reminds his readers that Wagner once described the fanfare that opens the final movement of Beethoven's Ninth as the "terror fanfare" and, then, that it was later quoted by Tippett in his commemorative Third Symphony. What Schmidt does not add, though he could have, is Adorno's warning to composers not to quote. Of course, in nearly all works, commemorative or not, musical quotation plays a significant role and admirably so, as, for example, in Ullmann's work. Surely Adorno does not intend to disparage the extensive knowledge of music that composers held in memory when in the camps. Nor is Adorno blind to Benjamin's extensive and sometimes even exclusive use of quotation. His warning, therefore, must be differently motivated, as, in fact, it is.

His argument against quotation has two prongs. First, he describes the danger implicit to any art that capitulates through quotation to a form of communication. The danger would be to assume that a quoted and thus presumably well-known image or word could capture the horror of the act or the torment and suffering it caused. In this situation, no image or word can do justice to that which it attempts to refer.[39] Second, he warns against calling up well-known images or words for fear that the artwork, and by extension the act, will turn an alienated experience into one that puts recognition and familiarity at its center. In an argument more against technology than against commemorative art (an argument to which I return in chapter 7), Adorno describes the severe reduction of experience when musical works or plays are repeatedly broadcast. He recalls an elderly woman who, having just heard *Hamlet*, remarks on how the play seems to her to consist entirely of quotations.[40] She has heard it all before—or so she believes. Adorno wants commemorative art to avoid eliciting such a response. When images of terroristic acts are attended by the feeling that they are already known, digested, and understood, this leads too quickly to the same feeling about the acts themselves.

Adorno wants to keep the shock of the image and event in place and thus, by extension, its inexplicability and indigestibility. He recognizes the difficulty of doing so. Why should commemorative art be any different from other art or any more able to resist eliciting normalized responses as it is increasingly subjected to domesticating structures of repetition? Focusing on quotation, Adorno shows what is at stake when any art becomes by easy association or repetition an art of pacification, reconciliation, and acceptance. This, interestingly, is an argument about quotation considered from the perspective more of form than of content, as, in fact, is his argument regarding commemorative art overall. For here, too, it is only through form that his preferred negative terms of noncommunication, loneliness, silence, withdrawal, and refusal attain meaning. The silence or lonely speech of Schoenberg's music, he thus writes without any paradox at all, *speaks more* about suffering and the social condition than does any explicitly communicative discourse.[41]

Schmidt mentions one critic's opinion that, in commemorating the prisoners of concentration camps, there was only one work "worthy of being played" and that was Ullmann's *Kaiser*. Why the critic chose this work is not hard to imagine. Yet Schmidt correctly dismisses the idea that there could be only one appropriate work. With Adorno, but even more with Thomas Mann, he argues for the more general appropriateness of works of lamentation or mourning: a music of tears, like that, he notes, described at the end of *Doktor Faustus*, where the failures of modernity are left raw, unabated, and undisplaced. However, all these thinkers remain aware that even a music of tears might fall into sentimentality, into kitsch, or even into displacing gestures of universal messaging. The harder it resists, the more likely it falls, which leads one to wonder whether a music of tears wouldn't better be conceived as a music about the contemporary impossibility of tears, about tears that cannot and, artistically speaking, should not be shed.

Adorno offers no safe formula for what a work of mourning should be. He only describes examples of what a noncompromised music might be. Concluding his obituary essay on Schoenberg, he considers productions of the later life that, failing to be works, showed "paradigms of a possible music" instead. In diminishment, withdrawal, or brevity, the works, in refusing to be works, approached the character of "the *fragment.*" Recalling Benjamin's thought, written in his essay on Goethe's *Elective Affinities,* Adorno writes that, splintered, the works moved, like Ottilie, toward "shriveled diction," and, by lasting six minutes, *A Survivor from Warsaw* outweighed the production of any lengthy oratorio or biblical opera.[42]

In Schoenberg's late nonwork works, Adorno finds an expressive core or anxiety that identifies itself with persons terrorized by an "agony of death" as administered by the terms of "total domination." The music belonging to these persons expresses the impotence to which they feel now fated, the terror that has been inflicted on humanity as a whole. Of *A Survivor,* he writes, "never has horror rung so true in music." In recollecting horror, the music regains its power through negation. Its final song, "Sh'ma Yisroel," is a musical expression of humanity's protest against myth.[43]

In speaking about humanity, Adorno gestures not toward a universalizing or reconciling sentiment but toward a contradiction, the sort he finds expressed in Schoenberg's *Survivor* the moment the chanting of the prayer counters the terrifying music that precedes it. By analogy, one might consider whether the prisoners in the camps ever sang the prayers, if ever they "sang" at all, to drown or block out what Laks termed the "sirenic music" that was sometimes played around them. This is a case where one music is used against another—offering a true consolation to oppose a false one—if, once more, we choose, as I think we should, to speak of music in the camps in terms of music at all.

Schoenberg's *Survivor* does not remain immune to Adorno's criticism. In this piece, he says he finds something embarrassing, for even if it refuses to repress the memory of what many postwar Germans tried to repress, as a work of art it cannot help but contribute to appeasing their shame. However violent the images and sounds, its violence is displaced by a sublimating pleasure: the image "of the sheer physical pain of people beaten to the ground by rifle-butts contains, however remotely, the power to produce enjoyment."[44]

If even the most resistant artworks cannot surpass their status as art, likewise, they cannot surpass the material, social, or historical conditions of their production. Even if the most resistant artworks produced as afterimages (*Nachbilder*) are like the survivors who live in their afterlives (*Nachleben*) with their suffering, Moses's words (in the opera) remind us that even the most withdrawn expression cannot withdraw completely from a world made up of words and works. No genuine art can thus overcome its contradictory character: that as form it strives to sublimate its material, or that as a work it strives to reconcile its internal oppositions, or that, finally, in wanting to withdraw into silence or speechlessness, an artwork only effectively withdraws by speaking.

Adorno argues finally against any commemorative work that would attempt to offer a utopian image of another world. Instead, he recommends works that resist in this world the gun that is so repeatedly "put to our heads." In a late essay written to move beyond the Sartrean and Brechtian commitment to engaged art, he maintains that an art that is properly responsive to its times is not one that produces images and messages about the times but one that remains true to art in its present condition. "What is demanded by our time is not [therefore] political art," he argues, but a genuinely autonomous art and precisely the art that others falsely reject on the grounds of its purported impotence. Just like politics, Adorno explains, art has had to migrate into an exiled space, which means that, just like politics, art is *most political* under contemporary conditions when it resists overt content or messaging. Yet, what an exiled art or politics must avoid is the sort of idealized speech that also tends to become quotable and thus quoted back (as the camp guard quoted back the poet's ideals), having been appropriated by the society it opposes. Only works, Adorno concludes, that *appear* as "politically dead," because they commit themselves to genuinely autonomous form, have a chance of being "uncompromisingly radical."

In this view, though now in my terms, an art of mourning does not require artists to decide about how best to portray the horror of a specific act, because this would be to think about the art in terms of its copying or representing the world as it *appears*. Rather, the demand is for an art that, in its formal or expressive capacity as art, reveals something about the concealed violence of a society that allows explicitly violent acts to be performed without objection in its name. To displace our attention from *representation* to *expression* is one way how not to take "the name" in vain. This is also my theme in chapter 7.

If there is a residual theological dimension of this withdrawn art of commemoration, it becomes evident the moment Adorno likens music to demythologized prayer. Such music frees itself from the magic of making anything happen in a world in which everything or anything is now claimed to be possible. Just as the humanist ideal of universal brotherhood thrived by exclusion, so the principle that everything is possible thrives paradoxically by eliminating, first, the possible in favor of the actual and, second, the different in favor of the same. Adorno's argument is against the reduction of art to object and the identification of art with a social act. By preserving a difference in both cases, he is not led back to a Christian view of art as embodiment in which shame is mitigated by claims of universal suffering but sideward to a view of art in which the *Bilderverbot* is evoked whenever spectators forget that images necessarily distort.

An artworld in which anything goes is one that admits any image, perhaps because it is believed that images are all we now have. However, it is not just that discrimination and judgment seem to be lost in an artworld in which anything goes. The problem is much more that when no image is forbidden or excluded, it is because no act is forbidden in the world. *The Bilderverbot is about forbidding images if it is also about forbidding acts.* This is the final displacement in my own argument. Many philosophers speak about art and its objects, but far fewer about art and its acts. Given the latter, an artwork resists a social act only by refusing to mirror that for which the act stands. In this resistance, the artwork becomes antirepresentational both artistically and politically, and art begins to serve a politics of displaced representation by raising anew the question on behalf of whom an artwork now speaks.

In general, an aesthetics of displacement, worked out under the condition of the negative dialectic, is intended to preserve art's quieter violence as a form of political resistance against a politics whose violence would seek to rid the world of resistance altogether. This is what is most at stake for Adorno in thinking about how art confronts catastrophe. In his view, far too many works try to clean the blood from the floor, to displace the blood by aesthetic transcendence: the *sol* by the *ange* of Solange. These are works that fail to protest humanity's catastrophe, however loudly the words of protest are uttered. Adorno refuses this sort of protest; what he recommends in its place is a double-edged sword. For, at every moment when he describes the conditions of an art of mourning, he also asks whether art after Auschwitz or, indeed, art after any act of human violence is possible at all. This, in his view, is a profound contradiction that cannot and should not be resolved, for only as unresolved does it leave us with possibility—the gap, the space, and the almost as I have been describing it—in which contemporary art and acts go on in production and performance.

Nevertheless, in interpreting the *Bilderverbot* to accord with a resistant art, doesn't Adorno end up as much theologically placed as those who seek in the universalizing gestures of art a correlate to Christian eschatology? He does, for whether one takes the side of lonely individuals or humanity as a whole, a side is still taken and a side he takes. Yet, as we should now expect, he criticizes the dangers of the side even as he takes it, which is different, at least, from those who either commit themselves too blindly to a side or claim to take no side at all. In the negative dialectic, there is no way to leap out of the circle of judgment.

In this chapter, I have shown that the difficult issues of commemorative art turn less on the production of a special class of artworks and more on the question of what it means for any artwork to take a side genuinely different from that taken by undesirable acts performed in the world. Commemorative art is only about taking sides if to what this leads is a deep assessment of how art places itself and is placed in the world. This conclusion, alone, recommends a displacement of some of our most cherished philosophical beliefs about art, on the one hand, and life, on the other.

7 Film as Visual Music
Duplication, Dissonance, and Displacement

In Paris 1934, displaced by exile, Joseph Roth produced a piece of cultural criticism titled *Der Antichrist*. One of its eighteen parts was a criticism of Hollywood, interpreted as the productive industry of modern inhumanity.[1] Written two years before Benjamin's seminal essay on art and technological reproducibility, Roth's piece testified to the cultural, economic, and social pessimism heard so often in those times regarding modern technology put to advanced capitalistic or totalitarian use.

His criticism opened with a quotation from a Swiss Catholic theologian, Max Picard, a metaphysical theorist who wrote about silence as signifying not the absence of noise but the loss of the world's meaning. Roth quoted a passage from Picard's 1929 text *Das Menschengesicht* (*The Human Face*) about the sameness and difference once given by God to humanity as a gift: "That they were all different from each other was a sign of the inexhaustibility of God's abundance. At the same time, they were all similar insofar as one knew that the diversity stemmed from a single creative source."[2]

God's gift, allegedly, was no longer evident. Roth illustrated the loss by describing, first, what results when people communicate at great distances on the "technical wonder" of the telephone. What loss of understanding occurs when closeness is replaced by distance? Can we hear the "malice, falsity, or betrayal" in a voice when we do not see the face? Isn't it easier to lie when we do not see the other's eyes? Similarly, what results when we see shadows on a film screen that seem to move, to speak, or to sing? The film lies because reality lies, transferring meaning from the world to the screen and back again, until audiences are fully deceived into thinking that what they see on the screen is more real than life itself. It isn't difficult to copy reality if reality is devoid of meaning. Film goes wrong because there is something wrong with reality, especially when "reality" refers to the inhumanity that now makes it up.

Living people who become actors live without meaning. In becoming shadowy, they give their residual reality to the screen characters they play so that the characters now seem more real than they. Roth recalled meeting actors whose faces and bodies he recognized from films, and though he knew that persons were the creators of their screen images, he felt he addressed only their images. The more existence the images assume, the less life the persons have, until they have none at all. Persons become the doubles of their own doubles they project daily onto the screen. In one moment, the most fleeting of all fleeting things of our early existence is transformed into something quite real.

Though to be the double of a former self is already a terrible thing, the situation only worsens when a person dies, because only the filmic shadow now exists—and for eternity. The shadow, Roth explained, can't die because it's never lived. Having achieved the triumph of eternal existence, it becomes an honorary personage of Hollywood. Roth concluded that Hollywood provides what Hades once provided: a dwelling place for disembodied idols existing between life and death. But the implication of his critique went further. Embodied spirits in the world have gradually been displaced by ghosts in the Hollywood machine, or the artificial world that is Hollywood is what the real world has become. What once was double is now only one.

The Focus

In this chapter, I develop Roth's theme of the double to reorganize the aesthetic and philosophical arguments offered in the late 1920s (and after) regarding the role of music in film. That decade marked the moment when it was technologically possible to include music or sound more generally as an essential component of a film in the process of its being made. Before then, music had an external status of mere accompaniment, so it was said, contributing to a film's meaning after the fact. Two contrary claims followed the change: first, while music was technologically an accompaniment, film was prevented from becoming the total (operatic) artwork it sometimes aspired to be, but, second, film was perfectly satisfied having already become the kind of art it wanted to be—with or without music.

Early arguments about film music had as much to do with film conceived as a moving, visual art as with traditional concerns of musical aesthetics asking after music's expressive or representational meaning. The two concerns met when film was regarded as having inherited questions formerly raised by opera pertaining to the status of the work and to the metaphysical, aesthetic, and social function of music within it. Yet they also met when film was taken to have inherited questions belonging to the visual arts, theater, narrative art, and pantomime. Along whichever path of inheritance, the concepts explored in chapters 1 and 2, of *movement* and *musicality,* assumed a leading place. The concepts gave sense to two questions pertinent to film's early history. First, what role did music have in an art that was already, in virtue of the moving camera, claimed to be sufficiently musical? Second, what role had music in an art that was promising, challenging, or threatening the most advanced totalitarian identification of life with art? These two questions preoccupy me in the first half of this chapter.

In the second half, I consider three specific arguments of *doubling:* arguments of *duplication, dissonance,* and *displacement.* I favor the last. Though most arguments about film music have already been recorded in the extensive literature, they have not usually been scrutinized by referring to the modernist unease to which Roth gave expression: that, given the new technological medium of film, it wasn't possible to sustain the distinction between art and life that traditionally sustained bourgeois art. In this modernist critique, the technological production of doubles became a story about the loss of the double.

So stated, it looks as though unease toward modern technology always led to technology's condemnation, but it doesn't have to. Sometimes it was turned into optimistic expressions of what might yet be for film and for humanity. In general, that arguments about film music exhibit the tension between pessimism and optimism asks neither that this tension be resolved nor that the arguments be severed from the original modernist context of cultural criticism. However, they do ask to be carefully considered for what they tell us about the art of film when music was first able to make its entry.

All That Is Solid

Nowadays, to think about film in relation to ghosts in the machine is not original if all one claims is that film, once regarded as the most advanced art of technology, testifies to a significant loss of spirit or meaning. It is just as unoriginal to recall the early fear that spectators allegedly once felt watching ghostlike figures uncannily suspended on the screen between life and death. Although I draw on both these ideas, I focus more on the association of ghosts and shadows with a world that was seen as transitory, fleeting, even melting. When Marx and Engels proclaimed, "All that is solid melts into air," they were thinking not about film but about a profane or unholy life being lived out in its last moments by a bourgeoisie in a world of almost entirely petrified relations.

In her recent inquiry into the strange history of waxworks, Michelle Bloom links the production of wax figures to the Pygmalion myth. She shows how the unnerving transformation of figures of art into figures of life corroborated a view of the world as essentially malleable. Many traditional dichotomies, between the real and unreal, changeable and permanent, stable and unstable, substantial and fluid, even male and female, were dissolved by the emergence of a semidark Calligarian world of wax figures. Bloom notes an analogy with film and quotes Erwin Panofsky: "The appeal of the waxworks to the film-maker [was] enormous, how to breathe life into the inanimate."[3]

Consider the telephone or any early technology for the ear—the microphone, loudspeaker, or radio. Regarded as lifeless machines, they demanded that life be breathed into them, literally, through the human voice. Yet there was the suspicion that the human voice, rather than bringing the machine to life, would only meet it halfway. The voice would thus be reproduced merely as echo. In the murky space of modern echoes, more distinctions dissolved. What once was far, not heard, or unreachable was brought close—but only deceptively close for those, like Roth, who were most critical. In this context, Bloom refers to another early myth: "Only her voice and her bones were left, till finally her voice alone remained."[4] But perhaps we should say that not even her voice was left, to recall Ottilie, Mélisande, or so many other vocally withdrawn figures of modernity.

As I said, though many worried about the general dissolution, not everyone did. To quote Marx and Engels is also to suggest something liberating. However, to connect the melting of all that is solid to the idea of wax figures underemphasizes something crucial about what their famous phrase means. The translated phrase offers almost a mixed metaphor, when something *melts* into *air.* The origin of the translated phrase is found in Shakespeare's *Tempest,* though Marx and Engels's German suggests neither the English term "melting" nor even Schlegel's Shakespeare translation "aufgelöst in Luft." With their own German terms, the phrase suggests evaporation: "Alles Ständische und Stehende verdampft [everything settled (or socially stratified) and unmoving (even petrified) evaporates]."

Whereas the melting of wax suggests a loss of form, leaving a thick puddle or fondue on the ground, it does not suggest an entire transformation of material conditions—which is what Marx and Engels do suggest by almost conjuring up the fleeting and combustible, industrial passage of a steam engine. Following their philosophy of history, their phrase suggests a picture in which one form of life gives way to another. It refers to a world in which all distinctions are being transformed, a world fast receding into the past, having become old by its own internal momentum. The *Communist Manifesto* (from which the phrase comes) accordingly begins with the ghost (*Gespenst*) of communism moving across (*geht um*) Europe, yet the movement is dialectical. A ghost of the future moves through space and time, though it has *not yet* acquired living form. Still, as unmaterialized, it moves with the potential to transform the bourgeois world into a ghost of the past. In their dialectical image is the promise of progress.

What Bloom describes in terms of *dissolution* I describe (following chapter 6) in terms of *displacement.* Instead of speaking of distinctions dissolved, I speak of the fragile continuation of their opposing terms. Displacement retains the possibility of fluid, even if fraught, transitions of meaning. Where these transitions occur, confusions also sometimes occur, especially in those transitions leading to the belief that between once different things no differences remain. A social and cultural theory of displacement acknowledges the fear in modernity that all distinctions have been dissolved, yet it does not simply give in to the fear.

In film's early years, it was often suggested that how the camera eye relates to a cinematographic world matches how the body's eye relates to the everyday world. Consider Walter Serner's statement from 1913: "[Cinema] gives the eye what is the eye's and acts thanks to the eye; what the eye sees is no deception, and the greatest disillusion becomes for it the greatest illusion. Picture for picture in a true-to-life succession of movement: this is no state and no picture, this is life."[5] Is such an identity claim really so different from those made later by artists of the 1960s? Recalling chapter 3, aren't differences maintained and rendered all the more explicit the more forcefully such identity claims are made? And aren't celebrations of identity really only recognitions that life is now only *like* art because both have liberated themselves from petrified conceptions of their bourgeois autonomy? For some, of course, celebrations of likeness are always in order; for others more circumspect, the glasses are only ever half raised in the hope that petrified relations of sameness are not in truth as petrified under late bourgeois conditions as they seem.

To develop a theory of displacement is not to ally oneself with critics like Roth who, having described the dissolution of the distinction between film shadows and human souls, see only decline. Nor does it imply immediate allegiance with those who see in dissolution only a progressive revolutionary outcome. Displacement aligns itself to the philosophical ambition of a critical theory that demands that a means of deception be used indirectly to convey social and philosophical truth and not to produce more social deception. An early filmmaker once remarked that film's radical aim is to demystify its technique to demystify life. This is an exemplary statement of displacement, especially if "demystify" is accompanied by the term "demythify." Doing one thing (demythifying film) for the sake of doing or showing a different thing (demythifying life) does not submit to the pessimistic thought that there is nothing to be done about art or about life. But neither does it submit to the naive optimism that an art demythified is one whose beauty has thereby been restored or that a life demythified is a life lived again in safety.

The Moving Camera

It is often said that film, through the roving eye of the camera, was the first art to show the world in essential flux: malleable, indeterminate, incomplete. "Thus, we enjoy it," Herbert Tannenbaum wrote in 1912, "when we see how . . . everything lives and is in flux." A year later, Lukács declared cinema the art of "movement in itself, the eternal transience, the never resting change of things."[6]

Later on, film was claimed to be the only art consciously aimed at showing the world not as found but as made. "By the movement of the camera or the flickering of the montage," Béla Balázs argued, "even the physical immobility of such static conditions could be mobilized and dramatized. This is a means of expression *completely specific* to the film." Or Kracauer: in film it makes sense to speak of "multiple meanings [or] vague meaningfulness . . . *only* in connection with camera work."[7]

To see the real world as malleable or made by camera work matched the then-dominant theories of perspectivism and relativity such as offered by

Einstein in physics, Panofsky and Wölfflin in the visual arts, and Merleau-Ponty and Wittgenstein in philosophy. "It's strange," Wittgenstein noted, for example, that

> only when we philosophize, but not in ordinary life, are we troubled by the feeling that the phenomenon is slipping away from us, the constant flux of appearance. This indicates that what is in question here is an idea suggested by a misapplication of our language.
>
> The feeling we have is that the present disappears into the past without our being able to prevent it. And here we are obviously using the picture of a film strip remorselessly moving past us [*vorbeibewegt*], that we are unable to stop. . . . What we are looking at here is really the possibility of movement [*Bewegung*]: and so the logical form of movement.[8]

For early theorists and makers, the film showed a world in which people participate, a world no longer standing at a distance from passive and solitary egos, but an intersubjective or interactive world of their own making. "We came upon no ready-built city," Sergei Eisenstein remarked in relation to early Soviet cinema,[9] or again Balázs:

> In the cinema the camera carries the spectator into the film picture itself. We see everything from the inside as it were and are surrounded by the characters of the film. . . .
>
> Although we sit in our seats for which we have paid, we do not see Romeo and Juliet from there. We look up to Juliet's balcony with Romeo's eyes and look down on Romeo with Juliet's. Our eye and with it our consciousness is identified with the characters in the film. . . . Herein lies the psychological act of "identification."
>
> Nothing like this "identification" has ever occurred as the effect of any other system of art and it is here that the film manifests its absolute artistic novelty.[10]

In the history of visual arts, the eye was long held in place or preserved at a distance by available technologies, ideologies, and aesthetic theories. The moving camera brought home how impassive the eye is and had always been. With the moving camera came the technological motivation to let the eye roam, enter in, and construct a space, not just in front of it but also around it. With the moving camera, the embodied eye took possession of the world, private as well as public. Neither artists nor spectators needed to assume a bystander's position anymore; they could sit in their homes or walk the city streets as embodied participants in the cinematic and panoramic process. Many modernists compared metropolitan walking or cosmopolitan travel with thinking itself, sometimes with the confidence of those who feel at home though they are homeless—as we see in Charlie Chaplin's *City Lights*—or, in a Chaplinesque reversal, of those who experience homelessness despite their being at home. Others modernists found the drama of thinking taking place off the streets, as in Robert Siodmak's *Der Abschied,* a film about the internal workings of a boardinghouse with sounds comprising the negotiating noises of modern life: telephones, vacuum cleaners, and clocks.

Moving inside the world, the eye saw small bits of things formerly hidden from view. Film exploded the world's fixity by revealing the dynamic movement of its life. Kracauer, like Bloom, completed the thought by quoting Panofsky:

Owing to diverse camera activities, cutting and many special devices, films are able . . . to scan the whole visible world. The effort results in what Erwin Panofsky . . . defined as the "dynamization of space": "In a movie theater . . . the spectator has a fixed seat, but only physically. . . . Aesthetically, he is in permanent motion, as his eye identifies itself with the lens of the camera which permanently shifts in distance and direction."[11]

Recall from chapter 4 Benjamin's distinction between the artist as magician and the artist as surgeon, or between the painter's brush that leaves the world intact and the filmmaker's camera that cuts the world into bits and pieces.[12] With these distinctions, the words "world" and, by extension, "nature" shift in meaning. With one hand, a natural world is painted at a respectful distance by brushes of artists who nevertheless feel connected to the landscapes they depict. With the other, society and nature are rearranged by the depersonalized knives of inhumane labor. Yet, it is no longer obvious which view offers the greater deception in modern times—the harmonious world that appears to the eye as found, or the fractured world that seems entirely to be made.

For the critical theorists, there was obviously a danger in what Balázs described as the psychological act of identification, though there was also the potential for advance. To absorb oneself fully in film might encourage the belief that what film shows is reality itself. Benjamin described this sort of absorption as a new, modern form of distraction.[13] Breaking and entering into a film (more as a detective than criminal) is what one is meant to do if one *also* makes an exit, to let the thinking begin in a psychological place distanced from the addictive and rapid movement of visual images. Moving in and out of a film, the alienated or distracted eye might reconnect itself to an intelligent mind that wants to both participate and observe. If the camera makes the eye more flexible, it has the potential to make the self more flexible without, however, relinquishing the self's grip on what is real or on what really matters (the residue of the self's humanity). While critical theorists know that a self that opens itself up to change is a self at risk of being manipulated, they recognize that being manipulated is the risk the self has to take to liberate itself from increasingly petrified discourses and practices.

Thus, the new perspective granted by film was potentially liberating, even if it offered no guarantee. That was the point: to remove the moribund promise of certainty. Film might be the art par excellence for the transformation of consciousness and society, offering for both eye and mind what Benjamin called "the sequence of positional views."[14] Still, film was also believed to reveal the last move in a deadly dialectic between humanity and nature, according to which humanity achieved its total domination just when "the cutter" removed all distance and difference between the world he made and the social world outside.

What Benjamin called "the sequence of positional views" Adorno described as a series (*eine Reihe*) in which every positional view—as in the twelve-tone row of musical composition—is equally close to the center. Yet, this equality proved illusory in cases where the roving eye of the camera or the voice of the radio continued to dictate what was seen or heard, and when. Whereas later feminist theorists identified the camera's eye with the eye of the male, Adorno aligned it with the allegedly neutral eye of authority (which might be the same thing) to show the total control of all possible points of view. In this argument, false *equalization* was only one side of the coin that was totality. On its other side was false *identification*, where all distinctions that once preserved dignified distances between things were seemingly erased. The two sides stuck to each other in a new technology that distributed its messages ubiquitously or intruded indiscriminately into even the most private of a person's space. "The substitution of ends by means takes the place of the characteristics of humans themselves," Adorno wrote. At the end of the argument, Adorno agreed with Marshall McLuhan: the medium has been reduced to the message—or so this is *what* and *how* we are now being asked to believe when "civilization [is] at its most degraded."[15]

If everything is possible, anything is possible, anywhere and at any time, as Cole Porter told us in 1934, over radio, phonograph, and film. Writing about the Weimar "Twenties," when everything was permitted, Adorno stressed that a song or technique that claims to shock us out of our complacency can with too much repetition become a dead technique: "the ghost of a ghost." And long before Adorno, Lukács wrote specifically about the cinema that its never-ending succession of images proves not only that everything is possible but also that everything is "equally true and equally real." Here, the equality suggested less the identification of truth with relativism and more a conformist identification of possibility with reality and, thus also, with a static or coldly repetitive confirmation of the status quo.[16]

In a recent book, *The Material Ghost*, Gilberto Perez refers to a line from Herman Melville's *Billy Budd:* "To pass from a normal nature to him one must cross 'the deadly space between.'" To this Melville adds in the original, "And this is best done by indirection."[17] It was the indirection and movement that most threatened to be lost in the new modern mediums of identification. "The deadly space between" became all the more deadly the less it was acknowledged to be a space.

Movement and Musicality

In pursuing an argument for displacement, one could focus on the perfectly legitimate thesis that both the social danger and the emancipatory potential of film lie in its explicitly and subliminally conveyed messages. One could consider film's early and continued use as an instrument of propaganda. This would be an argument mostly regarding film's *content*. Alternatively, or in addition, one could focus on *form*: on how, with its new technological means and specifically with the moving eye of the camera, film promotes a perspectival view of the world. Perspectival through and through, the film is open to promoting social change, even though what some filmmakers desire for their society might well be most undesirable.

The more formal argument was promoted early on by filmmakers and theorists across the political, social, and aesthetic board: Balázs, Chaplin, Eisenstein, Kracauer, Münsterberg, Mamoulian, Pudovkin, Riefenstahl, and Vertov. I have little new to say about their arguments as film theory; that is not my expertise. However, their arguments assume an intriguing significance the moment one notices that when they spoke about the formal or abstract mobility of film, they used a musical language to do so. They described film as symphonic, improvisational, orchestrated, melodic, harmonic, syncopated, and contrapuntal as often as they referred to film's musical lines, rhythms, and curves. Some even called film optic, visual, or visualized music. References to visual music did not begin with film but already had a rich history pertaining to the other arts.[18] Still, tied to film, the consequences were profound. For, with these terms, they were not speaking about a film's music. This is the point, even the paradox. In the late 1920s, when film had the opportunity to embrace music as one of its essential components, objections by even the most musical of filmmakers were vigorous. Film was already a musical art, they insisted, *without music*.

In 1916, in his classic text on "silent photoplay," Hugo Münsterberg showed the sense of investigating "moving pictures" by analogy with the "mental processes of the hearing of tones and of chords, of harmonies and disharmonies."[19] Münsterberg was correct: film moves as music moves. This analogy was surpassed, however, when the claim was rendered considerably more metaphysical. When filmmakers used the language of music, they were thinking less about sound and more about an aesthetic of movement and musicality. This aesthetic infused discussion of all the arts throughout the late eighteenth and early nineteenth centuries. Just as the concept of musicality was used from the beginning to speak about painting, sculpture, and poetry, so, too, tied to the concept of movement, it shaped most of the theories that contributed to the founding of the cinematic art—theories of synesthetic and kinesthetic perception, abstraction, and symbolism.

The influence of Wagner and Schopenhauer in these theories was indisputable. If film was the natural successor to the art of theater, opera, or music drama, or the successor only to the traditional visual arts, this was because of its ability to give perfect outer form to an "inner musicality." Nonetheless, in making this claim, *recourse was not made to music*. What was inner, essential, living, symphonic, harmonizing, synthesizing, and even totalizing in film was explained by reference to cinematic or visual movement. Film's musicality was a visual matter and moved best in some sort of cinematic silence—or, perhaps one should say, with Wagner, in aesthetic light. As embodied movement, film offered a complete visual choreography of meaningful and expressive gesture. In claims like this, there was a shared assumption: a total artwork does not necessarily imply the use of every artistic medium if one medium can perform the total work that art is intended to do—*alone*.

Balázs wrote: "We know it no longer, how we learnt to see in this time. How we learned optically to associate, optically to deduce, optically to think, how familiar optical shortcuts, optical metaphors, optical symbols, optical concepts became to us."[20] Still, the consequence of this cinematic learning was to declare film musical.

Let me restate the paradox: the moment when so much musicality was claimed to belong to film as a visual art was just when it was possible to incorporate music fully into film. The claim and the possibility conflicted. With the "reinvention" of film in the 1920s, specifically as it fell under the concept of visual music, filmmakers left it unclear what significance a sounded-out music had. If film is the art par excellence of visual music, even a *Cinéma Pur* or *absolut Film*, to recall the long-standing adulation of *pure or absolute music*, sounding music is redundant. Sounding music might have a pragmatic or an accompanying use but not an essential one. For what need is there for a sounding language of music in an art that is already sufficiently musical? To adapt an oft-quoted line of René Clair: we do not need to *hear* the melodic movement if we can *see* it before our eyes. What Clair actually wrote was, "we do not need to *hear* the sound of clapping if we can *see* the clapping hands."[21] This remark pertains to the incorporation of sound into film, whether or not the sound assumes a musical form; the sound might also be speech or noise. The arguments for sound's incorporation generally, and those for music's specifically, are not always the same, though they are often run together. The confusion sometimes matters and sometimes not: sometimes it works to a particular film's advantage.

Clair's remark is deepened by an even earlier observation from 1904, recently recorded by sound film theorist Rick Altman. Women were observed covering their ears when they *saw*, though they did not *hear*, pistols being shot in *The Great Train Robbery*.[22] Regarded as predominantly visual, film doesn't need to use sound to sustain its movement because it assumes a particular phenomenology of absence and presence in which one spectatorial sense compensates for another when the other is deprived of its activity. According to the principle of Gestalt switching, based on psychological and physical need, what we do not or cannot hear we learn to see, and vice versa. This principle provides sustenance for the claim that film conveys all the musicality it wants, whether or not music, word, or noise is heard. "Vicarious senses," Nietzsche once declared: "'Our eyes are also intended for hearing,' said the old father confessor who had gone deaf: 'and among the blind he is king who has the longest ears'."[23]

What We See and What We Hear

Whatever the aesthetic and political commitments of filmmakers and theorists, and whether or not they spoke of films with or without actual music, references in the 1920s and 1930s to visual musicality and movement were abundant. Sometimes they were offered in the form of expressionist or gothic imagery, as in F. W. Murnau's *Nosferatu: Eine Symphonie des Grauens,* or sometimes in terms of the abstract relations and lyrical movements between kaleidoscopic images, as in Fernand Léger's *Le Ballet Mécanique,* René Clair's *Entr'acte,* Walther Ruttmann's *Berlin: Die Symphonie der Grossstadt,* and Hans Richter's Dada film, *Rhythmus 2.* Sometimes the references were intended to promote socially and aesthetically harmonious movements of spatial and temporal figurations, as in the military parades and sporty exercises in Leni Riefenstahl's *Triumph des Willens.* Sometimes they stressed the constantly altering movements of city life, as in Clair's *Sous les Toits de Paris* or G. W. Pabst's rendition of Brecht and Weill's *Die Dreigroschenoper.*

There are many other examples—American, Russian, Japanese—but suffice this list to suggest that when the camera moved, meanings were established as much through figurative movement as through representations or depictions of content. If film shifted our perspective, it did this by making a world appear from the inside out, as if emerging. In virtue of the "visual hieroglyphs," Kracauer wrote in partial quotation of Horace M. Kallen's work, film stories unfold the "unseen dynamics of human relations" or reflect "the inner life" of nations from which the films "emerge."[24]

Imagine watching the momentous movement of events in Riefenstahl's *Triumph of the Will* without Herbert Windt's devotedly Wagnerian soundtrack. The change in how we look is extraordinary. Separated from the cruder or more obvious manipulations of the music, the film assumes a stronger visual expressivity that derives from a documentary realism approximating the early silence of the newsreel. Seen this way, an uncanny resemblance is established between this film and a genuine newsreel—between Hitler's automobile entry into Nuremberg and Kennedy's final automobile exit out of Dallas. This comparison originates not with me but in the well-known observation that Hitler's political poses for the moving camera, like Churchill's on the other side of the channel, had an extraordinary influence on politicians of the future, in part because their gestures were among the first to be deliberately and publicly staged with the new technologies: politics as technological exhibition.

Along similar lines, an anecdote is often told about Hitchcock's 1943 war movie *Lifeboat* when it was still in production at 20th Century-Fox. Hitchcock decided against using music in this film other than at its beginning and end, the time for titles and credits. No background music is used when the handful of passengers of a shipwreck try to survive physically on a lifeboat and socially in a confined space. When one of Hitchcock's associates was asked to explain Hitchcock's decision, he responded: "Hitchcock feels that since the entire action of the film takes place in a lifeboat on the open ocean, where would the music come from?" To which apparently the composer Hugo W. Friedhofer retorted: "Ask Mr Hitchcock to explain where the camera [comes] from, and I'll tell him where the music comes from."[25] Whereas the composer was reminding the filmmaker that every part of the film is artificially produced, the filmmaker was rendering an artistic judgment about how best to hide this fact for the sake of a realism in which background music has no part. Film can do all it wants in the world—without music.

Music in Film That Is Hardly Heard as Music

The matter is more complicated than this, however, since the oft-repeated claim that Hitchcock used no music in this film is false. He did use music, though not *film music* or the sort of music produced by a modern, reproductive technology. (Of course, what counts as film music is the question under consideration.)

In Hitchcock's film, as in Riefenstahl's, the realist *effect* is a product of a cinematic artifice that corresponds to an equally carefully constructed *reality* outside, a reality designed to make triumph for one side or the other look inevitable. Such is the purpose of propaganda films. In both films, the question is raised as to what contribution music makes if, to turn the image into a political metaphor, a lifeboat is equally able to save humanity or let it drown in the middle of a perfectly silent world made of water. In both films, music is used as an ideological tool, even if in Hitchcock's film, and this is the point: one hardly notices the music as music.

Hitchcock's music is first heard—or hardly heard—when a passenger plays his pipe. Thirty minutes into the film, the music enters from the background, not as scored by Friedhofer, though he may well have had something to do with the selection. As background music inside the dramatic frame, it is played by the one passenger who also remains mostly in the background, the only African American on board. Later, the pipe is taken over by another passenger, who plays a part in the foreground, when he decides to accompany the only Nazi on board in singing German lullabies. One cannot say he is the only German on board, though this is how he is referred to, given two opening arguments the film makes: first, that not all Germans are Nazis and, second, that some of the Americans on board were once Germans and could be so again. "I prefer to call you by your original name Schmidt than your immigrant name Smith," more or less says the Nazi to one passenger whose life he twice helps to save but whom he then helps to die. Both arguments are then, for propagandistic reasons, rejected.

When we (as the audience) are supposed to pay attention to the song of the pipe, we already know that the singer is a Nazi, though the passengers are not yet fully aware of it. When we are not meant to pay attention to the pipe, it is played subliminally as if to warn the passengers (and us) of the Nazi deceit, emanating from Nuremberg, to which they are about to be subjected. They still want to believe that he is one of those "good Germans." It is as if the African American passenger were piping the song without yet fully understanding the message it conveys. On first hearing his notes, though they are hardly recognizable, one soon realizes they belong to Wagner. One immediately then expects that the song will echo Siegfried's private bird or the pipe heard in *Tristan*'s last act when Tristan awaits Isolde's arrival on a boat. But what one actually hears is what I suspect would already in those years have been associated with Nazi ideology: the music from *Die Meistersinger*. Still, none of the music of this opera's pomp and circumstance—say, the opening of the overture—is heard, only a very quiet rendition of the prize song's melody.

The reference is more subtle than the overall message the film conveys (too subtle, perhaps, given that when the film was premiered it was criticized as offering a far too sympathetic and attractive portrait of "the German," a criticism that entirely misses the point). Just as in the original opera's drama the prize song requires several repetitions or reconstructions to turn Walther von Stolzing's natural intuition into cultivated understanding, Hitchcock's film assumes a similar dramatic form—the repetitive seafaring form of a compass error, which is exactly what shapes the film's plot. However much the passengers are inclined to trust Germans, and they do keep trying to trust them, they learn that the German is after all a Nazi—just as Walther von Stolzing ends up, despite his resistance along the way, as a mastersinger apparently convinced that he, too, should henceforth sing to secure the future of German art. The German, Willy, in the film, who sings so well—who is so *gebildet*, cultured, and handsome, so good an actor within and without the film, a master of both medical and seafaring crafts who secretly carries a compass and who alone knows the direction toward which they all are heading—is no more to be trusted than the ignorant blond youth appearing at the end who holds a pistol directly to the passengers' heads. Both Germans are equally polite; both say *danke schön* on being pulled out of the water into the boat. Hans Sachs–Walther–Willy: ultimately it makes no difference—don't be fooled by culture! This is the message the audience is left with at the end, as much as they watch it resisted along the way: every time, in fact, one of the passengers reminds the others of the American creed of freedom that individual innocence or integrity should be the presumption before totalizing assumptions of national and cultural complicity.[26]

Moving Inside

When Schopenhauer argued that music alone expresses the movement of the world Will, he gave to the other arts their future song to sing: anything music can do, they can do better. All these arts had to do was surpass their representational limits by electing an aesthetic option or concept that would transform them into predominantly expressive or unmediated arts, if not also into performance arts. One way to defend film as a visually moving art was to prove that vision could be expressive or musical without music.

So far, the formal argument depends on the metaphorically rich claim that the camera could move inside a world to bring life to that world. Such terms, however, make it easy to run two separate ideas together. On the first, more metaphysical view, moving into the inside was often claimed to be a move toward the essence, toward something more real, certain, living, soulful. To capture the movement of a world in film was to capture the essence or *Innerlichkeit* of the world. Sometimes, when theorists or filmmakers spoke like this, the implications of their speech moved well past philosophical insight into the most disturbing political arenas. Riefenstahl's film is the most obvious example. On the second view, however, the appeal to a move inside was a more modest way that modernist philosophers and artists separated their views from one maintaining that the world was just the totality of (objective) facts. Here, reference to the inside supported a modernist perspectivism or constructionism of the sort we find in the work of Wittgenstein and Merleau-Ponty, given their bid to avoid the metaphysical and political extremes of subjectivism, objectivism, positivism, idealism, and absolutism.

The Fear of Music

As we know, there is a strong Hegelian tendency to theorize about an art after it has reached its final or consummate form. To focus on the 1920s, by contrast, is to return to film at an early stage, when its beginnings and ends were still being negotiated. In this period, many believed that film as a visual music had already fulfilled its ambition and resented any change in its status. They wanted film to transmute itself neither into a narrative art of "the talkies" nor into the symphonic form of a Wagnerian opera. Little in these arguments, unsurprisingly, was straightforward.

Consider this statement from 1924 in which D. W. Griffith expressed his conviction that when a century has passed

> all thought of our so-called speaking pictures will have been abandoned. It will never be possible to synchronize the voice with the pictures. This is true because the very nature of the films foregoes not only the necessity for but the propriety of the spoken voice. Music—fine music—will always be the voice of the silent drama. One hundred years from now will find the greatest composers devoting their skill and their genius to the creation of motion-picture music.[27]

Griffith was partially wrong but expressed a belief prevalent at the time that film was an art more of visual drama and accompanying music than of the heard word. In thinking this way, he undermined what others wanted to stress: film could be a perfect art *also* without music.

Griffith's prophecy prompted an interesting question: What would happen to film were its accompanying music to become the best it could be—even great? Would film become a genuinely symphonic or operatic art? Indeed, could music so successfully do the cinematic work of musicality as to render the camera redundant? Given what we now think about film, this seems to be an unfounded fear, but it was not. After all, what could happen to film happened to opera when the symphonic strands of the orchestra assumed so great a pride of place that opera was declared a primarily and even purely musical art. Couldn't the sheer volume of an ever-expanding orchestra one day outweigh even the greatest magnitude of cinematic vision? Again, the thought is odd, but it didn't prevent Ernst Bloch from declaring in 1919 (and thus long before Stanley Kubrick) that "now" is the moment when "music in film assumes its singular function: to take the place of all the other senses. . . . Here, the world is filmed all over again, this time as music."[28]

Recall from chapter 2 the argument that if an opera's music is to be great, it had better be composed to mediocre texts, because if the texts are great themselves, great music won't be needed in addition. That this argument didn't convince as given suggested that it was less mediocrity than redundancy that was the issue, an issue made urgent when artists felt the need to justify using more than one medium in an artwork when one medium was already enough. This need was felt most urgently around 1800 when the fine arts sought affinities to each other, each having achieved an independence that was at once celebrated and feared. The entire discussion was influenced by Lessing and his contemporaries. Increasingly, throughout the nineteenth century, the view was established that for a work of more than one medium to be great, each medium must make its unique contribution. Still, this didn't prevent the question of priority from being an urgent one, as shown in the writings of Schopenhauer and Wagner. This is the point: when film theorists turned back to Lessing's earlier Laoköonian discussion (as, for example, Rudolf Arnheim, to whom I turn below), they did so largely to counter the manifold influence of Schopenhauer and Wagner regarding music's threatening priority.[29] Even if music was present and however great its contribution, something other than music should take priority in film.

In 1929, Giuseppe Becce increased the anxiety that music would assume too dominant a role when he argued that film and music would both benefit were film to devote a large part of its ambition to presenting already existing great works of music as cinematic events. The provision of visual images would do more than merely accompany; they would give a new range of meanings to the works. (This argument also works in reverse: to provide visual images with music would give the images new meaning. Unlike many others, this argument would actually be a convincing argument for incorporating music into film.) Just imagine, Becce continued, turning Richard Strauss's "Death and Transfiguration" or Beethoven's Pastoral symphony into a *Tonfilm*. What could be better for film and what better for music? Becce was addressing the alleged "crisis" of the modern concert hall. Apparently, no one wanted just to listen anymore: they also wanted to look—though not just at the orchestra. Wouldn't the crisis of listening be solved were music to be distributed democratically to a great number of people in a manner that, rather than succumbing to "tastelessness," would educate them through their new and preferred medium?[30] Good music in better films, for a greater number of people: What possibly could be lost?

For many, however, the issue was not loss but gain. Brecht, for example, named the gain "music inflation" (*Musikinflation*). To inflate film with music and even worse with "great music" risked overindulging the film's culinary and narcotic dimensions. Linked to a capitalist economy of need and satisfaction, culinary film threatened to undercut film's revolutionary social potential. Thinking of the culinary, Brecht had the pleasurable diet of Wagner, Verdi, Bruckner, Puccini, and Strauss in his stomach, as did many of his contemporaries. This is not surprising: even in the earliest film, it was mostly this sort of *foreground* music that was used as *background* music.[31]

Imagine, now, the reaction to Herbert Ihering's declaration of 1931 informing filmmakers that "only by the outsiders," by which he meant musicians, can film be renewed. Or imagine Walther Ruttmann's experiment a year earlier, in which an eleven-minute, fragmented composition titled *Weekend* (shortly thereafter described as an "imageless film") demonstrated *via radio* the new auditory potential of *film*: that even *without images* a medium could conquer Berlin.[32]

Fear of Opera–Fear of Film

In the 1920s, theorists who most feared film's auditory potential were those who regarded film as primarily following painting and photography. For at least the naturalists among them, nature films were paradigmatic of the new art. Others regarded film as extending the narrative or dramatic arts and others as extending opera or even modern music theater. Why, given these different regards, couldn't one celebrate everything film could do by declaring film the real *Gesamtkunstwerk* of the future that did not need always or ever to give priority to music?

Strangely enough, it wasn't only the visual music faction that appreciated this last thought; some composers did, too, though for a perverse reason. If film assumed the responsibilities of the *Gesamtkunstwerk,* modern music and modern opera would thereby be freed from the burden. Here, the burden lay not with the difficulty of producing a total artwork of integrated mediums but with the fear that in the very production of a total work of art, one would not be able to avoid contributing to a totalizing, excessive, or decadent vision of the world. And this the contemporary composer didn't necessarily want to do.

Thus, though all recognized the relationship between film and opera and though some celebrated the relation, there were some composers arguing that film should not be opera's future. In the 1910s and increasingly by the late 1920s, especially in Germany, opera was declared to be in a severe crisis. Many composers looked to film to save it, but others resisted—not, I am saying, *by giving up on opera but by giving up on film*. What had become true of film— just because of the Wagnerian legacy—should not become true, they insisted, of modern opera. Schoenberg explained in 1926, in the *Berliner Tageblatt:*

It would be a shame to renounce the many possibilities the stage offers through the union of solo and ensemble singing, orchestra, and dramatic action on a grand scale. The theater crisis has been brought about in part by film, and opera finds itself in the same situation: neither can compete with the realism film offers. Film has spoiled the eye of the viewer, one sees not only truth and reality but also every illusion that would otherwise have been reserved for the stage, and that which was only intended as an illusion now presents itself in a fantastic way as reality. In order to avoid the comparison with film, therefore, opera will probably turn away from realism or must otherwise find an appropriate path for itself.[33]

Schoenberg's comment suggests something important about film's early history. Not only was film tormented by its *naturalistic* potential to deceive, to confuse illusion with reality; it could also deceive in ways so *fantastic* that it approximated Wagnerian opera. This is a crucial move in the overall argument of this chapter. Schoenberg's comment shows that the worry that reality was being confused with illusion was of a quite different order from the worry triggered by those thinking in the more traditional terms of a "copy theory" of art. Whereas the one worry had to do with expression and modernist loss, the other had to do with representation and ontology.

Representation and Expression

Consider the ontological argument first: that the end of the copy theory marked the beginning, paradoxically, of the age of perfect copies. Hence, the copy theory worked only as long as copies were imperfect. This is part of what was argued in relation to early film: film brought to an end a view of art as imitative because it leaped over the gap between copy and original, by getting the original, as it were, perfectly or directly right. Yet, when a copy is perfect, it is no longer a copy but the original itself; or, better, with Danto, the way film imitates shows that it produces neither a copy nor an original but an entirely different and independent ontological thing. (More on this below.)

The argument of immediate interest regards the worry that cinematic illusions did not *look like* the real world but *felt like* the real world, where the real world felt to many as though it were being moved by the most dangerous of social movements. Hence, when Danto first articulated his thesis on the end of art, he epigraphed his essay with words written in 1912 by Marius de Zayas in a journal pertinently called *Camera Work:* "The Sun Has Set" and "Art is dead." The "present movements" of art, De Zayas explained, show neither "indications of vitality" nor even "convulsions of agony prior to death" but only "the mechanical reflex actions of a corpse" that has submitted "to galvanic force."[34]

In general, one might think that the more film was defended as a visual art, the more it was defended as a representational art; still, this is the equation that was fractured the moment the visual turned itself over to expressive movement. For visual movement had to do less with what was discerned by the eye and more with how films could "come to mean." In this articulation, "representation" connotes only the idea of how things look, but this diminishes its possibilities. To regard representation as also meaning-engendering is to reconnect it to matters of expression. Reconnected, cinematic representation-expression shows how meanings emerge, how they are *made* more than simply *captured* by the camera. In the 1970s, this was the view so well reflected upon in the pitched ontology of Stanley Cavell. What cinematic expression gave back to representation too narrowly conceived was the possibility of reconnecting to a world of lost objects, of retrieving something that was and could not be caught in the act of mere copying.

In *The World Viewed,* Cavell captured many of the modernist anxieties associated with film's ability to displace, move, and produce the sort of automatism that breaks down desirable distances between art and life. Surprisingly, given his own musical background, he did not write much about music or musicality, though he did write about movement and voice. In his pitched and reflective ontology, as the subtitle of his book suggests, he showed his deep concern with both experience and commitment. He associated his *imperfect* memory of an earlier time in his life when the warlike rules of the game allowed the camera first to shoot its images for him to see and later to canonize its sounds for him to hear. "Memories of movies," he opened his "metaphysical memoir," are "strand over strand with memories" of his own life. That he qualified his statement of identity between movies and life with Wittgensteinian "strands" of recollection gave him his modernist theme. How matters look to us in movies and how in life cannot be separated from the deeper contexts of historical or temporal experience in which the imperfection of memory is invoked to overcome the felt experience of loss. For both Danto and Cavell, though certainly not only for them, it is as though film emerged from the first moment as a fated art producing galvanic tremors in a context of technological shock.

Films of Opera and Operatic Films

One reason for the prevalence of the language of music in film's early history is that many moving pictures took for their subject matter already existing operas and operettas. (Films were made of *Faust, Parsifal, Carmen, Butterfly,* and *The Barber.*) Even here, however, the story did not track a straight path. To explain why not, we need to explore further what it meant for film to want to shed itself of the desire merely to copy and, instead, to capture life emergently, *from the inside out.*

Consider three arguments about cinematic movement and the potential of the camera, each offered by reference to a musical event. The first comes from Kracauer. When music enters at some moment into a film, the camera, Kraucauer noted, tends to stop moving, like "a concertgoer" who suddenly "forgets to breathe because of his involvement in the score." With the cessation of the "camera-reality," the music sounds more like an intrusion than an integral part. The intrusion, he concluded, is experienced as a loss of life to which we tend to respond with resignation and ennui—but perhaps we should not.[35]

The second comes from Alberto Cavalcanti, who in 1939 wrote: "A musical performance is presumably worth looking at in a concert hall (because nearly everyone looks), but it is not worth looking at in a cinema."[36] He was right, though if "looking at" is all one did at a concert, one would miss the music's movement there as well. The point of his argument was to convince us that film's ambition should not be to represent a worldly event that has already taken place independently outside. Film could do more: show how a world is made and comes to mean. To catch a concert on film was not to take advantage of what the new technology could do as a constructive and productive art of interpretation and technique.

The third argument comes from Balázs, who told us that close-ups in film show us what in our lives we have lived without noticing: the shadows on our walls and the "speechless face and fate" of the mute objects that surround us. Before film, we looked at life like an uneducated audience listens to music, hearing only "the leading melody" and ignoring "the contrapuntal architecture." A good film, he insisted, could meet this contrapuntal demand by revealing what would otherwise remain hidden: namely, the polyphony of both art and life.[37] In the contrapuntal demand, the traditional mimetic requirement of visual art to *represent* the world merely as it *appears* was displaced. This displacement, as discussed in the preceding section, played a central role in the history of aesthetic theory in bringing to an end the traditional demand for mere imitation or copy. Mere copying had become like listening only for the melody, given that both were allegedly showing the diminishment of experience in modern times.

These three early arguments were brought together later, in 1952, in the brilliantly sardonic criticism of Hans Keller in a short editorial "Film Music: The Operatic Problem." Not seeing the advantage of using film only to document independent ongoing events, Keller suggested replacing the making of films *of* opera with the making of "genuine film-operas."[38] Film could do more than merely re-present an opera. The performance need not be an ontologically or temporally prior act caught and copied by the camera. The performance could be the film itself: a film version of an opera considered as a work in its own right.

Partly motivating Keller was his concern with time, specifically with the fact that whereas opera performances lasted for hours, films usually did not. Watching an entire opera on film taught him "the purely musical significance of intervals." Listening is hard work and one needs rest on the way. But more, he argued, if all one did was watch a performance on film, wouldn't it be preferable to see the real thing? In posing this question, Keller's motivation shifted over to technological considerations. Though sound or recording technology was much advanced by the 1950s, the synchronization of image and pitch maintenance was still apparently such as to produce more pain than pleasure for the audience. In general, Keller quipped, he'd rather not submit to torture, a torture, he added, that could be both visible and audible. When the camera started to move inside the opera, for example, it usually moved into the wrong inside, which is to say, not into the aesthetic inside but into the physical inside of the sweaty performance revealing the singer's tonsils. Producing music should not conjure up images of chewing a glass of milk, he declared — just as Goethe refused to view colors fractured through a prism. The sort of closeness achieved by close-ups was not necessarily to anyone's advantage.

Yet, for Keller, as for Balázs, film and opera had to find shared ways to fulfill their contrapuntal potential. If film and opera were to be brought close, moving in on the operatic event would have to mean something else: namely, radically rearranging the already existing work. Like many musicians, Keller was worried about changing less opera's images than its notes, especially if the notes were Mozart's. Change anything, but leave the notes alone. Of course, this demand was not peculiar to film, but regarding film it moved Keller to propose this solution: instead of producing films of traditional opera performances, new opera films should be produced for which the music is specifically composed to suit the new technological art. Whereas some had been persuaded to move film opera in the direction of the American musical, Keller opted for avant-garde models such as had already been tried in the cinematic productions of Stravinsky, Schoenberg, and Berg. Like so many others, he feared the loss of educated culture and wanted to defend the potential of film to become a genuinely "serious" art.

Keller concluded in a way that mirrors Schoenberg's words as quoted above. Film and opera were not so naturally suited given their opposing tendencies: toward realism and naturalism in film and toward style and symbolism in opera. So polarized, the question became, In a genuine film opera, should film become more like opera or opera more like film? For some, however, this was a false polarization, resting as it did on a no longer plausible aesthetic distinction. Why should a new art remain obedient to traditional aesthetic categories and tendencies? In 1913, when Lukács posed this question, he wondered what would become of the new art. "We never get out of the state of conceptual confusions," he wrote: "Something new and beautiful has arisen in our days, yet, instead of accepting it as it is, people want to classify it by all possible means in old, unfitting categories, to strip it of its true meaning and value."[39] Others, like Benjamin and Adorno, responded by asking what it meant in modern times to speak of "true meaning and value."

Technological Advance

Rick Altman treats the general claim surrounding film as visual music as a fallacy with "four and a half" manifestations. The historical and ontological manifestations are relevant here.[40] The historical fallacy was to treat film's history as one in which image came before sound and then to use this false historical fact to justify valuing the image more highly. The ontological fallacy was to treat film as essentially a visual art and then to resent any challenge to this essential nature. Altman stresses that the arguments presented in the late 1920s against the use of music in film were mostly disguised arguments for conceiving film as a visual art. But then he reminds us that the very idea that film was ever a purely visual art is belied by the fact that film, even if once called silent, was never as a rule experienced without music or sounds. This is correct even if in one sense it is beside the point. As Balázs noted (though here he excluded film), a metaphysically *silent* art is not necessarily a *soundless* art; indeed, haven't we always spoken metaphysically and metaphorically of music as silent?[41]

I agree that the conceptual and aesthetic questions of music's place in film became urgent in the late 1920s when it became technologically possible fully to integrate the former into the latter. Before then, despite many attempts to integrate "movietone," worries were less pronounced and even perhaps of a quite different sort. Altman records these arguments in detail. At this point, my concern is only to emphasize that though technological limitations held certain aesthetic arguments back, and vice versa, with some technological advances certain aesthetic arguments became available and, in the dialectical minds of some, even inevitable. Accordingly, this meant that although as technology advanced, resistance to incorporating music and sound increased, once the idea of incorporating sound was in the air, the idea couldn't be stopped. "Being a prophet is a hard fate," Balázs remarked: When sound "struck the first blow" at silent film,

> I said that it would destroy the already highly developed culture of the silent film. I added that this would be only temporary, until expression by means of sound would have developed to a higher level. I said that what had happened was a catastrophe, the like of which had never occurred before in the history of any other art. But I also said that a return to the silent film was impossible, for the evolution of technique is the evolution of the productive forces of mankind and the dangers it brings in its train cannot be averted by hampering its development. That would be senseless machine-wrecking. We cannot protect people from impending suffering by killing them.[42]

It is almost a given of modernist theory that aesthetic and technological arguments were brought into an inextricable, though anxious, relation by the new art of film. Consider an oft-cited example, *Singin' in the Rain* (1952). The title suggests a displacement of how and where one sings, even before such displacement becomes the film's subject matter. Just as weather was not the issue in Hitchcock's *Lifeboat,* it was not the issue for lovers singing in the rain—as opposed to where? In this film, we are told that a woman who speaks with a nicer vocal timbre, and whose voice we can now hear, is better fitted to love the man-cum-actor with whom, as an aspiring actress, she must sing, even if her looks less obviously fit the character's part. What would this film mean if it did not run together different arguments, technological and aesthetic, ones that play on all the complex connotations of speaking and singing, speaking and singing through microphones, hearing and seeing on stage and behind the stage, or watching persons in love and willing to get their feet wet turned into perfectly dry screen couples? The shifting between these perspectives gives this film its dramatic form and content but reveals most of all the modernist anxiety that motivated the film's having been made in the first place. For some, it is preferable to be seen but not heard, to play only when and where one feels completely safe.

Arguments for Film Music

The most plausible and effective arguments for film music were those that were willing to consider aesthetic arguments in relation to technological ones and to take serious account of film's claim to have become the paradigmatic *art of movement*. This was the position taken in 1936 by Kurt London, who argued against "the need" to explain film music by reference to mass psychology—say, by pointing out "that a crowd would listen in silence, but would not watch in silence"—and for "the need" to explain film music by reference to the form it could achieve by rhythm.[43] Over time, however, the sort of formal argument proposed by London was increasingly separated from other, more psychological and philosophical ones to the detriment of all. It was also overshadowed by an argument wanting to see music's role in film as no different from its role in song, opera, or operetta.[44] Whereas the latter argument suited those who saw film as the new opera, it far less suited those who saw film as making new technological and aesthetic demands on the traditional arts. For the former, music could just do what it had always done: saturate the ears with melodies so beautiful that all other senses would be overwhelmed. Those, moreover, who most resisted fitting music to the new technology were often those who feared that music's role would thereby be reduced to *sound*'s role in general and, thereby, that *music*'s particular aesthetic contribution to film would be underestimated. The worry was not unmotivated then as now, though the response was not necessarily to fall back on outdated aesthetic arguments. The greater challenge was to make music's aesthetic claim work on different terms with the new art.

In 1924, Fritz Lang noticed that when people spoke of "going to the movies," they regarded this form of speech sufficient. They didn't feel the need to fall back on traditional genre categories to specify what kind of film they were going to see. Lang approvingly thought this attitude illustrated film's independence though feared that it might undermine film's categorization as a serious art. When we go to the theater, we show how educated we are when we specify what kind of play we will see: a comedy, a tragedy, a revue. Should we not do the same in film, he wondered, though not so as to detract from its status as an independent art?[45]

Consider the argument in reverse, in Adornian terms. We used to think that when we went to the theater we cared what we saw. Now we get more pleasure from buying the ticket or simply attending the public event. Does this not show that all arts are reaching film's commodified condition or that film is showing what all arts have become in a late industrialized age? Perhaps—though neither Lang nor Adorno concluded this way. Their point of assessing film on its own terms was to save it from the allegedly late and wasted condition of the traditional arts. From this it followed, paradoxically, that whereas all the arts were approximating the condition of film, film had the most potential to resist that for which it was being made to stand in modern times: namely, the fate of art overall.

If technological and aesthetic arguments couldn't ultimately be kept apart, neither could sociological and aesthetic arguments, especially concerning the categories of high and low, serious and popular. Accordingly, contrary arguments were produced to the effect that if film is a serious art, its music should approximate the condition of traditional serious music or that if film is its own art, high or low, music should meet film's demands *before* it meets its own.

In the rest of this chapter, I present three specific arguments for film music: arguments of duplication, dissonance, and displacement. I recommend the third, though in allowing it to surpass the other two it must absorb what each gets right. In these terms, I present a dialectical or 3D approach to thinking about film music. The last argument takes the most time to unfold since it requires two detours on its way: through the themes, respectively, of the double and the ghost. None of the arguments is separable from the modernist anxieties described so far. One aim in this chapter is to persuade readers of this inseparability.

Duplication

The argument of duplication is usually considered the most conservative or at least the least avant-garde. It is linked to the realist or classical Hollywood film of the 1930s and after. It is an argument for the perfect construction of unbroken illusions and sustains the production of films with happy endings. It takes music's role to be essentially one of "Mickey Mousing," of imitating or illustrating what happens on the screen through melody, rhythm, and leitmotif.[46] Music is made to fit or to match the visual mood without question or comment. Music moves as images move, as though there were a one-to-one acceptance and correspondence between them: perfect synchronicity. Schoenberg famously took this argument to be one for the composition of "lovely music" for lovely films or, as others said, for "silly symphonies" after Walt Disney's films, the sort of redundant or *mezzo forte* music one hears but doesn't notice because it offers nothing or too little beyond the images. To speak of a film's sound track is to speak of music as tracking the images. To speak of a musical score is to hear the music as underscoring what is already given by the visual script. Music reinforces, pads, or completes a whole to produce something approximating an additive *Gesamtkunstwerk*. Consistent with this duplicative view was the early and vast production of film music manuals for silent and sounding films, which, like baroque practice, offered literally thousands of bits of music suitable for every mood and effect. (Interestingly, baroque music was rarely used in early film, even though its principles of construction, as exemplified in early, "occasional" music, would have suited it perfectly.)

I have presented the argument of duplication as already giving away the terms of its critique. Still, for those who favor it, it has a history of veritable film and film music to its credit. Lovely music for lovely films: this shouldn't automatically suggest the music's redundancy that reference to doubling up implies. Nor should this argument be assumed faulty just because it was associated with Hollywood, even if, for some critics, this association was enough.[47] Hollywood has always been as much a European as an American institution, as much out of as in sync with what mainstream America stands for, depending, of course, on what one thinks or hopes America stands for.

I return to this particular dynamic in chapter 8, but suffice it here to mention one difference of attitude among Europeans toward film produced in America. Many Europeans identified the origins of the movement thesis in American film. Before the formal movement of musicality was linked to Europe's modern cosmopolitan cities, it was linked to American notions of speed: to the open-air chase of the automobile or to the flight of the airplane. To be sure, although one entered a darkened room to watch a film, one was transported to a place of light where film as "camera work" was a site for "dream work" separated from the nightmares and stale air of the Old World. "Whereas the old world endures . . . [as] kitsch," Claire Goll wrote in 1920,

America's healthy will has created true film. In the good American film, any literary element is left out. . . . What happens or rather races by on the screen can no longer be called plot. It is a new dynamic, a breathless rhythm, action in an un-literary sense. Nor is it created and acted out in a glass house, but in the open air.

Film has replaced old words with pure "granite energy," the energy of "concentrated movement and pantomime."[48]

By contrast, when Kracauer arrived as an exile in the United States, he produced a history of early film that showed that it was in German film that the camera had *first* been rendered "completely mobile." This was a truth, he noted, evident to any "connoisseur."[49] He wasn't completely wrong, even as he knew about both European *Amerikanismus* and the contributions that early Soviet, American, and Japanese filmmakers had made to encourage Germany's cinematographic movement into mobility. Kracauer wanted what other exiles wanted: to salvage as best they could some part of Germany's history and culture from its Nazi appropriation. The remarkable history of film that began with Caligari could have had an end other than in the cinematic and social nightmare associated with Hitler's Reich.

Yet what Kracauer saw in Germany as having moved in the wrong direction he also saw in America, as its dreams were increasingly being sold by Hollywood. His book was not written, in other words, about only the Old World. He was not pleased by the loss of the word or by New World transformations of the word into caption and advertisement. In his criticism, he was not alone. Recall from chapter 1 the passage from Tennessee Williams's *The Glass Menagerie* (with the missing words now given), where we learn that boys from New York seeking flight in the open air seek it in the movies, then to discover that the movies prevent them from moving:

> Hollywood characters are supposed to have all the adventures for everybody in America, while everybody in America sits in a dark room and watches them have them! Yes, until there's a war. That's when adventure becomes available to the masses! *Everyone's* dish, not only Gable's! Then the people in the dark room come out. . . . But I'm not patient. I don't want to wait. . . . I'm tired of the *movies* and I am *about* to *move*!

One point is clear: "People go to the *movies* instead of *moving*." Notwithstanding, another thought is available—that in certain times of certain wars, it would be preferable were Tom to remain in the movie house, in Hollywood, dreaming to the accompaniment of all that lovely music.

Dissonance

The argument of dissonance is tied to the modernist and consciously anti-Hollywood film. Dissonant techniques are used to break through the deceptions and illusions of perfect wholes with happy endings by showing that the implicit contradictions in the film and in the world it portrays haven't been resolved. They are used to break the Hollywood aesthetic of false satisfaction or to crack the narcotic-hypnotic film trade. Dissonant techniques of interruption and shock are introduced to promote impatience and estrangement in the audience. Music serves not as accompaniment or illustration but as equal partner. Visual techniques of montage, close-up, and rupture find their analogues in musical form. The music neither directly tracks nor underscores the visual movement but moves sometimes along with and sometimes against it, sometimes forefronting, receding, anticipating, or holding itself back. The music stresses the differences of the constitutive mediums of film to break the habitual demand for sameness. It resists, as the camera and drama resist, the tendency to regard film as a totalizing, consummating, or harmonious work of art.

The most explicit argument for the dissonant approach was offered by Hanns Eisler and Adorno in their collaborative book, *Komposition für den Film*. Written in the 1940s, the book reflects their lives before and during exile. They drew significantly on the theories of others—mentioning Eisenstein and Kurt London—though also on their firsthand and secondhand experiences of filmmaking in Europe and America. In their view, to argue for the dissonant theory was to argue against duplication for the social and aesthetic reason that it was ineffective, unworkable, dishonest, and uneconomical. They knew that Hollywood film was not uneconomical in terms of what sells, but it was uneconomical if, by doubling up its mediums, it threatened the redundancy of any one. "Birdie sings, music sings," they quipped in criticizing what they termed "unhealthy doubling" (*schädliche Verdoppelung*). If you get the point by seeing it, you don't need also to hear it—if getting the point economically is the purpose of art. For them it was the point, just as it was for many modernists influenced by prevalent criticisms of ornamental excess in the arts and of the redundancy of persons under conditions of industrialized labor.[50]

As noted above, a strong tendency in developing arguments for film music is to borrow the theoretical moves of a traditional aesthetics of music, with the result that one tends to treat music as a language of emotion but not of cognition or concept. As such, the traditional approach to film music too easily plays into an old philosophical and even ideological divide between emotion and cognition that holds, most crudely, that what we *know* we know through the eye and what we *feel* we feel through the ear, denying the complex interaction between our senses and epistemological faculties. Thus, it is sometimes held that whereas a cognitive account might explain how *sound* and *noise* function in film in alliance with visual images or spoken text, only an emotive account will explain music's ability to track the movement of film's essentially audible mood (*Stimmung*).[51]

Following Benjamin (who referred to Paul Valéry), there is the contrary position that, given a new art or technology, one must entirely rethink the aesthetic and social terms. In rethinking these terms, Adorno and Eisler did not assume that cognitive and emotional elements should be divided as once they were. They urged a radical change in the traditional understanding of musical and specifically *aesthetic* discourse, to award music a both rational and sensuous role. This was stressed to the utmost in Adorno's preparatory notes, "Entwurf zum Filmmusikbuch," which began, "Es soll keine 'Ästhetik' der Musik im Film gegeben werden" ("the intention is not to offer an aesthetic of music in film"). What this meant was that film music was not yet sufficiently advanced as to call forth its *own* aesthetic and thus was still looking. Chapter 5 of Adorno and Eisler's published text began similarly, suggesting that Adorno was responsible for this carefully titled chapter, "Ideas toward an Aesthetic" ("Ideen zur Ästhetik," recalling chapter 4 of my own book regarding such titles). The translation sometimes given as "Elements of Aesthetics" fails to capture the extent to which Adorno and Eisler were investigating film and its music far more in terms of its potential than of its actuality.[52]

Film music, they argued, should look for its model in the expressionist, extreme, and inherently suspenseful developments of New Music. In the advanced use of "new musical material," rational construction and sensuousness were brought into antagonistic play. They rejected the idea that film should inherit without question the traditional illustrative, programmatic, or expressive tasks of a bourgeois music, particularly when the melody became so fetishized (*Melodiefetischismus*) that counterpoint was deemed unnecessary. Of course, melody would continue to be used, but only as adapted to film's contrapuntal demands. This meant rethinking how film conveys its musicality in order to liberate melody from conventional norms.[53]

New Music offered these authors something singularly appropriate to film, straightforwardly neither high nor low, fine nor popular, emotional nor rational. The way to reveal the overly polarized dualisms of traditional bourgeois categories was to occupy the uncomfortable and mediated places in between. On its own terms, New Music followed the law of autonomous musical development as all good music had always done. When used in film, however, this law could be suspended to allow the music to function alongside the film's dramatic and visual movement. In other words, the music could justifiably be broken up, freed from its traditional, developmental logic. Unlike music of the late symphonic age, New Music broke up easily since it already had techniques of rupture, patchwork, montage, gestural brevity, and condensation as part of its compositional and social conception.[54] In this regard, it was different from Wagner's lyrical, leitmotivic technique, since it neither implied an endless melody to mend or harmonize its disparate parts nor offered the sort of calling cards, as Debussy once called them, to announce Brünnhilde's imminent arrival on the set.

This view of dissonant film music rested on an independent musical argument to which Adorno and Eisler were already committed regarding the historical advance of one particular language of music—a dissonant one over a more traditional, harmonic language. Their primary ambition was to adapt an argument they had already given for advanced music to the film's new dissonant demands, instead of asking what music would best fit the film, given film's needs, without prior commitment to one sort of music over another. Some critics have noted this restriction in their approach by referring to the book's idiosyncratic character: that it was offered more as a primer for Eisler's own film music than as a general philosophical investigation; hence its pragmatic title. Here it was assumed that Eisler as composer would simply adapt to film what he had already achieved in the musical sphere. This interpretation is not unfounded, though it underemphasizes how attentive Eisler generally was to the demands the new technologies were making on the arts and especially on artists devoted to a left revolutionary politics. Before his collaboration with Adorno, his collaboration with Brecht had resulted in a worker's art of dialectical song. Through parody or farce, the new songs replaced old bourgeois songs by showing up the latter's inherent contradictions. For Eisler, all composing and not only "composing for film" was a revolutionary matter—of composing *for the times*.[55]

Adorno was similarly attentive to technology and to this dialectical argument, even if he was less swayed by explicit revolutionary demands. He wondered what was left of a bourgeois aesthetic and art, given the new technology. What he asked about film he asked about radio and phonograph: whether, say, the Wagnerian blended and soporific music didn't play too easily into a machine that, given its present not very good condition, had no choice but to sound *canned*. He described how the former cathedral-like, surround sound of a concert hall was reduced by the radio or phonograph to a small, neutered, or leveled-out sound. Wagner had described the space in his Festspielhaus as allowing the music to emanate from everywhere and nowhere, thus achieving a transcendent or ethereal unity. Conveyed by the radio, the sound was reduced to coming from anywhere and thus nowhere that mattered—the meaninglessness of the "here and there." If, for Adorno, Wagner's own music had resisted its soporific tendency in the live hall, it couldn't yet do this when played through the radio or through any other new reproductive medium, which meant dialectically that the latter technologies, even in their *unadvanced* state, were showing better than older ones the potential cultural-industrial dangers implicit in Wagner's music. From this Adorno concluded, so much the worse for this technology in its present form, and so much the worse for the music that is currently being processed through it.[56]

Adorno comparably considered the contemporary transmission of the highly differentiated movement of a Beethoven symphony. He asked whether the subtle dynamic or instrumental differences of the musical movement were yet technologically transmittable by the new media. If not, wouldn't it be better *for the time being* to produce a different sort of music more suited to the new media, a music specifically where the distinction between "technique" and "technology" was, if not completely erased, then brought into a new and appropriate relation?[57] Why didn't Adorno conclude that all new music should sound Wagnerian, given its alleged suitability to the new technology? Because there was always a choice, he insisted: to adapt already existing music to technology's present state or to encourage the technology to advance to meet the independent demands of a new and emancipated music—demands that, even if not fashionable, were more socially and aesthetically appropriate to the times. Thus, rather than resting content to hear already existing music, high or low, on inadequate equipment, Adorno encouraged the development of both: the music and the equipment. The outcome, he surmised, might be quite unexpected, especially if the technology advanced so well that listening to Beethoven's highly differentiated music once again became possible.[58]

By arguing for the use of New Music in film, Adorno and Eisler argued that no concession should be made by art to the present conditions of technology. New Music should be used as an indirect motivation to produce a technology to accommodate what is best or most important about art. However, they offered this argument not only to save art or to promote technology but also to save something of the experience that once was possible through the aesthetic use of our ears and eyes. If the dominant question was whether film could ever be an art on its own terms (a question Adorno actually despised), then the answer was yes, if it made a certain experience possible. In a medium that was claiming to double everything up, why did everything differentiated in human experience seem so quickly to melt into a meaningless, undifferentiated mass? And could film music do anything to help subvert this tendency? Adorno and Eisler thought it could.

Displacement

The argument for displacement acknowledges that music has multiple roles in film and that this music may result from all types of construction associated with classical, jazz, popular, and other traditions. It advances a complex auditory perspectivism to work alongside an equally complex visual perspectivism. The argument was developed recently by French theorists such as Gilles Deleuze and even more devotedly by the composer and film theorist Michel Chion. Both were influenced by Bergson's early writing on movement and by his conclusion that "the *mechanism of* [all] *our ordinary knowledge is of a cinematographical kind.*"[59]

Following Chion, music, and not just noise or sound, can be diegetic and nondiegetic, heard inside and outside, above, below, distant, near, and around. It can be heard, not heard, half-heard, heard in bits and pieces, drawing our attention to and away from it. It can serve as background music inside and outside the narrative frame. It can be foregrounded externally when it overwhelms the speech or image, say, through acceleration or increased dynamics, or internally when a character in the film bursts, as tenors used to like to do, into song. Music can be used to draw our emotional and cognitive attention to some element or person when we hear one person singing louder than those around them or when music is used to announce a coming storm. Shifting our attention through noise, sound, and music is what filmmakers consider when thinking about music for the sake of cinematographic movement. Their aim is to give credence to both the temporality and spatiality of sounds or to seek auditory analogues to the visual techniques of close-ups, sudden cuts, and camera shifts. They do not assume, however, that every shift in visual perspective must be matched by a musical shift. The argument for dissonance and difference is maintained. Nevertheless, difference or dissonance cannot always be the rule. Duplication and identification must be presupposed for dissonance to work. Or, as Balázs reminds us, distortion presupposes that some degree of realism is possible.[60]

Consider a view offered by phenomenologists that begins with the familiar claim that hearing is intentional. When we hear a sound, we hear a sound *of* something. This is not true and need not be true, however, of every musical sound or of every group thereof. It would be true only if one believed of an artwork or of an acoustic experience that every constitutive sound had to pick out a specific emotion, object, or mood for the whole to be meaningful. But this is the belief phenomenologists undermine when considering music's place in film. Music may generally be bound up with the visual and dramatic movement as a whole without requiring that each bit of music be specifically directed. "My perception is . . . not the sum of visual, tactile, and audible givens," Merleau-Ponty once wrote: "I perceive in a total way with my whole being; I grasp a unique structure of the thing, a unique way of being, which speaks to all my senses at once."[61]

Merleau-Ponty worked out this "unique way of being" by reference to how a subject experientially bonds with the world. Film demonstrates this mode of experience in a way, he argued, continuous with contemporary philosophy and psychology. What they all reveal is what Goethe revealed earlier in his poetic line: "what is inside is also outside." Goethe further described this truth as "a public secret" and as a holy truth grasped through the contemplation of nature, which leads me to the next point.[62] To regard music as bound up with the intentional whole of the film without demanding that it be intentionally pinned down in each instance in which it appears, one must be careful not then to reduce music to a merely duplicating function within the larger intentional space. Film music should be used as neither stopgap nor mere commentary but as communicating with a script of word and image that is *already,* Merleau-Ponty stressed, about sound and silence.[63] Music must thus be allowed to do what it does in relation to the intentional meaning produced by the film's other *musical* and *moving* components.

This claim may be enhanced via a conclusion drawn by John Belton: "In the sound cinema, we always see and hear events *through* images and sounds of them." Fine, but then he adds: "The cinema remains the phenomenological art par excellence, wedding, if indeed not collapsing, consciousness with the world."[64] Referring to this collapse, Belton arguably celebrates music's participation in an existentially harmonious wedding. On what assumption, however, does the wedding take place? Is it that when film is granted an intentional character it closes the gap between mind and world? Why not allow a divorce between consciousness and world where there should be one: namely, in the phenomenological experience of *art?* Why assume that a phenomenology of film works just like a phenomenology of everyday life or just like the pure contemplation of nature? Shouldn't the former accommodate the fact that one involves art as the latter do not, to avoid rendering art redundant?

In fact, this is Belton's argument, as it is Merleau-Ponty's. Despite assertions sometimes to the contrary, phenomenological accounts do not try to overcome the distance between film and world, however much the experience of one instructs us regarding that of the other. Whereas Belton pays attention to the technology that intervenes to prevent a straightforward collapse, Merleau-Ponty pays attention to how advances in technology occur together with advances in technique. Perhaps the wedding to which Belton refers is not so harmonious after all.

A phenomenological view of film sound assumes that sounds point to something, that they have an *of-ness* of meaning. This view is correct under these two conditions: first, that sounds assume meanings by pointing not to objects or moods in isolation but within complexes or Gestalt figures and, second, that the sorts of intentional meanings sounds help promote are different from those promoted by everyday sounds. These conditions are hardly controversial, yet they assume a new significance when combined with arguments once used to deny sound's entry into film.

Double or No Double

Merleau-Ponty offered a hint regarding this new significance when he drew on Roger Leenhardt's notion of "cinematographic rhythm":

> Just as a film is not merely a play photographed in motion and [just as] the choice and grouping of the shots constitutes an original means of expression for the moving picture, so, equally, the soundtrack is not a simple phonographic reproduction of noises and words but requires a certain internal organization which the film's creator must invent. The real ancestor of the movie soundtrack is not the phonograph but the radio play.[65]

What the radio play suggested, which the phonograph allegedly did not, was the idea that film might be an art of production without *re*production—hence, an art *without a double*. Out of this direct means of production emerged a new aesthetic and a new technique.

Consider now, in this matter of the missing double, how sight and sound have often been differentiated in the literature. Sounds cannot be isolated as images can; they motivate different kinds of identification. Sounds throw no shadow, have no double; they cannot be represented or forged. They have no tense and admit no conditional.[66] Whereas one image can stand behind another, sounds presumably of comparable decibels and competing for audible space don't cancel each other out but only amalgamate in more or less harmonious ways. Rudolf Arnheim drew on the claim that sound has no double to challenge music's integral incorporation into film, where the assumption was that a real sound is no different from an artistic sound. To incorporate music was, he insisted, to erode the representational gap between filmic fiction and reality, disqualifying film from what he wanted it to be: namely, a "pure art." However, to read Arnheim's argument ontologically (as many do) obscures its real motivation. Arnheim determined to keep film as a dominantly visual art and as an art of pure form, even, that is, if music, sound, or word were present. He wanted film to approach neither the sort of opera that put music first nor the sort of theater that put the word first. I think he also doubted that the basic ontological argument held, though in saying this one must be careful not to confuse arguments about *sound* with those about *music,* nor, indeed, arguments about *art* with those about *aesthetics.*

Hence, consider that even if sound admits no representational double, this does not mean that music brings to film an antiaesthetic element, even if, arguably, it introduces an antiartistic one. Recall Hitchcock's view that no mechanically reproduced music is heard in the natural or real world and therefore that there is nothing in the world for music to double up on as copy. That music admits no double doesn't thereby render it real but perhaps more purely aesthetic, at least if we follow Schopenhauer in arguing that music freed from mediated representation surpasses its status as a copying art. The inclusion of music in film might thus disqualify it from being an *art* but not from being purely aesthetic. Indeed, one might conclude that the moment music enters film, film is rendered more purely musical or aesthetic, and hence more expressive than it was before.

This argument works, paradoxically, only if music is treated metaphysically as *silent* and not empirically as *sounded* out. The moment music qua sound enters film, the lack of a double disqualifies film from being a pure art from the other direction. Since sounds qua sounds are real all the way through, they disqualify film from being purely "representational."

But this argument does not convince. Even if there can be no imitation of a real instance of the tone of C without its also being the real sound, there can be imitations of the trumpet sound of C when, say, the trumpet sound is produced by a computer. This is how many theorists distinguish musical works from the mere or basic sound events that constitute them, by referring to the sound's essential instrumental quality. No sound—whether noise, word, or music—enters a film as pure sound but already as a sound with artistic, aesthetic, or metaphorical properties. If, within a film, there are differences between noises, sounds, and music, these are differences of aesthetic, artistic, metaphorical, instrumental, and interpretative import and not of mere ontology. Clair made the point brilliantly and early on: "If imitation of real noises seems limited and disappointing, it is possible that an interpretation of noises may have more of a future in [film]. Sound cartoons, using 'real' noises, seem to point to interesting possibilities."[67] Here, interpretation counts more than imitation.

This argument recalls Danto's artworld argument of 1964. Considering primarily the art of Lichtenstein, Rauschenberg, and Johns, Danto describes how the contemporary art productions, say, of beds, were not intended to deceive anyone into thinking they were real beds because they were *not* produced as imitations. If anything, they seemed just to be the real things, which, if correct, meant that "any intended copy of a member of this class of objects [was] automatically a member of the class itself," hence, "these objects [were] logically inimitable." This, too, is what was claimed about sounds. Yet, though logically inimitable, the Rauschenberg beds were not thereby excluded from being art, just as cinematic sounds should not have been declared non-art because they ontologically threw no shadow. Film sounds, like art beds, following Danto, are in the end neither mere copies nor real things or events but have their own, unique status.[68]

What Danto called the artworld, early filmmakers called filmdom or filmland, the special institutional and historicized place where films are made, viewed, interpreted, and theorized. Whereas early filmmakers stressed the form of their films made in filmland, Danto drew on a later, more reflective stage of development in which interpretation, concept, and theory came to dominate both sense and form. For Danto, doubling up was no longer the issue and, with this, at least one anxiety associated with art's deception disappeared. However, for most other theorists confronting the loss of the double, the anxieties of deception remained. In his radio research, Adorno described how, despite the illusion of immediacy and presence, radio sound created a feeling of deep separation, as though the real sounds were produced only as echoes. Mirroring Roth's argument, radio sounds sounded like echoes because real sounds had become shadows of their former selves. If music was "antiartistic" in the modern age, this was a result of what technology had done and not of what ontology required.

Adorno described how the sort of presence formerly experienced in a concert hall, when listeners sat at a respectful distance from the orchestra, had been eroded by a technology that reduced aesthetic space to an empirical space defined by commercialized programming. The symphony that once promoted the illusion of pent-up time (recall chapter 1) was now experienced as identical to the forty-minute slot granted in the day, between meals, advertising, and newsbreaks. Little of the ritual of the live performance remained, especially the impression that behind a performance stood an "original" work. Like Roth, he concluded, the doubleness of the performance-work and the person-actor relationships had been displaced by another sort of doubleness that paradoxically had eradicated all difference.

Adorno wrote that live performances now sounded like their own phonograph reproductions (contra Merleau-Ponty's claim) or like radio reproductions because the real only replicates the already reproduced. One way to subvert this tendency toward identification, he suggested, was to produce radio music according to the condition of direct production as though musicians— like Merleau-Ponty's radio players—were playing directly onto the sound strips.[69] At least the music produced would be true to its technological condition by promising no double in the first place. Adorno drew on Benjamin's thesis that film represents the most advanced art when it relinquishes its claim magically to reproduce and admits its status as an art made for (re)production. When an art willingly relinquishes its status as a double, it reveals more social truth than when it becomes a double of a double to the nth (falsely) auratic degree: the proliferation of doubles without differentiation.

Later in life, in Darmstadt, when Adorno actually heard music directly produced on computers—as if somehow the computers were playing themselves—he didn't conclude that the technology had actualized its potential. Instead, he bemoaned the loss of tension of the work–live performance distinction. Was he contradicting himself? Maybe not, if what he now wanted to hear in film was different from what he wanted to hear in New Music. Whereas film music should go the way of technology, arguably New Music should not. This suggestion, however, contradicts his other view that, even in film, it would be preferable for technology to advance less to meet its own demands than those of the New Art. Perhaps he was corroborating another of his views: that even if technology and technique had *almost* collapsed into an identity, that collapse could be resisted the moment technique resumed the more dominant position. From this one could conclude that film music or radio music was truthful when it made explicit art's tendency to turn itself into a form of commodified and mechanized production. Here the truth was shown in commodified art's untruth as art. Or, contrarily, it was truthful, when, through the technique of the new, mechanically produced music resisted its own commodification and showed thereby that, even under modern conditions of technology, both art and aesthetic expression were still possible.

From Dissonance to Displacement

Adorno and Eisler rejected the idea that the correct way to think about film music was as inseparable from the film's prior commitment to visual musicality and movement. They rejected this idea to differentiate their view from the views of their influential predecessors, especially Eisenstein. They proclaimed the formalist view too narrowly formalist, too likely to collapse into an argument for duplication or perfect fit. The formalists, they wrote, "dealt predominantly with laws of movement (*Bewegung*) or color, the sequence, the cutting, or with vague categories such as 'inner rhythm.'"[70] Their claim is correct, even if as a criticism it wasn't completely fair. Mostly it expressed their unease that too pure a formal account would move film into a falsely autonomous aesthetic space divorced from any mediation of the social world or, contrarily, that aesthetic elements would be reduced to only the most crass materialism, leaving no tension within the aesthetic space or even for aesthetic space.

To avoid either risking the formal divorce of the aesthetic from the social or reducing music to a mere duplication of another artistic medium, they redirected their own argument. They started to make much of the radical nonsimultaneity or asynchronism of the eye and ear, of hearing and seeing, and of time and space. In the breaks given by nonsimultaneity, in the cracks in the harmonious whole, they saw the possibility of a movement that had dialectical consequences as much for society as for art. Yet they did not give up on a commitment to movement altogether, though they did tend to confine it to the most strictly dialectical of terms.

The argument for displacement also asks that auditory perspectivism be made to work alongside visual perspectivism without reducing musical or aesthetic matters to those of empirical or auditory perception. It asks what kind of knowledge one can attain through the technology of sight and sound. It seeks the kind of knowledge that is not only formal, phenomenological, or psychological but also socially critical. However, it does not commit itself strictly to a dialectical logic of dissonance—of question and answer, affirmation and negation, appearance and essence—which Adorno and Eisler's argument does in its explicit formulation, even if claims they make elsewhere sustain a theory of displacement in which a much greater range of movement is admitted.

More than the dialectical argument for dissonance, the broader argument for displacement emphasizes that a filmic world capable of movement is one that admits all manner of displacements between art and society. The point of the latter argument is to combine the formal theory of cinematic movement with the social theory of modernist displacement and modernist anxieties about deception, the sort of deception that motivated many modernist arguments about the arts.

Consider a scene recorded by theorist Arthur Knight, from Clair's film *À nous la liberté,* where the confusion of the real and unreal becomes the point of the scene itself. A young man gazes fondly at a woman who seems to be singing from a window. Something strange is heard in the song, since it seems to move in slow motion. Moments later, the girl appears in the street not singing, though still the song is heard. In this instant, we realize that we have been listening to a phonograph record from the next apartment.[71] This deception is similar to that Kant described when a young man's song sung from behind the bushes was mistaken for a song sung by a nightingale, and thus it assumes an increased significance as it plays into the anxiety that modern art celebrates its ability to deceive even when it allegedly claims not to.

In this matter, Adorno recalled an informal experiment in which he once participated when visiting friends near Frankfurt. In the countryside garden, he heard the nightingale's beautiful song in live performance. The Frankfurt Radio Station discovered the song and arranged to transmit it. The next time Adorno visited, he heard the live performance at the same moment as its broadcast. Still, between the two events he noticed a minuscule time delay, but not in the order he expected. Hearing the broadcast before the real event, he noted that the live song sounded suddenly like an echo of the transmitted version. Though he understood the scientific explanation, he was more interested in how the phenomenological illusion of immediacy and nearness produced by the radio had a quite different social character from the presence of a live performance.[72]

Warmth and Cold

One of the first arguments for film music was that music was needed to cover up the mechanical noise of the projector—for who, as one theorist asked, could ever believe that one's pleasure in film was produced by a machine?[73] I mentioned this claim in chapter 4 and noted there that the argument worked only if the music was produced live. If produced by machine, the machine character of film was maintained and even increased when the phonograph's drone proved louder than the projector's. This argument reflected an older argument for concealing the means of production for the phantasmagorical sake of creating a pure aesthetic illusion, either of a fictional world or, as with Hitchcock, of the real world. Even so, it did not convince. In 1909, Alfred Döblin argued that silent film, regardless of any mechanical noise, was already assaulting the visual senses with the gush and violence of the film's content and, therefore, that at least "better educated" persons could exit the cinema happy in the realization that their ears had been left intact.[74]

Döblin's remark countered another argument for allowing sound in: namely, that the sense of hearing did not *want* to be left out of the new art; indeed, that the ear *needed* something to do. "In the cinema, the ears should somehow be occupied," Frank Warschauer commented in 1929: "that is the origin of film music."[75] By itself, this is an argument for music's or sound's presence, though not for either's full incorporation into film. Music or sound effects might satisfy the ear even if heard only in the accompanying background. Presumably, then, Warschauer meant more: that the ear wants something aesthetic to do on a par with the activity of the eye. Yet this claim conflicts with what we know to be generally true in the visual arts: that the ear is perfectly satisfied being at rest when the eye is viewing paintings or sculptures. This is not to deny that hearing plays an active part in aesthetic imagination, even when or just because there is nothing literally to be heard. Charlie Chaplin defended silent film for just this reason: visual clues are enough to excite all the senses, touch and smell included—so why the *necessity* for sound?

Perhaps the claim is that the ear only needs something to do when the other senses fail us. What, as many asked, is the advantage of reading captions or lip-reading characters on the screen if one can hear what the characters are saying? Surely real voices are less distracting, because more normal, than the intermittent appearance of screen captions? Chaplin was not convinced, as Woody Allen, later, was not convinced: juxtaposing images and captions was normal, at least for Chaplin, just as it is normal in cartoons when captions produce a sort of choric commentary on the visual plot. Why, then, deny film its form or make the cinematic experience just like everyday life under the claim of "normalcy," especially when everyday life seems either to be what we want to escape from in the first place or the cause of our anxiety when we experience it directly or too realistically on film?[76]

Others argued that why our ears need something to do admitted of the same rationale as to why background music is needed in restaurants—to smooth over embarrassing silences between people who have lost the ability to converse. "Good," one might retort, "because we don't want people to talk in the cinema." Or, as Stravinsky apparently retorted, if this is the role music plays, let's stop calling it "music."[77] More than these retorts, the argument again reflects both artistic and sociological complexities.

In one argument, it was maintained that music was able to fill up an empty space created by an art that, though two-dimensional, promised the illusion of a three-dimensional reality. Again, however, if film was the successor to painting and photography, the argument was as inappropriate to film as it was to any other visual art. Did anyone ever seriously claim that music could solve the "problem" of two-dimensionality in painting, as if that were a problem? And what would we have been given: general music or specific bits to accompany each separate painting? (In the eighteenth century, arguments like these were in fact proffered, though in response to overcoming the ontological limitations of all the arts, not just painting.)

For those who regarded film as the successor to theater, opera, or drama, the argument was perhaps more plausible. Music could fill up an *emotional* void by giving life, breadth, and depth to a world that was otherwise experienced as lifeless, restricted, and superficial. On the assumption that music is the language par excellence of mood and emotion, it was claimed that music warmed up, enhanced, and even brought to color screen images that were by themselves flat, dimensionless, and monotone. "The movies," Aaron Copland concluded in 1940, "need music, and need it badly. By itself the screen is a pretty cold proposition. . . . Music is like a small flame put under the screen to help warm it."[78]

Kracauer offered a more subtle argument: music bolsters the materiality of visual or photographic images more than providing them emotional warmth:

No doubt musical accompaniment breathes life into the silent pictures. But it resuscitates them only to make them appear as what they are— photographs. . . . Music is not intended to restore mute spectacles to full reality . . .: it is added to draw the spectator into the very center of the silent images and have him experience their photographic life. Its function is to remove the need for sound, not to satisfy it.[79]

Film music was here legitimated by *serving* film as a visual art. New meaning was given to the silence of silent film because the silence was now a form of *animation* that admitted rather than excluded music. Silent film was not about the absence of sound but about the muteness of the image.

Adorno brought this argument to an anxious extreme by suggesting that music, and specifically one technologically produced, augmented the coldness, not the warmth. In its less-perfect technological state, silent film, he remembered, was warmer. When less was given as art, more was left for imagination and fantasy. When the ear was left out of film's equation, the ear was given a certain freedom denied it when the art reached a more technologically totalized state. With Horkheimer, Adorno justified these claims by reference to how "the whole world" was now being filtered seamlessly through the culture industry, leading moviegoers to find a perfect continuity between what they experienced in the cinema and what they experienced outside. The introduction of the sound film with its technique of "mechanical duplication" sustained this false finding. Unlike the traditional theater, they concluded, film denied its audience the free play of fantasy and instead asked only for immediate empathy and identification.[80] In a passage Adorno titled "How nice of you, doctor?" he added: "Every visit to the cinema leaves me, against all my vigilance, stupider and worse," less because film's content offends and more because the communication and sociability that cinema promises is false. It's like saying "Have a nice day": every day one's humanity is cooled and one's inhumanity is warmed.[81]

As long as film remained a black and white art, the eye resisted film's tendency either to saturate the sense or to produce the cheap but colorful illusion that film is identical to real life. Here, Adorno mirrored an argument he made about the radio. In its early stages, radio, in its *imperfection,* retained a space for genuine experience, even if most of the experience was given in Proustian mode as a memory of things past. The more advanced radio became, the more it offered a music reduced to commodity on the social side and to a trivial or sentimental expressiveness on the aesthetic side, a music in which even the traces held in memory were eradicated.[82]

Why did Adorno retreat to a form of art or technology before the moment of its alleged total petrification? So (in the spirit of the "almost") he could find something retrievable to help subvert the historical trajectory from reaching its most deadly form. Sometimes, like Cavell, he recalled the child's eye that still viewed the world in black and white; sometimes, as when collaborating with Eisler, he listened with an ear that had purportedly retained something of its archaic condition. "Hearing," he wrote with Eisler, "in comparison with seeing, is 'archaic,' and has not kept up with technique." While the eye is agile and discriminating and functions at the speed of the "late industrial age," the more passive ear remains a little oblivious.[83]

To consider the ear as lagging behind the already depleted eye allowed the ear, and the music composed for it, to express something that, were it fully advanced, it could no longer express. That something would be akin to what they described as a hidden, invisible, or repressed feeling for a collective that hadn't yet become completely drunk with its own power. For an example, they proposed Eisler's score for Brecht and Lang's *Hangmen Also Die* (1943). Later in life, Adorno also mentioned Maurizio Kagel's score for the 1965 film *Antithèse: Film for One Performer with Electronic and Everyday Sounds*, a film in which Adorno found what he most often found in works he considered genuinely new: a space for repressed individuals to speak through silence in opposition to the articulated and compromised word.[84]

It has often been noted that in *Hangmen Also Die,* at the end of the introductory music (*Titelmusik*), Eisler used a ten-pitch chord, heard the moment one is confronted with a portrait of Hitler. About this chord, Eisler and Adorno declared:

> There is hardly any traditional harmony that has the same power of expression as this extremely advanced sound. Only the twelve-tone chord at the moment of Lulu's death in Berg's opera comes close to producing the effect of film. While the film technique aims essentially at creating extreme tension, traditional music, with the dissonances it tolerates, knows of no equivalent material.[85]

To bring their point home, they contrasted their preferred music with the inadequate music offered for *San Francisco,* the moment the roof of a night bar collapsed, or for *King Kong,* when the elevated railway was hurled onto the streets in New York. Having been assimilated or familiarized by the ear, this music, they maintained, failed to register the real shocks of modern city life.

However, reconsider Eisler's ten-pitch chord. Though an amalgamated sound, it does not amalgamate harmoniously. It aimed to achieve what those other strong and brief chords of New Music allegedly achieved: to register singular protests approximating extreme screams. Yet, shouldn't Eisler and Adorno admit that though dissonant in aim, this particular chord only doubles up on the image already shown? Or isn't it enough to see Hitler's over-sized portrait on the wall?

Here there is a tension: Do they really think that images do not have the shock value that sounds now have, given the allegedly more compromised or advanced condition of the eye? Surely images and sounds can equally shock or fail to shock, both thus demonstrating their allegedly archaic or compromised condition. Why give the advantage to the ear? Aren't they falling back, despite their own assertions to the contrary, on an old argument that the ear stands in a different relation to society than the eye does? If this is an issue for Adorno and Eisler, it is for anyone who claims that the technology for the ear lags behind that for the eye. It does not and never has. Still, even if they had balanced their argument to avoid prioritizing one sense over another, this wouldn't have necessarily implied that hearing and seeing had now to move hand in hand. Perhaps, it suffices to recall the pragmatic aim of their book and to say that, because they wanted to show specifically what music offered to film as a potential art of the genuinely new, they overplayed the hand of the ear.

Ultimately, what Eisler and Adorno called genuinely New Music was music that was unlikely ever to become assimilated, even, I would add, in horror films, though not in the sort normally so classified in stores. Their point about dissonant film music was to reveal horror not when horror announced itself as such but when it did not: when it was hidden behind the ordered illusion of a society's "happy match." This is a basic principle also of the argument for displacement, though, as I insisted, it must apply as much to the function of the eye as to that of the ear, and, indeed, to the function of any other sense involved in the experience of film.

The Erotic Return of the Ghosts

The argument most often offered for the full incorporation of music into film affirmed music's ability to pacify or soothe the uncanny feeling that audiences allegedly experienced when they first saw ghostlike figures on the screen. Theorists usually noted, however, that it was unlikely a real fear of ghosts at stake and more the silent atmosphere of the darkened cinema when moving images flashed before their eyes. Kracauer recalled how, whenever the music suddenly broke down in the accompaniment of a silent film, a deathly hush became palpable. The images corporealized by music's presence were suddenly reduced to the mere shadows they really were.[86] (Maybe it was this memory that inspired him to argue also that music should be used to bring attention to the lifelessness of images even when the music doesn't break down.)

Generally motivating the ghostly discourse was the connection early film had to the shadow play, magic-lantern show, marionette theater, and pantomime. Given this connection, two questions arise. First, were audiences ever really so unnerved by film, given all their prior experience of moving images? Second, didn't the ghostly images suit what all these early mediums did so well—satisfy the erotic desire for horror and lust viewed at a safe distance in the dark? So far I have written nothing about the erotic experiences of images, but many early commentators did and often to express another fear. Yet, though eroticism entered significantly into the social criticism of film, the critics rarely went so far as to support the increasingly harsh censorship policies being introduced in their time to control both the medium and the desire.[87]

Consider how muddy the ghostly and erotic argument became the moment the question of music's entry into film arose. In the history of musical aesthetics, it was often claimed that whereas words and visual images offer a comfortable and humanized representation of the world, music is the most unnerving of the arts. How, then, could music be appealed to to pacify nerves if, when in full symphonic power, it led one down the Dionysian path? Hadn't the world of shadows or representation always offered comfort, even if a false comfort, denying knowledge to those who looked only at shadows? How, now, was this argument turned around to make music suddenly the most comforting of the arts? Certainly, music had always been praised for its soothing and medicinal qualities, yet this praise counters the Wagnerian environment in which film emerged, an environment in which music was now being regarded as the most dangerous and decadent of the arts.

Still, to regard film music as soothing or as capable of warming up the coldness of the modern world was one censorious way, I would suggest, that was developed to express the desire and need to domesticate film's potential violence or shock. How better to discipline film than with domesticated music? Film would require no formal government censorship were composers simply brought into the industry to dampen the impact of shocking images. And what better music to compose than a tamed Wagnerian music, so that a music that was thought to threaten most would now not threaten at all? For music to become a comfortable doubling-up art was for music to assume a copycat status, conforming exactly to what an oppressive society was demanding of its new media. In this view (and following chapter 6), music was stripped of its ability to shatter the false comforts of mere representation and made to keep these comforts in place. The ghosts having left town, film music turned film into a safe *socially representational* art.

Film Music as False Compensation

Eisler and Adorno discussed the ghostly argument vigorously. "The pure play of light must have had a ghostly effect similar to that of the shadowplay in which shadow and ghost have always belonged together." To appease "the evil spirits unconsciously dreaded," music must have been introduced as a kind of antidote (*Gegengift*).[88] Music, they argued, did not supply screen effigies with missing life; this became the aim only in the era of total ideological planning. Music then helped spectators to absorb the shock, by which these authors meant, the shock of the spectators' contemporary condition. This argument belonged less to Eisler than to Adorno, who borrowed it from Kurt London to turn it on its head. Philip Rosen, a recent commentator on Adorno, is one of the few to have noticed the dialectical use to which Adorno put the argument. He correctly records Adorno's view that if music humanized film in the Hollywood era of ideological planning, it did this by further concealing Hollywood's and, by extension, society's inhumanity from view.[89] Film with music thus doubly deceived. First, the images told us that all is right with the world, and then music entered the picture to reinforce rather than to contradict the message.

By enveloping people in lovely sound, or by turning listeners into happy participants, or even by making chilled strangers feel as though they sat next to each other in closenesss and warmth, the music contributed perfectly to society's attempt to absorb everything in its allegedly rational planning. To be overwhelmed by lovely music was to experience a gray world as saturated with panoramic color, even if no color, as no sound, had any genuine meaning left. Music as warmed-up color had the character of folderol, Adorno maintained: the only thing warmed up is the "desolation of the inner sense."[90]

Elsewhere, Adorno argued that Hollywood film, like television and radio, offered only substitute or displaced satisfactions. Overpowering by word, image, and music, film, rather than letting persons feel their fear, smoothed fear over with false comforts, screening the almost primordial fear audiences had when confronted with half-living effigies on the screen. What exactly did audiences fear? Again, not ghosts, but the fact that they had become the figures they were seeing before their eyes: empty, monotonous, and flat. The muteness or deadness they experienced was the sort of muteness that Adorno thought Beckett captured perfectly in his plays, even if more immediately it emanated from the experience of sitting in a restaurant in which, having lost their sense of living life, consumers waited endlessly for something to fill up the empty space. In these settings of experienced loss, music compensated, though impotently. The more the music was not Mozart's but only sounded *like* Mozart, the more *music* became *Musak*, the double of what, in fact, was never a double in the first place.

To say that spectators and listeners identified with what they heard or saw is to say that the dead images or withdrawn sounds reflected their own dead condition. What we saw in film was something *true to life*, but where the life to which film was true was as commodified or authoritative as the (musical) work to which we thought we were being true when we reproduced the work perfectly in its image. What we feared most about film was our submission to the high-fidelity illusion that this is just how life is. This is the final turn of the key in the argument of displacement, showing how the fear of art displaces our fear of life.

Deception Revisited

Kracauer recorded a comment once made by Frederic March that "the film actor must act as if he did not act at all but were a real person caught in the act by the camera. He must seem to *be* his character." Yet, he must also be himself. Adorno wondered whether such a double position was possible anymore. Whereas theater might once have been about character acting, film, following Benjamin, was constructed by "takes" and "shots." What Joseph Roth called ghosts, Adorno, Eisler, and Benjamin called "stars," but others called them "stuntmen" at the moment when the stars refused even to participate in their own shots.[91] Doubles of doubles of doubles—double prints and double exposures—all collapsed into the eternal sameness and endless deceptions of appearance (as, say, in the Quentin Tarantino film of 2007, *Deathproof*— which is anything but).

When Wagner developed his sacred space in Bayreuth, he dimmed the lights to create a world to which audiences could have immediate aesthetic access. Yet no one ever thought that the audiences were deceived into thinking that the world Wagner created was the real world itself. However, they did say this about film. What, I finally want to ask, accounts for the difference, if there is a difference? One answer would be to say that early anxious critics of film confused deception and illusion. Even if film depends, as in opera, on offering a convincing illusion, the illusion does not necessarily imply or even require deception. Another answer returns us to a distinction drawn earlier: whereas film aims for realism or naturalism, opera aims for stylization. But, in the end, cinematographic realism is also about style and even operatic style and, thus like opera, has everything to do with how things *appear*, especially when what this appearance reveals is how far film (or opera) contributes to reconstructing the world in its own image.

In 1916, Münsterberg wrote: "*Nevertheless we are never deceived; we are fully conscious of the depth, and yet do not take it for real depth.*" Why did he write this with emphasis? Because, though film offers us a "*reality with all its true dimensions,*" the reality it offers is an artistic mixture of "*fact and symbol*" and is thus different from the reality of "*hard facts.*" Similarly, Vertov wrote (as Danto might have written): "If a fake apple and a real apple are filmed so that one cannot be distinguished from another on the screen, this is not ability, but incompetence—inability to photograph."[92] Both these remarks address the idea that deception implies some sort of perceptual error. But there is another sort of deception that has more to do with social deception by aesthetic means, in which an audience is "taken in" by what they see and hear. It is this more all-enveloping social deception that Clair aimed to counter when he wrote:

> I have observed people leaving the cinema after seeing a talking film. They might have been leaving a music hall, for they showed no sign of the delightful numbness which used to overcome us after a passage through the silent land of pure images. They talked and laughed, and hummed the tunes they had just heard. *They had not lost their sense of reality.*[93]

What I finally suggest is that the entry of music into film displaced the problem of deception away from perceptual or copying error to expressive error, away, one might well say, from Plato's ontological concerns of book 10 back to his sociological concerns of book 3. When we fear music we do so because it leads us to believe false things and because it makes us *feel* satisfaction, when, from the perspective of truth, dissatisfaction ought to be the (dis)order of the day. From this it follows that film is much more like opera than some have claimed, especially those who have overly separated the *realism* and *naturalism* of one from the *style* or *high stylization* of the other. If

Wagnerian music drama deceives, it does so as film as visual music deceives: not by perceptual errors of imitation but by errors of phantasmagoric expression and form.

When Clair remarked that audiences did not lose their sense of reality, the question was whether this was something with which one should have commiserated or celebrated. Clair meant that audiences were not taken in by what they saw when they entered the cinema. But this should not mean that what audiences had at the end of their cinematic experience was only the reality they began with, because, then, there would be little cognitive or social point in entering the cinema in the first place. The aim of this argument is not to neutralize the deceptive potential of film by blind references to reality. Nor is it to encourage the view that film's deceptive potential is so complete that we end up believing that the real world as it presently appears in film is all that is the case.

Adorno ungenerously criticized his childhood friend Kracauer for falling prey to the undialectical claims of false immediacy, for failing to maintain a sufficiently dialectical movement between art and reality. He believed that what Kracauer aimed for with his idea of "camera work" was to reach the world without mediation.[94] To equate camera *work* with camera *life* undermined a difference Adorno aimed to preserve. The more camera work denies what it is—a technique of art governed by the rules of art—the more arty or artificial (*künstlich*) it becomes. Film takes us further away from the world and not closer to it. I have presented this argument many times in this book, as used by Adorno against Cage and against anything promoting itself as a new naturalism or realism. But consider a comparable expression of the argument now by Hofmannsthal: those who go to the cinema, he wrote, "feel that [the power of film] leads only deeper into the machinery and farther and farther away from actual life."[95] With this feeling, he continued, new bonds form between them in a way that temporarily separates them from the shackles of higher learning. Whether or not Hofmannsthal approved this temporary separation is not my concern here. Of more interest to me is the conclusion that his words afford us: that from the new bonds we might be granted something quite new and thus something more positive to take away with us when leaving the cinema.

Behind the arguments presented in this chapter, film has been regarded as a fated art, a disenchanted art, an art already signifying social death, given the time of its birth and development. But it was and arguably still is such an art also because of the potential it has to be the art of the new that tries constantly to leave the traditional arts in its wake. That the traditional arts fight back against film gives them, in turn, a present and future. Hence, one might well conclude that film as a late art arrived just in time to prevent the demise of art overall.

Like Adorno, Cavell described how film shows us a world of our own making or promotes the fantasy—for the skeptic who can't live with his skepticism—that this is a world given, already past and complete, as if its life has already been lived. This description matches a description offered in chapter 5 regarding the pastness of the work. It accords with the sort of modernist experience that is confined to the past tense because with this tense we think we can come to know the world with certainty. We look at films as photographs, Cavell explained, believing that as long as living persons stand in front of the camera, their life gives security or fixity to the meaning we see in the images. When we realize that what is alive or real is in fact already past, and that no living person stands behind the screen, our connection or conviction is broken, and, suddenly, it all feels very cold. At the opposite extreme to Adorno though meeting him at the conclusion, Cavell described how modernist loss is felt when we experience the film as having withdrawn the real from us by setting it into the past. In vain, we try to domesticate the loss through the pursuit of something onto which we can securely hold (childhood or memories), even if in truth we feel ourselves shipwrecked in the (Hitchcockian) lifeboat that is our present.

In his lectures on the increasing authoritarian posture of Hegel's philosophy, Adorno linked this pursuit of certainty, clarity, and timeless knowledge to the static gaze of a camera that sits on a tripod.[96] Unmoving, he quipped, the camera would rather shoot the world in place than allow the world to break free from its gaze. Philosophical thinking, if it can learn from film, as both Cavell and Adorno think it can, should thus be pitched so that the musicality of its movement does not make us too quickly accept the pastness of experience as *entirely past* or the presentness of experience as all there *is*. Submitted to critical reflection, film, like philosophy, is thereby awarded a future—and, as we know, sometimes a most marvelous one.

When Adorno and Eisler wrote about ghosts, they recalled Karl Kraus's critique of contemporary language, from which they concluded that language has fallen mute, emptied of its former human significance, the more it has become a shadow of what it once was. To this they added that film audiences are not scared of the ghostly silence but, ultimately, of their own inability to speak. Decades later, Chion developed this argument by referring to what he called phantom sound or audition. We not only see ghosts, he insisted, we also hear them, though what we hear when we hear ghosts is that there is, in fact, no longer anything left to hear in a world that has become silent through the intensity and pervasiveness of its noise. Chion described the anxiety audiences must have felt when first watching Fellini's 1957 *Nights of Cabiria,* in which, in a magical landscape that becomes a site of crime, "not a single birdsong is heard."[97]

Chion's example resonates with a long-standing trope of modernism, expressed early on by an unhappy European, who, having arrived in America, noticed that in the New World no nightingale yet sang. With this, I have the last sentence for this chapter and the first for my next. For my final chapter is about the hopes expressed and the hopes shattered by those who once left the Old World for the New, but who found themselves displaced, for good and for bad, at every step along the way.

8 Amerikamüde / Europamüde
The Actuality of American Opera

What is impossible in Europe is possible in America: what is impossible in
America is not possible at all!
—Ferdinand Kürnberger, *Der Amerikamüde*

This rotation of crops is the vulgar, inartistic rotation and is based on an
illusion. One is weary of living in the country and moves to the city; one is
weary of one's native land and goes abroad; one is *europamüde* and goes to
America etc.
—Søren Kierkegaard, *Either/Or*

In the late 1830s, Charles Sealsfield (born Karl Anton Postl), wrote a
novel titled *Die deutsch-amerikanischen Wahlverwandtschaften*. It was one of
many such novels of the period in which young men left Germany in search of
something better in America, typically a nightingale's song. Rarely were these
men oblivious to prevalent opinions held back home, that "the Americans"
are "totally oblivious" to spiritual life and prefer only the "dollars jingling
in their pockets" or that, with neither nightingales nor wine in their land,
they listen to mockingbirds while sipping apple cider.[1] When they arrived in
America, however, reality hit. Sometimes they found something better than
what they had expected and sometimes something far worse, but ultimately
nothing so radically different from the home they'd left behind. Sealsfield's
travel pictures were not completed and were later published as an extended
fragment. Adorno would argue a century later that fragmentation was the
most appropriate outcome in a too-complete story of German-American
relations.

The Subject

My subject is the concept of American opera. I situate a particular discourse about this concept within a more general one about actuality and possibility, weariness and hope, drawn from predominantly German-American philosophies of history and art. I produce two interwoven narratives: one focused on Adorno's work; the other moving back through the writings of the early nineteenth century to the "founding moment" of the New World when, so it once was said, "all the world was America."[2] For the last time, I situate Adorno's view within a broader narrative to show the pervasiveness of the narrative, on the one hand, and its dialectical movement, on the other—that is, the sort of movement that Adorno's immanent critique renders explicit.

Mostly I survey competing narratives regarding the concept of American opera around the time of the Second World War. First, I present the more abstract narratives, moving through Adorno back to earlier thinkers and times. Then I consider four concrete narratives: the polyglotic, the purist, the democratic, and the posthistoricist. Each is represented by a distinct theorist, only the last of whom is well known: Diane Kestin, William Saunders, Hans W. Heinsheimer, and John Cage. Each demonstrates something about teleological attitudes toward America that tend, I argue, to disenfranchise American opera, even as they are meant to empower it.

For much of its history, especially after the 1820s, American opera served as an *institutional* concept referring to any opera sung in English and produced in the United States: Weber in English, Rossini in English. The only operas that tended to be excluded were those by American composers. Around 1930, "American opera" predominated as a *classificatory* concept designating operas produced "of the people, by the people, for the people," which is to say, by Americans, for Americans, on American themes. Although this was a moment of liberation for the concept, it did little to bring opera by Americans into the institutional mainstream of operas performed in the United States. While the concept of American opera was won by Americans, the institution of opera in the United States was not.

The tension in the history may be variously expressed. The more that European, and specifically German, opera was thought to be in decline or even to have come to an end, the more hope was pinned on what American opera might be—as opera's only or last chance. Or just when American opera became a concept *for* America, it became a concept designed to capture the future of *all opera*. In both cases, what was supposed to be unique about *American* opera was drained of any substantial meaning. Alternatively, the more the concept was subsumed into a teleological narrative about the progress, decline, or end of Europe, the more it was severed from any real or actual empirical history of opera or music in the United States. This left the concept serving an ideal or ideological role far more than a constitutive one in an institution that continued to favor its European warhorses. Recall that just as America was once called "the land of the future" (Hegel), so a specific sort of German opera was once named "the music of the future" (Wagner). What sort of conceptual and political rearrangement, I ask, occurred to combine claims about America with claims about opera to make American opera the new opera of the future—and with what inexorable consequence?

Though my focus is given to a German-American dialectic, the issues pertain also to what happened in France, Britain, Italy, and Russia, or in Europe when Europeanism was contrasted with Americanism, or when the West was contrasted with the East.[3] References to "Germany" usually include Austria and other German-speaking lands; sometimes they connote Europe as a whole. "America" sometimes refers to the entire Americas as a continent or to the geopolitical entity that is the United States. As an adjective, "American" means, positively and negatively, utilitarian, pragmatic, republican, democratic, natural, romantic, uncivilized, or not yet civilized. As a movement from the 1920s, "Amerikanismus" refers to something happening in Europe; as a psychological condition, *Americomania*—well, this can occur anywhere to anyone at any time. To overrefine the terms only conceals the complexities of inclusion, exclusion, generality, and specificity in this history of turbid waters.

Though recent scholarship rightly warns against dualistic models that overpolarize differences, I engage the sort of critical theoretic approach that self-reflectively employs just such a model to expose what is most at stake in its sustained use of certain concepts and terms. Though entirely sympathetic to them, my approach differs from what one finds in John Dizikes's classic *Opera in America* or in Carol Oja's recent book about how music was made modern (and American) in the 1920s. Oja challenges the "enshrined myths" implied by the "chest-thumping," dualistic German-American discourse of "music in this new found land."[4] Like Dizikes, she draws a marvelous historical picture of what happened why and when, revealing the complexity of involvement between American and European attitudes. I offer something different, a critical history of the concept of American opera at a certain level of perpetuated and mythified abstraction, explicitly to expose assumptions that, despite all the recent dismantling work, remain prevalent.

Naming and Nationhood

I first became interested in the question of identifying opera according to its national character when granted the opportunity to write about Verdi's 1871 opera *Aida,* where 1871 marks a critical moment in the history of modern nations. Most intriguing was the fact that though this opera had vigorously and competitively been described as Italian, French, and Egyptian, it had never apparently occurred to anyone, not even to Edward Said, to name it, as if in an act of sympathetic baptism, an Ethiopian opera. To avoid this description, I argued, was to play into the hands of the opera itself, to treat the Ethiopians as they are treated within the opera: as the "underdogs" or "savages" (from the libretto) and thus as not worthy enough even to constitute a legitimate "side" in a nationalist war. I said that to identify an opera with a particular nation was too often an identification of assumed success, an identification in which the opera names the victor in advance and where the desire for victory necessitates the destruction of any person who gets in its way.

In these terms, I said, *Aida* is less an opera *about* a war between two nations and more a one-sided opera of colonialist achievement. Or, from its very first note, Ethiopia was chosen "for destruction" because, to recall the rationalization sung by the high priest Ramfis in militaristic echo of words uttered by the king of Prussia, God had already taken Egypt's side. Any victory would thus be an easy one—"facil vittoria." My argument was not against nationalism per se, nor did it rest ultimately with this particular reading of the opera. But it was aimed against the assumed success of one nationalist group against another and, more, against the sort of religious or historicist nationalism so often seen in opera, though not only there (following chapter 5), that proclaims victory before even the battle is fought.[5]

The second opportunity to think about nationalism in opera was awarded me when I was asked to participate in a conference initially titled American Opera—Opera in the Americas. I immediately became obsessed with the dash, wondering whether it implied an "and" or an "or." An "and" suggested an expansion in the concept of American opera to include the operas also of the Americas. But an "or" seemed to demand more: that the arguably unitary, exclusive, or closed concept of American opera be *replaced* by a clearly more inclusive or open one. The language of openness well accommodated a conference aimed, so it seemed, at fully democratizing the concept of American opera in large part to reenfranchise what had allegedly been excluded from its domain.

When the conference took place, those interested in opera in the Americas happily proved by both word and deed that the first operas on the American continent were performed in the Americas around 1700. More, they showed that opera's history in the Americas had occurred without any particular *need* to develop a concept of American opera, and this, despite vigorous debate in the different countries of the Americas over the national identity of their arts. Once this became apparent, most of the discussion turned back to the United States and its concept of American opera.

However, the discussion generated anxiety. Few could decide what sort of concept American opera was supposed to be: a classificatory concept; a concept delimited by geographical boundaries; or a concept expressing cultural, social, or political ideals? And how much did it include: any opera written by an American composer? any production performed in an American opera house? any opera with an American theme? any opera with a distinctively American musical idiom? Could an American opera also be a piece of Broadway theater, or a performance piece from the American, experimental avant-garde, or even an early Marx Brothers musical film like *Cocoanuts* (as one participant suggested)?

From these questions, another tension emerged. Most participants were inclined to treat American opera as a classificatory concept referring to an impressive body of works but yet were content to pronounce the institution of American opera in crisis, and hence to treat the concept as *institutional*. I wondered whether attempts either to democratize or not to democratize the concept had contributed to the institution's alleged crisis. Or did the problem lie elsewhere—perhaps with the very idea of producing opera in the United States even more than with the idea of producing specifically American opera?

I wondered also whether the conference might not finally be called "Operas in the Americas" to do justice to both terms, to "America" and to "opera." Again a problem arose, for when the term "opera" was first coined, it was already the plural of the singular term "opus" or "work." Only later, and especially with the emergence of national operas, did "opera" assume a substantive and singular connotation to mark not only a specific musical-theatrical genre—Italian opera or French opera, say—but also and increasingly a specific production of individual great works. One needed only to track how earlier and more popular French and Italian traditions of grand opera had gradually become dominated by a Wagnerian and increasingly dedicated search for absolute works of the future. Clearly, any inquiry into the concept of American

opera had to be twofold, to account for what it meant both for American opera to be *American* and for American opera to be committed to the production of *works.*

Still, might not a decision about the former determine the scope of the
latter? This question prompted two more: What if the conceptual inquiry
showed that up to a given point an American opera had hardly ever been
performed in the United States, because its history had mostly meant the production of European opera in American opera houses? And what if the political ideal of being American proved so out of sync with the specific form of
cultural production—with a serious or elite production of works—that the
very concept of American opera turned out to be a contradiction in terms?
These questions proved fruitful even as they suggested something dreadful,
rather too akin to the European high- or male-mindedness that several German philosophers once exhibited when asking whether to speak of educated
women is a contradiction in terms.[6]

More after the conference than before, I pursued an inquiry that gave me
a specific historical beginning and end. It was premised on the idea that much
of the anxiety surrounding American opera originated in the need to transform what was clearly a European practice of opera production in the United
States into something more suitably homespun (minus the derogatory connotation of this term). With the anxiety so stated, I decided that that original
dash was best interpreted as an "or," but the sort of "or" going back to the
early enlightenment when the Marquis de Sade wrote his infamous *Juliette ou
les Prospérités du Vice.* De Sade used his *or* to show the contradiction in the
figure that is Juliette, a figure subject both to the freedoms and constraints
of what Horkheimer and Adorno later called (in their *Dialectic of Enlightenment*) "Aufklärung und Moral."[7] With this in mind, I decided to offer a history of opera in the United States as a history of both freedom and constraint
determined at different times by the particular content given to the concept
of American opera. At the very least, the history would both fit and complete
the project of the present book.

Life Doesn't Live Here Anymore

When Adorno attempted between the last months of 1932 and the early, fateful months of 1933 to compose an opera based on Mark Twain's *Adventures
of Tom Sawyer,* did he try to compose an American opera? This is not an easy
question to answer, though prima facie one would answer "no." Not only

did he give his work a German title—"Der Schatz des Indianer-Joe"; he also decided to set his own libretto to music approximating the high modernist style of his composition teacher, Alban Berg. The only thing American was the story, though even this—a violent account of murder, needless death, and revenge—he selected for its relevance to the country in which he still (just about) lived.

Adorno failed to finish the opera. Only two songs are handed down to posterity as completed. These are usually criticized, if not plain ridiculed, for their evidently contradictory character, for their mixing of a subject matter belonging to the New World with a musical form belonging to the Old. Perhaps the mixing had its point, however. Was it not usually the very point of Adorno's work to show just such a contradictory mixture as this? It was. Still, he didn't finish his opera.

Perhaps Adorno was not a good enough composer or not a good enough composer of operas. Maybe he became too distraught by the extreme circumstances in which he found himself, circumstances that forced him to leave Germany, eventually to live in exile in the United States. However, a more interesting explanation turns on Adorno's increasing awareness of the extreme difficulty, if not the impossibility, of composing an opera for the sake of a possibility he believed had a minimal chance of being realized in contemporary times: the possibility of social justice.

Late in life, having returned to Germany after the war, Adorno opened his *Negative Dialectics* with a singular thought: "Philosophy, which once seemed obsolete, holds on to life because the moment to realize it was missed."[8] He didn't confine this thought to philosophy alone but extended it to art and even to opera, when in 1963 he described Schoenberg's *Moses und Aron* as a "sacred fragment."[9] With this description, Adorno gestured toward the contemporary impossibility of producing an opera, or any other kind of great work, in a world in which the historical passage of secularization had left both the sacred and the just in ruin. However, the critical question remained open: Under what conditions could opera hold onto life—and was Adorno's own failure to complete his project, like Schoenberg's, meant to provide an answer?

In some sense, "yes," or so Adorno argued regarding Schoenberg's failure to complete his own opera. He thus wrote of Schoenberg's work that the "final sentence" of its second act "becomes music" just when Moses laments the loss of the word: "O Word, O Word that I lack." Having become music, Moses's final thought remains unarticulated, though it is protected now by its silence. Why the need to withdraw from articulation? As we know, to demonstrate the impossibility of expressing a sacred thought in the form of a work that has become too authoritative in a commodified world. Adorno interpreted Schoenberg's work as refusing its status as a total work to become, instead, an unarticulated or mimetic cipher of "a supreme, unnamable truth." He distinguished what the early romantics did—when, in tragic vein, they demonstrated in their fragments the "insoluble conflict between the finite and the infinite"—from what some modernists did when they showed in their art the contemporary impossibility of producing great works. To produce a fragment was all one could and should now do if one's art was to hold onto the sacred, as one holds onto life, in a world in which a work, as a life, "can no longer be lived."[10]

In a broader version of the argument, written in response to his "intellectual experiences in America," Adorno referred to Alexis de Tocqueville and Ferdinand Kürnberger to suggest the contemporary impossibility of producing anything that formerly went by the name "culture." "Unless one withdraws behind a barricade of elitism," he remarked, "one cannot avoid asking . . . whether the very concept of culture with which one grew up has become old."[11] Adorno described a historical tendency that had "befallen" bourgeois culture overall—the tendency for culture to sever itself from the society to which it belonged. By claiming to exist in a separate sphere, the sacred was now conceived falsely, as though it could somehow survive autonomously, untouched by any concrete or social conditions of the real. What followed from this dangerous separation of the spheres was that society paid culture back for its claim to autonomy by reducing its purportedly sacred products to commodity status. Culture was rendered meaningless by the double reduction: first, by its aesthetic claim to have nothing to do with society (the reduction of the aesthetic to itself); second, by society's reduction of the aesthetic to society's social terms.

Adorno did not conclude, however, that culture should simply accept its own befallen condition but, instead, that it seek the albeit fragmented terms of continued life. He found these terms both in the Europe he left temporarily behind and in the country that provided him safety while in exile. In 1949, he observed that what had occurred in Europe to separate the cultural and social spheres had *not yet* happened in America. This thought strikes an equally optimistic and pessimistic note—first, that not all was lost in America, but, second, that America was following along Europe's trajectory. The deep significance of his comment lies in the *not yet*, gesturing as these words do toward a possibility that hasn't *yet* been eliminated by what presently exists.[12]

That America is the country of the not yet was a deeply engrained thought shared by many in Europe who put their hopes in the New World. However, is this thought retainable in any form even after a person arrives on America's shores? Here, the thought takes a dialectical U-turn, threatening the very enterprise of the dreamer whose hopes are fixed on an imaginary place that then becomes an actual place.

When Adorno wrote his *Minima Moralia* in exile—on one shore of the United States—he produced an epigraph of a damaged thought with words already aged. He drew the words from a poem from the past because of their continuing relevance (*Aktualität*) in the present. The poetic line reads, "life does not live" (*das Leben lebt nicht*) and originates in Ferdinand Kürnberger's novel of 1855, the title of which has the same world-weary effect: *Der Amerikamüde*—he who is tired of America. In the poem, though even more in Kürnberger's Viennese discourse surrounding it, Adorno found two models: one to compare the differences between German and American music, and another to demonstrate how the ideals, dreams, and hopes of *Amerika,* born out of the failure of the 1848 revolution in Germany, were shattered by the reality of the *United States*.[13]

Kürnberger constructed his travel narrative in his imagination: America as a *fata morgana*. It has been described as a "romantic apotheosis," a psychological novel about hopes and disappointments, or an explicitly "tendentious" novel, reflecting the social and political aspirations of a period against the backdrop of failure.[14] His narrative conjures up a view of modernity characterized by boredom, lateness, or agedness, against which hope and futurity are constructed. Yet, though gazing afar to America, the descriptions are *always also* about what stands closest before our eyes: our home.[15]

In the more general discourse to which this novel contributes, *Amerika* is distinguished from the United States to separate myth from fact, potentiality from actuality, and dream from reality. Representing a past or future paradise, a utopia, an Atlantis, a safe haven or refuge from wandering and exile, *Amerika* overcomes a Germany of limits and constraints. *Amerika* comes to stand for what Germany no longer is or has never been though still aspires to be—a future place "without borders" offering "unlimited possibilities."[16] However, what Kürnberger actually ends up showing is that the reality one invests in the future, or in any other elsewhere, might turn out to be no better or worse than the reality known at home, leaving one uneasily suspended between a New World that promises to be different yet proves not different enough and an Old World whose actuality has already been refused.

Kürnberger's narrative has abundant precedents. One of them is the (then partially published) memoir of Lorenzo Da Ponte. Da Ponte appears in Kürnberger's novel at its end, walking ghostlike through the streets of Manhattan, weary from his strenuous efforts to bring Italian opera and learning to America. He shares both a glass of wine (not cider) and a sad narrative with the novel's protagonist, Moorfield (modeled on Nikolaus Lenau). He dreams of returning to Europe, having apparently forgotten the Don Giovannian circumstances of his life that drove him away in the first place. Knowing he will not return, Da Ponte determines to write a memoir instead. It will testify in part to the literary greatness of *Don Giovanni* even more, he insists, than to the greatness of Mozart's music.[17] A proud Stone Guest in New York, but once a living Don Giovanni back home, this dialectical pair gives color to what otherwise is a rather gray model of German-American affinities, a critical model on which Kürnberger relied in constructing his narrative and Adorno, a century later, in constructing his.

Kürnberger did not travel to the United States; Adorno did. Shouldn't this fact make a difference? Shouldn't the imaginary components of the dialectic have been overwhelmed by Adorno's concrete experiences? I am not sure they were, since Adorno's dialectic remains uncannily in place. This has led critics to suggest that Adorno underestimated or offered only caricatures of his concrete experiences. But it also prompts one to consider whether what Adorno found produced, even as caricature, in the German imagination about America, he then found so engrained in some part of America's consciousness of itself, that for him to experience the country for real was just to experience the country as defined by the imagination.

Consider the matter this way. When Adorno insisted that life can no longer be lived in truth in a world that is untrue, was he thinking more about Germany than America or more about America than Germany? Was he contrasting a rotten German past with a better American present or a rotten American present with a better German or European past? I think he was doing both equally, as many before him, on both sides of the Atlantic and throughout the long nineteenth century. For, in the general discourse, it was claimed with one voice that what occurred in Germany or Europe hadn't yet occurred in the United States, and with another that Germany or Europe was becoming what America already stood for. Janus-faced, the double claim was sometimes rosily intended, even as it displayed pricking thorns whenever it insinuated itself into pro- or anti-modern, cosmopolitan, republican, democratic, socialist, or capitalist attitudes regarding Germany and the United States, conceived as antitheses in a dialectical argument.

Benjamin drew on Klee's *Angelus Novus* to tell us about a bird of history who gazes with split vision.[18] One might say that what the bird saw in the future, it also saw in the past—or when the bird tired of America, it was partly because it was already tired of Europe. As early as the 1830s, past fatigue was introduced as a pessimistic antidote, to warn anyone seeking future happiness in America (or elsewhere) that their dreams were likely to be disappointed (too). This weary thought was then repeated in 1951, when one exile, Erich Kahler, told another, Thomas Mann, that were one an immigrant traveling on a boat, one would be crazy in present times to sail toward either Europe or America—leaving Mann wondering whether the modernist bird should not just remain in flight, suspended in the middle of the Atlantic, this being the only place—or nonplace—left for any hope.[19]

Adorno also liked to refer to the space suggested by the term "almost," a negative nonplace, even a shipwrecked place, a space from which to prevent his own sentences reaching just the sort of totality they described. In this chapter, I describe the general dialectic between Germany and America in terms of what is "now," "no longer," and "not yet," which Adorno transformed into a negative dialectic moving between the terms of "the real," "the possible," and "the impossible." When he speaks of the real, he speaks of the impossible, and when of the no longer, he speaks both of what was once possible and of what is now impossible. When he speaks of the not yet, he speaks of what might be possible once again. Adorno used these terms to reverse a positivistic dialectic of optimism and pessimism on which it had grown too easy for too many to depend, and to reverse a fateful philosophy of history that had come to dominate thinking about opera and nationhood on both sides of the sea.

Operas of Amerikanismus

Did Adorno intend to compose an *American* opera or, should one say, an American *opera*? The fact that his project coincided with a moment around 1930 when opera was most proclaimed to be in crisis, persuaded him, as others, to seek alternative and sometimes even blatantly antiopera or antiwork descriptions for their works. They called their works variously "music theater pieces," "play operas," "musical plays," "musical picture-sheets," and "epic-operas," or, in Germany, "Lehrstücke," "Stücke mit Musik," and "Singspiele." Adorno chose the last designation—*ein Singspiel*—to describe his project modeled "*after Mark Twain.*"[20] But that he, as others, sometimes refused the name "opera" was also a way of asking after the conditions of opera's continuation.

Put differently, though he experimented with alternative terminology, Adorno did not give up entirely on traditional terms, even or most especially when they had been abused. In this matter, he aligned himself with other composers who experimented with new names and produced antiopera works, although, as in the following examples, they eventually reverted to calling their productions operas: Ernst Krenek's *Jonny spielt auf,* Darius Milhaud's *Christopher Columbus,* Eugen d'Albert's *Die schwarze Orchidee,* Max Brand's *Maschinist Hopkins,* George Antheil's *Transatlantik* (*Transatlantic* or *Transatlantique*), Karol Rathaus's *Fremde Erde,* and, finally, Brecht and Weill's *Aufstieg und Fall der Stadt Mahagonny.*[21]

Had Adorno completed his *Singspiel,* maybe he would have reverted to calling it an opera. Still, what reason did he have for thinking about producing a *Singspiel* in the first place? One provocative answer was offered some years later when, in 1938, he was no longer thinking about his own project but about the entire history of opera going back to that key enlightenment moment in the late eighteenth century when Mozart produced his quintessential Singspiel: *Die Zauberflöte.* What made it quintessential? Apparently, "the pleasure of the *Singspielcouplet*" so perfectly coincided with "the utopia of emancipation" that it marked an absolute historical moment "unto itself." After this moment, what had made that naive opera simultaneously both "serious and light" could not (like Humpty Dumpty) "be put back together again" without artificial or sentimental "force."[22] What Adorno wrote about serious and light music he also wrote about freedom and constraint, libertinage and authority, construction and sensuousness, the sacred and secular—that is, about nearly all the oppositions on which his dialectic of enlightenment depends.

So what was Adorno attempting when, at the other end of enlightenment, he thought about composing what was arguably an American opera under the condition of the *Singspiel?* Did he want to show that the moment for doing this had been missed because the moment was long past, or, more suggestively, that American opera was possible only in that Mozartian moment when Da Ponte tried to bring Mozartian opera to America's shores? In part, the latter was his point, but only if it indicated something as significant about the end of the dialectical story as about its beginning. Thus, if *Amerika* held out the promise for opera in 1930, this was because it was trying to retrieve something classical from the opening operatic bids for enlightenment—when the *Singspiel* was not only possible but also, in that Mozartian moment, actual.

Here Adorno was following Schoenberg, Krenek, and Brecht, though explicitly Kurt Weill, who one year earlier, in 1937, in his "The Future of Opera in the United States," penned an almost identical statement about *Die Zauberflöte*. Weill argued that even if the future of American opera lay with Broadway theater or with the musical movies, it would only succeed in being genuinely new if it rebuilt something from the classical form according to contemporary needs. In a country, Weill wrote, not yet "burdened with an opera tradition" (a complex observation to which I return below), "we can see a field for the building of a new form."[23] Much depended on what was meant by retrieving something of that Mozartian moment. Whereas Weill produced American operas in the United States, Adorno was left deeply tormented by the thought that what Weill was doing might be impossible to do now—that the positive or naive moment for composing American opera had been missed, making it possible only to produce sentimental or fragmented operas, demonstrating opera's contemporary impossibility.

In this argument between Adorno and Weill, it is a genuine question who maintained the preferable position. Consider the operas I mentioned above, called operas despite their antioperatic gestures and form. Part of what they were meant to do around 1930 was to stand opposed to a certain European—and particularly German—political and operatic tradition, by aligning themselves with a presumably progressive politics and musicality associated with the New World. For this reason, these works are well named operas of *Amerikanismus*. Yet it is also true that some of these works—and *Mahagonny* is exemplary—refused what they initially seemed to hope for, the more it was shown what the New World or America was fast coming to stand for: namely, capitalism at its late extreme. Accordingly, some of these operas had their attention directed elsewhere, mostly to the East, either to the Soviet Union or to Asia, these being the other elsewheres for those who desired geopolitically to relocate the new. However, though looking eastward is obviously a central theme in the history of modernist opera and music, I pursue it no further. I only investigate what happened when German composers turned their ears—critical or approving—to the United States, since this story is complicated enough.

Shortly after the first, and sometimes many, extremely successful performances of these operas of *Amerikanismus* in Germany, their composers were forced to leave. Mostly they went to the United States as exiles, and this despite their sometimes already very critical stance toward this country. In this move, the *Amerikanismus* that had guided their compositional production back home was transported and transformed into a consideration about what

American opera should become in the United States. This was a key moment, if not *the* key moment, in the history of the concept of American opera. For, in the transition from *Amerikanismus* to *Americanism,* a new nationalist element emerged that, though intended to move American opera forward, started to close the concept down. Already by 1939, Ernst Krenek, living in exile, remarked that the cost of searching for a specifically American music had grown too high, "reminiscent" as it had become "of that tide of nationalism" that had so recently arisen "to menace everything worthwhile in Europe."[24] As early as 1939, the warning was in the air that those once enamored of *Amerika* and now enamored of *America* should be careful what they wished for. The warning was double-edged. Not only was it being asked what it meant for composers to produce operas in the United States but also what exactly the appellation "American" would add to their products. To what was Krenek responding? Exactly to that to which Adorno was responding: namely, to a teleological sort of talk they were hearing all around them.

Old World–New World

This talk drew on a teleological philosophy of history and may be couched in Hegelian terms; hence, it begins with its end. When the concept of American opera arrived on the shores of the United States, roughly during the period of the Second World War, this was the moment of its realization. At this moment, and despite differences of political sympathy, American opera assumed the task formerly claimed by German opera: to be the true opera of the future. For American opera to be this, other already established, nationalist operas had to be relegated to the past. At this moment, the operas of Europe became old. To so conceive of American opera had two consequences: its concept was used, first, to endorse an ideal of futurity and the new in which all hope was placed but, second, to endorse a myth of America concealing the actual history of opera and music in the United States from view.

At the moment of alleged realization, the concept of American opera stood less for what was and more for what might be. Implicit in this claim is a normative understanding of what it means for a concept to realize itself. Recall part of what it meant for Hegel for the concept of art to realize itself—that when art became "a thing of the past," the concept was withdrawn from a perceived contemporary state of decline. Or, at the moment of realization, the concept of art was also *eternalized,* and art became Idea, as though the realization of World History depended on history, art, and philosophy suitably detaching themselves from certain unwanted or contingent aspects of the presently or existing real.

To describe the realization of the concept of American opera as occurring at a given historical time demanded that something be said about the history or protohistory of American opera before the concept's realization. According to one narrative, the history of American opera was just the history of opera in the United States going back to the country's beginnings. This history exhausts the concept with an empirical history, whereas an idealist or teleological history finds a contradiction between the concept of American opera and the history of opera in the United States. For, just when the concept assumed its authority, it set an internal empirical history aside in order then to regulate a narrative imported from Europe. To say that American opera arrived as a concept on America's shores is thus to regard the critical historical development as occurring primarily in Europe though reaching its culmination in the United States. What happened in the United States was, on one side of the dialectic, part of a European development of the concept of American opera and, on the other side, part of a protohistory of American opera, which was then redescribed, once the concept was in place, as a purely American history of opera in the United States.

In this story, before the realization of the concept, there was no well-formed American opera yet in the United States, and, to the extent that there was a *concept* of American opera, it served significantly as an ideal for the future sake of European opera. Let us return momentarily to the question whether Adorno intended to compose an American opera. At first, I answered tentatively with a no but moved toward a yes, by interpreting his project as part of that Weimar *Amerikanismus* that projected ideals onto America, given the current state of society at home. Hence, for a young German composer to compose an American opera or even an American antiopera at home might well have been for him to compose for the future sake of a society with a specific dialectical disregard for the reality of opera and music in the United States.

Thus, according to the teleological model, it did not matter that the empirical history of opera, either in the United States or in the Americas, was nearly as old as the history of opera in Italy, France, and Germany. Because, despite its age, age is what the concept of American opera was meant least to invoke. Here American opera joined the chorus singing about America itself as retrieving what had been lost in Europe when Europe became old. What Europe called the good, the true, and the beautiful would now be kept safe by all that in America was forever young, new, and possible. As is well known, this song of America extended back to America's very beginnings.

The discourse of the new has long been a mode of rhetoric designed to persuade an audience of something new or not already known to them by making what is unfamiliar seem entirely familiar. By extension, to come to see what was new about America was to assimilate its difference into values already held at home in Europe.[25] America was accordingly conceived as an extension, even if also as a better version, of Europe itself. Apparently, it was thought better to see America this way than to accommodate what was genuinely unfamiliar, should that unfamiliarity challenge the values already established at home. To discover a *new found land* was really to discover a *ready-made land* made in the image of the discoverers.

This argument was complicated when the history the Europeans told of America was accepted as the internal discourse of America itself. What this meant was that any genuinely new terms had to assume, even for Americans, the aura of the already self-evident. American opera or even America might have been clothed in the new, but the mantle of the already known back home became its undetachable shadow.

The terms of the new were linked to the modern terms of nationhood. Nations were often described anthropomorphically in terms of their age, with their birth, immaturity, and youth pitted against their age, maturity, and death. They were also described in terms of their rise and fall or in terms of their development and decline, as part of a world history of the so-called ages of man. However, nations were also described in terms originating with Aristotle that later shaped the enlightenment and then idealist discourse of nations on which Adorno and others relied. These were the terms of possibility, realization, actuality, and ideality.

A mere glance at Aristotle's *Metaphysics* or *De Anima* shows these terms playing their part in sophisticated means-ends theses regarding form, matter, deed, energy, and potential. By the nineteenth century, the terms had shifted in meaning. Consider the term "Aktualität," a term often used by Adorno. In fact, in any essay in which he asked after the *Aktualität* of something, be it of philosophy (as he asked in 1931), of "bourgeois opera" (in 1955), or of Wagner (in 1967), he deliberately set the modern meaning against an earlier or older one. In contemporary German-English dictionaries, *Aktualität* is translated only with its modern meanings: "modish," "topical," "up to date," or "relevance to the present." In the reverse direction, however, the English words "actuality" and "actually" are aligned to the German "Aktualität," given the latter's original associations with reality, realism, and factuality. With Adorno, one might too cleverly declare that the more the German term comes to mean relevance, the more it loses its grip on the genuinely real. Thus, what

Adorno argued *against* was the idea that the more up-to-date or modish the philosophy or opera, the more mature or new necessarily the thought. But what he argued *for* is that we always ask of philosophy or art whether it still has meaning in a society or culture in which meaning has been eradicated. His answer to this last question was yes, though only if the residual meaning was expressed by the sort of fragmentation of form that connoted possibility, since only as so expressed would philosophy or art show that it was still able to do the dialectical work of cutting through the untruthful appearances of the presently existing real.[26]

Adorno's play with the term "Aktualität" as possibility recalled Nietzsche's "untimely reflections" on timeliness. It also revised the meaning that the term assumed in the late nineteenth century, when it was incorporated by the neo-Kantian theorist Oswald Külpe into what he named *Aktualitätstheorie*. Külpe deliberately handed the term over to the spiritual or ideal development of the soul to contrast it with its real development, thus leading another of the theory's chief exponents, Wilhelm Wundt, to write, "So viel Aktualität, so viel Realität,"[27] thereby allowing *Aktualität* to do the idealizing or spiritual work that "reality" wasn't presently doing itself.

Under these conditions, the question of the relevance (*Aktualität*) of American opera was transformed into a question more about possibility or promise than about existing reality. Yet, as Adorno repeatedly warned, in a dialectical model in which actuality is promised as possibility, the actuality will only be relevant if it remains sufficiently mediated by the real. Only then will what is *real* separate itself from its conformist need to identify with what currently *exists*. Here Adorno's thought recalled Hegel's detailed discussion of actuality-as-possibility offered in his *Encyclopedia of Philosophical Sciences*.

Insofar as American opera was regarded as a concept of possibility, it was often connected to the language of newness and youth. The connection worked if the concept served European interests as a prior condition to serving the eventual interests of the United States. After that, the proclaimed newness and youthfulness would have to be tied to terms more associated with realization, achievement, and self-evidence. In other words, the concept of American opera would only release itself from this prioritizing of interests when it released itself from its European past, not by being born again but by proclaiming a self-incurred maturity.

Nothing in this story should lead one to think that the description of a country as new or young applied uniquely to America. Germany was named *Junges Deutschland* partly under the influence of Heinrich Heine and just when the play between *der Europamüde* and *der Amerikamüde* explicitly began. Other countries were named new and young, too. However, whereas newness for most countries was usually tied to the historical notion of renewal, of leaving a past behind, in America the newness was interestingly attached first to the absence then to the presence of a particular political order. Thus, it was argued (often by Europeans) that before its founding or finding, America existed without a political order; after its founding, it acquired an order and no less a self-evident one to which all countries should aspire—which is a claim Americans were also more or less happy to encourage. When, in the 1980s, Israeli writer A. B. Yehoshua remarked that America treats democracy as its unburnable skin, whereas all other countries treat it as a suit that may or may not be worn, he picked up perfectly on the earlier Tocquevillean thought that America's political order required no history or becoming because it was already in some sense realized, its history having occurred elsewhere. Its Constitution might call for constant reinterpretation, but this was different from its requiring a historical development to legitimate its standing in the first place.[28]

Consider a teleological claim derived from Francis Fukuyama's thesis on "the end of history and the last man." With the realization of history, history found itself in just the place where it was least needed, in a country where the political order of democracy was already realized at least as a matter of declaration. But if this claim is right, what sense does it now make to speak of America as the country of the young or the new, if America is, at the same time, born already old or, more accurately, fully formed? Why not collapse these tensed terms into a discourse of extended *nowness* to suit a posthistorist country that, without past and future, exists only in the expanded present? This suggestion has been made seriously more than once and not just recently. It has two distinct forms, one more critical and one more celebratory.

From the critical perspective, America was described as a country without history, with the consequence that "she"—America—was liberated from history's burden and from account. *Amerika* was described as "Raum ohne Geschichte," a "geschichtsloses Land der Gegenwart," a country without Hegels or Hamlets—that is, without knowledgeable men able to think responsibly about "the whole." Instead, it was said, America was populated by "rootless" or "barbaric" children playing in "all that is the case," with only the merely or contingently present.[29] Rarely was this implicit contrast between Europe and America offered without dialectical ambition. For the nowness found in America, or the here and now of the present, was separated from the eternal or European *now* that included only what in the past, present, and future was able truly to stand the test of time. Excluded from historical account, America might have been liberated, but this was *not yet* the sort of liberation one should celebrate. Or, America might be the country of the not yet, but this was said to justify describing the rational passage of thought as still occurring only in Europe.

Hegel supported this view in his oft-quoted statement from his lectures on the philosophy of history that America is "not a state but a territory." He drew this distinction to show the necessary dialectical division of "the *Old*" from "the *New*," where the New was new in two ways. First, it came to "our" attention "only of late"; second, it was "altogether new" (*überhaupt neu*) regarding its physical and spiritual makeup. Given the second meaning, but serving the first, he concluded that America was so new that one was justified in calling it the "land of the future." From this, two consequences followed: one for the person with an ordinary or historical (*historische*) perspective, and the other for the philosopher of *Geschichte*. For the first, *Amerika* could serve as a place of longing (*Sehnsucht*) for those "bored [*gelangweilt*] of the historic arsenal that is old Europe." (Here Hegel quoted Napoleon's *europamüde* statement, "Cette vieille Europe m'ennuie.") For the philosopher, however, America had to be excluded from the pursuit of "eternal reason," since what had taken place there did not yet belong to world history and thus could not constitute part of the timeless or philosophical "what is." Nevertheless, in the future, America, as the land of the future, would have to be taken into account.

Hegel briefly turned his attention toward cultural production to conclude that what was "original" or "genuine" was to be identified more with what "is" and thereby "eternal" than with what was "new." Accordingly, what the New World *up to now* had produced was not its *own* products but only those echoing or mimicking the Old World, hence, only immature goods with an alien, borrowed, or quickly packaged vitality.[30] The ramifications of this way of thinking were pervasive. That America was soon deemed a "culture of copies" emanated from just this sort of philosophy of history, as we see in Tocqueville and Marx. Or even in Wagner, I would suggest, when he turned this sort of view of a nation into a corrupt diatribe against the "second-handedness" of "Jewish culture," which only too soon became identified (though not by Wagner) with "American culture." Walther von Stolzing might have sung a song that sounded so new yet was so old, but the bird singing in "the sweetness of May" did not yet sing in America.

From the other perspective, many writers in this same period chose to side with the New World and her "dreams" (Hegel's term). These were thinkers who were willing to leave Old World History behind in favor of a preferred

New World History or a New World that claimed no pastness, oldness, or age at all. Despite the fact that in one sense of "nation" Germany was younger than America, Germany was treated not as America was, as forever young, but as already old, as somehow having arrived *zu spät*. Goethe's oft-quoted poetic lines of 1827 suffice to express the sentiment, challenging as they do the increasingly grandiose mentality described in chapter 5, in which art and politics found far too much national security in proclaiming themselves born in a state of already monumentalized ruin:

> America, you have it better
> Than our continent, the old one.
> You have no ruined castles
> And no aged stones [*Basalt*].[31]

The contrast between these attitudes pervaded the nineteenth century in Europe and continued to do so in the twentieth, even—and this is my point—when the whole debate was transported onto American soil. From one perspective, one heard the sort of celebratory description endorsed by John Cage when, in composing his perfectly named *Europeras* (more on these below), he continued his project to articulate a *new* aesthetic which he cleverly couched in terms of the ahistorical *now*. From another perspective, the German thought of historical lateness was turned over to America itself the moment it was asked, as by Adorno, whether "the moment" for American opera had been "missed."

Adorno's question suggested two different things: first, that it was too late for American opera as it was now for any opera to show itself in anything other than a reflective or fragmented mode of production; second, that American opera arrived too late in the United States just because too few Americans were willing to remove the fallen castles and aged stones from the almost exclusively European stages of their already very successful institutions of opera.

A Short History of American Opera

Throughout most of the early history of opera in the United States—from roughly 1700 to 1930—the explicit concept of American opera was not often employed. When it was, it was used to group together the many extant examples of oratorios, ballad operas, comic operas, melodramas, and pantomimes, as early "English" productions tended to be named. After the 1820s especially, it was used to group more exclusively and broadly any opera proper or any opera-*libretto* sung in the English or American-English language. Hence, Weber in English, Rossini in English—all fell under the institutional umbrella of American opera.

Unsurprisingly, the umbrella did not hold the rain off for very long. American opera, regarded increasingly as opera in translation, remained uncomfortably foreign even when sung in the vernacular. Even more troublesome, the more status the immigrant concept attained, the more it excluded any opera composed by an American. That this was a story of class, of social status, and of where, how, and by whom opera was supported is obvious. What is less often noted is that singing in the rain of American opera was mostly a matter of foreigners singing in America's rain.

When theorists argued that *all* opera could become American opera if good enough translations were produced, they brought home how much opera needing no translation was excluded. Or, when in 1885, the financial failure of the newly founded American Opera Company was explained on the grounds that opera audiences in the United States generally disliked anything in opera that was "American"—be it the libretto, subject, composers, singers, performers, conductors, or directors—one understands why in the 1800s opera in the United States was so often accused of being anti-American.[32]

In the 1880s, Frédéric Ritter recorded how in January 1855 a prize was offered by Philadelphia's Academy of Music for an "opera by an American composer." In the description of the prize, Ole Bull, the Norwegian-born manager of the company, informed all "American Composers" that the academy wanted the "best original grand opera . . . upon a strictly *American subject.*" And that the academy wanted this so that it would stop being merely "a home of refined and intellectual amusement" and would become "an *academy in reality,* whose principal object shall be the encouragement, the development, and elevation of American art and artists." Within just two months, however, the academy was closed and the prize was not awarded. Ritter explained the failure as part of a larger story, according to which the patronage for opera in the United States was beset by deep inequalities when it came to supporting American opera by American artists on American themes, and that while this was the case, American opera would remain almost exclusively a foreign enterprise. He wasn't dismayed by this conclusion. Commenting on the "systematic effort" to "extinguish" American operas from "American opera," he wrote unsympathetically: "They could hardly extinguish that which had no existence."[33]

To be sure, the problem of American opera was largely an extension of the problem of opera in toto. Beyond the increasingly elite, foreign-opera audiences, many audiences claimed not to want opera of any sort, as long as they were being asked to pay high prices for an art from the Old World which lasted too long and usually was not comprehensible, even when sung in translation. Yet they were not willing necessarily to give up on opera altogether. If opera, some said, would only become more like the popular theater it once was (before the best of Italian, French, and German opera arrived to conquer the American turf), then American opera would have its own future. Ritter quoted a critic from 1830, who, after an allegedly botched production of *Die Zauberflöte* in New York, wrote: "Our national character is so strongly marked with the love of novelty and singularity, that, like the men of Athens, we are perpetually in search of something *new*."[34] But still, what was wanted as new was arguably something already known, something opera once was when, as in the eighteenth century, it was dominated by the popular production of all manner of ballad operas, comic operas, and pantomimes, something perhaps approximating those Dionysian festivals of Athens!

A generally imported attitude persisted, especially when the more dominant critics expressed with pain (or was it pleasure?) the practical problems of producing "opera proper" in the United States. They commented ceaselessly on the fact that, if one didn't have the space, the performers, or the appropriately trained audiences, at best what one would get were bits and pieces of operas produced as entertaining excerpts. What one wouldn't get, as a German visitor commented in 1828, were whole works: "The performance of a whole opera is not to be thought of."[35] How, he continued, could one even expect adequate performances if the only oboist in North America lived in Baltimore? To which one might have replied: If Mozart could adapt to the performers he had available, why not admire the same potential flexibility in America? Why shouldn't opera in translation also mean adaptable opera, an opera indicative of cultural transformation?

Throughout the 1800s, two options that need not have been mutually exclusive seem to have tugged with increasing impatience on critics, musicians, and audiences: either to wait for the time when opera could be produced successfully—according to the allegedly more elite strictures of the work concept—or to encourage the development of opera as a more popular or genuinely theatrical art offered at low prices. Opinions were divided. Ritter clearly worried that as long as opera was performed in bits and pieces, no sense would ever be made of leitmotivic technique in Wagnerian opera—since the technique demanded a hearing of the whole—and thus that it would "probably be many years before the lyrical drama rises to the importance of an American national art-work."[36]

Other critics suggested that something *other* than the Wagnerian model might guide the development of American opera, but only if American musicians started to have a say in the determination of their art. As one critic noted in 1906, little would change regarding American opera or American music while the stars continued to be imported, or while the singers, composers, and conductors of continental Europe (broadly conceived) were *alone* made into the new American wares of the opera industry. A self-proclaimed American composer of several American operas, this critic was the first to set "America the Beautiful" to music.[37]

Given these opposing options, the question constantly arose: Who was more the friend and who more the enemy of American opera—the critic who saw American opera as aspiring to become what opera had already become in Europe, or the one who saw American opera as taking European opera's place? Much of the argument depended on the critical opinion of European opera: whether it was disliked for being opera or disliked for being European. The argument continues today, not only through the persistence of the awful friends and enemies language toward art but also regarding the double trouble of American opera. We know that New World attitudes toward Old World opera are complicated, but add the epithet "American" to "opera" and the trouble only compounds.

The critic who spoke of national character and the search for something new was also the critic who claimed in 1830 that the failure of Italian opera in the United States was the same as that of opera in English, and thus the same as the failure of *all* opera. If audiences didn't even like operas that express familiar values or operas performed "in a familiar tongue," they were not going to like operas that struck them as "wholly foreign." The critic drew two conclusions. First, opera was about to disappear from "the cisatlantic shores," where, for him, what remained of a popular tradition did not even enter into consideration. Second, given the "rational" development of the people (which apparently wasn't yet "rational" enough), opera would not likely reappear until "a century hence." To this Ritter, having recorded these conclusions, responded in 1880: "Our prophet does not seem to have been far from a true one."[38] Strangely, Ritter was right, but only because American opera in 1930 was still mostly identified with what was predominantly an imported art.

Around 1930, however, something changed. This was more or less the moment when the concept of American opera, in being opened at last to operas by Americans, started systematically closing itself off to operas that were "foreign." At this moment, American opera became a classificatory concept to refer more singularly to operas made in America—produced by Americans for Americans, in American style, and sung by American singers. For some this was an advance, for the perverse reason that the best opera houses of the United States now felt justified in producing foreign operas as foreign, which meant in their original languages! For others, celebration was appropriate because everything and anything now seemed possible for American opera.

American opera evidently flowered under these new conditions. Still, the optimism was soured by several new tensions. First, American opera as an art in which everything was possible found itself supported less by the mainstream than by sidelined experimental houses that presented no real challenge to the major institutions of opera in the United States. This left American opera cut off or severely marginalized from the mainstream institutions that continued to produce European or foreign works. Second, having excluded foreign operas from its domain, the concept of American opera now functioned by further excluding anything not truly deserving of America's name. Despite the openness of the claim that America should embrace all, American opera threatened to embrace only that which conformed to a specific ideal America had come to have of itself. Third, despite its having excluded opera composed in foreign languages on foreign themes, the concept of American opera retained much of its imported character, significantly because of the exiles who arrived during these years and became its staunchest advocates. Despite all intentions for American opera not to be what European opera was, much of what was thought to now be lost in Europe was given over to America by the exiles in the form of opera's future promise. Regarding the last tension specifically, it is important to note that to speak of the concept as having an imported quality is not a problem if what this acknowledges is that most people at some point came to America to make the United States all that it is. However, to speak about the concept of American opera as imported is just as problematic as thinking about it as homebred—two bad sides of a nationalist coin, motivating Krenek to issue his warning with urgency in 1938.[39]

If conceptual negotiations proved urgent in the 1930s, they remained so in the 1950s. In 1951, Herbert Graf, the new, Viennese stage director at New York's Metropolitan Opera wrote: "Twenty, even ten, years ago, the question was whether there was a place for opera in the American Community. Today the question is, How can its artistic existence be made secure?" He penned these words in his book of that year, *Opera for the People*, after which he described what American opera should now be. Like Papageno, he was tempted to snare in his net all works "throughout the land": Broadway theater, the

American musical, even productions at the Met, where, he noted, the representation of American operas was something of an embarrassment.[40]

One way Graf tried to open up the concept of American opera so that it would actually include operas by Americans was by insisting that American composers take courage. Whatever names they elected to give to their productions, the products were "operas just the same."[41] Graf intended to undermine the ongoing fear American composers apparently still had—that calling their works operas would guarantee their dismissal, first because they were operas and then because they were American. His message was to be proud of both.

Graf agreed with Weill. In Germany, when Weill, with Brecht, explored alternative names for their joint productions, they continued to use the term "opera" in part to show what opera had been, for good and for bad. However, in New York, in 1947, when Weill considered how best to describe his new production, called *Street Scene,* he used not the generic term "opera" but the more specific "American opera" (after considering "Broadway opera"), as if to show the affinity that the very idea of opera had with the New World. For Weill, remember, the point was not only to turn one's hope toward America but also to renew the genre in its name.

In further sympathy with Weill (and Adorno), Graf encouraged the emancipation of American opera by turning his gaze back to the Old World, to opera before its fall—to that first Mozartian moment. If American opera was to be truly "of the people, by the people, for the people," it was a matter of referring not to America's Declaration of Independence but to that first European promise of operatic enlightenment when Mozart produced both *Zauberflöte* and *Don Giovanni.* Graf recalled Goethe's famous epistolary lines to Schiller, expressing the thought that contemporary theater should be reformed in the spirit of what he had just experienced watching Mozart's opera. Graf adapted the thought: if American opera is to become open, it must turn away from the tradition of European opera that has separated the Mozartian moment from today. Or, to liberate that first moment from Europe is to hand it over to America. But would this handoff work? Only, Graf insisted, if Americans remembered what Goethe and Schiller looked for in Mozart's reform: namely, something capable of leading people, and now Americans, away from their alleged preoccupation with the real, the pragmatic, or the useful and toward a genuine appreciation of feeling. Despite good intentions, Graf imported from Europe a rather too well established anti-American motif: that Americans are more interested in profit than in the nightingale's song. For, as German opera formerly found its musicality in Italy, so American opera would become opera when Americans got over their fear of emotion. In a final gesture of empathy and identification, Graf wrote: "Let *us* not be afraid of opera."[42]

Yet, should we not ask whether Graf didn't too quickly forget where too little fear of opera led, or to what too great an appeal to emotion helped to promote in the Europe he left behind? Between that Mozartian moment and the 1950s (and onto today) is a history full of increasingly damaging nationalistic appeals to musicality, a history that cannot simply be remaindered by optimistic new Americans who would rather forget the world of yesteryear.

In the next part of this inquiry, I consider four accounts: two by Americans, one by a German exile to America, and one by a European who lived and remained in Europe, in Great Britain. Though their views range over the political, philosophical, and musical landscape, each is aimed at delimiting the proper scope of American opera. Despite claims to the contrary, each leaves it unclear whether the elected concept is meant to transform an old one, replace an old one, or proclaim no predecessor at all. In this ambiguity, the tension in the concept is exposed: whether the concept is meant to regulate a national opera in the United States specifically or the future of opera altogether.

The Folkloric Narrative

The folkloric narrative was offered mostly by scholars wanting to establish that "serious" American opera had been around in the United States since the beginning of modernity and enlightenment. In this story, in 1794, one of the most often-mentioned dates, a composer named James Hewitt set an antifederalist libretto written by Ann Julia Hatton (an African American) to music, and in so doing produced the first American opera. The topic was the Spanish persecution of the Cherokees, and the title was *Tammany or the Indian Chief.* Here is the "or" in the title, a use that reminds us that when de Sade formulated his title, he drew on a literary convention already so widespread that without any trouble it captured the first American opera.[43]

This narrative was offered explicitly in 1957 by an anthropologist, Diane Kestin, writing not for a musicology journal but for the California journal *Western Folklore,* founded in January 1942. Titling her article "Western Folklore in Modern American Opera," she aimed to establish that "native folklore has interested our composers since the eighteenth century," though most evidently in the operas of "our" own time.[44] She offered her argument in a listlike manner, recording the names, composers, and themes of many operas produced in the United States from the 1790s to her present. Characteristic of many operas was their preoccupation with pioneering and migration. She mentioned Douglas Moore's 1949 *Giants in the Earth,* an opera about the presumably tall Norwegians who settled in the Dakotas in the 1870s. Kestin acknowledged the influence of European opera, mentioning Da Ponte and the many other Europeans who landed either temporarily or permanently on America's shores. Walter Damrosch's opera of 1935–37, interestingly named *The Man Without a Country* after a novel by a Bostonian, was reported as being too familiar, by which the critics meant that it sounded too much like what they already knew from Beethoven and Wagner.[45] Still, it testified to the sort of continuity and cross-fertilization between European and American traditions that Kestin wanted to encourage. She mentioned the European *Amerikanismus* of Germany and Italy. Puccini's *La fanciulla del West* was a perfect example of what opera might sound like in the United States and of what it might represent in terms of the American dream in which (in my words), given a society of malcontents, the more rebellious individuals seek a better life elsewhere.

Consider another opera Kestin mentioned, Lukas Foss's 1949 one-act *The Jumping Frog of Calaveras County.* Though drawn from a story by Mark Twain, it was set to music described as being of European, neoclassical form. In the opera's libretto by Jean Karsavina, the story of the "stranger" is mixed with that of a "dance-hall girl" named Lulu—suggesting (in my terms again) that Jack the Ripper had a less successful night in London than one had previously thought or, entirely rhetorically, that Berg's opera had to wait for its completion in America.[46]

Kestin mentioned many American operas by composers of more or less renown, ranging from Aaron Copland's *The Tender Land* to Josef Marai's *Tony Beaver* and Thomas Fenyo's *Rise of Her Bloom.* Given her list, Kestin concluded that "the most effective results are achieved when the composer derives his inspiration from folk sources, when he becomes imperceptively immersed in folk expression and arises from this national influence to express American opera in singular stylistic terms." "Imperceptively" is a subtle term: what Kestin meant is that composers should so immerse themselves in folk expression that their expressions would strike us as natural. But "imperceptively" shouldn't mean "imperceptible," because unless we notice the expression we presumably won't grasp why the work is American. Still, Kestin never suggested that American opera or American musical style should be assessed according to a singular "determinist philosophy"—the dominant German model against which she was reacting—but according only to the demands that the dramatic situations chosen by the composers made on the individual works. Yet, she added, musical style should not be imposed on the works, since only freed from this imposition could America speak with what "by [its] very nature" it stood for: the tongue of "a musical polyglot."

How unrestricted was the tongue? Surely it included the Connecticut Yankee, Paul Bunyan, and the Mother of Us All, but did it include the tongue of Nashville or the Southern blues, or even the Broadway musical, especially when the East Side story moved over to the West? For Kestin, did it all count if one were to be true to the concept of being American, and this despite the fact that not every singing tongue actually sang the song of opera? Kestin spoke more about the idea of being American than about the scope of the genre. What began as a classificatory argument listing operas ended with a politicization of the concept of being American, a demonstration of what would be possible in America were it true to the ideal of speaking many languages.

Kestin's politicization of the concept was only loosely bound to notions of freedom, pluralism, and democracy. She was more concerned with ideas or ideals of the folkloric and the regional. Even so, she didn't give much independent attention to these concepts. Yet the appeal to the folkloric, as that which gave specificity to American opera, did allow her to avoid classifying American opera according to geography or national boundaries too literally stipulated or to where composers were born. This was a sensible strategy, given that very few of the composers she mentions were born in the United States, even the composer of purportedly the first American opera. In the end, the decisive point for Kestin was that American opera should make no purist or determinist demand, either on the works or on the composers, that they be of "one definite" kind, origin, or character.

The Purist Narrative

The next two narratives show significant differences of approach, largely because they were offered either by writers not living in the United States or by recent exiles to the United States. In posing the question "What is American opera?" they asked whether there was such a thing, as if there might not be, and then, if there was, whether it had *yet* arrived. The first reaction to this last question is to ask sarcastically, "Arrived from where?" as though the idea being promoted were a Eurocentric one: that European opera arrived at some point in the United States and in so arriving constituted what henceforth would be called American opera. In fact, this was the claim, but only because by "arrival" the arguers intended to capture something teleological. Hence, their question, "Has American opera arrived?" should be read either as "Has American opera as a sui generis concept arrived?" or as "Has the very concept of opera arrived by coming to America?" One answer was that though the concept of opera had already arrived in Europe, it hadn't yet arrived in America. Another answer was that the concept of opera would realize itself only once a particular course of history had played itself out in Europe, but since that history was going to end in the United States, the concept would realize itself only by becoming all that "being American" stood for.

One of these narratives was offered by a Scot, William Saunders, whose gaze was directed mostly toward Germany. He argued that the concept of opera realized itself in Europe, supremely in Italy, Germany, France, and, with qualifications, in Russia and England. (He expressed disapproval of a Celtic bid for independence.) Establishing the national sovereignty of each great country, Saunders claimed that were America to follow in Europe's best path, its opera would realize itself, too. Yet, for opera to realize itself, the country would also have to realize the political dream of establishing itself as a true nation, by which Saunders meant "a pure nation." And by "realization," he was clearly thinking about the achievement of a cultural state.

Saunders, an established scholar of Weber, wrote for established journals. His argument was produced over the course of eight critical years. A 1932 article, "The American Opera: Has It Arrived," was a follow-up piece to his 1927 article on the general topic of national opera and a forerunner to his 1935 article on the virtues of German song (virtues, for Saunders, that recently had become visible with the success of the "German Nazi Revolution of 1933").[47] In 1927, Saunders defined "nationalism" in terms of a nation's development of *Geist*, a development shown in the ability of different nations to establish their own techniques, styles, and subject matters. Verdi's *Aida,* he declared, is "one of the greatest operas the world has ever known"—"truly indigenous" to its soil.[48] Thinking thereafter about the possibility of American opera, he wrote:

> There is a decided urge in the United States toward the creation of a distinctively national type of opera, and although nothing of a highly outstanding character has yet emerged, one may trace the same tendencies and draw the same inferences as can be elucidated from the experience of the European nations during the past three centuries.[49]

By 1932, nationalism had come to mean something more dependent on a given country relinquishing its "indiscriminate immigration policy." An opera that concedes to "Jewish demands" stifles its own genuine possibility. Or, to produce an "indigenous form of opera," one needs a strong, "pure and unsullied" race. Saunders described the need for the melting pot finally to melt, by which he seemed to mean the reduction of all foreign or racial differences to that which is indigenous—which, for him, meant "English." Asking whether American opera had yet arrived, he answered: it exists as potential but not as actualized. We must be patient, for it cannot "too often [be] repeated that there can be no American opera until there is a pure and distinctive American people." While the pot is still melting, "only half-baked and immature matter" will be produced.[50]

So far, the argument was straightforward. Suddenly, Saunders complicated it by concluding: "There is however nothing surer than the fact that the future of opera lies largely with America." I think the implication was that, if America became more like what Germany was promising to be in 1932, American opera would realize its potential. But if this is what he meant, why didn't he conclude the same of Germany in 1932, or even the same of Italy, France, England, or Russia? Why, in other words, in 1932, did he pin his hopes largely on America? He never gave a convincing answer, though he offered some provocative and distasteful thoughts along the way.

In 1935, Saunders expressed his admiration for the new German songs of the revolution. He recorded how he had recently asked his "very good friends" in the (Nazi) SA and SS about the character of their songs, only to come to understand that, despite their seeming to be full of racist and violent content, the songs really expressed the most noble aspirations of the German nation. Saunders picked out one song he heard sung by his uniformed friends, which despite its harsh words against Jews, was a "gem," he said, evidencing Germany's indigenous musicality and inherent genius for song. Yet he wasn't entirely convinced by his or their argument. Indeed, he showed increasing skepticism regarding the path Germany was taking. Maybe he had to express skepticism in an article written for a British readership or perhaps he was genuinely skeptical. The latter seems right, given his next argument: that one can well appreciate the advance of a culture, and especially of music, independently of what goes on politically.

Where before he allied American opera to the political or social development of the nation, he now challenged that alliance by stating that, though the revolution had "transformed the entire *Reich* into a veritable 'nest of singing birds,'" this fact had nothing to do with the dictatorial policies of its "revolutionary" leader. The culture the revolution had produced was more subtle than the politics it had produced and certainly more lasting in showing how a people could "keep time and tune in their singing." Hitler, he quipped, is "but as the blowing of a summer zephyr," and, hence, "[a] nation that can sing, as Germany is doing through all her triumphs and troubles, has little to fear, even from her own so-called rulers, and dictators." Still, he concluded: "When all is said and done, *what* [the nation] sings matters not a whit."[51]

It's a tricky ending. Though Saunders distanced himself from the dictator's recent policies, he remained sympathetic to the songs of his inspired revolutionary "friends." He left it ambiguous, however, as to what he thought about the content of the songs. Did their words lie on the side of the political policy of which he disapproved, or were they by-products of a cultural ideal of which he continued to approve? I think he opted more for the former than for the latter idea every time he remarked that the music was better than the words. That the Germans were singing was clearly more important than what they sang about. Nevertheless, we must ask: Can a nest of singing birds merely piping out their tunes really be separated so neatly from the master bird who makes their nest?

Given the trajectory of this argument, it is now even less clear why Saunders turned his attention to America. Maybe he believed that even if opera had realized itself in Europe, the political ideals of which he dreamed had not. And, ideally, though culture and politics were separable, wouldn't it be better were they to work hand in hand? The reasoning does not work. When Saunders described the history of opera in the United States, he said little about the politics of the country. He spoke only of the possibility of an indigenous musicality, as if suggesting that America was on the correct political path. But this suggestion for America was belied by what he had already said about Germany, since, as we heard, even if a country's dictator pursues a wrong policy, its indigenous musicality may still be realized in song. In the end, Saunders argued for a separation not of culture from politics per se but of an ideal cultural politics from an actual politics. With this distinction, culture could serve as a safety net or protected space for a *political ideal*—say, of pure nationhood—that was not presently being realized in political terms.

The distinction is important. First, it is one on which many modernist theorists of the right and left during this period relied, a matter to which I return. Second, when Saunders turned to what looked like a purely musicological story of the history of opera in the United States, he did not, despite a neutralized appearance, backtrack on anything he had previously written. Nothing of the political content of his concept of American opera was deflated, even if the more distasteful elements were concealed. Thus, even when he appeared neutrally to encourage more American composers to compose more American operas, he was still hoping for an America that would sing with an eventually pure tongue.

In his brief history of opera in the United States, Saunders challenged the claim that American opera began in 1790. He stated that the "first operatic performance ever given in America" was a ballad opera composed in England in 1729 by one John Hippisley but performed in Charleston, South Carolina, in 1735, as *Flora, or Hob in the Well*.[52] All Saunders confirms here, contra Kestin, is that the history of American opera in the United States includes more than the composing of American operas. In his view, the history of opera in the United States is a history of *performing* any opera, American or not, in the United States—a view that more accurately accords with the early meaning of "American opera." However, he promoted this view only as a background (or protohistory) to his more important claim, now implicit, that though American opera had its roots in the operatic goings-on in the United States throughout the eighteenth and nineteenth centuries, the pure concept had not yet arrived.

Saunders described the lively performance tradition of opera in the 1760s. He recorded how that tradition took a decisive turn in the 1790s when, largely under Europe's influence, it became a tradition of grand opera. Though long dominated thereafter by foreign works, European workers, singers, conductors, and directors, to which Saunders had no objection, there were signs of indigenous growth whenever American composers were encouraged to compose American operas. He did not explain to what the term "American" referred. He only mentioned operas that might one day form, I assume, part of a pure history of pure American opera, as opposed to an impure history of unmelted opera in the United States: operas by Victor Herbert, Edward F. Schneider, Henry K. Hadley, and Arthur Nevin. Whatever his political sympathies, the only European prejudice exhibited at this moment rested with his assumption that what Europe had already developed as opera was what American opera ought to copy. That the operas he listed by American composers had not become well known did nothing to deflate his hope in the American opera of the future: he had simply to be patient and wait for the pot to melt.

At the end of his narrative, one is still left wondering why Saunders accorded special favor to the development of American opera. Was it because he found nothing better in the contemporary European operas being composed back home? Nothing in his writing suggested that, though he did discuss the state of opera in the respective countries in a mix of positive and negative terms. More, he was assuming what so many others were also assuming at this time: that because America was the country of the not yet, it represented the best dialectical alternative to a Europe that in reality was not presently pursuing the right course, even if, for Saunders, in Germany, it ideally or spiritually was trying to. Hence, what began as an account regarding the indigenous roots of American opera ended up assuming the successful importation of that toward which European opera had already strived. The future might lie largely with America, but this was only because what the future would demonstrate as the new was what Saunders already knew as the old.

The Democratic Narrative

The democratic narrative was offered by a former Austrian critic and musician, Hans W. Heinsheimer, once a colleague of Adorno's, a modernist who wrote for, among others, the journal *Anbruch*, after which, as an exile living in America, he wrote for the music journal *Tempo*. He argued for the potential of American opera and said that, were this potential to be realized, it would be the realization of the concept of opera *überhaupt*. This argument moved beyond Saunders's claim that the future of opera lay only "largely" with America.

Like Saunders, Heinsheimer produced three articles relevant to our concerns: one in 1945, "Opera in America," and another in 1947, "Music and the American Radio," for the journal *Tempo*, and a third in 1951, "Opera in America Today," for *Musical Quarterly*. With Saunders and Kestin, he traced opera's history in the United States or the protohistory of American opera—a history before the concept of American opera was realized. However, his argument distinguished itself by the stress it gave to American opera regarded as a thick social institution and thus extending beyond a list of works or performances.

For most of its history, Heinsheimer reminded us, the institution was dominated by foreigners and elite, European attitudes. This is not surprising, given that "America did not begin her musical history in the days of Palestrina or Bach or even of Richard Wagner." We know this is wrong and that this is a European attitude. However, Heinsheimer argued this way, like Weill, to turn a teleological argument on its head. If opera came to America only "of late" (Hegel), then what this meant was that America was essentially freed from the "burden" (Weill) of having to continue a tradition. Unburdened, Heinsheimer rejoiced, "everything that happens here in music is different and new and exciting"—"It is all just a beginning."[53]

Heinsheimer set aside nearly all of the more popular forms of opera and music production throughout the long nineteenth century of the United States so that he could mark the beginning of his interest as going back only as far as the founding of New York's elite Metropolitan Opera—in 1883. He did this to sustain his conclusion that only now (at the end of the Second World War) did the institution of American opera have the chance to reveal itself as what it *should* be: namely, a democratic institution, more popular in appeal and more suitably directed toward the full range of American interests and tastes. What Heinsheimer wanted for American opera was for it to be radically out of sync with what the exemplary Metropolitan Opera had so far offered during its short and predominantly European history: namely, an elite opera of European inclination. "The democratic age of opera [has] arrived," he announced almost gleefully, leaving Gatti Casazza to abandon the Met because "opera can no longer be done the way [Casazza] did it."[54] This argument presupposed a subtle but crucial shift, assuming that what was brought from Europe to America was only an elite form of production and not a popular one. It was assumed elite not because it reflected the conditions of opera in Europe—conditions that were always as much popular as elite—but because the elite came to be identified with the imported, as the popular was with the homespun.

Whereas Kestin and Saunders set their hopes on the folkloric and the indigenous, Heinsheimer bound the concept of American opera to a concept of American democracy as something that had only recently triumphed over the Europe he had left behind. With American democracy came the realization of the concept of opera, as the *institution* he desired it to be. Against this background, he remarked in 1951 on the "sudden and rapid growth of American musical culture," which —and here comes the teleological assumption—"long retarded for obvious historic reasons" tended to produce "many strange and revolutionary patterns," of which the most recent was also the most significant.[55]

Heinsheimer focused on New York's Metropolitan Opera to tell a history of a closed European institution severed from the spiritual and cultural development of the country as a whole. Receiving no government subsidy, which was not the focus of his complaint, opera had so far appealed only to those with money, gowns, and jewels, or to those rich Americans whose eyes were forever gazing toward Europe. The history of opera in the United States had been an elite history of European opera. His argument was not quite this crude. He acknowledged how many opera houses had sprung up across the country as a whole and how much traveling singers, directors, and conductors had contributed to spreading the song. And more than anything else, he looked for recent evidence of changes in class and social status that had already brought about a partial democratization of American opera. He thus approved of the contribution that radio had made with its already famed broadcasts from the Met, both to the allied war effort and to bringing opera to an ever-greater number of listeners. Turning his attention to what was produced in the opera houses, he complained that for too long American composers had not been sufficiently encouraged to compose operas, given the few opportunities they had had for performances in preferred venues. By 1951, when Heinsheimer returned to this theme, he was pleased to record the notable increase in opportunity.

Between 1945 and 1951, he began to change his attitude toward the radio. He started to see the demise of live performance in favor of what he called, with Adorno, canned radio shows and a preference for horse and soap operas, especially since television began to enter the home. In this view, a genuine democracy shouldn't encourage *every* sort of so-called popular culture. Moreover, he noticed how much modern American opera, as something pursued seriously for the sake of democracy, was already being cut off from the standardized opera houses and radio stations that were promoting performances only of the old European warhorses. Cut off, true American opera was supported less by mainstream houses and more by universities, say, Columbia University and Indiana University–Bloomington. What Heinsheimer might have written in 1951, Herbert Graf did write: "Opera at Columbia is small scale, experimental, and not a bit grand, but it is opera, it's American, and it's exciting because its concern is with the future."[56] Though Heinsheimer admired these university programs, he feared that if it was not careful, American opera would miss its moment. Nevertheless, he was optimistic: the time "is ripe" for American opera and her composers to take the lead, free and unconstrained in the new "decentralized" institution: "Anything can happen. . . . There are no limitations."[57]

Thoroughly opposed to Saunders's purism, Heinsheimer nevertheless shared his idea that the preferred state of culture (whatever it was) did not necessarily mirror what was then going on in the country at large. This attitude was shown implicitly in an interesting explanation Heinsheimer offered in 1945 as to why German opera was boycotted during the First World War but not during the Second. He recalled the recent spectacular success of Wagner's *Ring* and the spontaneous decision by the Met management to repeat the performance. But why, he asked, the difference of policy between the two wars? He did not suggest any difference in sympathy toward Germany or lack thereof. Instead, he suggested, in the Second World War there was just so much more at stake that it would have been an unnecessary waste of one's energies trying to boycott German music.[58] From this thought it seemed to follow that, despite one's interest in music, one should never forget what was politically at stake or that to be preoccupied with boycotting music was a mere luxury in a time when there were really important concerns with which to occupy oneself. The thought was especially problematic when it is used to disenfranchise culture. Even if music matters, he seemed to be saying, when compared with other matters, it matters, recalling Saunders's words, "not a whit."

Recall Thomas Mann's famous remark, here adapted, that wherever he went as an exile from Nazi Germany, he would take a true or better Germany with him, by which he mostly meant the culture misappropriated by the Nazis, that of Goethe, Schiller, Beethoven, and Wagner.[59] Though Mann, on arrival in the United States, favorably connected culture to democracy, he remained convinced that, when needed, there must be writers like him to produce works and protect the culture. Although a country's social condition guarantees nothing about the worth of its culture, since culture is not directly made by a society, a society can still destroy a culture by destroying its exemplary producers. The relation between politics and culture is not equal: culture will protect an ideal political concept even when the actual politics of a country is failing. Mann felt the need to protect culture and politics in 1933 in Germany and again in 1951 in McCarthyite America, but he worried increasingly that protection might be possible only if the writer remained shipwrecked somewhere in the middle of the ocean. Heinsheimer found a different protected space in the margins of American culture, in the few institutions where democratic American opera was being produced. Even if "American opera has no role" yet "in the United States as a nation," he hoped, perhaps it will have one in the future.[60]

Consider a more interesting turn that Heinsheimer's argument could have taken, the moment he suggested that a concern with opera in a time of war is a luxury. He could have argued that opera, even when sung in German, merits no censorious assessment, given its elite place in the culture. Only effective culture need be censored in a time of war, as it was. This thought throws a wrench into the entire argument. For, so far in this chapter, the question of opera's actuality or relevance to the United States has not been questioned. That opera matters to the future of the nation has simply been assumed. But what if one were to claim that opera did not have the potential to become an indigenous art of the United States, or, despite its long history in this country, that one should not have wanted it to have this potential? Why should it have shed itself of its European heritage if it was already good as it was, a mischmasch or cross-fertilization of many different, high and popular, European traditions mixed up with a plentiful representation of American contributions (in the form of singers, performers, conductors, critics, and fans, and, by the 1950s, increasingly more composers)? Maybe the question of American opera is just not so critical when it comes to thinking about the history of American music in the United States.

Arguably, this thought was suggested by the Marx Brothers' 1929 film *The Cocoanuts*, in a scene in which a man who has lost his shirt tells his audience, to the accompaniment of the most famous tune in Bizet's *Carmen,* that this is the best reason why a tenor in America ought to sing unto death. Doesn't this song ask us to consider the possible mismatch of American interest and cultural genre at every single American night at the opera? Or is this a disenfranchising question? I think it is, as I show below. However, my present interest is only to ask what would happen to the entire argument were attention turned to quite another art or part of culture, one more obviously indigenous to the United States or arguably more in line with the popular ballad and comic traditions of the eighteenth century. And what about the tradition of African American jazz? Wouldn't the entire "chest-thumping" dialectic between Europe and America be threatened? Likely and perhaps deservingly. Still, this matter was usually suppressed by those for whom there was something genuinely at stake in the song America sang in the time of war, most especially when that song was seen to retrieve something thought now lost to Europe.

Heinsheimer thus concluded by almost begging his readers in 1945 to pay attention to George Gershwin's "folk opera" *Porgy and Bess* (or, as some called it, "the first real American opera") if they really wanted to understand the social potential of opera as a whole. Despite its poor reception on Broadway in 1935, the work had to be embraced to alter our "entire attitude." For only with this alteration would American opera replace that "old European cradle of opera" that had just gone down "in flame and destruction." Why did we need a "unique sort" of "American creative genius" right at that very moment? Apparently, so that we could continue "to develop" [presumably only the best] "traditions of the old world."[61] But this only prompts the question of what exactly would be "unique" about the American creative genius if it were also meant to be a continuation. Whereas earlier Heinsheimer celebrated a fully emancipated "anything goes" attitude, in the end he fell back on the traditions he had known back home.

Heinsheimer's attitude was finally quite typical of those exiles who, having seen what happened in their old home, sought a different (but not too different) home in the place in which they arrived. Put extremely, opera arrived in the United States when they arrived, because only then could they pursue something still European, despite protestations to the contrary, no longer pursuable in Europe. American opera thus symbolized their hope, on the one side, of a modernist dialectic, on the other side of which was the living memory of a destroyed and suffering Europe.

In the narratives I have considered, the authors took little interest in the operas of the *Americas,* though each acknowledged the presence of, say, musicians from the Americas on the shores of the United States. This confirms my impression that the anxiety over American opera is mostly directed toward opera in the United States. Moreover, each author showed, to a greater and lesser degree, an interest in the question more of national identity than of genre. Each promoted his or her ideal of American opera more or less in disregard of the empirical history of opera in the United States: Kestin, less, and Heinsheimer, more, while Saunders occupied, despite his political and cultural convictions, a middle position. Finally, in each narrative, a normative distinction was implied between *what is* from *what is wanted* or *should be,* which only became problematic when that distinction also implied a contradiction. Think of the contradiction this way: To be interested in American opera was not necessarily to be interested in opera in the United States, and this became increasingly clear the more American opera began to express what *any* country should want of its art. In this sense, all the world was still America, as long at least as "America" was not defined geopolitically as a nation but ideally as the Land of the Future. But what, then, was the advantage of speaking about American opera at all? Here was the paradox: the more the concept of American opera was empowered, the more redundant became the terms—both "American" and "opera."

The Posthistoricist Narrative

The posthistoricist narrative was suggested by a particular project of opera or, better, of antiopera, produced by John Cage. Whether Cage was really a posthistoricist is too complex a matter to discuss here. I show only his tendency toward this position—when, after commenting that "America has an intellectual climate suitable for radical experimentation," he added, by alluding to Gertrude Stein, that America is "the oldest country of the twentieth century" in its "way of knowing nowness."[62] Cage used the defamiliarizing term "nowness" to separate his view from a commitment to the sort of newness that suggests continuation with the old. Thus (to recall chapter 4), when someone once remarked to Cage that "it must be very difficult" for him to write music in America, given how far he was from the centers of the tradition, he responded by saying, on the contrary, it would be more difficult to write music in Europe by being too close. What Cage demanded was an impatience and excitement associated with the nowness of the present, a nowness that would shed itself of the historicist or at least European commitment to waiting for either the right time or a suitable period of time to pass. If American music and, by extension, American opera were going to happen, they would do so in posthistoricist happenings severed from any reference to past or future. In wanting this, however, Cage also wanted an American music and opera exemplary of what all music now should be.

Cage told us a lot about what American opera should be by telling us what it should no longer be. Consider the project in which he engaged a few years before his death. Beginning in Frankfurt in 1987 as *Europera 1 & 2*, this project moved through London as *Europera 3 & 4* and ended with *Europera 5* in Buffalo, New York. Altogether just about the length of a Wagnerian opera, Cage's swan song, as it has been described, was meant to put European opera to rest. Its commissioners from Frankfurt, Heinz-Klaus Metzger and Reiner Riehm, asked for an "irreversible negation of opera," to break opera's rules of form, content, length, and performance location.[63]

In Adornian terms, this antiopera opera was produced in fragmentary form, not to cipher the aesthetic only to quote it. In fragmented form, *Europera 1 & 2* showed what the operatic aesthetic had become in the modern age: a set of empty and random quotations from our best-loved European operas, produced anywhere, anytime, in a society in which anything goes. As patchworks of quotations from Wagner, Verdi, and Puccini, produced by performers or record players, Cage's products appeared ready-made to show what was always ready-made about Old Europe. If Europe once founded America as ready-made—as a culture of copies—then Cage handed back a Europe now made in America's image, a Europe of dead operatic space that could not shed itself of the burden of tradition. "For 200 years the Europeans have sent us their operas," he wrote: "Now I am returning them."[64] Maybe Europe would see what it had become—a culture of copies of European images, the historical meanings of which are so eroded that the images serve only as fodder for an up-to-date American art of the consumer image, popping up as in pop art wherever and whenever one opens one's ears or eyes.

In his *Europeras*, Cage urged a reductionism of space, time, utterance, and movement such that the performances ended in "nothingness." This was the ultimate negation of the work concept that had culminated in the total and authoritative work of art. Cage conceived of his project as a radical demonstration of what many Europeans were demanding of their own opera houses—that they be blown up—and this all the more urgently, given their arguably too quick, postwar restoration. Cage's project also aligned itself with what the surrealists did earlier, when they damaged the authority of the work concept by making radical gestures of art and producing manifestos for what art ought to be. Certainly, the *Europeras* were as much manifestos as reflective acts of art or music, exactly on a par with Warholian forms of image making or quotation making in the modern age of technological reproducibility.

Yet Cage's projects were denied entry where they were needed most: to the opera houses. In Europe and in America, they were performed in alternative spaces where their inconvenient truth was conveniently ignored. Paradoxically, the space for a genuinely American art found more support in Europe than in the United States, though when there was support in the latter, it was always in places a little too far north or south on Broadway to matter to the mainstream. Recall Cage's proclamation of nowness and how it suspended an allegiance to world-historical differentiations of time to separate what presently existed from what should or could exist if America "would only support it." The nowness to which he appealed was thus not the *now* of the presently existing but the normative *now* associated with a possibility, which, when actualized, found itself almost completely marginalized. Might it not be worthwhile, he wondered, to seek venues for American opera elsewhere? Interestingly, in this story, the failure of what might have been a future for American opera (Cage style) contradicted the unequivocal success of American visual art (Warhol style), which far more successfully took over from the sidelines the mainstream museums of American art.

To Be or Not to Be

In 1966, Douglas Moore's *The Ballad of Baby Doe* was declared the "great American opera." In so declaring the work, few seemed worried that the *work* showed obvious European influence. Its *composer,* apparently, was sufficiently American. Still, the description of greatness didn't stick.[65] But isn't this the point? Otherwise put, shouldn't we worry that attributing greatness to an American opera might be out of sync with the democratic spirit? Maybe American operas are not meant to last, freed from a philosophy of history that demands the passing of historical time as art's evaluative test. Maybe the point of American opera is not to produce "great works." To be a work or not to be a work: that was almost the question one critic asked in Berlin in 1924. Actually, he wrote: "*Kultur oder Unkultur* . . . that is a European question," but then immediately criticized the Germans who asked it for their deplorable and incurable monomania.[66] Comparably, in denying America the question of workhood or greatness, is America liberated from a burden or only further deprived from playing on the field of history? Isn't there a tendency to disenfranchise American opera in every attempt to empower it via exclusionary tactics?

In 2006, Alex Ross, music critic for the *New Yorker,* reviewed three new or fairly new works of American opera: Stephen Hartke's *The Greater Good, or the Passion of Boule de Suif* (after Maupassant), Ned Rorem's *Our Town* (after Thornton Wilder), and Elliott Carter's *What Next?,* an antiopera with a Beckett-like libretto written by Paul Griffiths. Ross asked:

> Are any of these new operas towering masterworks that will alter the course of music history while winning the hearts of millions? People have been asking that loaded question for a hundred years, and the way they phrase it almost demands a negative answer. Better to ask whether a new work is strong enough to hold the stage. If it does, it has a future, and the masterpiece-sorting can be done by later generations.[67]

Ross's suggestion is not immediately transparent. Instead of tossing out the question of masterpieces, he leaves it intact, putting it off for future critics to answer. A masterpiece is still that which stands the test of time, and time must pass before the judgment can be made. Given this delaying tactic, Ross diverts his thought to the apparently more pressing issue: what it means for a work to "hold the stage." He does not seem to be saying that works need adequate productions to show them as the masterpieces they are; rather, that works need adequate productions to establish them as masterpieces in the first place, which follows Benjamin's view urging us no longer to think of works as requiring production but as being made *for* production. If this is what Ross wants, it is a subtle move, because, by putting off the question of sorting out masterpieces, he is really putting the question off altogether in favor of an assessment more fitting to what one might call the New Stage Age of Reproducibility. That "stage" is here synonymous with "production" suggests a New Produced Art for Reproducibility.

To hold the stage or not to hold the stage: Is this the question for the future of American opera? Perhaps. But if it is, wasn't it always the question, as Adorno suggested when he described Mozart's achievement in the last naive moment of operatic production? Consider Peter Sellars's recent production of Mozart's *Zaide*. From the one perspective, Sellars produced a work for repro- duction because there was no complete work or no work at all to begin with. What he produced on and for a stage is an American opera, even perhaps a *Singspiel* about the emancipatory impulses of African Americans set against late industrialized conditions of labor. From the other perspective, Sellars produced an incomplete work by Mozart to show where too much complete- ness of the operatic work had led: namely, to its own radical fragmentation. Juxtaposing these two perspectives, Sellars's production in 2006 recalls not only the Mozartian moment but also those earlier operas of *Amerikanismus* with which this chapter began. We have come full circle.

American Opera or American *Opera*

In 1930, when Adorno arguably tried to compose an American opera, he was also becoming a philosophical critic of the same. His early critical aims tell us something about his compositional aims. Consider his review of Antheil's *Transatlantic* in the journal *Modern Music*. This opera, the first "American opera" to be premiered in Europe, was produced in Frankfurt on May 25, 1930, but not in the United States until 1981. Born in New Jersey in 1900 and dying in New York in 1959, Antheil has been described as an American com- poser of German descent, and then like this:

> In 1926, Antheil was hailed by Aaron Copland as the most promising of a trio of radical composers. . . . In less than a year, however, his Parisian sup- porters were denouncing his turn from iconoclasm to neo-classicism. . . . Faced with artistic dethronement, Antheil accepted the critic H. H. Stuckenschmidt's invitation to participate in the operatic renaissance in Germany, and in 1928 he moved to Vienna to begin work on his "politi- cal" opera *Transatlantic,* a work he later viewed as the beginning of his search to shape a "fundamentally American style." . . . [Antheil] returned permanently to the USA in 1933 and spent more than a decade trying to recover the compositional momentum of his early European years.[68]

Why did Antheil choose to compose his first American opera in Germany? Because there, he answered himself, there are "eighty-two immensely active opera houses." In the same journal in which Adorno reviewed his work, An- theil published an article with the Wild West title, "Wanted—Opera by and for Americans." American opera, he argued, should be captured alive rather than dead. Americans should do some "quick thinking," to recognize how much European operas produced on American themes were capturing better the potential of America than American operas themselves. Most of all, Antheil wanted America to stop "making excuses that [it was] still a young nation musically, which," he added, "is obviously hokum." He blamed the ultraconservative Europeans for this view, particularly those who betrayed America's future by maintaining the country's own sense of its immaturity—though, as we have seen, it wasn't only the ultraconservatives who thought this way.

Three years younger than Antheil, Adorno opened his review by describing America as young, though not necessarily as immature, as if wanting to identify himself with the possibility America represented at its best. Adorno insisted on the importance of reviewing young composers and young works, but not so as to license the "die-hard reactionaries" to reject the young works by aligning them immediately with the left. Rather than aligning works politically or tendentiously at all, it would be better, he said, to look in detail inside a work if one wanted properly to expose its aesthetic and social content.[69] At just the moment when Benjamin criticized Adorno's own opera project for its "romantic idyllization," despite the modernism of its social theme, Adorno criticized Antheil's work for the same. The more its aesthetic form capitulates to something romantic, the more the social subject matter is left suspended (undialectically) above the work.

Noticing this tension, Adorno asked whether it was possible at all to produce an *opera* about present-day *America*. Whereas opera tended, in its romantic impulse, to capture the essence of reality, Americanism in art (and in film paradigmatically, as discussed in chapter 7) tended toward "naturalistic reflection." "In Antheil's opera," he wrote, we are not shown "the mythos of America" but only "a series of non-historical episodes" suggesting modern life. We are shown only "the façade of modernity" onto which capitalists displace their concerns, by showing more interest in champagne and dancing than in production and sales—or, given the American president, more interest in love affairs than in political programs. Everything to do with "eternal values" of love and hate are made primitive and familiar in this phantasmagoric "parade of accessories."

Though Adorno appreciated the work's theatricality, he rejected its tendency to "unravel rather than to manipulate the clichés of civilization." Musically, what might have been a critical manipulation of rhythm, jazz, or even folkloric elements was turned into an antimodern acceptance of traditional harmony and polyphony. Ultimately, he declared the work young but now also immature. Wasn't the point of this opera, he asked, "to imagine an America more 'American' than this?" Adorno said no more, leaving us only with the enchantment he experienced in observing this fantastical portrayal of New York, admitting, however, that the portrayal had catered perfectly to his still young European imagination.

What might he have meant by imagining an America more American than this? What he did not mean was an America of enchanted fantasy. Nor did he show any subtle appreciation of façade (contra Benjamin or, later, Warhol and Cage). He only looked for evidence of the sort of clichés that could be manipulated first by a work and then by its philosophical critique. When he tried to compose his own opera, he read the works of Mark Twain and Richard Hughes, seeking to borrow an immanent critical stance on a country he himself did not (yet) have. But why, finally, did he look across the Atlantic at all if what he really sought was something already available at home? Why not look inside Germany, especially given how much Germany was at this moment either electing or rejecting affinities with America?

Adorno posed the same question when, in another review of 1930, he considered Brecht and Weill's *Mahagonny*. Despite Cocteau's earlier productions, Adorno declared this work the "first surrealist opera." With its tension between construction and sensuousness, this opera was arguably, in my view, the most sentimental or reflective *Zauberflöte* of modern times. For Adorno, as for Brecht and Weill, the term "opera" was deliberately retained for this work to put into question what opera could be under the contemporary conditions of capitalism, where capitalism was what was used to identify America. If American opera was a contradiction in terms, it was because capitalism was beset by contradiction. Being an opera about consumerism, false pleasures, and unfulfilled promises, *Mahagonny* betrayed (and thus revealed) what opera always promised—to be culinary without social cost—and what America promised most to be: a place of social justice.[70]

For an opera to be produced for the sake of social justice, Adorno concluded, it had to be produced under contemporary conditions in the fragmented form of a broken promise. One cannot simply save a genre by continuing blindly or naively to compose operas. If opera was trying to survive by turning its gaze toward America, the attempt should be worked out in terms of persistent possibility in order to break the illusion that happiness or social justice already exists somewhere else—just not here.

What is preserved here of the dialectical model of Germany and America neither confuses the possible with the actual nor ends up taking sides. Whichever side of the ocean one finds oneself on, that side must be subjected to critique. Hence one hears, on one side, the *Cocoanuts* tenor singing to Bizet's music of his having lost his shirt and, on the other, *Mahagonny's* fat man proclaiming that "one can speak of great times, one can also forget great times, and though we can put a clean shirt on a dead man, we can do nothing further to help him." Yet, as Adorno well knew, the tenor or the fat man will continue to sing every time he gazes to some faraway place—as in *Mahagonny*, of a golden age, a better age, or, with Jenny, the moon in Alabama.

What Adorno suggested in 1930 is something he later could make explicit: though the dialectic between Germany and America, or the Old and the New, seems to give us a choice, it is really no choice at all, just as there is no real choice between *American* opera and American *opera*. Dialectical models do not give us "either-ors" unless they are dialectical either-ors showing both sides as participating "in the same history." The "or" is a dialectical "or" belonging to enlightenment history as much at its beginning as at its end. If this is correct, what should one conclude regarding the very idea of American opera? It is often supposed that once the baggage that thickens a concept has become too heavy or large, it would be better to stop using the concept. However, if the concept is not retained, will we find better terms with which to consider the future of a country and its art? Another option, which I prefer, is to maintain the concept as the sort that allows criticism to be ongoing within a practice that would rather keep its terms too comfortably in place. To use a concept critically against its own specific applications is one way to show the immanent tension in a practice that, with one hand, proclaims its openness but, with the other, threatens constantly to close its borders. To paraphrase the 1929 words of an exiled critic (who once had to break a leg to stay alive): what promises unlimited possibilities usually delivers impossible limitations.[71]

In the fragile space between unlimited possibility and impossible limitations, the double trouble of American opera rests its case, leaving us asking: Does America need an opera and, if it does, does it need one that is American? If my argument has gone through, the significance of this question extends far beyond the geographical borders of the United States, sending us back once more to the complex history of opera and nationalism in Europe.

Afterword

In *The Seduction of Culture in German History,* a book about how culture seduces the other as also itself, Wolf Lepenies concludes with an argument against the monumentalizing of our questions and attitudes and for their lo-calization. His motivation is painfully up to date—*aktuell*—the more he wit-nesses current events interpreted as world-historical events. In this context he mentions an article whose theme might well have preoccupied me in my own chapter on intentional ruins. The article was written by Don DeLillo for *Harper's Magazine* in December 2001 and titled, "In the Ruins of the Future: Reflections on Loss and Terror in the Shadow of September." DeLillo wrote:

> We like to think that America invented the future. We are comfortable with the future, intimate with it. But there are disturbances now, in large and small ways, a chain of reconsiderations. Where we live, how we travel, what we think about when we look at our children. For many people, the event has changed the grain of the most routine moment.[72]

DeLillo's lines are marvelous for their deconstructive movement: they be-gin large but end small, producing disturbances on their way in what has be-come most routine in our daily lives. If those disturbances lead us away from the comfort of our grandest thoughts, then this seems to be the very best outcome of what are otherwise left floating above our lives as untouchable world-historical events. The move from the great to the small, from large to small gestures, is the trajectory of all the arguments in my book, movements toward deflation and diminishment. The more a philosophy demands this sort of ending, however, the more urgent and extreme seems to be its sen-tences, as though the move toward the small is always triggered by something cataclysmic or catastrophic. When philosophers end up wanting to tend to their gardens, they mostly do this as an escape from world-shattering events. Usually as acts of retreat, resignation, or despair, they determine to produce philosophies writ small as antidotes to world histories writ large. Few philoso-phers begin in the garden, though this is where most end up.

Having made this trajectory explicit, how now does one end a book with-out too much clichéd diminishment or too much clichéd grandeur? I recall once asking my colleagues why they thought it was that students never ap-plauded my classes at the end of the semester. They asked how I ended the class. I described the negative but hopeful Socratic message that I offered the students: that at least they might have learned how much they did not know and how this might leave them wanting to read more philosophy. No wonder, my colleagues retorted: Why would you expect applause for that? Or, even better, why do you expect applause at all? The latter was the best response I could have been given, reminding me as it did of Nietzsche's appropriately cutting remark to anyone overly preoccupied by success: "A thinker needs no applause and clapping of hands provided he is sure of his own clapping of hands."[73] Nevertheless, I admit that I have continued to experiment with class endings, just as in my writing about philosophy, music, and opera I have continued to investigate the upbeats, downbeats, no beats at all, big bows, little bows, questioning glances, final endings, open endings, ambiguous endings, and promising endings to encourage new beginnings. Like almost every other scholar interested in modernism, I find Samuel Beckett's line to be the most appealing: avoid the terrific end, and go for the middle, even if what the middle offers is only a temporary cessation of the pain.

I began this book with the conceit of rewriting a very great story. I end by doing the same. This story was written by Mark Twain as a self-described "tramp abroad" and begins in Munich in a concert, where like Eduard in Goethe's *Elective Affinities,* the performance proceeds on time and without too much disturbance to the end. Rather than being offered intermittently, the applause is reserved for the end, though for an end following rather than being simultaneous with the last notes. In America, Twain remarks, we always smash into the ending with an earthquake of applause, but in Germany they usually wait for "the closing strain of a fine solo or duet." Why, he asks, are Americans so willing "to rob [themselves] of the sweetest part of the treat?" We "get the whisky" but miss "the sugar in the bottom of the glass."[74]

The different approaches toward applause suggest differences between German and American audiences. Twain recognizes the need to appreciate an actor or a singer's gestures at the moment of occurrence. Lively and immediate response is a good thing, he notes, whereas the "deathly silences" of a German audience can be dreadful. But he also seems to fear that an American audience might so interrupt a performance that the traditional distance between reality and art will be eroded altogether. In many places in this book, I have described the gap, the space, and the "almost" on which theorists have depended to preserve differences between ideas or things that modern culture and society have tended to collapse. In my story, the threat of this reduction stems specifically from an audience that cannot hold back from demanding of art that it gratify its most immediate needs.

Twain's story recalls the king of Bavaria, who, though very fond of opera, prefers to sit alone in an empty auditorium. Typically, the king arrives at the opera after its end, demanding that the work be performed as an encore for him alone. On one occasion, the king, rather than being content to watch the *imitation* of a storm on stage, demands that a *real storm* be produced by opening the theater's water pipes. The opera proceeds with as near a real storm as possible: "The mimic thunder began to mutter, the mimic wind began to wail and sough, and the mimic rain to patter." Dissatisfied with the mimicking, the king demands more reality by demanding more water. If only reality were so easily produced—or maybe this is the point: reality is this easily produced. The singers singing in the rain are thoroughly drenched, while the king applauds from his dry seat. The storm over, the king demands a repetition of the event, a demand to which the unhappy manager finds a both convenient and witty reply. He tells the king that the demand for repetition is already reward enough for the singers, who ought not be further allowed to indulge their vanity by singing again. That the king is persuaded by the reply is proof enough of the king's moderation—the sort of "royal" or "German" moderation that ultimately keeps art where it belongs, on the stage, with the audience placed at a respectful distance in their seats. Would an American audience be so moderate? Twain concludes, probably not. With a "gladsome" absence of reflection, they would rather bring art to its end by having the storm entirely drown the singers on the stage.

But let me ask for the last time whether it is evidence of an absence of reflection or, rather, of too much reflection that motivates the American audience to act this way. I answer simply by recalling the confident words written in 1849 by Walt Whitman, though they could also have been written a century later—or even last week:

> As for us of America, we have long enough followed obedient and child-like in the track of the Old World. We have received her tenors and her buffos, her operatic troupes and her vocalists, of all grades and complexions; listened to and applauded the songs made for a different state of society—made perhaps by royal genius, but made to please royal ears likewise; and it is time that such listening and receiving should cease.[75]

Nevertheless, as I have argued throughout this book, to ask for a cessation of influence or even for an end is often to ask for a liberation that turns out to be just another disenfranchisement. Between liberation and disenfranchisement is an extremely fine line: there are no guarantees. Drowning singers on the stage is one way to close down an American institution that refuses to let its own homespun opera in. Yet doing this runs the risk that the singers who sing best will simply go elsewhere, to sing with their magic flutes, to forget once more the threat of extinction with which they are faced, even here, in a place they have come to think of as home. Or, to quote Nietzsche:

Oh, the poor bird that has felt free and now strikes the walls of this cage! Woe, when homesickness for the land overcomes you, as if there had been more *freedom* there—and [now] there is no more "land"!

Notes

Chapter 1

1. These opening paragraphs are drawn from pt. 1, chs. 4 and 8, of Goethe's *Elective Affinities*, 109–17, 130–32 (transl. amended); *Die Wahlverwandtschaften*, 309–20, 338–41.

2. According to Benjamin ("Goethe's *Elective Affinities*," in *Selected Writings* 1:330; *GS2* 1.1:168), the references to recitation and storytelling come from, respectively, Georg Simmel and R. M. Meyer.

3. Adorno often employs this sort of formulation not to reify or prioritize one side but to preserve the tension between the two sides. In each case, he shows by appeal to the one side what is lost as the other side has become more dominant.

4. Adorno, *B*, 116 (transl. amended); B^G, 170.

5. Adorno, *Two Pieces for String Quartet*, op. 2 (1925), and *Six Short Orchestra Pieces*, op. 4 (1929).

6. Entry "Satz" in Eggebrecht, *Brockhaus-Riemann Musiklexikon*, 444 (my transl.).

7. Rousseau, "Mouvement," in *Dictionnaire de musique, Oeuvres Complètes*, 5:913–14.

8. Quoting Robert and James Adam, *Works in Architecture,* preface 3 note (London: 1773–78), cited in *Oxford English Dictionary,* s.v. "movement."

9. Williams, *Glass Menagerie,* 61. I return to this passage in chapter 7.

10. Quoting *Pall Mall,* 1 Dec. 1885, 4/1, cited in *Oxford English Dictionary,* s.v. "movement."

11. Hanslick, *VMS,* 27. Unless otherwise specified, all translations of Hanslick's text are my own.

12. Scruton, *Aesthetics of Music,* 96.

13. Cf. Kivy's discussions in "How Music Moves," in *Music Alone,* 146–72, and "Movements and 'Movements,'" in *New Essays on Musical Understanding,* 168–82.

14. Adorno wrote these lines in 1960 with explicit allusion to Goethe's *Wilhelm Meisters Lehrjahre* ("Mignon's Song"), "Music and New Music," in Adorno, *QF,* 265; *QF*G, 490.

15. *Faust* I, Intermezzo to the "Walpurgisnachtstraum," lines 4239–40, in Goethe, *Texte,* 182 (my transl.).

16. Hanslick, *VMS,* 64, 72.

17. Ibid., preface of September 11, 1891, vi.

18. Ibid., 59.

19. In thinking about the translation of this phrase, note that Hanslick chose a poetic, and not a more straightforward, construction. He could have written *tönende bewegende* or *bewegliche Formen.*

20. For part survey and part new treatment of these topics, see Hasty, *Meter as Rhythm.* Moving beyond traditional limitations, Hasty places contemporary thinking about rhythm, meter, and time into the context of broader musical, philosophical, and historical debates. Scruton also contextualizes his account by reference to traditional accounts, offered, among others, by Victor Zuckerkandl and Leonard B. Meyer.

21. In surprisingly similar terms, Adorno rejects Rudolf Kolisch's argument on character in music (see Kolisch, "Tempo and Character in Beethoven's Music"), when arguing specifically against the positivistic or mechanistic construction of general "types." The "knowledge," Adorno responds in a letter to Kolisch dated Nov. 16, 1943 (*B,* 179–81; *B*G, 255–57), "must be concrete and must yield overarching connections through the movement from one particular moment to another, and not through establishing general features [characteristics or types]" (180).

22. Hanslick, *VMS,* 29.

23. Ibid., 62; transl. partly taken from Payzant, *On the Musically Beautiful,* 30.

24. Schopenhauer's remarks on music are offered almost entirely in *WWR,* 1:255–67 and 2:447–57, and *WWV,* 1:356–72 and 2:573–86.

25. Schopenhauer, *WWR,* 1:256, 264; *WWV,* 1:357, 369.

26. Schopenhauer, *WWR,* 1:264 (transl. amended); *WWV,* 1:369–70.

27. Schopenhauer, *WWR,* 1:258 (transl. amended); *WWV,* 1:360.

28. For more on Schopenhauer's account of analogy in relation to the anagogical principle, see Goehr, "Schopenhauer and the Musicians."

29. Mann, "Schopenhauer," in *Essays of Three Decades*, 394.

30. I say more about Hotho's revisions of Hegel's text in chapter 2.

31. Hegel, *HA*, 2:928 (transl. amended); *VA*, 15:183.

32. Hegel, "Elective Affinities," in *Science of Logic*, 354–55.

33. Hegel, *HA*, 2:890, 897; *VA*, 15:134, 143.

34. Hegel, *HA*, 2:914; *VA*, 15:164–65.

35. Hegel, *HA*, 2:928; *VA*, 15:183–84.

36. Hegel, *HA*, 2:928 (transl. amended); *VA*, 15:184.

37. Hegel, *PS*, 11; *PG*, 24.

38. Hegel, *PS*, 12; *PG*, 26.

39. Hegel, *PS*, 38 (transl. amended); *PG*, 59. For more on *Schweben*, see Goehr, "Adorno, Schoenberg, and the *Totentanz der Prinzipien*."

40. Hegel, *PS*, 35–36; *PG*, 56.

41. Adorno, *ND*, 27; *ND*ᴳ, 38.

42. Adorno, *ND*, 8 (transl. amended); *ND*ᴳ, 20. In this book, I often juxtapose more- and less-sympathetic readings of Hegel's philosophy. In the last paragraphs of his treatise, Hanslick criticizes Hegel for finding in music only a generalized expression of a nonindividualized *Inneres* (inwardness) that overlooks and thus seriously underestimates the particular, formal (objective) activity of the composer (*VMS*, 173).

43. Adorno, *AT*, 51; *ÄT*, 82: "Hegel arrests [*stellt*] the aesthetic dialectic by his static definition of the beautiful as the sensuous appearance of the idea" (transl. amended); also *AT* 219; *ÄT*, 326: "Hegel failed to recognize [art's impulse to objectify the fleeting, not the permanent] and for this reason, in the midst of the dialectic, failed to recognize the temporal core of art's truth content" (transl. amended). What motivates Adorno to read Hegel this way is an explicit theme of chapter 5.

44. Adorno, *TMR*, 228 (my transl.). Adorno often speaks of liquidation—a fluid and almost Goethean term—whenever he wants to ask whether something is still possible, be it philosophy, music, art, or even life, especially after the catastrophe of World War II. In a letter to Benjamin of March 18, 1936, he writes: "You are well aware that the question of the 'liquidation' of art has been a motivating force behind my own aesthetic studies for many years" (Adorno and Benjamin, *Complete Correspondence*, 128).

45. Adorno, *ND*, 361 (transl. amended); *ND*ᴳ, 354.

46. Adorno, *MM*, 245 (transl. amended); *MM*ᴳ, 280.

47. Adorno, *MM*, 152; *MM*ᴳ, 173.

48. Adorno, *ND*, 377–78; *ND*ᴳ, 370.

49. Adorno, *ND*ᴳ, 62 (my transl.).

50. Adorno, *AT*, 181; *ÄT*, 270. References to knots are numerous in the works of German idealism (from Hegel to Kierkegaard), as well as in writings on drama and opera throughout the eighteenth and nineteenth centuries (from Lessing to Nietzsche).

51. On how metaphysics emerges in response to specific needs, see Adorno, *MCP*, esp. chs. 11 and 12 on *Bewegung*.

52. Adorno, *ND*, 406 (transl. amended); *ND*^G, 397.

53. For Adorno, much of what we hope for is what we can no longer have and, more drastically, no longer even hope for, despite our continuing to do so—namely, for reconciliation between subject and object. The hope is expressed as a negative or anti-utopian gesture. Cf. Wellmer, *Persistence of Modernity.*

54. Goethe, *Elective Affinities,* 262 (transl. amended); *Die Wahlverwandtschaften,* 401.

55. Benjamin, "Goethe's *Elective Affinities,*" 349, 356; *GS2* 1.1:193, 201.

56. Adorno, "Zur Schlussszene des Faust," in *NL*^G, 138 (my transl.).

57. All these claims appear in the final section of Adorno, *ND*^G, 397–400.

58. Benjamin, "Goethe's *Elective Affinities,*" 333; *GS2* 1.1:171. Benjamin also often employs the term "diminuendo." For more on this theme, see Corngold, "Genuine Obscurity Shadows the Semblance Whose Obliteration Promises Redemption."

59. The contrast here between Webern and Berg is not sharp; hence, Adorno also writes about Webern's music in Hegelian terms, describing, for example, its brevity as a "fury of disappearance" (Adorno, *SF,* 94; *SF*^G, 113). I return to the theme of Webern's brevity briefly below.

60. Adorno, *AB,* 39; *GS* 13:374. Adorno also uses the term "Doppelbewegung" in a discussion of Hegel, specifically when describing the double character of art as at once aesthetic and social (*AT,* 118; *ÄT,* 180). For another approach to the "doppel" aspect of *Bewegung* in the history of German aesthetic theory, see Menninghaus, *Unendliche Verdoppelung.*

61. Adorno, *ND,* 270 (transl. amended); *ND*^G, 266–67.

62. Adorno, "Skoteinos, or How to Read Hegel," in *HS,* 133; *DSt,* 363. In the terms of social theory, Adorno explores "the subject's hand" as social labor. Borrowing from Marx, he criticizes Hegel for not describing society's *Bewegung* in the material terms of human and social labor. Hegel goes astray in allowing "the quiescence of movement"—that is, "the absolute"—to become identified with "the reconciled life, the life of the pacified drive," which no longer recognizes either the deficiency or excess of social labor that has gone into producing the illusion of reconciliation in the first place (Adorno, "Aspects of Hegel's Philosophy," in *HS,* 32; *DSt,* 277).

63. Adorno, *ND,* 156–57; *ND*^G, 159.

64. It is not uncommon in this sort of thinking to write as if languages or modes of thinking had their own agency, thus the yearning between music and philosophy. The agency should not be taken too literally, even if it is Adorno's point to show that what happens to languages and disciplines happens also to persons (and their agency) given the social conditions under within which they more or less "live." (For more on life and the possibility of its being lived, see chapters 5 and 8).

65. Adorno often asks about the contemporary possibility of experience, aesthetic or otherwise. I return to this theme constantly but most explicitly in chapter 8.

66. Adorno, *AT,* 358; *ÄT,* 531.

67. In *B*, Adorno remarks on Schnabel's "overvivid rendition of sung melodies" (127) and in *AT*, on Schnabel's nominalist attempt to replace the indeterminate "expressivo" with a specific thing expressed (104–5). Adorno also takes up the theme of "melody" in his obituary essay honoring Schoenberg, in *Prisms*, 152–53, to counter the constant and destructive reproach that New Music is antimelodic. Though he criticizes the attention paid to melody at the expense of contrapuntal harmony, he refuses to hand over melody to those who seek to appropriate it for their own and, in his view, regressive use. I resume this theme in chapter 2. One might, however, recall here (a little tongue in cheek) Wittgenstein's alleged ability to whistle an entire symphony, as if whistling the melody were all that is required to whistle the whole. For his talent, he was rightly congratulated; for the reductionist act, he was rarely criticized.

68. Despite the metaphysical status of the claim, it is also historical, from which it follows that Adorno is thinking only about a specific dialectic between work and performance that obtains in a particular historical form of Western/European musical practice and thus not about all music whatever its conceptual, social, or musical form.

69. Adorno, *AT*, 358 (transl. amended); *ÄT* 531.

70. Adorno, *MM*, 50; *MM*^{G}, 55.

71. Adorno, "The Experiential Content of Hegel's Philosophy," in *HS*, 66; *DSt*, 305.

72. Adorno, "Skoteinos," in *HS* 109–10; *DSt*, 342.

73. Ibid., in *HS* 123–24; *DSt*, 353–54. For a pertinent and more recent musicological consideration of the relation between the movement of music, thought, and language, see Treitler, "Beethoven's 'Expressive' Markings," 89–111.

74. Adorno, *HS*, 51, 123 (transl. amended); *DSt*, 294, 354. Here, Adorno is quoting the poet Rudolf Burchardt, "Ich habe nichts als Rauschen" (used also as the epigraph for his essay "Skoteinos," in *HS*, 89).

75. Adorno, *B*, 43 (transl. amended); *B*^{G} 74.

76. Ibid.

77. Adorno, *HS*, 136; *DSt*, 366.

78. Adorno, *B*, 13–15; *B*^{G}, 34–36. For more on phantasmagoria and second nature, see chapter 3 and for Adorno's explicit definition of "musical work," see Adorno, *COM*, 633.

79. Adorno, "On the Contemporary Relationship Between Philosophy and Music," in *AEM*, 144; *GS* 18:159; also *AT*, 222 (transl. amended); *ÄT*, 330; also *B*, 18; *B*^{G}, 41: "Herein lies the real coincidence with Hegel: from this standpoint, their relationship can be defined as one of logical unfolding, *not* of analogy."

80. Adorno, *B*, 21; *B*^{G}, 45.

81. Adorno, *MM*, 126–28; *MM*^{G}, 143–45. This is a key passage in Adorno's writings to which I often return. In this passage, Adorno also describes dialectical thinking in terms of its fragility (see my chapter 4) or its necessary divergence from apparently established facts (my chapter 5).

82. Adorno, *B*, III; *B*^G, 164.

83. Adorno, *B*, 118–19; *B*^G, 174–79. This idea is offered within Adorno's critique of "the radio symphony" (see my chapter 7). There is a danger in this principle when it is assumed that from the first note we already know the last, as though the work's movement was fated all along. For more on fate, see my chapter 5 but also Goehr, "Aida and the Empire of the Emotions," and Goehr, "Undoing the Discourse of Fate."

84. Adorno, *AT*, 137–38, 85; *ÄT*, 207–08, 132. Cf. Ernst Bloch's "Deaccelerated Time, Accelerated Time, and Space," in *Literary Essays*, 482–86, for relevantly related descriptions of the "pent up" experience of music and of the uncanny quality of time's having been "snatched up" and stretched, suddenly lapsing, being reduced, reaching a "diminuendo," or as having achieved moments of compression and blissful suspension. Bloch shifts attention from everyday experience to the aesthetic experience of artworks, specifically to musical and operatic works where, for example, he hears a paradigmatic expression of how time accelerates and decelerates, as in the *Zeitlupe* (time loop) of Melusine's box. In opera, Bloch finds particularly pregnant or uncanny moments of intensity, in the experience of the "the totality of a world . . . coming [musically] to itself."

85. Goethe's complete line reads: "Die Hoffnung fuhr wie ein Stern, der vom Himmel fällt, über ihre Häupter weg." Benjamin, "Goethe's *Elective Affinities*," 354–55; *GS2* 1.1:199–200.

86. Adorno, *AT*, 188 (transl. amended); *ÄT*, 279. The example is used again and the measures indicated in Adorno, "'Beautiful Passages' in Beethoven," in *B*, 184; *B*^G, 260.

87. Lewy, *Zur Sprache des alten Goethe*. Cf. Adorno, "Beethoven's Late Style," in *B*, 187; *B*^G, 266.

88. Adorno, "Beethoven's Late Style." Elsewhere, in *MMP*, Adorno describes Beethoven's use of the reprise in terms of the idealist demand for final identity. Here, Mahler is the elected figure in whose music one still finds something like a Proustian expression of the "irrecoverability" of lost time (94).

89. Goethe, *Maximen und Reflexionen*, 279: "Alter. stufenweises Zurücktreten aus der Erscheinung." Adorno refers to Goethe's phrase several times in his writings, but writes "von der Erscheinung" instead of "aus der Erscheinung." The difference between stepping *back from* and stepping *away from* appearance is subtle; both phrases differ from what Henri Lonitz (in Adorno and Berg, *Correspondence*, 209) has argued is actually implied by Goethe's phrase: namely, "stepping *out of* phenomena" (my emphasis). In my view, Adorno may have arrived at his Goethean phrase by confusing it with another he quotes in reference to Husserl—namely, "Unabhängigkeit von der Erscheinung" (Adorno, *Philosophische Frühschriften*, in *GS* 1:48). However, contra Lonitz, I don't think that either Goethe or Adorno intended to speak of stepping out of phenomena, which means that the prepositional slippage does not imply a confusion of meaning.

90. Adorno, *B*, 188 (transl. amended); *B*^G, 266.

91. Adorno, *AT,* 23–24, 178–81; Adorno, "Vers une musique informelle," in *QF,* 295–98, 285, 312.

92. Adorno, *CM,* 384–85.

93. Goethe, *Elective Affinities,* 115–16; *Die Wahlverwandtschaften,* 318.

Chapter 2

1. Hanslick, *VMS,* 90–92n. All discussion of Hanslick in this essay is drawn from this extended footnote.

2. Wagner, *DS* 5:310 (my transl.).

3. For example, Hinton, "Not 'Which' Tones? The Crux of Beethoven's Ninth."

4. For example, Buch, *Beethoven's Ninth;* Cook, *Beethoven: Symphony No. 9;* Daverio, *Nineteenth-Century German Music and the German Romantic Ideology;* and Dennis, *Beethoven in German Politics.* In chapter 6, I briefly discuss the use of Beethoven's Ninth in the 2000 commemoration of the victims of the Mauthausen concentration camp.

5. Berlioz, *À Travers Chant,* 49–59.

6. For example, Treitler, *Music and the Historical Imagination,* 25.

7. The phrase appears in a letter to Gräfin Marie Erdödy, Sept. 15, 1815, written by Beethoven in sympathy for her ailing condition (Beethoven, *Briefwechsel Gesamtausgabe,* 3:161–62).

8. For another history of "das Musikalische," see Naumann, *Musikalisches Ideen-Instrument.* Naumann locates early and implicit uses of the term also in the work of Diderot, Gulden, and Heinse. Though she does not pay attention to Schiller's explicit use, she does suggest that "musikalisch" changed from an adjectival to a noun form when it was confused with "Musik"; that is, when late-eighteenth-century writers began to speak of the other arts in terms of "music" (2). For recent discussion of Rousseau's particular use of the term "music," see Strong, "Theatricality, Public Space, and Music in Rousseau." For more on Schiller, see Dahlhaus, *Klassische und romantische Musikästhetik,* 67–85, and Clark, "The Union of the Arts." In the latter, Clark shows with pertinent quotations how strong Herder's influence was on Schiller in developing ideas of both musicality and the total work of art. In this matter, I am also grateful to Gesa Frömming for pointing out an early noun use of the term by Herder from the 1760s, from his *Erstes kritisches Wäldchen* (*Critical Forests: First Grove, Selected Writings,* 141). However, though Herder employed the term, he did not, as Schiller does, simultaneously reflect on its use. There are many other sources for the concept I am investigating, in the writings of Jean Paul, Novalis, and, later, Kierkegaard, but instead of providing an exhaustive history, I record only the developments pertaining to my argument.

9. Schiller, *SW,* 22:271.

10. Schiller, *On the Aesthetic Education of Man,* Letters 15 and 25, 100–109, 182–89.

11. Nietzsche, *BT,* 14–19. Nietzsche discusses musicality and mood also in *BT,* 28–40.

12. Translated by Susan H. Gillespie.

13. Schiller, *SW,* 26:141–42 (my emphasis; my transl.).

14. Schiller, "On Naïve and Sentimental Poetry," in Nisbet, *German Aesthetic and Literary Criticism,* 293 note m (transl. amended); *SW,* 20:455n.

15. Quoted in Longyear, *Schiller and Music,* 90 (my transl.).

16. Beethoven, *Letters, Journals and Conversations,* 223.

17. Cf. Schiller's letter to Körner, Oct. 21, 1800, in *SW,* 30:206–7. In discussing the same issue, Clark notes that "Gluck had written that the agreement between the words and the music must be such that neither should seem to be made for each other. But even Gluck had departed from his theory in his setting of Klopstock's odes" ("The Union of the Arts," 1141).

18. Schiller, letter to Zelter, Feb. 20, 1798; quoted in Longyear, *Schiller and Music,* 90 (transl. amended); *SW,* 37:248.

19. Schelling, *Philosophie der Kunst,* 494, 496; Schelling, *Philosophy of Art,* 111–12. I first came across the different phrases in this text in a conversation with David Farrell Krell; see Krell's own "Brazen Wheels."

20. Schelling, *Philosophy of Art,* 112; *Philosophie der Kunst,* 496.

21. Ibid.

22. Such a phrase prompts comparison with Hanslick's "tönend bewegte Formen."

23. Schelling, *Philosophy of Art,* 112; *Philosophie der Kunst,* 496. Schopenhauer, *WWR,* 1:263; *WWV,* 1:368.

24. Schelling, *Philosophy of Art,* 113; *Philosophie der Kunst,* 497.

25. Ibid.

26. Schelling, *Philosophy of Art,* 115; *Philosophie der Kunst,* 500. Schelling explores ideas of yearning and striving in terms of affinity, attraction, and *Bewegung* throughout his work, especially in his writings on the philosophy of nature.

27. Schelling, *Philosophy of Art,* 116; *Philosophie der Kunst,* 501.

28. Schelling, *Philosophy of Art,* 280; *Philosophie der Kunst,* 736.

29. Ibid.

30. Schelling's discussion of the chorus appears at the end of the lectures within a discussion of tragedy and comedy: *Philosophy of Art,* 251–61; *Philosophie der Kunst,* 693–708. For Wagner on "ersichtlich gewordene Thaten der Musik," see his "*Über die Benennung 'Musikdrama,'*" in *DS,* 9:276. This is an extraordinarily interesting essay, about which I have more recently written (Goehr, "Musikdrama"), given Wagner's attempt to weigh up the benefits of linking the term "Drama" to that of "Musik" (as in *Musikdrama*) as opposed to "musikalisch" (as in *ein musikalisches Drama*) (272). He also pertinently discusses the difference between "deed" (*Tat*) and "action" (*Handlung*).

31. Schiller, *SW,* 10:7–18.

32. Schiller, "Über die tragische Kunst," in *SW,* 20:157.

33. Schiller, *SW,* 10:13.

34. Wagner, *DS,* 9:12–28.

35. For more on the womb, see Nietzsche, *BT,* 54–59; see also Borchmeyer, *Richard Wagner,* 167–68.

36. Cf. Keil, "'Gebt mir Rossinische Musik,'" 89.

37. Schoenberg, "Criteria for the Evaluation of New Music," in *Style and Idea,* 136.

38. Schopenhauer, *WWR,* 2:435–36; *WWV,* 2:559–60.

39. Schopenhauer, *WWR,* 1:262 (transl. amended); *WWV,* 1:366.

40. The term "allein" plays a significant role in the writings of this period, particularly regarding issues of autonomy, freedom, and cultural optimism in the face of political pessimism. In his *Letters,* Schiller uses the term "allein" some twenty-six times, to suggest that *only* via *aesthetic* education is the restoration of culture and society possible. Whether "allein" is attached to the more general idea of the aesthetic or is used to maintain the arts in separation from one another often differentiates one view from another.

41. Schopenhauer, *WWR* 2:450–52; *WWV,* 2:579–81.

42. Schopenhauer, *WWR,* 2:450; *WWV,* 2:579.

43. Schopenhauer, *PP,* 2:431, 433; *PP*G, 509–11.

44. Schopenhauer, *WWR,* 1:262 (transl. amended); *WWV,* 1:365; *PP,* 2:431; *PP*G, 509.

45. Schopenhauer, *PP,* 2:432–34; *PP*G, 509–12.

46. Just when the work of musicality is given to the more abstract movement of music and taken away from the chorus, the theme of difficulty appears in the philosophical and everyday discourse of musical criticism. The topic is pursued by Schopenhauer, Hegel, and Hanslick and later by Adorno in his essay "Difficulties," in *AEM,* 644–79; *GS* 17:253–73.

47. Schopenhauer, *PP,* 2:432–34; *PP*G, 509–12.

48. Nietzsche, *BT,* 76–80.

49. Ibid., 163; Wagner, *DS,* 7:328. As Borchmeyer notes in *Richard Wagner,* 170, this Wagnerian idea was influenced by Lessing's arguments offered in his *Hamburgische Dramaturgie* of 1767.

50. Olivier, "Das Musikkapitel aus Hegels Ästhetikvorlesung," 34.

51. Quoted in Gethmann-Siefert, "Phänomen versus System," 210 (my transl.). Note here Hegel's modern use of the term "music" to refer to music produced by instruments in contrast to "song" which refers to singing (accompanied by instruments). Hegel's lectures of 1826 have recently appeared under the title *Philosophie der Kunst: Vorlesung von 1826.*

52. *HA,* 2:900; *VA,* 15:147.

53. Quoted in Olivier, "Das Musikkapitel aus Hegels Ästhetikvorlesung," 35.

54. For example, De Vos, review of Hegel's *Vorlesungen über die Philosophie der Kunst;* Gethmann-Siefert, "Phänomen versus System"; Hegel, *Vorlesung über Ästhetik;* Olivier, "Das Musikkapitel aus Hegels Ästhetikvorlesung"; Pöggeler, *Hegel in Berlin;*

and Schneider and Gethmann-Siefert, "Über Nachschriften zu Hegels Vorlesungen." For a recent assessment of Hotho's contribution that concentrates on the preference Hegel gave to painting, see Gaiger, "Catching up with History," where, he argues, "Hotho strives to be more Hegelian than Hegel" (163).

55. Keil, "'Gebt mir Rossinische Musik,'" 87.

56. See Knox's note in *HA*, 2:950; Pöggeler, *Hegel in Berlin*, 91–93; and Olivier, "Das Musikkapitel aus Hegels Ästhetikvorlesung," 17.

57. Olivier, "Das Musikkapitel aus Hegels Ästhetikvorlesung," 15; Keil, "'Gebt mir Rossinische Musik,'" 91. See also Knox's note in *HA*, 2:901.

58. See Hegel's remarks even in Hotho's version, *HA*, 1:595–600; *VA*, 14:223–29.

59. Hegel, *HA*, 1:158, 2:935; *VA*, 13:209, 15:192.

60. Gethmann-Siefert, "Phänomen versus System," 190.

61. Hegel, *HA*, 2:951 (transl. amended); *VA*, 15:213.

62. Following Gethmann-Siefert, the fact that Hegel's remarks on opera appeared next to those on tragedy might have raised opera's standing by association, but it also encouraged interpreters to think that Hegel was demonstrating a preference for instrumental music in his pages devoted specifically to music. Hotho apparently encouraged this idea as much as he could.

63. Olivier, "Das Musikkapitel aus Hegels Ästhetikvorlesung," 41.

64. Hegel, *HA*, 2:1175; *VA*, 15:497. I return to this thought in chapter 5.

65. For this chapter I benefited also from reading Kramer, "Harem Threshold"; Levy, *Beethoven;* Martin, *Nietzsche and Schiller;* Selfridge-Field, "Beethoven and Greek Classicism"; Solomon, *Late Beethoven;* Stendhal, *Life of Rossini;* and Wallace, *Beethoven's Critics.*

Chapter 3

1. Kant, *CJ*, 182; *KU*, 236.

2. Hegel, *HA*, 1:42–46; *VA*, 13:64–69.

3. Wilde, "The Nightingale and the Rose," in *Works of Oscar Wilde*, 295.

4. In chapter 1, the point was reversed: that although Adorno appreciated Stockhausen's writings on time, he thought his works belied his stated aims. In other contexts, Adorno appreciated, say, some of Cage's works more than the rationalizations Cage offered on their behalf. For a complete coverage of the Darmstadt festival, see Borio and Danuser, *Im Zenit der Moderne.*

5. See the more detailed historical narrative I provided of the role of birdsong in opera and music in an earlier version of this essay, in Goehr, "For the Birds/Against the Birds."

6. Hegel, *HA*, 1:9 (transl. amended); *VA*, 13:23.

7. Cage, *Bird Cage* (2000).

8. Quoted in Beyst, "John Cage: Europeras."

9. Danto, *PDA,* and Horkeimer and Adorno, *DE.* For discussion of Oedipus's blindness and Odysseus's deafness to the songs of the "old metaphysical bird catchers," see Nietzsche, *Beyond Good and Evil,* 123; *KSA* 5:169.

10. Quoted in Mertens, *American Minimal Music,* 21, 109.

11. Adorno, "Vers une musique informelle," in *QF,* 321; *QF*^G, 539.

12. A modification to the argument is needed. There is an extensive literature regarding how artworks are treated as philosophical works and vice versa. I have put the point as I have, to direct attention toward what I believe is more importantly being claimed by Danto and Adorno. In *MM,* Adorno argues that in a certain sense every artwork aims to bring art to an end by claiming to have perfectly instantiated the concept, though in another sense, the work must also fail in this aim in order to remain a work of art. Partially, this idea develops Kierkegaard's claim that each great work is an incomparable classic, though it also brings to light another more obvious way of thinking about "the end of art," where "end" is just taken to mean aim or final purpose.

13. This is an argument to which Schoenberg vehemently objected: that Adorno knew better philosophically what was going on in Schoenberg's compositions than the composer himself. See Goehr, "Dissonant Works and the Listening Public."

14. To present Danto's view in this chapter, I draw on "Artworld," *TC,* and the essays in *PDA.* Note also his recent *Unnatural Wonders,* with its pertinent subtitle, *Essays from the Gap Between Art and Life.*

15. I prefer the term "posthistoricist" to Danto's "posthistorical" for reasons I offer in chapter 5 and in my "Afterwords," written as an introduction to Danto's *NK.* Danto does not offer an end of history thesis, but he does argue for the cessation of a historicist approach to the philosophy of history.

16. Walter Braunfels's opera *Die Vögel* of 1920 was based on Aristophanes's play. The opera tells of a society (Germany after World War I) being built anew, trying to escape the problems of the old society, only to end up in a condition much worse, where the birds assume control even of the air. The freedom promised by the naturalized society of birds becomes totalitarian control, such that the birds are equally severed from nature and the gods. In a proud moment, the birds sing of their power and control; nevertheless, their words forecast their inevitable fall.

17. Danto began pursuing the theme of catching the world's conscience, by reference to how Hamlet caught the conscience of the king, in 1964 in "Artworld."

18. This said, Danto articulated his end of art thesis only in the early 1980s, though he planted the seeds two decades earlier.

19. Quoted in Mertens, *American Minimal Music,* 71.

20. In introducing Testadura in 1964, Danto also referred to Hegel's "sham grapes of Zeuxis" ("Artworld," 575). In this article, he also used the language of transfiguration and enfranchisement that later became so central to his thought (573). Testadura also appears in Danto's philosophy of history of the same period.

21. Andersen, "The Nightingale," 144–45 (transl. amended).

22. Hanslick, *VMS,* 150 (my transl.). For Kant's discussion of art's relation to "raw materials" (*blosse rohe Materie*) of nature, see *CJ,* 240; *KU,* 314–15. Danto might not be aware of Hanslick's argument, but he is aware of the general philosophical point, as evidenced in his quoting from William Butler Yeats: "Once out of nature I shall never take/ My bodily form from any natural thing" ("Artworld," 582). Yeats's poem "Sailing to Byzantium" is also about the monumentalism of history and art, which is my topic in chapter 5.

23. Danto, "Upper West Side Buddhism," 56.

24. For more, see Shultis, "Silencing the Sounded Self," 319; Mertens, *American Minimal Music,* 104; and Cage, *Silence,* 3–13.

25. Danto, "Upper West Side Buddhism," 57.

26. Ibid., 51.

27. Adorno offers extended discussions of nature and art and of natural and artistic beauty in his *AT.* I complicate the current argument below when I present Adorno's argument to the effect that art takes nature's side when it refuses what humanity has done to nature, art, and itself.

28. Adorno, "Vers une musique informelle," in *QF,* 283 (transl. amended); *QF*^G, 505. Adorno criticizes not only the attempt to imitate heroic strength but also the very idea of heroic strength when it gives way to false claims of strength on the part of totalitarian leaders (*MM,* 143).

29. Adorno's opening sentence in *AT* has several meanings: partly it asks whether art is possible at all, but then whether this question can genuinely be posed, given a situation in which even the question becomes voided of meaning by becoming too self-evident. The ramifications of asking whether art is still possible testify to a critical social and aesthetic situation (ramifications I pursue throughout this book).

30. In his letter of March 18, 1936, to Benjamin, Adorno argues that only a musical work that consistently pursues its own formal laws is able to show the real freedom inherent in something that is consciously produced or made (*Complete Correspondence,* 129).

31. Adorno, *QF,* 275–76; *QF*^G, 499.

32. Kant, *CJ,* 126 (5:243); *KU,* 164. Kant worried about the boredom experienced when hearing the same song repeatedly, that once we grasped the point or rule of a song's pattern, there would be nothing left to stimulate the imagination. Here his worry cut across the distinction he drew between the real and the artificial nightingale because it was the repetition alone that annoyed him, whether naturally or artificially produced. Kant wondered whether one ever really enjoys song of any kind: even in the case of a genuine birdsong, he asked, might we not really be appreciating only the little bird that produces it?

33. Adorno, *AT,* 67–68; *ÄT,* 105–6.

34. Adorno, "Vers une musique informelle," in *QF,* 314–15; *QF*^G, 533.

35. Cf. Adorno's remarks on Karl Kraus's "What Has the World Done to Us" in "Schoenberg," in *Prisms,* 152; *GS* 10.1:156.

36. Cage, *Silence*, 12.

37. Quoted in Tomkins, *Bride and the Bachelor*, 97, 104.

38. Adorno, *AT,* 68; *ÄT,* 107.

39. Quoted in Mertens, *American Minimal Music*, 45.

40. Adorno, *AT,* 73; *ÄT,* 114.

41. Adorno, *AT,* 66; *ÄT,* 104

42. Cf. Hannah Arendt's thesis on the banality of evil read as a critique of the commonplace and self-evident, developed in her *Origins of Totalitarianism,* where she epigraphs part 3 with a line from David Rousset: "Normal men do not know that everything is possible" (287). By quoting this sentence (taken from Rousset's commentary on what was done to humanity in labor and concentration camps), she compels us to ask what normality should be in contrast to what it has become normal to think that it is. Adorno takes up the theme of banality in connection to the "self-evident" in *MM,* 128–29 and 148–50, and in "Opinion, Delusion, Society," in *CM,* 121–22. I pursue this theme in subsequent chapters.

43. Adorno, "Vers une musique informelle," in *QF,* 322 (transl. amended); *QF*G, 540.

44. Keats, "Ode on a Grecian Urn" (1819), in *Poems,* 373. Adorno quotes this line as an epigraph to "Schoenberg," in *Prisms,* 147; *GS* 10.1:152.

Chapter 4

1. Adorno, *QF,* 65–67; *QF*G, 309. Cf. Horkheimer and Adorno in *DE,* 27 (*DA,* 51): "The fettered man listens to a concert, as immobilized as audiences later, and his enthusiastic call for liberation goes unheard as applause."

2. Horkheimer and Adorno, *DE,* 1; *DA,* 19. In their own note, the authors refer to the twelfth letter of Voltaire's *Lettres philosophiques* for the source of their reference to Bacon as "the father of experimental philosophy." Thereafter, in their account, they imitate both the tone and language of this letter.

3. Adorno, "Actuality of Philosophy," 132 (transl. amended); *GS* 1:343.

4. Adorno, "The Essay as Form," in *NL,* 1:9; *NL*G, 17.

5. Bacon, *Advancement of Learning,* 2:145–46.

6. Cassirer, *Platonic Renaissance in England,* 48–49.

7. Cf. Pesic, "Wrestling with Proteus." Pesic cites Gross, *Rhetoric of Science:* "Although the sentiment is Baconian, the phrase is from Leibniz." See also Mathews, *Francis Bacon;* Bossy, "'Torturing the Truth'"; and Merchant, "The Scientific Revolution and the Death of Nature."

8. Apollonio, *Futurist Manifestos,* 74–88. For futurism's reception in music, see Payton, "Music of Futurism."

9. Wind, *Art and Anarchy,* 20–21.

10. Goethe, *Zur Farbenlehre,* 45. Cf. Schöne, *Goethes Farbentheologie,* 64–66.

11. Horkheimer and Adorno, *DE*, 1–2; *DA*, 20.

12. Quoted in Schöne, *Goethes Farbentheologie*, 64–66.

13. Schiller, *On the Aesthetic Education of Man*, 4–5.

14. Cage, *Silence*, 7–12, 13–17, 67–75.

15. Ibid., 72.

16. For more on the open work in Cage, see Perloff, "John Cage," 62–69.

17. Cage, *Silence*, 72.

18. Ibid., 69, 13, 15.

19. Ibid., 8.

20. In recent philosophy of science, there has been a marked effort to identify the theatrical qualities of experimentalism in early scientific experiments. Much of this effort has involved rereading the history of science back to Bacon to determine what was lost in later, overly positivistic interpretations of that history. See Stephen Shapin's exemplary article, "The House of Experiment in Seventeenth-Century England."

21. Cage, *Silence*, 73.

22. Pesic, "Wrestling with Proteus," 86, quoted from Bacon, "Of the Wisdom of the Ancients," in *Works of Francis Bacon*, 6:726.

23. Bacon, *New Organon*, 33.

24. For more on Platonic themes in Bacon and his experiments in music, see Pesic, "Wrestling with Proteus," and Gouk, *Music, Science and Natural Magic in Seventeenth-Century England*.

25. Bruce, *Three Early Modern Utopias*, 180.

26. Horkheimer and Adorno, *DE*, 2 (transl. amended); *DA*, 20.

27. Bacon, *New Organon*, 142, and *Advancement of Learning* 2:75. Cf. a parallel claim increasingly made in the eighteenth century, that because nature's forms do not appear directly, with distinction and clarity, they should be investigated by the indirect means of art. This claim matches Bacon's idea that art gives away its secret more willingly than nature. For Adorno, later, it then follows that the less art chooses to give away its secret, the more it takes nature's side.

28. Bacon, *Advancement of Learning*, 2:75.

29. Adorno, *AT*, 26 (transl. amended); *ÄT*, 47; Cf. Horkheimer's remark: "The illusion of performative freedom is belied by the instructions produced, where instead of allowing spontaneity within a score, one is constantly following impersonal instructions as driving instructions on a road" (*Eclipse of Reason*, 98). For other critical writings on experimental music, see Ballantine, "Towards an Aesthetic of Experimental Music"; Boulez, *Orientations*, esp. ch. 42; Metzger, "Abortive Concepts in the Theory and Criticism of Music"; Nyman, *Experimental Music*; Palombini, "Pierre Schaeffer, 1953"; and Smalley, "Experimental Music."

30. Adorno, *PNM*, 30; *PNM*G, 37.

31. Adorno, "Vers une musique informelle," in *QF*, 303 (transl. amended); *QF*G, 523.

32. Adorno, "Schoenberg," in *Prisms*, 154–55 (transl. amended); *GS* 10.1:160.

33. Adorno, "Das Experiment," in *GS* 18:26–27.

34. Adorno, *NL,* 2:103; *NL*^G, 440; *AT,* 34; *ÄT,* 58; *AEM,* 651 (transl. amended); *GS* 17:262. Adorno uses two terms, *überleben* (to survive) and *Nachleben* (afterlife), terms that I reintroduce in subsequent chapters.

35. Adorno, "Vers une musique informelle," in *QF,* 302–3; *GS* 16:523.

36. Adorno, *GS* 19:631; *AT,* 37-39; *ÄT,* 62–65.

37. Cf. Cavell, "Music Discomposed," in *Must We Mean What We Say?,* 180–212.

38. Adorno, *GS* 8:92; *GS* 14: 427; *ISM,* 223; *AT,* 23; *ÄT,* 41.

39. Adorno. *AT,* 85 (transl. amended); *ÄT,* 131.

Chapter 5

1. I am thinking here of the brilliant discussion of artworks as historical objects in Riegl, "Modern Cult of Monuments."

2. In Goehr, *Imaginary Museum,* I focused on the crystallization of a generic work concept in music around 1800. In this chapter I broaden the claim, but not to suggest that there was no work concept in the arts in general before 1800, though I do think a new centrality was given to the work concept in all the artistic domains around this time.

3. I discuss this phrase also in Goehr, "Afterwords," in Danto, *NK,* which I wrote as a companion piece to the present chapter.

4. Halbwachs, *Collective Memory,* 52; quoted also in Crane, *Collecting and Historical Consciousness,* 152. Some historical detail in the present chapter is borrowed from Crane.

5. Hegel, *IPH,* 5 (transl. amended); *VPG,* 14.

6. Hegel, *IPH,* 76; *VPG,* 98.

7. In recent studies, Hegel is interpreted as both a systematic and antisystematic thinker and thus as responding to the many sides of enlightenment's conflicted passage. See, for example, Pinkard (*Hegel*), Pippin (*Hegel's Idealism*), and Neuhouser (*Actualizing Freedom*).

8. Hegel, *IPH,* 82 (transl. amended); *VPG,* 104–5.

9. Hegel, *HA,* 2:1175 (transl. amended); *VA,* 15:496–97. In chapter 2, I introduce the idea that Hegel was specifying a German problem.

10. Hegel, *HA,* 1:11 (transl. amended); *VA,* 13:25–26.

11. Hegel, *IPH,* 82; *VPG,* 105.

12. Leopold von Ranke introduced this provocative phrase in 1824, while (incidentally) a colleague of Hegel's in Berlin. Rather than judging the past, Ranke aimed only to show (*blos(s) zeigen*) how it actually was (see the opening pages to his *Geschichte der romanischen und germanischen Völker*). Hegel referred to Ranke's principle in *HA,* 2:986; *VA,* 15:257, but not as T. M. Knox's English translation suggests with Ranke's specific phrase, but instead indirectly in terms of that which really happened: "das

wirklich Geschehene." Hegel referred to Ranke's attitude toward history precisely to distinguish his own.

13. Hegel, *IPH,* 17 (transl. amended); *VPG,* 27.

14. Hegel, *IPH,* 32–33; *VPG,* 45.

15. Hegel, *HA,* 1:279–80; *VA,* 13:361–62.

16. Hegel, *IPH,* 81; *VPG,* 104.

17. Nietzsche, *Gay Science,* 117; *KSA* 3:477.

18. Hegel, *PS,* 492; *PG,* 590–91.

19. *HA,* 2:870; *VA,* 15:108–9. When describing the living spectacle, Hegel stressed its chronological character, which is relevant, given the debate among his contemporaries regarding how paintings would be hung, chronologically or by an alternative principle, in Berlin's new Royal Museum. "The greatest aid," Hegel insisted "to study and intelligent enjoyment is an *historical* arrangement. Such a collection . . . we shall soon have an opportunity to admire in the picture gallery of the Royal Museum." Hegel had his reasons for being so insistent. Looking at the collection, he argued, two sorts of history had to be recognized simultaneously: "the external history of painting" and "the essential progress [of its] inner history." Nevertheless, it would be interesting to speculate how some sort of ahistorical ordering of artworks in the museums might have undermined his historical method. For more on the background to the museum debate, see Osterkamp, "Gesamtbildung und freier Genuss. Wechselwirkungen zwischen Goethe und Wilhelm von Humboldt," in *Wechselwirkungen,* 133–54.

20. Burgin, *Remembered Film,* 85.

21. Before even the terrible reality hit, the idea of airships dropping bombs (otherwise called sausages or flying machines) was described by H. G. Wells in his 1908 novel, *The War in the Air,* 159.

22. Co and Polano, "Interview with Albert Speer," and Speer, *Inside the Third Reich,* chs. 5–6. My discussion of Speer and quotations are drawn mostly from these two chapters.

23. Angela Schönberger ("Die Staatsbauten des Tausendjährigen Reiches") argues that the question of materials was seriously constrained by Hitler's total reorganization of industry and that, further, industrial and military constraints made it impossible to reinforce the stone constructions, say, in the Nuremberg field with iron, which, in turn, promoted the view that the buildings became ruins earlier than they might, had there been more available iron.

24. Mittig, "Dauerhaftigkeit, einst Denkmalargument," 21.

25. Ruskin, *Seven Lamps of Architecture,* 186. In her introduction to *Le Désert de Retz* (2–4) Diana Ketcham remarks, first, on the exaggerated character of ruins that were just a bit too large, too tall, as if preempting a surrealist mockery of the buildings they were copying, and, second, on the paradox that what was an intentional ruin in the late eighteenth century later became in the twentieth a genuine ruin.

26. The complexity here takes us momentarily to Herder's discussion of "decay." Herder wrote of how God gave man limitations or imperfections for him to surpass.

Just as folly (*Torheit*) exists, that wisdom may conquer it, so by analogy does decay in works of art. Their ruin or decaying breakability (*zerfallende Brechlichkeit*) is part of their essential matter (even their beauty). It allows artists to work on art as men work on the limits of what they know, to overcome those limits for the sake of progress. In the pursuit of art or wisdom, one must be in a constant state of exercise and improvement—which is the state separating man from beast (*Ideen zur Philosophie der Geschichte der Menschheit*, 342). The idea of decay as imperfection, as something to be overcome, is different from a monumentalized view in which decay as imperfection is excluded from the very concept, just as a view of progress or victory as an ideal toward which one strives is different from the claim that progress or victory is something assumed or already achieved. It is the ease or difficulty of the transition between the first and second views that is constantly at work in a progressivist philosophy of history.

27. Riccardo Martinelli correctly reminded me that Mussolini could not have built Rome as a ruin, since so many ruins already made up the city. This suggests, first, that the Nazi vision should not automatically be equated with the fascist vision and, second, that any account of pastness must also be reconciled with (Italy's) futurist visions. Still, though there are concrete political and aesthetic differences, pastness and futurist visions often make up two sides of the same totalizing coin in a philosophy of world history.

28. Speer, *Die Bauten Adolf Hitlers*.

29. For more, see Taylor, *The Word in Stone*, and Schönberger, *Die neue Reichskanzlei von Albert Speer*, 168–69.

30. Speer, *Inside the Third Reich*, 93.

31. Benjamin, *WOA*, 101–33. Goebbels's argument is documented in Lutz Hachmeister's 2004 film, *The Goebbels Experiment*.

32. Speer, *Inside the Third Reich*, 118.

33. Cf. Adorno's response to Benjamin's WOA, in his letter of March, 18, 1936 (*Complete Correspondence*, 127–34). Though Adorno claimed Benjamin's argument "insufficiently dialectical," he was content to see exposed the false rationalizations of a monumentalizing ideology serving totalitarian ends.

34. Henderson, *Failure of a Mission*, 66–67.

35. Speer, *Inside the Third Reich*, 97. In chapter 6, I refer to what the Nazis euphemistically called *Kristallnacht* or *Reichskristallnacht*, sometimes translated Night of Broken Glass. This, too, was a spectacle whose idea survived, though obviously in a form much worse and more total than that connoted by the name.

36. Speer, *Inside the Third Reich*, 101. Cf. Sontag on Riefenstahl in *Under the Sign of Saturn*, 73–105. See also Spotts, *Hitler and the Power of the Aesthetic*, 67 and 54, specifically for discussion of how stagecraft and statecraft became indistinguishable. This matter has been taken up more recently by Lepenies, *Seduction of Culture*, 41.

37. In 1935, Adorno wrote to Horkheimer to report on his visit with Gretel to Nuremberg: they were "quite alone, no one was there, no guards keeping watch, noth-

ing; the whole thing was somehow decayed and pathetic, in no way *aere perennius*" (*Briefwechsel* 1:341; my transl.).

38. For example, Scobie, *Hitler's State Architecture,* 133–34.

39. When Danto wrote his *Analytical Philosophy of History* (later, *NK*) he also wrote *Nietzsche as Philosopher.*

40. Nietzsche, *Gay Science,* 60; *KSA* 3:412.

41. Here and in the following sections, I draw on Danto's *NK, TC, PDA,* and *BB.* The end of history thesis makes a brief appearance in Danto's work at the end of his first essay on "the end of art" (*PDA,* 111–15), but it does not play a decisive role in Danto's own "analytical philosophy of history."

42. Many of Danto's critics have discussed the difficult problems raised by his distinction between essential and historical meaning. For example, Rollins, ed., *Danto and His Critics,* esp. the essay by Carroll, "Essence, Expression, and History"; see also Horowitz and Huhn, *Wake of Art,* 1–56.

43. I use this loaded term to reflect Danto's own use when, in 1965, in introducing *NK,* he followed Thomas Kuhn in describing what positivism had done to science (xi). Danto then remarked on the irony of Kuhn's having written his revolutionary book, designed to expose substantive conceits, for the *Encyclopedia of Unified Science.*

44. In this section I draw mostly on Adorno's *AT,* which is largely a "résumé" of his life's work, though he deliberately puts into question what sort of life could have been constituted by such work. Benjamin also posed this question in relation to Goethe, in his essay "Elective Affinities," in *Selected Writings.*

45. Cf. Adorno, *MM,* 235–38.

46. Adorno, *MM,* 151 (transl. amended); *MM*G, 172.

47. Cf. Adorno, *MM,* 126–28. See also Horowitz, *Sustaining Loss.*

48. Adorno, *Prisms,* 184 (transl. amended); *GS* 10.1:181–94. Cf. Adorno *MM,* 112: "To happiness the same applies as to truth: one does not have it, but is in it"; *MM*G, 126. Adorno mentions the cult of ruins (*Kultus der Ruine*) in *AT,* 64; *ÄT,* 101, amid discussion of the Kantian and post-Kantian thesis on natural beauty that I introduce in chapter 3. Further, one should recall here Adorno's argument from "Bach Defended Against His Devotees" (*Prisms,* 133–46; *GS* 10.1:138–51), which focuses on how Bach was made by his *idolizers,* under historicist conditions, into a canonic or neutralized cultural monument, and thus subjected to the sort of anachronism that dispensed paradoxically with any genuine sense of loving either Bach or his music.

49. Nora, "Between Memory and History," 7.

50. Sartre, *What Is Literature?,* 41–42

51. Mann, "Disorder and Early Sorrow," in *Stories of Three Decades,* 500–528. Danto discusses this story in *NK,* 316.

52. Scott, *Antiquary,* 95.

53. Yerushalmi, *Zakhor,* 81–102.

54. For this section, three articles were helpful: Crane, "Writing the Individual Back into Collective Memory"; Hutton, "Recent Scholarship on Memory and History"; and White, "The Burden of History."

55. For a devoted treatment of this problem, see Kelly, *Iconoclasm in Aesthetics.*

56. Danto, "American Sublime."

57. Smithson, *Robert Smithson*, 10–23, 68–74.

58. Danto, "American Sublime."

Chapter 6

1. A different but compatible conception of the analogy between art and terror is offered by Lentricchia and McAuliffe, *Crimes of Art and Terror.*

2. Klemperer, *The Language of the Third Reich.* In German, several terms are used for displacement, as we see even just in Adorno's writings: "Verschiebung," "Verlagerung," and "Ersetzung."

3. This film has not been publicly released. Because I was able to view it only once, it remains unclear to me how consistent the documentary maker's sympathies were with the footage and imagery he presented.

4. All quotations of the play are from Harwood, *Taking Sides.* Although the views expressed in the play more or less match the real Furtwängler's views, they are, for the drama's sake, clearly amended. Hence, see Furtwängler's own *Notebooks 1924–1954;* see also the fascinating, though entirely too sympathetic, portrait offered before the war's end by Geissmar, *Baton and the Jackboot.*

5. Adams, *Death of Klinghoffer,* program note by Stephen Pettitt, 7.

6. Genet, *Maids,* 99–100. I found the ending of Bengston's opera convincing in its refusal to culminate in something approximating a *Liebestod.* The final notes tended rather toward the nothingness of the remains, leaving the violence unabated, in place.

7. Adams, *Death of Klinghoffer,* program note by Pettitt, 43–45. All quotations from Kien's libretto are from *Der Kaiser von Atlantis;* some of the translations by Paula Kennedy from the program notes have been amended.

8. Schlegel, *Philosophical Fragments,* 92 (transl. amended); *Kritische Friedrich-Schlegel-Ausgabe* 2:254.

9. Quoted by Sartre in *Saint Genet,* 523–24.

10. There is extensive coverage on the internet relating to the Stockhausen "case" of misinterpreted words, claims, and rejoinders.

11. For some, this particular displacement into art did not take place. On the days after 9/11, those who searched for bodies in the rubble reported hearing the musical ring of cell phones. If, here, music offered hope, it did by pointing the way to persons still living. Days later that hope was gone, but the music played on, having assumed a most macabre character. I thank Marta Tafalla for this example.

12. All mention of Tzvetan Todorov in this chapter draws on his *Facing the Extreme,* esp. 97–107.

13. Adorno, "On the Fetish-Character in Music and the Regression of Listening," in *AEM,* 288 (transl. amended); *GS* 14:14.

14. Danto, "Art and Disturbation," in *PDA,* 117–34. In this essay, Danto writes about the late paintings of Leon Golub. The rest of Danto's argument is given in his *PDA,* 1–22.

15. Danto, "Art and the Towering Sadness," 42.

16. Sartre, *What Is Literature?,* 135.

17. Adorno, "Sacred Fragment," in *QF,* 235; *QF*^{G}, 462.

18. Said, "Die Tote Stadt, Fidelio, The Death of Klinghoffer," 597.

19. Benjamin wrote: "There is no document of culture which is not at the same time a document of barbarism" ("On the Concept of History," in *Selected Writings* 4:392). This scene from *Klinghoffer* recalls one from the 1965 film *The Ship of Fools,* when an elderly man lecturing in a wheelchair is thrown to the ground as the upbeat to a Bacchanalian dance and fight among the unprivileged passengers.

20. For a history of this work's reception, see Fink, "Klinghoffer in Brooklyn Heights." Fink also connects the issue of taking sides to an aesthetic of displacement.

21. What makes an event unexpected admits different explanations. It might be an unpredicted natural occurrence or a freak event, or a political act unexpected for a particular group, or an event that has an unexpected outcome, where, contrary to intention, a performance artist dies or doesn't die by his or her own hand. These sorts of differences prompt one to ask whether there are any ontological limits, aside from moral limits, to what an artwork can be regarding, say, the extent of its time and space, when an event is too big, long, chaotic, or underdetermined, even when, pacé Danto, the imitation condition is surpassed by artists who intend to produce an artwork indiscernible from a real thing.

22. Laks, *Music of Another World,* 70.

23. Laks noted that music was not played at the crematoria, only to transport prisoners to work (*Music of Another World,* 58). He also deliberately contrasted his position with the "pompous" positions of Furtwängler and Albert Speer (85–86). Cf. here Abbate's recent description of how music is often used to give absolute credence to beliefs: "The point is that these ideas and truths are being made monumental and given aura by music" ("Music: Drastic or Gnostic," 520).

24. Levi, *If This Is a Man,* 57.

25. Hegel, from a section aptly titled "Love as the Transcendence of Penal Justice," in *Early Theological Writings,* 232.

26. Quoted in Wiggerhaus, *Frankfurt School,* 506, drawn from Adorno's response to Horkheimer's letter of Sept. 14, 1941, on the nature of language and speech in the concentration camps.

27. Laks, *Music of Another World*, 117. Cf. Adorno: "The chaotic anarchy in the human work conditions, which is established by the system itself, finds expression by displacing the guilt onto the victims" (*PNM*^G, 49; my transl.). See also Adorno's pertinent passage titled *Melange* in *MM*, 102–3; *MM*^G, 115.

28. Todorov, *Facing the Extreme*, 106.

29. Barenboim and Said, *Parallels and Paradoxes*, 6–10. I thank Chris Washburn and Ana Maria Ochoa for discussion of these examples.

30. Nelson, *Guys*, 23.

31. Adorno, *PNM*, 131–32; *PNM*^G, 163.

32. Said, "Die Tote Stadt, Fidelio, the Death of Klinghoffer," 598.

33. For more, see Tippett, *Tippett on Music*; Kemp, *Tippett*; and Gloag and Rushton, *Tippett*.

34. Hegel, *Lectures on the Philosophy of World History*, 83; Hegel, *Early Theological Writings*, 238.

35. Huyssen, *Present Pasts*, 163.

36. Borges, *Collected Fictions*, 234.

37. Huhn, "Kantian Sublime and the Nostalgia for Violence."

38. Adorno, "Sacred Fragment," in *QF*, 243; *QF*^G, 16:469.

39. Adorno, *AT*, 237; *ÄT*, 352.

40. Cf. Adorno, *COM*, 238.

41. Adorno, *PNM*, 38; *PNM*^G, 47.

42. The reference to Ottilie appears in Adorno's letter to Benjamin of March 18, 1936 (Adorno and Benjamin, *Complete Correspondence*, 129).

43. Adorno, "Schoenberg," in *Prisms*, 172; *GS* 10.1:180.

44. This thought and those following, including my "quotations" of Adorno, are drawn from "Commitment," in *NL* 2:76–94; *NL*^G, 409–30. See also Goehr, "Understanding the Engaged Philosopher."

Chapter 7

1. Roth, "Hollywood: Der Hades des Modernen Menschen," in *Werke* 3:571–73.

2. Ibid., 571 (my transl.).

3. Bloom, *Waxworks*, 123. For an early reference to film and waxworks, see Döblin, "Theater of the Little People of 1909," 1–3.

4. Bloom, *Waxworks*, 50.

5. Serner, "Cinema and the Desire to Watch," 19.

6. Tannenbaum, "Art at the Cinema," 5; Lukács, "Thoughts on an Aesthetics of Cinema," 13.

7. Balázs, *Theory of the Film*, 85 (my emphasis); Kracauer, *Theory of Film*, 20 (my emphasis).

8. Wittgenstein, *Philosophical Remarks,* 83 (transl. amended); *Philosophische Bemerkungen,* 83–84.

9. Eisenstein, *Film Form,* 3. Note that whereas I use Eisenstein's words to suggest that cities are not found but made, he used them more specifically to record the fact that on arrival in a "cinematropolis" in the Soviet Union, he found that the film city for his project had not yet been constructed.

10. Balázs, *Theory of the Film,* 48.

11. Kracauer, *From Caligari to Hitler,* 6. In his *Theory of Film,* Kracauer repeated that one should not treat the camera like the spectator who must sit in stony silence, unmovable, or stuck in place (146). Panofsky's words are from his "Style and Medium in the Moving Pictures," 124–25.

12. Benjamin, *WOA,* 112–13. Benjamin's comparison of the filmmaker to the surgeon might well have been inspired by the many early films devoted to anatomical investigations of human and animal bodies.

13. Ibid., 114–17.

14. Ibid., 119–20.

15. Adorno *GS* 10, 2772 (my transl.). On critical theory's relation to feminist film theory, see Koch, "Ex-changing the Gaze." I have written more about Adorno and McLuhan in Goehr, "'Three Blind Mice.'"

16. Adorno, *CM,* 42; *GS* 10.2:500. Lukács, "Thoughts on an Aesthetics of Cinema," 13. For Adorno on Porter's "Anything Goes," see "Transparencies on Film," in *CI,* 158.

17. Perez, *Material Ghost,* 123. Perez devotes a chapter to the "deadly space between" amid discussion of Murnau's *Nosferatu.* The additional line from Melville, as the line quoted by Perez, is from *Billy Budd,* 41.

18. Kracauer devoted a section to "visualized music," in *Theory of Film,* 152–53; broad discussion of different sorts of visual musicality, physiognomic and decorative, is found in Balázs, *Theory of the Film;* see esp. the section "Optische Musik," in *Der Geist des Films,* 50–51. For an excellent overview of cinematic musicality in the 1920s, see Prox, "Perspektiven einer Wiederaufarbeitung von Stummfilmmusik." In this context, note the etymological associations between the words "cinema" (or "kinein") and "movement" (or "Bewegung"). For references to visual music in the other arts, see Vergo, *That Divine Order,* esp. 247–76.

19. Münsterberg, *Film,* 19. Before film was referred to as silent film, it was referred to as "silent drama" or "silent photoplay." These English phrases were introduced around World War I. Film might have assumed the language of "film without words" or "film without sound" after the romantic "song without words," though neither expression would have been appropriate. Even if words weren't heard in silent film, they were seen, and even if music wasn't heard inside the film, it was heard outside. When the German term "Stummfilm" was introduced around 1910, it seems to have been in recognition more of music's internal absence than of the word's heard absence.

20. Balázs, *Der Geist des Films,* 11 (my transl.).

21. Clair, "Art of Sound," 92. Cf. Eisenstein's recollection of a comedian who suddenly having to substitute for a bass singer at the operetta, although he had no singing voice himself, remarked: "Whatever notes I can't take with my voice, I'll show with my hands" (*Film Form,* 18).

22. Altman, "Silence of the Silents," 648. Altman's work is developed in his edited collection *Sound Theory and Sound Practice* and culminates in his *Silent Film Sound.* Altman focuses on the early American development of film. Here I attend more to the European arguments and mostly German ones to continue my project of describing the background that most motivated Adorno to argue as he did (despite his experiences in America).

23. Nietzsche, *Gay Science,* 144. In 1913, Hanns Heinz Ewers remarked specifically on his interest in writing scripts for films when words (like music) were not at one's disposal ("Film and I," 23), and in 1920, Herbert Ihering defined a "good film" as not one that "obscures the absence of the word" but one "whose actions would be disturbed by the word": "The rhythm of the silence that voids language through the structure of gesture is the end and the goal" ("An Expressionist Film," 49).

24. Kracauer, *From Caligari to Hitler,* 7. Recall my reading of Cage's aesthetic as an emergent naturalism in chapters 3 and 4.

25. The quotation though not my subsequent interpretation is taken from McCann, "New Introduction" to Adorno and Eisler's *CF,* vii, a book I discuss below. For a similar remark apparently made by Max Steiner, see Gorbman, "Why Music?," 37.

26. For more on repetition and its lesson in Wagner's *Meistersinger,* see Goehr, "Dangers of Satisfaction." In describing the hypnotic power of film, Brecht remarked on the high value presently given to the sort of music that isn't heard, because sometimes it works most effectively when it's not noticed ("Über Bühnenbau und Musik," in *Gesammelte Werke* 15:489).

27. Quoted in Hofmann, *Sounds for Silents,* n.p.

28. Bloch, "On Music in the Cinema," in *Literary Essays,* 158.

29. Arnheim, *Film as Art,* 199–230.

30. Becce, "Tonfilm und Künstlerische Filmmusik." The theme of "concert films" is also taken up by London, *Film Music,* 145–48.

31. Brecht, "Über Bühnenbau," in *Gesammelte Werke* 15:488. Cf. Wittgenstein: "In the days of silent films all the classics were played . . . except Brahms & Wagner. Not Brahms because he [was] too abstract. I can imagine an exciting scene . . . accompanied with music by Beethoven or Schubert & might gain some sort of understanding of the music from the film. But not an understanding of music by Brahms. Bruckner on the other hand does go with a film" (*Culture and Value,* 29).

32. Quoted by Prox, "Perspektiven einer Wiederaufarbeitung," 22. And cf. Witt, writing about Godard: "The concept of imageless cinema has been with us since the early sound period, [ranging] from Walter Ruttmann's 'sound film without images', *Weekend* (1930), a remarkable experiment in . . . musique concrète, to promotional records for early Godard" ("Shapeshifter," 82).

33. Schoenberg, "Is There an Opera Crisis?," in *A Schoenberg Reader,* 193 (transl. amended); "Gibt es eine Krise der Oper?," 209. Schoenberg continued his criticism in 1940 in "Art and the Moving Pictures," in *Style and Idea,* 153–57. For more on opera's crisis and its relation to film, see the special issue of *Musikblätter des Anbruch,* 26:5, and Paul Bekker, "Krise des Operntheaters."

34. Danto, *PDA,* 81.

35. Kracauer, *Theory of Film,* 148.

36. Cavalcanti, "Sound in Films," 105.

37. Balázs, *Theory of the Film,* 55 (transl. amended).

38. Keller, "Film Music," 549. For more on Keller's film-music criticism, see his *Film Music and Beyond.*

39. Lukács, "Thoughts on an Aesthetics of Cinema," 11.

40. Altman, *Sound Theory and Sound Practice,* 35–45, or Altman, *Silent Film Sound,* 51–52.

41. Balázs, "From *The Visible Human,*" 91.

42. Balázs, *Theory of the Film,* 194.

43. London, *Film Music,* 35. Before moving to England as an exile, where this book first appeared (with an endorsement by Constant Lambert), London wrote many insightful reviews on early technological and aesthetic experiments in film music.

44. Cf. Hermann Danuser's correct insistence that the history of film music is not exhausted by merely a history and aesthetics of music (*Die Musik des 20. Jahrhunderts,* 270).

45. Lang, "Artistic Composition of the Film Drama," 63.

46. London, *Film Music,* 149, and Bordwell and Thompson, "Fundamental Aesthetics of Sound in the Cinema," 189.

47. For more complex readings of Hollywood film music, see Flinn, *Strains of Utopia,* and Duncan, *Charms That Soothe.* On specific composers composing for Hollywood film, see Palmer, *Composer in Hollywood.*

48. Goll, "American Cinema," 51 (transl. amended).

49. Kracauer, *From Caligari to Hitler,* 3. For an earlier expression of European and American attitudes toward film, see Murnau, "Ideal Picture Needs No Titles," 66–68.

50. Adorno and Eisler, *CF,* 6; *KF,* 13, and *CF,* 12; *KF,* 19. This book was published first in English in 1947 by Oxford University Press, then in German in 1949, in East Germany under the lone name of Eisler. In his German preface (5), Eisler stressed how much this book was written in reaction to the culture industry in America. Why Adorno's name was removed was a complex matter having to do as much with McCarthyism in the United States as with the authors' returns to different sides of a divided Germany. A new German edition (*KF*) of 2006 with names restored includes an excellent introduction, a DVD of Eisler's projects, and the telling notes made by Adorno

in preparation for the book. I am grateful to its editor, Johannes Gall, for having made these notes available to me prior to publication.

51. Cf. here, Doane, "Ideology and the Practice of Sound Editing and Mixing," 55. Doane makes clear that she is recording in her own argument the arguments of Roland Barthes.

52. Adorno and Eisler, *KF,* 147–54.

53. Ibid., *CF,* 6–9; *KF,* 13–15.

54. Ibid., *CF,* 4–6, 32–38; *KF,* 12–13, 35–40.

55. For more on Eisler's background in relation to the film project, see the many excellent articles in *Historical Journal of Film, Radio, and Television* (special issue) 18/4 (October 1998).

56. Cf. Adorno, *COM,* 128–45 on "Space Ubiquity."

57. Cf. Adorno, "Transparencies on Film," in *CI,* 155; *COM,* 173–82; and particularly "On the Fetish Character of Music," in *AEM,* 301, where he writes: "The dynamic is so predetermined that there are no longer any tensions at all. The contradictions of the musical material are so inexorably resolved in the moment of sound that it never arrives at the synthesis, the self-production of the work, which reveals the meaning of every Beethoven symphony." In this quotation, the symphony is regarded as now under the authoritative spell of the industrialized work concept, a regard that leads Adorno to ask: "What is the point of the symphonic effort when the material on which that effort was to be tested has already been ground up?" The idea of something's being already ground up is connected to Adorno's general critique of a culture that offers "baby food" that is repeatedly consumed as if or because always already eaten. This idea is also connected to his critique of the sort of experimentalism that treats an experiment as somehow dictating its outcome in advance of the actual testing (my chapter 4) and to his critique of quotation (my chapter 6).

58. This argument resonates with another Adorno offers: that by learning to listen to Schoenberg's "difficult" music, one might come to recognize the difficulty of listening to all music—especially Beethoven's—that is now shrouded in familiarity. I developed this argument in Goehr, "Dissonant Works and the Listening Public."

59. Bergson, *Creative Evolution,* 305–6; Deleuze, *Cinema 1* and *Cinema 2;* and Chion, *Audio-Vision.*

60. Balázs, *Theory of the Film,* 101–2.

61. Merleau-Ponty, "Film and the New Psychology," in *Sense and Non-Sense,* 50.

62. Ibid., 59. Goethe (c. 1819), *Selected Poems,* 12:158.

63. Merleau-Ponty, "Film and the New Psychology," in *Sense and Non-Sense,* 56.

64. Belton, "Technology and Aesthetics of Film Sound," 71.

65. Merleau-Ponty, "Film and the New Psychology," in *Sense and Non-Sense,* 55.

66. For more, see Balázs, *Theory of the Film,* 211, and Jeff Smith, "Movie Music as Moving Music."

67. Clair, "Art of Sound," 93.

68. Danto, "Artworld," 574–75.

69. Adorno, *COM*, 81, 140–45, 173–82. In *Film Music*, London devotes a section to the changes brought about to film with the emergence of "the handwritten soundtrack" (195–99), a procedure, invented by Rudolf Pfenniger, intended to eliminate the need for live performers.

70. Adorno and Eisler, CF, 62 (transl. amended); *KF*, 58.

71. Knight, "Movies Learn to Talk," 217.

72. Adorno, *COM*, 120–21, 143.

73. London, *Film Music*, 27–28.

74. Döblin, "Theater of the Little People," 3

75. Warschauer, "Filmmusik," 132.

76. For an argument to remove even the captions, see Murnau, "Ideal Picture Needs No Titles," 66–68.

77. Reported in Kracauer, *Theory of Film*, 38. Adorno discussed background music in *AEM*, 506–10, and London in *Film Music*, 123–27.

78. Quoted by Hofmann, *Sounds for Silents*, and Kracauer, *Theory of Film*, 138. Tannenbaum contrarily noted in 1912 that one problem with introducing sound into film was that the sound wouldn't fit what one was actually seeing, for one could never convince oneself that two-dimensional images were actually talking. One should thus resign oneself to the fact (and he celebrated the conclusion) that "that film art is a mute art" ("Art at the Cinema," 5).

79. Kracauer, *Theory of Film*, 135.

80. Horkheimer and Adorno, *DE*, 99–100; *DA*, 147–48.

81. Adorno, *MM*, 26.

82. Adorno, *COM*, 242.

83. Adorno and Eisler, *KF*, 25 (my transl.).

84. Adorno, "Transparencies on Film," in *CI*, 158.

85. Adorno and Eisler, *CF*, 36–37 (transl. amended); *KF*, 39. This example is also discussed by Schebera, "Hangmen Also Die."

86. Kracauer, *Theory of Film*, 134.

87. Cf. Serner, "Cinema and the Desire to Watch," 17.

88. Adorno and Eisler, *CF*, 75 (transl. amended); *KF*, 68.

89. Rosen, "Adorno and Film Music."

90. Adorno, "Function," in *ISM*, 46–47; *GS* 14:228.

91. Cf. Kisch, *Paradies Amerika*, 127.

92. Münsterberg, *Film*, 23, 30. Vertov quoted by Fisher ("Enthusiasm," 253), whose article contains much material relevant to the present argument.

93. Clair, "Art of Sound," 95.

94. Adorno, "Art and the Arts," 386–87.

95. Hofmannsthal, "Substitute for Dreams," 54.

96. Adorno, *HS*, 99–100.

97. Chion, *Audio-Vision*, 125, 133.

Chapter 8

1. Nikolas Lenau (1832): "Der Amerikaner hat keinen Wein, keine Nachtigall! Mag er bei einem Glase Cider seine Spottdrossel behorchen mit seinen Dollars in der Tasche" (quoted in Birker, *Nikolaus Lenau, Blick in den Strom*, 25). The reference to the mockingbird is found also in Kürnberger, *Amerikamüde*. In *Ideology, Mimesis, Fantasy,* Jeffrey Sammons remarks that the quality of birds found in America (or wherever else one happened to be) was an "international" concern expressed by numerous authors, including Jefferson and Keats (211). One of Keats's poems of 1819 begins, "What can I do to drive away/ Remembrance from my eyes?" and continues later, "There flowers have no scent, birds no sweet song,/ And great unerring Nature once seems wrong." Recall from chapter 3, Keats's "Ode to the Nightingale," also from 1819.

2. Locke, *Second Treatise on Government*, 29.

3. When, for example, Heinrich Heine borrowed and then developed the idea of *europamüde* from Napoleon ("Cette vieille Europe m'ennuie"), he referred not only to Wellington in Britain but also to Mohammed in the East ("Englische Fragmente," in *Sämtliche Schriften*, 594).

4. Oja, *Making Music Modern*, 6. The reference to "music in a new found land" is to the title of Wilfred Mellors's book of 1964.

5. See Goehr, "*Aida* and the Empire of Emotions."

6. Recall one of the earliest resentments expressed toward "America," which regarded "her" early emancipation of women and thus her "stunted" development in the (serious) arts. For more, see Hammond, *American Paradise*, 98–105.

7. I discuss this use of "or" further in Goehr, "*Juliette fährt nach Mahagonny* or a Critical Reading of Surrealist Opera."

8. Adorno, *ND*[G], 15 (my transl.).

9. Adorno, "Sacred Fragment," in *QF*, 225–48.

10. I return to this phase below. One could well discuss here the case of Hanns Eisler, who also began several opera projects that he never completed. I thank Joy Calico for reminding me of this and for several other useful comments on this chapter.

11. Adorno, "Intellectual Experiences in America," in *CM*, 241 (transl. of both title and quotation amended); *GS* 10.2:736–37.

12. Ibid.

13. Kürnberger, *Amerikamüde*, 451. Adorno's argument was influenced by Bloch's *The Principle of Hope* and by Max Weber's description of the United States as *not yet* fully bureaucratized. Weber and Adorno are discussed together in Offe, *Reflections on America*. In his *Protestant Ethic,* Weber refers to Kürnberger's line: "They make tallow out of cattle and money out of men"—to which he responds that this "philosophy of avarice . . . is not simply a means of making one's way in the world, but a peculiar ethic" (51).

14. On weariness as a general condition of modernity, see Imhoof, *Der "Europamüde."* *Die Europamüden* was a book title also used in 1838 by Ernst Willkomm.

Adorno often used the phrase "fata morgana" and, given present concerns, most relevantly to conclude his essay on American Utopianism, "Aldous Huxley and Utopia," in *Prisms,* 117; *GS* 10.1:122. Mention of Kürnberger's novel as a "romantic apotheosis" in found in Nettl, *Other Casanova,* 271.

15. Cf. Wittgenstein's quotation of Grillparzer: "How easy it is to move about in broad distant regions, how hard to grasp what is individual & near at hand" (*Culture and Value,* 13). Recall, also, Wittgenstein's motto for his *Tractatus*—"whatever a man knows, whatever is not mere rumbling and roaring in his head, can be said in three words"—drawn from Kürnberger, whose influence on Viennese, fin-de-siècle thinkers (esp. Karl Kraus) was notable.

16. In 1827, Charles Sealsfield (while in London) published a series of sketches pertinently and originally entitled *Austria as It Is, or Sketches of Continental Courts.* (The phrase "as it is" interests me most, given the contrast it suggests with how things *might* be.) The reference to "unlimited possibilities" refers to Goldberger's influential text on economics, *Das Land der unbegrenzten Möglichkeiten.* Adorno referred to this text when he described America as no more the place of "unlimited possibilities" in his "Intellectual Experiences," in *CM,* 240.

17. Kürnberger, *Amerikamüde,* 563–68. Other precedents for this text are found in the works of Goethe, Schiller, Heine, Duden, and Lenau and also in Dickens, specifically his *Martin Chuzzlewit.* After Kürnberger, writers as various as Karl May, Feuerbach, Marx, Spengler, Arnold, Twain, Santayana, Kafka, and Dewey addressed these themes, as did Freud in his 1930 *Civilization and Its Discontents.* In describing a general weariness or resignation, Freud wrote of the damage to civilization done by America, about which he then remarked that he'd rather write no more (63).

18. Benjamin, "On the Concept of History," in *Selected Writings* 4:392–93.

19. In the correspondence between Kahler and Mann, India was mentioned as perhaps the last possible refuge for the intellectual (April 14, 1951), to which Mann responded (April 23): though "we live in a world of doom from which there is no longer any chance of escaping," probably "the man sailing westward is just a trace crazier" than the immigrant traveling back to Europe (*An Exceptional Friendship,* 154–57). I first read this anecdote in Lepenies, *Seduction of Culture,* 188.

20. Cf. Tiedemann, "Adorno's *Tom Sawyer* Opera Singspiel," 162–65, and Müller-Doohm, *Adorno,* 162–65.

21. I am grateful to Joy Calico for part of this list. For more, see Danuser and Gottschewski, *Amerikanismus–Americanism–Weill.*

22. I have imported Schillerian terms into Adorno's thought to make explicit the sort of damage about which he was thinking in his "On the Fetish-Character," in *AEM,* 290 (transl. amended); *GS* 14:17. Adorno devoted a section to the *Magic Flute* and enlightenment also in *MM,* 224, where he played on the *magic* associated with art's beauty and its subsequent loss—as Mann in *Der Zauberberg*—to show how much beauty was brought in by the enlightenment aesthetic even as it was increasingly ex-

cluded under modern conditions of domination. The theme of the magic flute and enlightenment was also taken up by Bloch and then later by Subotnik in her excellent article, "Whose 'Magic Flute?'"

23. Weill, "Future of Opera in America Today," 183. For more, see Kowalke, "Kurt Weill, Modernism and Popular Culture."

24. Krenek, "Transplanted Composer," 26.

25. Cf. here Fitzmaurice "Classical Rhetoric and the Promotion of the New World," and Todorov, *Conquest of America.*

26. For more, see Pensky, *Actuality of Adorno.*

27. Quoted in entry "Aktualitätstheorie," in Eisler, *Wörterbuch,* 1:12. I thank Willi Goetschel for alerting me to this theory.

28. Yehoshua, "Modern Democracy and the Novel," 43. See also Offe, *Reflections on America,* 4–5, 13 n.26, quoting Tocqueville: "The great advantage of the Americans is that they have arrived at a state of democracy without having to endure a democratic revolution, and that they are born equal instead of becoming so." For a musical discussion, see Gutman, "Young Germany, 1930."

29. Here, I am drawing on writings of Goethe, Hegel, Sealsfield, Burckhardt, and Kisch. In praising the Greeks, Nietzsche referred to them as eternal children (*BT,* 80–85), showing that not every reference to children was intended negatively.

30. Hegel, *IPH,* 84–91; *VPG,* 107–16.

31. Goethe, "Den Vereinigten Staaten," in *Poetische Werke,* 384 (my transl.).

32. Cf. Charles Edward Russell's discussion of the suggestion that, in general, opera companies should avoid using the "handicap" epithet of "American" and use "national" instead (*American Opera and Theodore Thomas,* 174).

33. Ritter, *Music in America,* 293–97.

34. Ibid., 199–200.

35. Ibid., 293.

36. Ibid., 338–39.

37. Pratt, "Plan and Plea for American Opera."

38. Ritter, *Music in America,* 197.

39. In Europe, the concept, say, of Italian opera was introduced less in Italy where the presence of opera sufficed and more in foreign countries. For, in Italy, it is enough to refer to opera; "Italian opera" in Italy would be unnecessary. However, German opera was introduced into Germany precisely when it was felt most urgent to resist the dominance of Italian and French opera in Germany. Clearly, the relation of "native" or "imported" national concepts to "home" or "foreign" countries is as complicated in Europe and elsewhere as in the United States.

40. Graf, *Opera for the People,* 186.

41. Ibid., 178.

42. Ibid., 244 (my emphasis).

43. From the early eighteenth century to the present, this titular convention has remained in place—in theater and opera, on Broadway, in African American music

theater traditions—in America and elsewhere, which warns against overassigning it significance.

44. All quotations of Kestin's words are drawn from her "Western Folklore in Modern American Opera."

45. Recorded in Ledbetter, "Damrosch, Walter (Johannes)."

46. Berg's opera was left incomplete at his death and was completed by Friedrich Cerha forty years later, though not in America.

47. Saunders, "National Opera, Comparatively Considered," "American Opera: Has It Arrived?," and "Songs of the German Revolution." In another article of 1928, after surveying the history of great sea shanties, Saunders concluded that the greatest of all came from the opening of Wagner's *Flying Dutchman* as a prefiguration of Senta's lyrical ballad ("Sailor Songs and Songs of the Sea").

48. Saunders, "National Opera," 73–74.

49. Ibid., 82.

50. Saunders, "American Opera," 152, 154. In this article, Saunders only mentioned how Bizet's resistance to "Jewish demands" allowed him to remain true to himself. I hope I am not extrapolating too unfairly from his thought.

51. Saunders, "Songs of the German Revolution," 50, 57.

52. For more background, see usOperaweb (www.usoperaweb.com) devoted to "American opera."

53. Heinsheimer, "Music and the American Radio," 13.

54. Heinsheimer, "Opera in America," 7.

55. Heinsheimer, "Opera in America Today," 315.

56. Graf, *Opera for the People*, 193. For more, see Sponaugle, "Columbia University, the Columbia University Opera Workshop and the Efflorescence of American Opera in the 1940s and 1950s."

57. Heinsheimer, "Opera in America Today," 329.

58. Heinsheimer, "Opera in America," 8. In *Seduction of Culture*, in a section titled "A Country Without an Opera," Wolf Lepenies clarifies the confusion surrounding the idea that the Met was even temporarily closed during World War II. He mentions the very few times it was ever closed and how important it was to Americans to keep it open, especially when this allowed them to send their missive out for Joseph Goebbels to hear across the sea: that he had been wrong in telling them in 1942 that their banning of opera proved their cultural inferiority. (The Met was closed when President John F. Kennedy was assassinated, as it was on the days after 9/11 in 2001.)

59. On arrival in the United States, Mann wrote: "Where I am, there is Germany. I carry my German culture in me. I have contact with the world and I do not consider myself fallen" (*New York Times*, February 22, 1938). These words were partially drawn and adapted from a 1934 poem of a Stefan George student, Karl Wolfskehl, "An die Deutschen." Wolfskehl reworked the poem for ten years though never apparently changed the line: "Wo ich bin, ist deutscher Geist" (Voit, *Karl Wolfskehl*, 63).

60. Heinsheimer, "Opera in America," 6.

61. Ibid., 9.

62. Cage, *Silence,* 73.

63. Descriptive details are drawn from Beyst, "John Cage."

64. Quoted in ibid.

65. Noted in Stiller, "Moore, Douglas S(tuart)."

66. Quoted in Tucholsky, "Ein Frühling in Amerika," 350.

67. Ross, "What Next?," 88–89.

68. Whitesitt, "Antheil, George [Georg] (Carl Johann)."

69. All references here are to Adorno's review, "Transatlantic," in *GS* 19:179–80.

70. I discuss Adorno's surrealist and culinary reading of *Mahagonny* in Goehr, "Hardboiled Disillusionment."

71. Quoted in Ward B. Lewis, "Egon Erwin Kisch," 255.

72. DeLillo, "In the Ruins of the Future," 37–38.

73. Nietzsche, *Gay Science,* 184.

74. Twain, *Tramp Abroad,* 51–57; quotations at 54, 56.

75. Quoted in Faner, *Walt Whitman and Opera,* 39–40.

Bibliography

Frequently Cited Texts

Theodor W. Adorno

AB   *Alban Berg: Master of the Smallest Link.* Trans. Juliane Brand and Christopher Hailey. Cambridge: Cambridge University Press, 1991.

AEM   *Adorno: Essays on Music.* Ed. Richard Leppert. Berkeley: University of California Press, 2002.

AT   *Aesthetic Theory.* Trans. Robert Hullot-Kentor. Minneapolis: University of Minnesota Press, 1997.

ÄT   *Ästhetische Theorie. GS* 7 (1970).

B   *Beethoven: The Philosophy of Music.* Ed. Rolf Tiedemann. Trans. Edmund Jephcott. Stanford: Stanford University Press, 1998.

B^G   *Beethoven: Philosophie der Music.* Frankfurt: Suhrkamp, 1993.

CF   (Coauthor with Hanns Eisler) *Composing for the Films.* Intro. Graham McCann. London: Athlone, 1994.

CI   *The Culture Industry: Selected Essays on Mass Culture.* Ed. J.M. Bernstein. London: Routledge, 1991.

CM   *Critical Models: Interventions and Catchwords.* Trans. Henry W. Pickford. Intro. Lydia Goehr. New York: Columbia University Press, 2005.

COM   *Current of Music: Elements of a Radio Theory.* Ed. Robert Hullot-Kentor. Frankfurt: Suhrkamp, 2006.

DA   (Coauthor with Max Horkheimer) *Dialektik der Aufklärung: Philosophische Fragmente. GS* 3 (1981).

DE   (Coauthor with Max Horkheimer) *Dialectic of Enlightenment: Philosophical Fragments.* Ed. Gunzelin Schmid Noerr. Trans. Edmund Jephcott. Stanford: Stanford University Press, 2002.

DSt   *Drei Studien zu Hegel. GS* 5 (1970).

GS   *Gesammelte Schriften.* 20 vols. Ed. Rolf Tiedemann. Frankfurt: Suhrkamp, 1997.

HS   *Hegel: Three Studies.* Trans. Shierry Weber Nicholsen. Cambridge: MIT Press, 1993.

ISM   *Introduction to the Sociology of Music.* Trans. E. B. Ashton. New York: Continuum, 1988.

KF   (Coauthor with Hanns Eisler) *Komposition für den Film.* Ed. Johannes C. Gall. Frankfurt: Suhrkamp, 2006.

MCP   *Metaphysics: Concept and Problems.* Ed. Rolf Tiedemann. Trans. Edmund Jephcott. Stanford: Stanford University Press, 2001.

MM   *Minima Moralia: Reflections from Damaged Life.* Trans. E. F. N. Jephcott. London: Verso, 1974.

MM^G *Minima Moralia: Reflexionen aus dem beschädigten Leben. GS* 4 (1951).

MMP   *Mahler: A Musical Physiognomy.* Trans. Edmund Jephcott. Chicago: University of Chicago Press, 1992.

ND   *Negative Dialectics.* Trans. E. B. Ashton. London: Routledge, 1973.

ND^G *Negative Dialektik. GS* 6 (1970).

NL   *Notes to Literature.* 2 vols. Ed. Rolf Tiedemann. Trans. Shierry Weber Nicholsen. New York: Columbia University Press, 1991–92.

NL^G *Noten zur Literatur. GS* 11 (1974).

PNM   *Philosophy of New Music.* Trans. Robert Hullot-Kentor. Minneapolis: University of Minnesota Press, 2006.

PNM^G *Philosophie der Neuen Musik. GS* 12 (1975).

QF   *Quasi una Fantasia: Essays on Modern Music.* Trans. Rodney Livingstone. London: Verso, 1992.

QF^G *Quasi una Fantasia. GS* 16 (1978).

SF   *Sound Figures.* Trans. Rodney Livingstone. Stanford: Stanford University Press, 1999.

SF^G *Klangfiguren. GS* 16 (1978).

TMR   *Zu einer Theorie der musikalischen Reproduktion.* Ed. Henri Lonitz. Frankfurt: Suhrkamp, 2001.

Walter Benjamin

GS2   *Gesammelte Schriften.* 7 vols. in 14 parts. Ed. Rolf Tiedemann. Frankfurt: Suhrkamp, 2005.

WOA   "The Work of Art in the Age of Its Technological Reproducibility." In *Selected Writings.* Vol. 3, *1925–1938.* Ed. Michael W. Jennings, 101–33. Cambridge: Harvard University Press, 2002.

Arthur C. Danto

BB   *The Body/Body Problem: Selected Essays.* Berkeley: University of California Press, 1999.

NK   *Narration and Knowledge (Including His Analytical Philosophy of History).* New York: Columbia University Press, 2007.

PDA   *The Philosophical Disenfranchisement of Art.* New York: Columbia University Press, 1986.

TC   *The Transfiguration of the Commonplace: A Philosophy of Art.* Cambridge: Harvard University Press, 1981.

Eduard Hanslick

VMS   *Vom Musikalisch-Schönen: Ein Beitrag zur Revision der Ästhetik der Tonkunst.* Wiesbaden: Breitkopf and Härtel, 1966.

Georg Wilhelm Friedrich Hegel

HA   *Aesthetics: Lectures on Fine Arts.* 2 vols. Trans. T.M. Knox. Oxford: Clarendon, 1975.

IPH   *Introduction to the Philosophy of History.* Trans. Leo Rauch. Indianapolis: Hackett, 1988.

PG   *Phänomenologie des Geistes.* Vol. 3 of *Werke.* Ed. Eva Moldenhauer and Karl Markus Michel. Frankfurt: Suhrkamp, 1970.

PS   *Phenomenology of Spirit.* Trans. A.V. Miller. Oxford: Oxford University Press, 1977.

VA   *Vorlesungen über die Ästhetik.* Vols. 13–15 of *Werke.* Ed. Eva Moldenhauer and Karl Markus Michel. Frankfurt: Suhrkamp, 1970.

VPG   *Vorlesungen über die Philosophie der Geschichte.* Vol. 12 of *Werke.* Ed. Eva Moldenhauer and Karl Markus Michel. Frankfurt: Suhrkamp, 1970.

Immanuel Kant

CJ   *Critique of the Power of Judgment.* Trans. Paul Guyer and Eric Matthews. Cambridge: Cambridge University Press, 2000.

KU   *Kritik der Urteilskraft.* Vol. 10 of *Werkeausgabe.* 12 vols. Ed. Wilhelm
        Weischedel. Frankfurt: Suhrkamp, 1977.

Friedrich Nietzsche

BT   *The Birth of Tragedy and Other Writings.* Ed. Raymond Geuss and Ronald
        Speirs. Trans. Ronald Speirs. Cambridge: Cambridge University Press, 1999.
KSA   *Sämtliche Werke: Kritische Studienausgabe.* 15 vols. Ed. Giorgio Colli and
        Mazzino Montinari. Berlin: de Gruyter, 1980.

Friedrich von Schiller

SW   *Schillers Werke (Nationalausgabe).* 56 vols. to date. Ed. Benno von Wiese.
        Weimar: Goethe and Schiller Archiv, various dates.

Arthur Schopenhauer

PP   *Parerga and Paralipomena: Short Philosophical Essays.* 2 vols. Trans. E. F. J.
        Payne. Oxford: Clarendon, 1974.
PP^G   *Parerga und Paralipomena II.* Vol. 5 of *Sämtliche Werke.* Frankfurt: Suhrkamp,
        1986.
WWR   *The World as Will and Representation.* 2 vols. Trans. E. F. J. Payne. New York:
        Dover, 1958, 1969.
WWV   *Die Welt als Wille und Vorstellung: Sämtliche Werke.* 2 vols. Ed. Wolfgang
        Frhr. von Löhneysen. Frankfurt: Suhrkamp, 1960.

Richard Wagner

DS   *Dichtungen und Schriften.* 10 vols. Ed. Dieter Borchmeyer. Frankfurt: Insel,
        1983.

Books and Articles

Abbate, Carolyn. *In Search of Opera.* Princeton: Princeton University Press, 2003.
Abbate, Carolyn. "Music: Drastic or Gnostic." *Critical Inquiry* 30, no. 3 (2004):
    505–36.
Adams, John. *The Death of Klinghoffer.* DVD, Decca B0001515-09, 2003.
Adorno, T. W. "The Actuality of Philosophy." *Telos* 31 (1977): 120–32.
Adorno, T. W. "Art and the Arts." In *Can One Live After Auschwitz: A Philosophical
    Reader,* ed. Rolf Tiedemann, 386–87. Stanford: Stanford University Press, 2003.
Adorno, T. W. *History and Freedom: Lectures, 1964–1965.* Ed. Rolf Tiedemann. Trans.
    Rodney Livingstone. Cambridge: Polity, 2006.
Adorno, T. W. *In Search of Wagner.* Trans. Rodney Livingstone. London: Verso, 1981.

Adorno, T.W. *The Jargon of Authenticity.* Trans. Knut Tarnowski and Frederic Will. Evanston, Ill.: Northwestern University Press, 1973.

Adorno, T.W. *Kompositionen.* Mainz: Schott Wergo Music Media, 1990.

Adorno, T.W. *Prisms.* Trans. Samuel and Shierry Weber. Cambridge: MIT Press, 1981.

Adorno, T.W. Review "Transatlantic." In *Gesammelte Schriften.* Ed. Rolf Tiedemann, vol. 19, 179–80. Frankfurt: Suhrkamp, 1997.

Adorno, T.W., and Walter Benjamin. *The Complete Correspondence, 1928–1940.* Ed. Henri Lonitz. Trans. Nicholas Walker. Cambridge: Harvard University Press, 1999.

Adorno, T.W., and Alban Berg. *Correspondence, 1925–1935.* Ed. Henri Lonitz. Trans. Wieland Hoban. Cambridge: Polity, 2006.

Adorno, T.W., and Max Horkheimer. *Briefwechsel, 1927–1937.* Frankfurt: Suhrkamp, 2003.

Altman, Rick, "The Silence of the Silents." *Musical Quarterly* 80, no. 4 (1996): 648–718.

Altman, Rick. *Silent Film Sound.* New York: Columbia University Press, 2004.

Altman, Rick, ed. *Sound Theory and Sound Practice.* New York: Routledge, 1992.

Andersen, Hans Christian. *The Stories of Hans Christian Andersen.* Trans. Diana Crone Frank. New York: Houghton Mifflin, 2003.

Antheil, George. "Wanted—Opera by and for Americans." *Modern Music* 7, no. 4 (1930): 11–16.

Apollonio, Umbro, ed. *Futurist Manifestos.* Boston: Museum of Fine Arts, 2001.

Arendt, Hannah. *The Origins of Totalitarianism.* New York: Harvest, 1973.

Arnheim, Rudolf. *Film as Art.* Berkeley: University of California Press, 1957.

Bacon, Francis. *The Advancement of Learning.* Books 1–2. New York: Random House, 2001.

Bacon, Francis. *The New Organon.* Ed. Lisa Jardine and Michael Silverthorne. Cambridge: Cambridge University Press, 2000.

Bacon, Francis. *The Works of Francis Bacon.* Vol. 6. Ed. James Spedding, Robert Leslie Ellis, and Douglas Denon Heath. London: Longman, 1870.

Bass, Jacquelynn, and Mary Jane Jacobs, eds. *Buddha Mind in Contemporary Art.* Berkeley: University of California Press, 2004.

Balázs, Béla. "From *The Visible Human.*" In *German Essays on Film,* ed. Richard W. McCormick and Alison Guenther-Pal, 69–98. New York: Continuum, 2004.

Balázs, Béla. *Der Geist des Films.* Frankfurt: Suhrkamp, 2001.

Balázs, Béla. *Theory of the Film: Character and Growth of a New Art.* Trans. Edith Bone. New York: Dover, 1970.

Ballantine, Christopher. "Towards an Aesthetic of Experimental Music." *Music Quarterly* 63, no. 2 (1977): 224–46.

Barenboim, Daniel, and Edward Said. *Parallels and Paradoxes: Explorations in Music and Society.* New York: Vintage, 2004.

Becce, Giuseppe. "Tonfilm und Künstlerische Filmmusik." *Musikblätter des Anbruch* 3 (1929): 140–42.

Beethoven, Ludwig von. *Briefwechsel Gesamtausgabe.* 7 vols. Ed. Sieghard Brandenburg. Munich: G. Henle, 1996–1998.

Beethoven, Ludwig von. *Letters, Journals and Conversations.* Ed. Michael Hamburger. New York: Putnam, 1951.

Bekker, Paul. "Krise des Operntheaters." *Musik und Gesellschaft: Arbeitsblätter für soziale Musikpflege und Musikpolitik* 1 (1930): 206–9.

Belton, John. "Technology and Aesthetics of Film Sound." In *Film Sound: Theory and Practice,* ed. Elisabeth Weis and John Belton, 63–72. New York: Columbia University Press, 1985.

Benjamin, Andrew, ed. *The Problems of Modernity: Adorno and Benjamin.* London: Routledge, 1989.

Benjamin, Walter. *Selected Writings.* Ed. Michael W. Jennings. 4 vols. Cambridge: Harvard University Press, 1996–2003.

Bergson, Henri. *Creative Evolution.* Trans. Arthur Mitchell. New York: Holt, 1911.

Berlioz, Hector. *À Travers Chant.* Hants, England: Gregg International, 1970.

Bernstein, Jay M. *The Fate of Art: Aesthetic Alienation from Kant to Derrida and Adorno.* University Park: Pennsylvania State University Press, 1992.

Bertens, Hans, and Joseph Natoli, eds. *Postmodernism: The Key Figures.* Oxford: Blackwell, 2002.

Beyst, Stefan. "John Cage: Europeras—A Light- and Soundscape as Musical Manifesto." Trans. Brian Cole. August 2005. At http://d-sites.net/english/cage.htm. Accessed June 24, 2007.

Biagioli, Mario, ed. *The Science Studies Reader.* London: Routledge, 1999.

Birker, Werner, ed. *Nikolaus Lenau, Blick in den Strom.* Graz: Stiasny, 1961.

Bloch, Ernst. *Literary Essays.* Ed. Werner Hamacher and David E. Wellbery. Trans. Andrew Joron and Others. Stanford: Stanford University Press, 1998.

Bloch, Ernst. *The Principle of Hope.* Trans. Neville Plaice, Stephen Plaice, and Paul Knight. 3 vols. Cambridge: MIT Press, 1995.

Bloom, Michelle E. *Waxworks: A Cultural Obsession.* Minneapolis: University of Minnesota Press, 2003.

Borchmeyer, Dieter. *Richard Wagner: Theory and Theatre.* Oxford: Clarendon, 1991.

Bordwell, David, and Kristin Thompson. "Fundamental Aesthetics of Sound in the Cinema." In *Film Sound: Theory and Practice,* ed. Elisabeth Weis and John Belton, 181–99. New York: Columbia University Press, 1985.

Borges, Jorge Luis. *Collected Fictions.* Trans. Andrew Hurley. New York: Penguin, 1998.

Borio, Gianmario, and Hermann Danuser, eds. *Im Zenit der Moderne: Die Internationalen Ferienkurse für Neue Musik, Darmstadt, 1946–1966.* 4 vols. Freiburg: Rombach, 1997.

Bossy, John. "'Torturing the Truth.' Is There a Connection Between Bacon's Science and His Statecraft?" *Times Literary Supplement,* 11 October 1996, 3–4.

Boulez, Pierre. *Orientations: Collected Writings.* Ed. Martin Cooper. Trans. Jean-Jacques Nattiez. Cambridge: Harvard University Press, 1990.

Bowie, Andrew. *From Romanticism to Critical Theory: The Philosophy of German Literary Theory*. London: Routledge, 1996.

Brandstetter, Gabriele, and Sibylle Peters, eds. *De figura: Rhetorik-Bewegung-Gestalt*. Munich: Wilhelm Fink, 2002.

Brecht, Bertolt. *Gesammelte Werke*. 15 vols. Frankfurt: Suhrkamp, 1967.

Brecht, Bertolt. *The Resistable Rise of Arturo Ui*. New York: Methuen, 1981.

Bruce, Susan, ed. *Three Early Modern Utopias* [Including *The New Atlantis*]. Oxford: Oxford University Press, 1999.

Brunkhorst, Hauke, ed. *Adorno and Critical Theory*. Cardiff: University of Wales Press, 1999.

Buch, Esteban. *Beethoven's Ninth: A Political History*. Chicago: University of Chicago Press, 2003.

Buck-Morss, Susan. *The Origin of Negative Dialectics: Theodor W. Adorno, Walter Benjamin, and the Frankfurt Institute*. New York: Free Press, 1977.

Burckhardt, Jacob. *Reflections on History*. Indianapolis: Liberty Fund, 1979.

Burgin, Victor. *The Remembered Film*. London: Reaktion, 2004.

Burns, Rick. *Andy Warhol: A Documentary*. American Masters, PBS, 2006.

Cage, John. *Bird Cage*. CD, EMF 013, 2000.

Cage, John. *For the Birds: John Cage in Conversation with Daniel Charles*. London: Marion Boyars, 1981.

Cage, John. *Silence: Lecture and Writings*. Middletown, Conn.: Wesleyan University Press, 1973.

Carman, Taylor, and Mark B. N. Hansen, eds. *The Cambridge Companion to Merleau-Ponty*. Cambridge: Cambridge University Press, 2004.

Carroll, Noël. "Essence, Expression, and History: Arthur Danto's Philosophy of Art." In *Danto and His Critics*, ed. Mark Rollins, 79–106. Oxford: Blackwell, 1993.

Cassirer, Ernst. *The Platonic Renaissance in England*. Trans. James P. Pettegrove. Austin: University of Texas Press, 1953.

Cavalcanti, Alberto. "Sound in Films." In *Film Sound: Theory and Practice*, ed. Elisabeth Weis and John Belton, 98–111. New York: Columbia University Press, 1985.

Cavell, Stanley. *Must We Mean What We Say?* New York: Scribner, 1969.

Cavell, Stanley. "A Philosopher Goes to the Movies." Conversation with Harry Kreisler, Institute of International Studies, University of California at Berkeley, 7 February 2002. At http://globetrotter.berkeley.edu/people2/Cavell/cavell-con0 .html. Accessed June 24, 2007.

Cavell, Stanley. *The Pitch of Philosophy: Autobiographical Exercises*. Cambridge: Harvard University Press, 1994.

Cavell, Stanley. *The World Viewed: Reflections on the Ontology of Film*. Cambridge: Harvard University Press, 1979.

Chion, Michel. *Audio-Vision: Sound on Screen*. Trans. Claudia Gorbman. New York: Columbia University Press, 1994.

Clair, René. "The Art of Sound." In *Film Sound: Theory and Practice,* ed. Elisabeth Weis and John Belton, 92–95. New York: Columbia University Press, 1985.

Clark, Robert T. "The Union of the Arts in *Die Braut von Messina.*" *Proceedings of the Modern Language Association* 52, no. 4 (1937): 1135–46.

Co, Franceso Dal, and Sergio Polano. "Interview with Albert Speer." *Oppositions* 12 (1977/78): 38–53.

Cohen, Peter. *The Architect of Doom.* Documentary. DVD, Sweden, 1989.

Coleridge, Samuel Taylor. *Biographia Literaria: Biographical Sketches of My Literary Life and Opinions.* Ed. James Engell and W. Jackson Bate. Princeton: Princeton University Press, 1985.

Cook, Nicholas. *Beethoven: Symphony No. 9.* Cambridge: Cambridge University Press, 1993.

Corngold, Stanley. "Genuine Obscurity Shadows the Semblance Whose Obliteration Promises Redemption: Reflections on Benjamin's 'Goethe's *Elective Affinities.*'" In *Benjamin's Ghosts,* ed. Gerhard Richter, 154–68. Stanford: Stanford University Press, 2002.

Crane, Susan. "Writing the Individual Back into Collective Memory." *American Historical Review* 102, no. 5 (1997): 1372–85.

Crane, Susan A. *Collecting and Historical Consciousness in Early Nineteenth-Century Germany.* Ithaca, N.Y.: Cornell University Press, 2000.

Dahlhaus, Carl, ed. *Klassische und romantische Musikästhetik.* Laaber: Laaber-Verlag, 1988.

Danto, Arthur C. *The Abuse of Beauty: Aesthetics and the Concept of Art.* Chicago: Open Court, 2003.

Danto, Arthur C. "The American Sublime: Robert Smithson and *Spiral Jetty.*" *Nation* 281 (September 19, 2005): 34–36.

Danto, Arthur C. "Art and the Towering Sadness." *Nation* 273 (November 12, 2001): 42–43.

Danto, Arthur C. "The Artworld." *Journal of Philosophy* 61, no. 19 (1964): 571–84.

Danto, Arthur C. *Nietzsche as Philosopher.* New York: Columbia University Press, 1965.

Danto, Arthur C. *Unnatural Wonders: Essays from the Gap Between Art and Life.* New York: Farrar, Straus Giroux, 2005.

Danto, Arthur C. "Upper West Side Buddhism." In *Buddha Mind in Contemporary Art,* ed. Jacquelynn Baas and Mary Jane Jacob, 49–59. Berkeley: University of California Press, 2004.

Danuser, Hermann. *Die Musik des 20. Jahrhunderts.* Neues Handbuch der Musikwissenschaft 7, ed. Carl Dahlhaus. Laaber: Laaber-Verlag, 1984.

Danuser, Hermann, and Hermann Gottschewski, eds. *Amerikanismus–Americanism–Weill: Die Suche nach kultureller Identität in der Moderne.* Schliengen: Argus, 2003.

Daverio, John. *Nineteenth-Century German Music and the German Romantic Ideology.* New York: Schirmer, 1993.

Deleuze, Gilles. *Cinema 1: The Movement-Image.* Trans. Hugh Tomlinson and Barbara Habberjam. Minneapolis: University of Minnesota Press, 1986.

Deleuze, Gilles. *Cinema 2: The Time-Image.* Trans. Hugh Tomlinson and Robert Galeta. Minneapolis: University of Minnesota Press, 1989.

Deligiorgi, Katerina, ed. *Hegel: New Directions.* Montreal: McGill-Queens University Press, 2006.

DeLillo, Don. "In the Ruins of the Future: Reflections on Loss and Terror in the Shadow of September." *Harper,* December 2001, 33–41.

Dennis, David B. *Beethoven in German Politics, 1870–1989.* New Haven: Yale University Press, 1996.

DeNora, Tia. *After Adorno: Rethinking Music Sociology.* Cambridge: Cambridge University Press, 2003.

De Quincey, Thomas. *On Murder.* New York: Oxford University Press, 2006.

De Vos, Lu. "Review of Hegel's *Vorlesungen über die Philosophie der Kunst.*" *Hegel-Studien* 34 (1999): 195–203.

De Zayas, Marius. "The Sun Has Set." *Camera Work* 39 (July 1912): 17–21.

Dickinson, Kay, ed. *Movie Music: The Film Reader.* London: Routledge, 2003.

Diers, Michael, ed. *Mo(nu)mente: Formen und Funktionen ephemerer Denkmäler.* Berlin: Akademie-Verlag, 1998.

Dizikes, John. *Opera in America: A Cultural History.* New Haven: Yale University Press, 1993.

Doane, Mary Ann. "Ideology and the Practice of Sound Editing and Mixing." In *Film Sound: Theory and Practice,* ed. Elisabeth Weis and John Belton, 54–62. New York: Columbia University Press, 1985.

Döblin, Alfred. "The Theater of the Little People (1909)." In *German Essays on Film,* ed. Richard W. McCormick and Alison Guenther-Pal, 1–3. New York: Continuum, 2004.

Duncan, Dean. *Charms That Soothe: Classical Music and the Narrative Film.* New York: Fordham University Press, 2003.

Eagleton, Terry. *The Ideology of the Aesthetic.* Oxford: Basil Blackwell, 1990.

Eggebrecht, H. H., ed. *Brockhaus-Riemann Musiklexikon.* Mainz: Schott, 1979.

Eisenstein, Sergei. *Film Form: Essays in Film Theory.* Ed. and trans. Jay Leyda. San Diego: Harvest, 1977.

Eisler, Rudolf. *Wörterbuch der philosophischen Begriffe.* 2 vols. Berlin: Mittler, 1904.

Ewers, Hanns Heinz. "Film and I." In *German Essays on Film,* ed. Richard W. McCormick and Alison Guenther-Pal, 22–24. New York: Continuum, 2004.

Faner, Robert D. *Walt Whitman and Opera.* Carbondale: Southern Illinois University Press, 1951.

Fink, Robert. "Klinghoffer in Brooklyn Heights: Opera, Anti-Semitism, and the Politics of Representation." *Cambridge Opera Journal* 17, no. 2 (2005): 173–213.

Fisher, Lucy. "Enthusiasm: From Kino-Eye to Radio-Eye." In *Film Sound: Theory and Practice,* ed. Elisabeth Weis and John Belton, 247–64. New York: Columbia University Press, 1985.

Fitzmaurice, Andrew. "Classical Rhetoric and the Promotion of the New World." *Journal of the History of Ideas* 58, no. 2 (1997): 221–43.

Flinn, Caryl. *Strains of Utopia: Gender, Nostalgia, and Hollywood Film Music.* Princeton: Princeton University Press, 1992.

Freud, Sigmund. *Civilization and Its Discontents.* Trans. James Strachey. New York: Norton, 1961.

Fukuyama, Francis. *The End of History and the Last Man.* New York: Free Press, 2006.

Furtwängler, Wilhelm. *Notebooks, 1924–1954.* Ed. Michael Tanner. Trans. Shaun Whiteside. London: Quartet, 1989.

Gaiger, Jason. "Catching up with History: Hegel and Abstract Painting." In *Hegel: New Directions,* ed. Katerina Deligiorgi, 159–76. Montreal: McGill-Queens University Press, 2006.

Geissmar, Berta. *The Baton and the Jackboot.* London: Hamish Hamilton, 1945.

Genet, Jean. *The Maids and Deathwatch.* Trans. Bernard Fretchman. Intro. Jean-Paul Sartre. New York: Grove, 1954.

Gethmann-Siefert, Annemarie. "Phänomen versus System: Zum Verhältnis von philosophischer Systematik und Kunsturteil in Hegels Berliner Vorlesungen über Ästhetik oder Philosophie der Kunst." *Hegel-Studien* 34 (1992).

Geuss, Raymond. *History and Illusion in Politics.* Cambridge: Cambridge University Press, 2001.

Geuss, Raymond. *Morality, Culture, and History: Essays on German Philosophy.* Cambridge: Cambridge University Press, 1999.

Gilmore, Jonathan. *The Life of a Style: Beginnings and Endings in the Narrative History of Art.* Ithaca, N.Y.: Cornell University Press, 2000.

Geulen, Eva. *The End of Art: Readings in a Rumor After Hegel.* Trans. James McFarland. Stanford: Stanford University Press, 2006.

Gloag, Kenneth, and Julian Rushton. *Tippett: A Child of Our Time.* Cambridge: Cambridge University Press, 1999.

Goehr, Lydia. "Adorno, Schoenberg, and the *Totentanz der Prinzipien*—in Thirteen Steps." *Journal of the American Musicological Society* 56, no. 3 (2003): 595–636.

Goehr, Lydia. "*Aida* and the Empire of Emotions: Theodor W. Adorno, Edward Said and Alexander Kluge." Unpublished ms.

Goehr, Lydia. "The Dangers of Satisfaction: On Songs, Rehearsals, and Repetition in Wagner's *Die Meistersinger.*" In *Wagner's Meistersinger: Performance, History, Representation,* ed. Nicholas Vazsonyi, 56–70. Rochester, N.Y.: University of Rochester Press, 2003.

Goehr, Lydia. "Dissonant Works and the Listening Public." In *The Cambridge Companion to Adorno,* ed. Tom Huhn, 222–47. Cambridge: Cambridge University Press, 2004.

Goehr, Lydia. "For the Birds/Against the Birds: Modernist Narratives on the End of Art." In *Action, Art, History: Engagement with Arthur Danto,* ed. Daniel Herwitz and Michael Kelly, 43–73. New York: Columbia University Press, 2007.

Goehr, Lydia. "Gegen die Vögel: Theodor W. Adorno über Musik, Konzept und dialektische Bewegung." In *Conceptualisms in Musik, Kunst und Film,* ed. Christoph Metzger, 97–113. Berlin: Akademie der Künste, 2003.

Goehr, Lydia. "Hardboiled Disillusionment: *Mahagonny* as the Last Culinary Opera." *Cultural Critique* 68 (Winter 2008): 3–37.

Goehr, Lydia. *The Imaginary Museum of Musical Works: An Essay in the Philosophy of Music.* Oxford: Clarendon, 1992; reprinted, New York: Oxford University Press, 2007.

Goehr, Lydia. "*Juliette fährt nach Mahagonny* or a Critical Reading of Surrealist Opera." *Opera Quarterly* 21, no. 4 (2005): 647–74.

Goehr, Lydia. "Musikdrama." In *Wagner und Nietzsche: Kultur-Werk-Wirkung—Ein Handbuch,* ed. Stefan Lorenz Sorgner, James H. Birx, and Nikolaus Knoepffler, 215–46. Reinbek b. Hamburg: Rowohlt, 2008.

Goehr, Lydia. *The Quest for Voice: Music, Politics, and the Limits of Philosophy.* Oxford: Clarendon, 1998.

Goehr, Lydia. "Reviewing Adorno." In Theodor W. Adorno, *Critical Models: Interventions and Catchwords,* xiii–lxi. New York: Columbia University Press, 2005.

Goehr, Lydia. "Schopenhauer and the Musicians: An Inquiry into the Sounds of Silence and the Limits of Philosophizing About Music." In *Schopenhauer, Philosophy, and the Arts,* ed. Dale Jacquette, 200–228. Cambridge: Cambridge University Press, 1996.

Goehr, Lydia. "'Three Blind Mice': Goodman, McLuhan, and Adorno on the Art of Music and Listening in the Age of Global Transmission." *New German Critique* 104 (2008): 1–31.

Goehr, Lydia. "Understanding the Engaged Philosopher: On Politics, Philosophy, and Art." In *The Cambridge Companion to Merleau-Ponty,* ed. Taylor Carman and Mark B. N. Hansen, 318–51. Cambridge: Cambridge University Press, 2004.

Goehr, Lydia. "Undoing the Discourse of Fate: The Case of *Der Fliegende Holländer.*" *Opera Quarterly* 21, no. 3 (2005): 430–51.

Goethe, Johann Wolfgang. *Elective Affinities.* Vol. 11 of *The Collected Works.* Ed. David E. Wellbery. Trans. Victor Lange and Judith Ryan. Princeton: Princeton University Press, 1988.

Goethe, Johann Wolfgang. *Faust I and II.* Vol. 2 of *The Collected Works.* Ed. and trans. Stuart Atkins. Princeton: Princeton University Press, 1994.

Goethe, Johann Wolfgang. *The Man of Fifty.* Trans. Andrew Piper. London: Hesperus, 2005.

Goethe, Johann Wolfgang. *Maximen und Reflexionen.* Weimar: Goethe-Gesellschaft, 1907.

Goethe, Johann Wolfgang. *Poetische Werke: Gedichte—Nachlese und Nachlass*. Vol. 2. Ed. Siegfried Seidel. Berlin: Aufbau, 1973.

Goethe, Johann Wolfgang. *Selected Poems*. Vol. 12 of *The Collected Works*. Ed. Christopher Middleton. Princeton: Princeton University Press, 1984.

Goethe, Johann Wolfgang. *Texte*. Ed. Albrecht Schöne. Frankfurt: Deutscher Klassiker Verlag, 1999.

Goethe, Johann Wolfgang. *Die Wahlverwandtschaften: Ein Roman*. In *Sämtliche Werke nach Epochen seines Schaffens*. Vol. 9, *Epoche der Wahlverwandtschaften, 1807–1814*. Ed. Karl Richter. Munich: Hanser, 1987.

Goethe, Johann Wolfgang. *Zur Farbenlehre: Polemischer Teil*. Vol. 5 of *Die Schriften zur Naturwissenschaft*. Ed. Dorothea Kuhn and Wolf von Engelhardt. Weimar: Rupprecht Matthaei, 1958.

Goldberger, Ludwig Max. *Das Land der unbegrenzten Möglichkeiten: Betrachtungen über das Wirtschaftsleben der Vereinigten Staaten von Amerika*. Berlin: Fontana, 1903.

Goll, Claire. "American Cinema." In *German Essays on Film*, ed. Richard W. McCormick and Alison Guenther-Pal, 50–52. New York: Continuum, 2004.

Gorbman, Claudia. "Why Music? The Sound Film and Its Spectator." In *Movie Music: The Film Reader*, ed. Kay Dickinson, 37–47. London: Routledge, 2003.

Gouk, Penelope M. *Music, Science and Natural Magic in Seventeenth-Century England*. New Haven: Yale University Press, 1999.

Graf, Herbert. *Opera for the People*. Minneapolis: University of Minnesota Press, 1951.

Gross, Alan G. *The Rhetoric of Science*. Cambridge: Harvard University Press, 1990.

Gutman, Hans. "Young Germany, 1930." *Modern Music* 7, no. 2 (1930): 3–10.

Habermas, Jürgen. *On the Logic of the Social Sciences*. Trans. Shierry Weber Nicholsen and Jerry A. Stark. Cambridge: MIT Press, 1996.

Hachmeister, Lutz. *The Goebbels Experiment*. DVD, 2004.

Halbwachs, Maurice. *The Collective Memory*. Trans. Francis J. Ditter and Vida Yazdi Ditter. New York: Harper and Row, 1980.

Hammer, Espen. *Adorno and the Political*. London: Routledge, 2005.

Hammond, Theresa Mayer. *American Paradise: German Travel Literature from Duden to Kisch*. Heidelberg: Carl Winter Universitätsverlag, 1980.

Hanslick, Eduard. *On the Musically Beautiful*. Trans. Geoffrey Payzant. Indianapolis: Hackett, 1986.

Harwood, Ronald. *Taking Sides*. New York: Dramatists Play Service, 1995.

Hasty, Christopher. *Meter as Rhythm*. New York: Oxford University Press, 1997.

Hegel, Georg Wilhelm Friedrich. *Early Theological Writings*. Trans. T. M. Knox. Philadelphia: University of Pennsylvania Press, 1975.

Hegel, Georg Wilhelm Friedrich. *Grundlinien der Philosophie des Rechts oder Naturrecht und Staatswissenschaft im Grundrisse*. Frankfurt: Suhrkamp, 1986.

Hegel, Georg Wilhelm Friedrich. *Lectures on the Philosophy of World History*. Trans. H. B. Nisbet. Cambridge: Cambridge University Press, 1975.

Hegel, Georg Wilhelm Friedrich. *Philosophie der Kunst: Vorlesung von 1826*. Ed. Annemarie Gethmann-Siefert, Jeong-Im Kwon, and Karsten Barr. Frankfurt: Suhrkamp, 2004.

Hegel, Georg Wilhelm Friedrich. *Philosophy of Right*. Trans. T. M. Knox. London: Oxford University Press, 1962.

Hegel, Georg Wilhelm Friedrich. *Science of Logic*. Trans. A. V. Miller. London: George Allen and Unwin, 1969.

Hegel, Georg Wilhelm Friedrich. *Vorlesung über Ästhetik: Berlin, 1820–21—Eine Nachshrift*. Ed. Helmut Schneider. Frankfurt: Peter Lang, 1995.

Heidegger, Martin. *Poetry, Language, Thought*. Trans. Albert Hofstadter. New York: Harper and Row, 1971.

Heine, Heinrich. *Sämtliche Schriften*. Vol. 3: *1822–1831*. Ed. Klaus Briegleb. Munich: Hanser, 1976.

Heinsheimer, H. W. "Music and the American Radio." *Tempo* 3 (1947): 10, 13–14.

Heinsheimer, H. W. "Opera in America." *Tempo* 11 (1945): 6–9.

Heinsheimer, H. W. "Opera in America Today." *Musical Quarterly* 37, no. 3 (1951): 315–29.

Henderson, Sir Neville. *Failure of a Mission*. New York: Putnam, 1940.

Herder, Johann Gottfried. *Ideen zur Philosophie der Geschichte der Menschheit*. Ed. Heinz Stolpe. Berlin: Aufbau, 1965.

Herder, Johann Gottfried. *Philosophical Writings*. Ed. Michael Forster. Cambridge: Cambridge University Press, 2002.

Herder, Johann Gottfried. *Selected Writings on Aesthetics*. Trans. and ed. Gregory Moore. Princeton: Princeton University Press, 2006.

Hermand, Jost, and Gerhard Richter, eds. *Sound Figures of Modernity*. Madison: University of Wisconsin Press, 2006.

Herwitz, Daniel, and Michael Kelly, eds. *Action, Art, History: Engagements with Arthur Danto*. New York: Columbia University Press, 2007.

Hinton, Stephen. "Not 'Which' Tones? The Crux of Beethoven's Ninth." *19th-Century Music* 22, no. 1 (1998): 61–77.

Hobsbawm, Eric. *The Invention of Tradition*. Cambridge: Cambridge University Press, 1992.

Hoeckner, Berthold. *Programming the Absolute: Nineteenth-Century German Music and the Hermeneutics of the Moment*. Princeton: Princeton University Press, 2002.

Hofmann, Charles. *Sounds for Silents*. New York: Drama Book Specialists [DBS], 1970.

Hofmannsthal, Hugo von. "The Substitute for Dreams." In *German Essays on Film*, ed. Richard W. McCormick and Alison Guenther-Pal, 52–56. New York: Continuum, 2004.

Hohendahl, Peter Uwe. *Prismatic Thought: Theodor W. Adorno*. Lincoln: University of Nebraska Press, 1995.

Horkheimer, Max. *The Eclipse of Reason*. New York: Continuum, 1974.

Horowitz, Gregg. *Sustaining Loss: Art and Mournful Life*. Stanford: Stanford University Press, 2001.

Horowitz, Gregg, and Tom Huhn, eds. *The Wake of Art*. London: G+B Arts International, 1998.

Horváth, Ödön von. *Ein Kind unserer Zeit*. Vol. 14 of *Gesammelte Werke*. 14 vols. Frankfurt: Suhrkamp, 1985.

Huhn, Thomas. "The Kantian Sublime and the Nostalgia for Violence." *Journal of Aesthetics and Art Criticism* 53, no. 3 (1995): 269–75.

Huhn, Tom, ed. *The Cambridge Companion to Adorno*. Cambridge: Cambridge University Press, 2004.

Hullot-Kentor, Robert. *Things Beyond Resemblance: Collected Essays on Theodor W. Adorno*. New York: Columbia University Press, 2006.

Hutton, Patrick. "Recent Scholarship on Memory and History." *History Teacher* 33, no. 4 (2000): 533–48.

Huyssen, Andreas. *Present Pasts: Urban Palimpsests and the Politics of Memory*. Stanford: Stanford University Press, 2003.

Ihering, Herbert. "An Expressionist Film." In *German Essays on Film*, ed. Richard W. McCormick and Alison Guenther-Pal, 48–50. New York: Continuum, 2004.

Imhoof, Walter. *Der "Europamüde" in der deutschen Erzählungliteratur*. Horgen-Zurich: Münster-Presse, 1930.

Jacquette, Dale, ed. *Schopenhauer, Philosophy, and the Arts*. Cambridge: Cambridge University Press, 1996.

Jameson, Fredric. *Late Marxism: Adorno, or the Persistence of the Dialectic*. London: Verso, 1990.

Jameson, Fredric. *Marxism and Form: Twentieth-Century Dialectical Theories of Literature*. Princeton: Princeton University Press, 1971.

Jarvis, Simon. *Adorno: A Critical Introduction*. Cambridge: Polity, 1998.

Jay, Martin. *Adorno*. London: Fontana, 1984.

Jay, Martin. *The Dialectical Imagination: A History of the Frankfurt School and the Institute of Social Research, 1923–1950*. Boston: Little, Brown, 1973.

Jay, Martin. *Permanent Exiles: Essays on the Intellectual Migration from Germany to America*. New York: Columbia University Press, 1985.

Kaes, Anton, ed. *Kino-Debatte: Texte zum Verhältnis von Literatur und Film, 1909–1929*. Tübingen: Deutscher Taschenbuchverlag, 1978.

Kahler, Erich, and Thomas Mann. *An Exceptional Friendship: The Correspondence of Thomas Mann and Erich Kahler*. Trans. Richard Winston and Clara Winston. Ithaca, N.Y.: Cornell University Press, 1975.

Kant, I. *Critique of Pure Reason*. Ed. Paul Guyer. Cambridge: Cambridge University Press, 1999.

Keats, John. *The Poems*. Ed. Jack Stillinger. London: Heinemann, 1978.

Keil, Werner. "'Gebt mir Rossinische Musik, die da spricht ohne Worte!'—Parallelen in Schopenhauers und Hegels Musikanschauung." In *Augsburger Jahrbuch für*

Musikwissenschaft, ed. Franz Krautwurst, vol. 7, 87–116. Tutzing: Hans Schneider, 1990.

Keller, Hans. "Film Music: The Operatic Problem." *Musical Times* 96, no. 1352 (1952): 549.

Keller, Hans. *Film Music and Beyond: Writings on Music and the Screen, 1946–59.* Ed. Christopher Wintle. London: Plumbago, 2006.

Kelly, Michael. *Iconoclasm in Aesthetics.* Cambridge: Cambridge University Press, 2003.

Kemp, Ian. *Tippett: The Composer and His Music.* New York: Da Capo, 1984.

Kestin, Diane. "Western Folklore in Modern American Opera." *Western Folklore* 16, no. 1 (1957): 1–7.

Ketcham, Diana. *Le Désert de Retz: A Late Eighteenth-Century French Folly Garden.* Cambridge: MIT Press, 1997.

Kierkegaard, Søren. *Either/Or.* Vol. 1. Ed. and trans. Howard V. Hong and Edna H. Hong. Princeton: Princeton University Press, 1987.

Kisch, Egon Erwin. *Paradies Amerika.* Berlin: Erich Reiss, 1930.

Kivy, Peter. *Music Alone: Philosophical Reflections on the Purely Musical Experience.* Ithaca, N.Y.: Cornell University Press, 1990.

Kivy, Peter. "Music in the Movies: A Philosophical Inquiry." In *Film Theory and Philosophy,* ed. Murray Smith and Robert C. Allen, 308–28. Oxford: Clarendon, 1997.

Kivy, Peter. *New Essays on Musical Understanding.* Oxford: Oxford University Press, 2001.

Klemperer, Victor. *The Language of the Third Reich: LTI—Lingua Tertii Imperii.* Trans. Martin Brady. London: Athlone, 2000.

Knight, Arthur. "The Movies Learn to Talk: Ernst Lubitsch, René Clair, and Rouben Mamoulian." In *Film Sound: Theory and Practice,* ed. Elisabeth Weis and John Belton, 213–20. New York: Columbia University Press, 1985.

Koch, Gertrud. "Ex-changing the Gaze: Re-visioning Feminist Film Theory." *New German Critique* 34 (1985): 139–53.

Koch, Gertrud. *Siegfried Kracauer: An Introduction.* Trans. Jeremy Gaines. Princeton: Princeton University Press, 2000.

Koch, Heinrich Christoph. *Musikalisches Lexikon.* Frankfurt: J. André, 1802.

Kolisch, Rudolph. "Tempo and Character in Beethoven's Music." *Musical Quarterly* 29, no. 1 (1943): 169–87, and 29, no. 3 (1943): 291–312.

Kolodin, Irving. *The Story of the Metropolitan Opera, 1883–1950: A Candid History.* New York: Knopf, 1953.

Kowalke, Kim H. "Kurt Weill, Modernism and Popular Culture: *Öffentlichkeit als Stil, Modernism/Modernity* 2, no. 1 (1995): 27–69.

Kracauer, Siegfried. *From Caligari to Hitler: A Psychological History of the German Film.* Ed. Leonardo Quaresima. Princeton: Princeton University Press, 2004.

Kracauer, Siegfried. *Theory of Film: The Redemption of Physical Reality.* Princeton: Princeton University Press, 1997.

Kramer, Lawrence. "The Harem Threshold: Turkish Music and Greek Love in Beethoven's 'Ode to Joy.'" *19th-Century Music* 22, no. 1 (1998): 78–90.

Krenek, Ernst. "The Transplanted Composer." *Modern Music* 16, no. 1 (1938): 23–27.

Krell, David Farrell. "Brazen Wheels: F. W. J. Schelling on the Origins of Music and Tragedy." In *Sound Figures of Modernity,* ed. Jost Hermand and Gerhard Richter, 64–91. Madison: University of Wisconsin Press, 2006.

Kürnberger, Ferdinand. *Der Amerikamüde.* Frankfurt: Insel Verlag, 1986.

Laks, Syzmon. *Music of Another World.* Trans. Chester A. Kisiel. Evanston, Ill.: Northwestern University Press, 1989.

Lang, Fritz. "The Artistic Composition of the Film Drama." In *German Essays on Film,* ed. Richard W. McCormick and Alison Guenther-Pal, 60–66. New York: Continuum, 2004.

Ledbetter, Steven. "Damrosch, Walter (Johannes)." In *Grove Music Online,* ed. L. Macy. At http://www.grovemusic.com.arugula.cc.columbia.edu:2048. Accessed June 24, 2007.

Lentricchia, Frank, and Jody McAuliffe. *Crimes of Art and Terror.* Chicago: University of Chicago Press, 2003.

Lepenies, Wolf. *The Seduction of Culture in German History.* Princeton: Princeton University Press, 2006.

Lessing, Gotthold Ephraim. *Hamburgische Dramaturgie.* Vol. 4 of *Werke.* Munich: Deutscher Taschenbuchverlag, 1973.

Levi, Primo. *If This Is a Man.* Trans. Stuart Woolf. Middlesex: Penguin, 1979.

Levinson, Jerrrold. *Music, Art, and Metaphysics: Essays in Philosophical Aesthetics.* Ithaca, N.Y.: Cornell University Press, 1991.

Levy, David Benjamin. *Beethoven: The Ninth Symphony.* New Haven: Yale University Press, 2003.

Lewis, Ward B. "Egon Erwin Kisch beehrt sich darzubieten: Paradies Amerika." *German Studies Review* 13, no. 2 (May 1990): 253–68.

Lewy, Ernst. *Zur Sprache des alten Goethe: Ein Versuch über die Sprache des Einzelnen.* Berlin: Paul Cassirer, 1913.

Locke, John. *Second Treatise on Government.* Ed. C. B. Macpherson. Indianapolis: Hackett, 1980.

London, Kurt. *Film Music: A Summary of the Characteristic Features of Its History, Aesthetics, Technique, and Possible Developments.* Trans. Eric S. Bensinger. London: Faber and Faber, 1936.

Longyear, Ronald M. *Schiller and Music.* Chapel Hill: University of North Carolina Press, 1966.

Löwith, Karl. *Meaning in History.* Chicago: University of Chicago Press, 1949.

Lukács, Georg. *History and Class Consciousness: Studies in Marxist Dialectics.* Trans. Rodney Livingstone. Cambridge: MIT Press, 1972.

Lukács, Georg. "Thoughts on an Aesthetics of Cinema." In *German Essays on Film,* ed. Richard W. McCormick and Alison Guenther-Pal, 11–16. New York: Continuum, 2004.

Mann, Thomas. *Essays of Three Decades.* Trans. H.T. Lowe-Porter. New York: Knopf, 1947.

Mann, Thomas. *Stories of Three Decades.* Trans. H.T. Lowe-Porter. New York: Modern Library, 1979.

Mann, Thomas, and Erich Kahler. *An Exceptional Friendship: The Correspondence of Thomas Mann and Erich Kahler.* Trans. Richard Winston and Clara Winston. Ithaca, N.Y.: Cornell University Press, 1975.

Martin, Nicholas. *Nietzsche and Schiller: Untimely Aesthetics.* Oxford: Clarendon, 1996.

Marx, Karl, and Friedrich Engels. *Werke.* 43 vols. Ed. Institut für Marxismus-Leninismus. Berlin: Dietz, 1956.

Mathews, Nieves. *Francis Bacon: The History of a Character Assassination.* New Haven: Yale University Press, 1996.

McCormick, Richard W., and Alison Guenther-Pal, eds. *German Essays on Film.* New York: Continuum, 2004.

McKay, David. "*The Fashionable Lady:* The First Opera by an American." *Musical Quarterly* 65 (1979): 360–67.

Mellors, Wilfred. *Music in a New Found Land: Themes and Development in the History of American Music.* London: Barrie and Rockliff, 1964.

Melville, Herman. *Billy Budd.* New York: Tom Doherty, 1988.

Melzer, Arthur M., Jerry Weinberger, and M. Richard Zinman, eds. *Democracy and the Arts.* Ithaca, N.Y.: Cornell University Press, 1999.

Menke, Christoph. *The Sovereignty of Art: Aesthetic Negativity in Adorno and Derrida.* Trans. Neil Solomon. Cambridge: MIT Press, 1999.

Menninghaus, Winfried. *Unendliche Verdoppelung: Die frühromantische Grundlegung der Kunsttheorie im Begriff absoluter Selbstreflexion.* Frankfurt: Suhrkamp, 1987.

Merchant, Carolyn. "The Scientific Revolution and the Death of Nature." *Isis* 97 (2006): 513–33.

Merleau-Ponty, Maurice. *Humanism and Terror: An Essay on the Communist Problem.* Boston: Beacon, 1969.

Merleau-Ponty, Maurice. *Phenomenology of Perception.* Trans. Colin Smith. London: Routledge and Kegan Paul, 1962.

Merleau-Ponty, Maurice. *The Primacy of Perception.* Ed. James M. Edie. Evanston, Ill.: Northwestern University Press, 1964.

Merleau-Ponty, Maurice. *Sense and Non-Sense.* Trans. Hubert L. Dreyfus and Patricia Allen Dreyfus. Evanston, Ill.: Northwestern University Press, 1964.

Mertens, Wim. *American Minimal Music: LaMonte Young, Terry Riley, Steve Reich, Philip Glass.* Trans. J. Hautekiet. London: Kahn and Averill, 1983.

Metzger, Christoph, ed. *Conceptualisms in Musik, Kunst und Film.* Berlin: Akademie der Künste, 2003.

Metzger, Heinz-Klaus. "Abortive Concepts in the Theory and Criticism of Music." *Die Reihe* 5 (1961): 21–29.

Mittig, Hans-Ernst. "Dauerhaftigkeit, einst Denkmalargument." In *Mo(nu)mente: Formen und Funktionen ephemerer Denkmäler,* ed. Michael Diers, 11–24. Berlin: Akademie-Verlag, 1998.

Molderings, Herbert. "Film, Photographie und ihr Einfluss auf die Malerei in Paris um 1910: Marcel Duchamp - Jacques Villon - Frank Kupka." In *Wallraf-Richartz-Jahrbuch,* 247–86. Cologne: M. Dumont Schauberg, 1975.

Müller-Doohm, Stefan. *Adorno: A Biography.* Trans. Rodney Livingstone. Cambridge: Polity, 2005.

Münsterberg, Hugo. *The Film: A Psychological Study—The Silent Photoplay in 1916.* New York: Dover, 1970.

Murnau, F. W. "The Ideal Picture Needs No Titles: By Its Very Nature the Art of the Screen Should Tell a Complete Story Pictorially" (1928). In *German Essays on Film,* ed. Richard W. McCormick and Alison Guenther-Pal, 66–68. New York: Continuum, 2004.

Naumann, Barbara. *Musikalisches Ideen-Instrument: Das Musikalische in Poetik und Sprachtheorie der Frühromantik.* Stuttgart: Metzler, 1990.

Nelson, Ann. *The Guys.* New York: Dramatists Play Service, 2003.

Nettl, Paul. *The Other Casanova.* New York: Da Capo, 1970.

Neuhouser, Frederick. *Actualizing Freedom: Foundations of Hegel's Social Theory.* Cambridge: Harvard University Press, 2003.

Nicholsen, Shierry Weber. *Exact Imagination, Late Work: On Adorno's Aesthetics.* Cambridge: MIT Press, 1999.

Nietzsche, Friedrich. *Beyond Good and Evil: Prelude to a Philosophy of the Future.* Ed. Judith Norman and Rolf-Peter Horstmann. Cambridge: Cambridge University Press, 2002.

Nietzsche, Friedrich. *The Gay Science.* Trans. Josefine Nauckhoff. Cambridge: Cambridge University Press, 2001.

Nisbet, H. B., ed. *German Aesthetic and Literary Criticism: Winckelmann, Lessing, Hamann, Herder, Schiller, Goethe.* Cambridge: Cambridge University Press, 1985.

Nora, Pierre. "Between Memory and History: *Les Lieux de Mémoire.*" Trans. Marc Roudebush. *Representations* 26 (Spring 1989): 7–24.

Nyman, Michael. *Experimental Music: Cage and Beyond.* Cambridge: Cambridge University Press, 1999.

O'Connor, Brian. *Adorno's Negative Dialectic: Philosophy and the Possibility of Critical Rationality.* Cambridge: MIT Press, 2005.

Offe, Claus. *Reflections on America: Tocqueville, Weber, and Adorno in the United States.* Trans. Patrick Camiller. Cambridge: Polity, 2005.

Oja, Carol J. *Making Music Modern: New York in the 1920s.* New York: Oxford University Press, 2000.

Olivier, Alain, ed. "Das Musikkapitel aus Hegels Ästhetikvorlesung von 1826." *Hegel-Studien* 33 (1998): 9–52.

Osterkamp, Ernst, ed. *Wechselwirkungen: Kunst und Wissenschaft in Berlin und Weimar im Zeichen Goethes.* Bern: Peter Lang, 2002.

Paddison, Max. *Adorno, Modernism and Mass Culture: Essays in Critical Theory and Music.* London: Kahn and Averill, 2004.

Paddison, Max. *Adorno's Aesthetics of Music.* Cambridge: Cambridge University Press, 1998.

Palmer, Christopher. *The Composer in Hollywood.* London: Marion Bayers, 1990.

Palombini, Carlos. "Pierre Schaeffer, 1953: Towards an Experimental Music." *Music and Letters* 72, no. 4 (1993): 542–57.

Panofsky, Erwin. "Style and Medium in the Moving Pictures." *Transition* 26 (1937): 124–25.

Payton, Rodney J. "The Music of Futurism: Concerts and Polemics." *Musical Quarterly* 62, no. 1 (1976): 25–45.

Pensky, Max, ed. *The Actuality of Adorno: Critical Essays on Adorno and the Postmodern.* Albany: SUNY Press, 1997.

Perez, Gilberto. *The Material Ghost: Films and Their Medium.* Baltimore: Johns Hopkins University Press, 1998.

Perloff, Nancy. "John Cage." In *Postmodernism: The Key Figures,* ed. Hans Bertens and Joseph Natoli, 62–69. Oxford: Blackwell, 2002.

Pesic, Peter. "Wrestling with Proteus: Francis Bacon and the 'Torture' of Nature." *Isis* 90, no. 1 (1999): 81–94.

Pinkard, Terry. *Hegel.* Cambridge: Cambridge University Press, 2001.

Pippin, Robert. *Hegel's Idealism: The Satisfactions of Self-Consciousness.* Cambridge: Cambridge University Press, 1989.

Plantinga, Carl, and Greg M. Smith, eds. *Passionate Views: Film, Cognition, and Emotion.* Baltimore: Johns Hopkins University Press, 1999.

Pöggeler, Otto. *Hegel in Berlin.* Berlin: Staatsbibliothek Preussischer Kulturbesitz, 1982.

Pratt, Silas G. "A Plan and a Plea for American Opera." *Forum* 15 (1893): 88–92.

Prendergast, Roy. *Film Music: A Neglected Art.* New York: Norton, 1977.

Prox, Lothar. "Perspektiven einer Wiederaufarbeitung von Stummfilmmusik." In *Stummfilm gestern und heute,* ed. Walter Seidler, 9–25. Berlin: Volker Spiess, 1979.

Ranke, Leopold von. *Geschichte der romanischen und germanischen Völker von 1494 bis 1514.* Hamburg: Standard Verlag, 1957.

Reijen, Willem van. *Adorno: An Introduction.* Philadelphia: Pennbridge, 1992.

Richter, Gerhard, ed. *Benjamin's Ghosts.* Stanford: Stanford University Press, 2002.

Riegl, Alois. "The Modern Cult of Monuments: Its Character and Its Origin (1903)." Trans. Kurt W. Forster and Diane Ghirardo. *Oppositions* 25 (1982): 21–51.

Ritter, Frédéric Louis. *Music in America.* New York: Scribner, 1883.

Robinson, Suzanne. "An English Composer Sees America: Benjamin Britten and the North American Press, 1939–42." *American Music* 15, no. 3 (1997): 321–51.

Rollins, Mark, ed. *Danto and His Critics.* Oxford: Blackwell, 1993.

Rose, Gillian. *The Melancholy Science: An Introduction to the Thought of Theodor W. Adorno.* London: Macmillan, 1978.

Rosen, Philip. "Adorno and Film Music: Theoretical Notes on Composing for the Films." *Yale French Studies* 60 (1980): 157–82.

Ross, Alex. "What Next?" *New Yorker,* August 21, 2006, 88–89.

Roth, Joseph. *Das Journalistische Werk, 1929–1939.* Vol. 3 of *Werke.* Ed. Klaus Westermann. Cologne: Kiepenheuer and Witsch, 1991.

Rousseau, J. J. *Dictionnaire de musique, Oeuvres complètes.* Vol. 5. Paris: Gallimard, 1995.

Ruskin, John. *The Seven Lamps of Architecture.* New York: Dover, 1989.

Russell, Charles Edward. *The American Opera and Theodore Thomas.* New York: Doubleday, 1927.

Said, Edward. "Die Tote Stadt, Fidelio, The Death of Klinghoffer." *Nation* 253 (November 11, 1991): 596–600.

Sammons, Jeffrey L. *Ideology, Mimesis, Fantasy: Charles Sealsfield, Friedrich Gerstäcker, Karl May, and Other German Novelists of America.* Chapel Hill: University of North Carolina Press, 1998.

Sartre, Jean-Paul. *Saint Genet: Actor and Martyr.* New York: New American Library, 1963.

Sartre, Jean-Paul. *"What Is Literature?" and Other Essays.* Cambridge: Harvard University Press, 1988.

Saunders, William. "The American Opera: Has It Arrived?" *Music and Letters* 13, no. 2 (1932): 147–55.

Saunders, William. "National Opera, Comparatively Considered." *Musical Quarterly* 13, no. 1 (1927): 72–84.

Saunders, Williams. "Sailor Songs and Songs of the Sea." *Musical Quarterly* 14, no. 3 (1928): 339–57.

Saunders, William. "Songs of the German Revolution." *Music and Letters* 16, no. 1 (1935): 50–57.

Schaeffer, Pierre. "Vers une musique expérimentale." *La Revue Musicale* 236 (1957): 11–27.

Schebera, Jürgen. "Hangmen Also Die (1943): Hollywood's Brecht-Eisler Collaboration." *Historical Journal of Film, Radio, and Television* 18, no. 5 (1998): 567–74.

Schelling, Friedrich Wilhelm Joseph. *Philosophie der Kunst.* Vol. 5 of *Sämtliche Werke.* Stuttgart: J. G. Cotta, 1859.

Schelling, Friedrich Wilhelm Joseph. *The Philosophy of Art.* Ed. Douglas W. Stott. Minneapolis: University of Minnesota Press, 1989.

von Schiller, Friedrich. *On the Aesthetic Education of Man in a Series of Letters.* Trans. Elizabeth M. Wilkinson and L.A. Willoughby. Oxford: Clarendon, 1967.

Schlegel, Karl Wilhelm Friedrich. *Kritische Friedrich-Schlegel-Ausgabe.* 35 vols. Ed. Ernst Behler. Munich: Thomas Schöninghaus, 1958–2002.

Schlegel, Karl Wilhelm Friedrich. *Philosophical Fragments.* Trans. Peter Firchow. Minneapolis: University of Minnesota Press, 1991.

Schmidt, James. "'Not These Sounds': Beethoven at Mauthausen." *Philosophy and Literature* 29, no. 1 (2005): 146–63.

Schneider, Helmut, and Anne Marie Gethmann-Siefert. "Über Nachschriften zu Hegels Vorlesungen." *Hegel-Studien* 26 (1991): 89–111.

Schoenberg, Arnold. "Gibt es eine Krise der Oper?" *Musikblätter des Anbruch* 5 (1926): 209.

Schoenberg, Arnold. *A Schoenberg Reader: Documents of a Life.* Ed. Joseph Auner. New Haven: Yale University Press, 2003.

Schoenberg, Arnold. *Style and Idea: Selected Writings of Arnold Schoenberg.* Ed. Leonard Stein. Berkeley: University of California Press, 1975.

Schönberger, Angela. *Die neue Reichskanzlei von Albert Speer: Zum Zusammenhang von nationalsozialistischer Ideologie und Architektur.* Berlin: Mann, 1981.

Schönberger, Angela. "Die Staatsbauten des Tausendjährhrigen Reiches als vorprogrammierte Ruinen? Zu Albert Speers Ruinenwerttheorie." *Idea* 6 (1987): 97–107.

Schöne, Albrecht. *Goethes Farbentheologie.* Munich: C.H. Beck, 1987.

Scobie, Alexander. *Hitler's State Architecture: The Impact of Classical Antiquity.* University Park: Pennsylvania State University Press, 1990.

Scott, Sir Walter. *The Antiquary.* Oxford: Oxford University Press, 2002.

Scruton, Roger. *The Aesthetics of Music.* Oxford: Clarendon, 1999.

Sebald, W.G. *On the Natural History of Destruction.* Trans. Anthea Bell. New York: Modern Library, 2003.

Seidler, Walter, ed. *Stummfilm gestern und heute.* Berlin: Volker Spiess, 1979.

Selfridge-Field, Eleonor. "Beethoven and Greek Classicism." *Journal of the History of Ideas* 33, no. 4 (1972): 577–95.

Serner, Walter. "Cinema and the Desire to Watch" (1913). In *German Essays on Film,* ed. Richard W. McCormick and Alison Guenther-Pal, 17–22. New York: Continuum, 2004.

Shapin, Stephen. "The House of Experiment in Seventeenth-Century England." In *Science Studies Reader,* ed. Mario Biagioli, 479–504. London: Routledge, 1999.

Shultis, Christopher. "Silencing the Sounded Self: John Cage and the Intentionality of Nonintention." *Musical Quarterly* 79, no. 2 (1995): 312–50.

Smalley, Roger. "Experimental Music." *Musical Times* 116, no. 1583 (1975): 23–26.

Smith, Jeff. "Movie Music as Moving Music: Emotion, Cognition, and the Film Score." In *Passionate Views: Film, Cognition, and Emotion,* ed. Carl Plantinga and Greg M. Smith, 146–67. Baltimore: Johns Hopkins University Press, 1999.

Smith, Murray, and Robert C. Allen, eds. *Film Theory and Philosophy.* Oxford: Clarendon, 1997.

Smithson, Robert. *Robert Smithson: The Collected Writings.* Ed. Jack Flam. Berkeley: University of California Press, 1996.

Solomon, Maynard. *Late Beethoven: Music, Thought, Imagination.* Berkeley: University of California Press, 2004.

Sonneck, O. G. *Early Opera in America.* New York: Schirmer, 1915.

Sontag, Susan. *Under the Sign of Saturn.* New York: Picador, 2002.

Speer, Albert. *Die Bauten Adolf Hitlers* (1938). International Historic Films, 1996.

Speer, Albert. *Erinnerungen.* Berlin: Ullstein, 2005.

Speer, Albert. *Inside the Third Reich.* Trans. Richard and Clara Winston. New York: Avon, 1970.

Sponaugle, Harlie. "Columbia University, the Columbia University Opera Workshop and the Efflorescence of American Opera in the 1940s and 1950s." September 2002. At www.usoperaweb.com. Accessed June 24, 2007.

Spotts, Frederic. *Hitler and the Power of the Aesthetic.* Woodstock, N.Y.: Overlook, 2004.

Steigman, B. M. "The Great American Opera." *Music and Letters* 6, no. 4 (1925): 359–67.

Steinberg, Michael P. *Listening to Reason: Culture, Subjectivity, and Nineteenth-Century Music.* Princeton: Princeton University Press, 2006.

Stendhal, *Life of Rossini.* Trans. Richard N. Coe. London: Riverrun, 1985.

Stiller, Andrew. "Moore, Douglas S(tuart)." In *Grove Music Online,* ed. L. Macy. At http://www.grovemusic.com.arugula.cc.columbia.edu:2048. Accessed June 24, 2007.

Strong, Tracy B. "Theatricality, Public Space, and Music in Rousseau." Special Issue: Politics on Stage. *SubStance* 25, no. 2 (1996): 110–27.

Subotnik, Rose Rosengard. *Deconstructive Variations: Music and Reason in Western Society.* Minneapolis: University of Minnesota Press, 1995.

Subotnik, Rose Rosengard. *Developing Variations: Style and Ideology in Western Music.* Minneapolis: University of Minnesota Press, 1991.

Subotnik, Rose Rosengard. "Whose 'Magic Flute?' Intimations of Reality at the Gates of the Enlightenment." *19th-Century Music* 15, no. 2 (1991): 132–50.

Szabo, Istvan, *Taking Sides.* DVD, 2001.

Tannenbaum, Herbert. "Art at the Cinema." In *German Essays on Film,* ed. Richard W. McCormick and Alison Guenther-Pal, 3–7. New York: Continuum, 2004.

Taylor, Robert. *The Word in Stone: The Role of Architecture in the National Socialist Ideology.* Berkeley: University of California Press, 1974.

Theunissen, Michael. *Negative Theologie der Zeit.* Frankfurt: Suhrkamp, 1991.

Tiedemann, Rolf. "Adorno's *Tom Sawyer* Opera Singspiel." In *The Cambridge Companion to Adorno,* ed. Tom Huhn, 376–94. Cambridge: Cambridge University Press, 2004.

Tiedemann, Rolf, ed. *Can One Live After Auschwitz: A Philosophical Reader*. Stanford: Stanford University Press, 2003.

Tippett, Michael. *Tippett on Music*. Ed. Meirion Bowen. Oxford: Oxford University Press, 1995.

Todorov, Tzvetan. *The Conquest of America: The Question of the Other*. Trans. Richard Howard. New York: Harper, 1984.

Todorov, Tzvetan. *Facing the Extreme: Moral Life in the Concentration Camps*. Trans. Arthur Denner and Abigail Pollak. New York: Metropolitan, 1996.

Tomkins, Calvin. *The Bride and the Bachelors: Five Masters of the Avant-Garde*. London: Penguin, 1968.

Treitler, Leo. "Beethoven's 'Expressive' Markings." *Beethoven Forum* 7 (1999), 89–111.

Trietler, Leo. *Music and the Historical Imagination*. Cambridge: Harvard University Press, 1989.

Tucholsky, Kurt. "Ein Frühling in Amerika." *Die Weltbühne* 11 (1924): 350.

Twain, Mark. *A Tramp Abroad*. Ed. Robert Gray Bruce and Hamlin Hill. New York: Penguin, 1997.

Ullmann, Viktor. *Der Kaiser von Atlantis*. DVD, Decca 440 854–2, 1994.

Vazsonyi, Nicholas, ed. *Wagner's Meistersinger: Performance, History, Representation*. Rochester, N.Y.: University of Rochester Press, 2003.

Vergo, Peter. *That Divine Order: Music and the Visual Arts from Antiquity to the Eighteenth Century*. New York: Phaidon, 2005.

Voit, Friedrich. *Karl Wolfskehl: Leben und Werk im Exil*. Göttingen: Wallstein Verlag, 2005.

Voltaire, François Marie Arouet de. *Letters on the English*. New York: P. F. Collier, 1909.

Wallace, Robin. *Beethoven's Critics: Aesthetic Dilemmas and Resolutions During the Composer's Lifetime*. Cambridge: Cambridge University Press, 1986.

Warschauer, Frank. "Filmmusik." *Anbruch* 3 (1929): 130–34.

Weber, Max. *The Protestant Ethic and the Spirit of Capitalism*. Trans. Talcott Parsons. New York: Scribner, 1958.

Weill, Kurt. "The Future of Opera in America Today." *Modern Music* 14, no. 4 (1937): 183–88.

Weis, Elisabeth, and Belton, John, eds. *Film Sound: Theory and Practice*. New York: Columbia University Press, 1985.

Wellmer, Albrecht. *The Persistence of Modernity: Essays on Aesthetics, Ethics, and Postmodernism*. Cambridge: MIT Press, 1993.

Wells, H. G. *The War in the Air*. Kila, Mont.: Kessinger, 2004.

White, Hayden V. "The Burden of History." *History and Theory* 5, no 2 (1966): 111–134.

White, Hayden. *Metahistory: The Historical Imagination in Nineteenth-Century Europe*. Baltimore: Johns Hopkins University Press, 1975.

Whitesitt, Linda. "Antheil, George [Georg] (Carl Johann)." In *Grove Music Online*, ed. L. Macy. At http://www.grovemusic.com.arugula.cc.columbia.edu:2048. Accessed June 24, 2007.

Wiggerhaus, Rolf. *The Frankfurt School: Its History, Theories, and Political Significance.* Trans. Michael Robertson. Cambridge: MIT Press, 1995.

Wilde, Oscar. *The Works of Oscar Wilde.* Leicester: Blitz, 1990.

Williams, Tennessee. *The Glass Menagerie.* Ed. Robert Bray. New York: New Directions, 1999.

Willkomm, Ernst. *Die Europamüden: Modernes Lebensbild.* Ed. Otto Neuendorff. Göttingen: Vandenhoeck and Ruprecht, 1968.

Wind, Edgar. *Art and Anarchy.* Evanston, Ill.: Northwestern University Press, 1985.

Witt, Michael. "Shapeshifter: Godard as Multimedia Installation Artist." *New Left Review* 29 (2004): 73–88.

Wittgenstein, Ludwig. *Culture and Value.* Oxford: Blackwell, 1977.

Wittgenstein, Ludwig. *Philosophical Grammar.* Ed. Rush Rhees. Oxford: Blackwell, 1974.

Wittgenstein, Ludwig. *Philosophical Remarks.* Ed. Rush Rhees. Oxford: Blackwell, 1975.

Wittgenstein, Ludwig. *Philosophische Bemerkungen.* Ed. Rush Rhees. Frankfurt: Suhrkamp, 1964.

Yerushalmi, Yosef Hayim. *Zakhor: Jewish History and Jewish Memory.* Seattle: University of Washington Press, 1996.

Yehoshua, A. B. "Modern Democracy and the Novel." In *Democracy and the Arts,* ed. Arthur M. Melzer, Jerry Weinberger, and M. Richard Zinman, 42–55. Ithaca, N.Y.: Cornell University Press, 1999.

Zuidervaart, Lambert. *Adorno's Aesthetic Theory: The Redemption of Illusion.* Cambridge: MIT Press, 1993.

Zuidervaart, Lambert. *Social Philosophy After Adorno.* Cambridge: Cambridge University Press, 2007.

Index